Danny Gronmaier
The US Sports Film: A Genre of American Dream Time

Cinepoetics

Edited by
Hermann Kappelhoff and Michael Wedel

Volume 11

Danny Gronmaier

The US Sports Film: A Genre of American Dream Time

DE GRUYTER

Approved Dissertation Freie Universität Berlin 2021 – D 188.

ISBN 978-3-11-152963-9
e-ISBN (PDF) 978-3-11-076035-4
e-ISBN (EPUB) 978-3-11-076039-2
ISSN 2569-4294

Library of Congress Control Number: 2022941356

Bibliographic information published by the Deutsche Nationalbibliothek
The Deutsche Nationalbibliothek lists this publication in the Deutsche Nationalbibliografie; detailed bibliographic data are available on the internet at http://dnb.dnb.de.

© 2024 Walter de Gruyter GmbH, Berlin/Boston
This volume is text- and page-identical with the hardback published in 2023.
Cover image: jpbcpa/E+/Getty Images
Typesetting: Integra Software Services Pvt.

www.degruyter.com

"Very soon the crowd is no crowd at all but a community, a small town of people sharing neither work nor pain nor deprivation nor anger but the common experience of being released to enjoy the moment, even those moments of intense disappointment or defeat, moments made better, after all, precisely because our fan is part of a large family of those similarly affected, part of a city of grievers." (Giamatti 1989, 32)

"The imagination is defined here as a contractile power [...]. This is by no means a memory, nor indeed an operation of the understanding: contraction is not a matter of reflection. Properly speaking, it forms a synthesis of time. A succession of instants does not constitute time any more than it causes it to disappear; it indicates only its constantly aborted moment of birth. Time is constituted only in the originary synthesis which operates on the repetition of instants. This synthesis contracts the successive independent instants into one another, thereby constituting the lived, or living, present. It is in this present that time is deployed. To it belongs both the past and the future: the past in so far as the preceding instants are retained in the contraction; the future because its expectation is anticipated in this same contraction." (Deleuze 2014 [1968], 94)

"One cannot criticize the American dream for being only a dream: this is what it wants to be, drawing all its power from the fact that it is a dream." (Deleuze 2013a [1983], 152)

Acknowledgement

I wrote this book in English, but the first language of most people who supported me in doing this is German (as is mine). I want to thank everyone in their mother tongue, so please excuse that most of these thank-you notes here are in German.

Bedanken möchte ich mich zuallererst bei meinem Doktorvater Hermann Kappelhoff, der früh an diese Arbeit und – noch viel wichtiger – an mich als Geisteswissenschaftler geglaubt hat. Sein von fordernder Schärfe und unbändiger Offenheit geprägtes Denken war und ist immer wieder Inspiration und Antrieb, das von ihm geschaffene, von Anspruch, Anerkennung, Sicherheit und Fürsorge geprägte Arbeitsumfeld der nötige Halt.

Ein ganz herzlicher Dank gilt auch meinem Zweitbetreuer Michael Wedel, dessen unerschöpfliche, mit Besonnenheit und Witz vorgebrachte Expertise mich nach wie vor jede Woche beeindruckt und dessen insbesondere filmgeschichtstheoretischen Überlegungen meine Arbeit noch einmal neu perspektiviert haben und dies immer noch tun.

Bedanken möchte ich mich außerdem bei Jan-Hendrik Bakels, Matthias Grotkopp und Christina Schmitt – nicht nur dafür, dass sie unter widrigen Bedingungen meine Promotionskommission vervollständigt haben, sondern und vor allem für viele Jahre sehr produktiver und kollegialer Zusammenarbeit.

Sehr wichtig für die Entwicklung dieser Arbeit und mein Wohlbefinden während deren Ausarbeitung war das Dissertations-Colloquium der Kolleg-Forschungsgruppe „Cinepoetics – Poetologien audiovisueller Bilder", das über die vielen Jahre so viel mehr als bloß ein institutioneller Rahmen war. Vielen Dank an alle Teilnehmer:innen und im Besonderen an Regina Brückner, Björn Hochschild, Thomas Scherer, Jasper Stratil, Michael Ufer und Hannes Wesselkämper.

Ganz besonders und für ganz vieles möchte ich mich bei Hanno Berger bedanken: Als aufgeschlossener Kommilitone und freundschaftlich verbundener Kollege hat er insbesondere meine ersten Jahre in Berlin und an der Freien Universität um so viel Gutes und Lustiges bereichert, als erster Leser und wohlgesonnen-überlegter Kommentator die Dissertation, auf der dieses Buch beruht, entscheidend geprägt und voran gebracht. TP ftw!

A huge thank you goes to Naomi Vaughan, who not only read and extensively commented on every chapter of this book, but also provided a lot of emotional support and introduced me to inspiring new ways of thinking, living and feeling. Full of critical debate, loving friendship and disarming honesty, I do not want to miss any second of the times shared in Ann Arbor and Berlin.

Bei Alena Horbelt, Elisabeth Mohr, Maja Roth, Octavia Rudek und Alexander Wiese möchte ich mich ganz herzlich für die Unterstützung bei der Erstellung des Manuskripts bedanken. I also want to thank Amber Shields for final edits!

Ein großes Dankeschön geht an meine Familie: Ohne jemals wirklich zu wissen, was ich da eigentlich treibe, hat mir jedes ihrer Mitglieder zu jeder Zeit Zutrauen und Kraft geschenkt, mich abgelenkt, aufgefangen und nicht zuletzt gefeiert. Dass solch eine Arbeit für mich überhaupt in den Bereich des Möglichen rücken konnte, verdanke ich meinem Vater Harald, der mich früh mit der Freiheit des Denkens bekannt machte, sowie meinem Stiefvater Rudi, der meine Begeisterung für Popkultur entfacht hat.

Der allergrößte Dank gebührt meiner Freundin Annabelle, die nicht nur jeden Tag schöner macht und mich mit starken Schultern und scheinbar unerschütterlicher Liebe durch die dunklen Täler des Dissertation-Schreibens geführt hat, sondern der diese Arbeit auch einen Großteil ihrer inhaltlichen und formalen Prägnanz zu verdanken hat. „Über uns das Sternenzelt, unter uns die weite Welt. Du gibst mir einen Kuss und dann wird es auch schon hell ..."

Widmen möchte ich dieses Buch meiner Mutter Angelika, auch wenn kein Wort dieser Welt ihrer bedingungslosen Liebe und Fürsorge gerecht werden kann, sowie meiner Tochter Liv, an die wir hoffentlich so viel wie möglich davon weitergeben können.

Berlin, den 29.07.2022

Contents

Acknowledgement —— VII

1 Introduction —— 1
    A Start: Spectator Sports and Media Sports —— 1
    Perimeters: The US Team Sports Feature Film —— 3
    Intervention I: Aesthetic Analysis and the Poiesis of Film-Viewing —— 5
    Real and Imagined Sporting Worlds —— 8
    The Sports Film Viewer's Involvement —— 10
    Intervention II: A Different Approach to Genre —— 12
    The American Dream as Constitutive Conflict —— 14
    Corporeal Temporalities and an Audiovisual Discourse of Time as Crystal —— 16

2 The Haunting Question of Genre —— 20
    2.1 The Shortcomings of Narrative Analysis —— 20
          Sports as Textual Material —— 23
          The Necessity to Cease from Narrative Content as Holy Grail —— 29
    2.2 A Genre-Theoretical Reperspectivation —— 30
          Historicizing the Transgression of Convention and the Notion of a Sporting Culture —— 30
          Genre as a System of Modalities of Experience —— 34
          The Sports Film's Allegorical Play with Time —— 37
          Genre Reflexivity —— 39
          American Dream Time as the Sports Film Genre's Constitutive Conflict —— 42
    2.3 Encountering Genre History on the FIELD OF DREAMS —— 47
          The Field as Mise en Scène and Imaginative Space —— 47
          Nostalgia for Pure Pasts and the Problem of Agency —— 49
          The Horror of the Voice —— 52
          A Future Vision of the Past —— 55
          Between Strangeness and Intimacy: The First Encounter as Western Duel —— 57
          The Personal Is Public: A PTA Meeting as (Comic) Courtroom Drama —— 61
          Time Traveling in Film History —— 66
          Encountering Genre Film as Time Crystal —— 70

A Community of Spectators of and as the Myth
of America —— 73
History as Filmic Experience of Deep Temporality and the
Negotiation of Belonging —— 78

3 Becoming What We Were and Will Be Again: The American Dream —— 84

3.1 The Shortcomings of the American Dream as Narrative and Narrativized Ideologeme —— 84
    Middlemen of Prescribed Meaning —— 88
    A Community-Building Idea of Lived Time —— 92
    Exploiting Utopian Sensibility and Distracting from Social Reality —— 93
    Films as Secondary Containers of (Un-)Faithful Correspondence —— 96
    The Mediated Sporting Star and Film as Sugar on the Ideology Pill —— 98
    A Seemingly Stable and Transparent Reality as Ineluctable Template —— 101
    The Structuring Absences of Historical Complexity —— 102
    Film as the Sensory Constitution of Audiovisual Space —— 106

3.2 The American Dream as Time-Image of Community-Building Historicity —— 107
    A Matter of the Imaginary —— 110
    A Dream Is a Dream —— 111
    The American Dream as a Romantic Mode and a Sense of Crystallized Time —— 113
    Deleuze on Melville: The American Dream as Becoming-We as Fractal Unity —— 114
    In View of a Past and a Future: The Declaration of Independence —— 120
    Lived Time and a Reality Making Itself in a Reality Unmaking Itself —— 123
    The American Dream as an Aesthetic Regime of Becoming Community —— 125
    The Paradox of the Declaration of Independence as Constative and Performative Act —— 128
    Utopia America: Fractal Unity and an Endless Process of Poetic Redescription —— 130

4 Still to Come and Having Already Happened: The Moment as Crystal —— 136

4.1 Time-Philosophical Considerations —— 136
The One Moment in Time as Time-Giving and Time-Consuming —— 136
The Decisive Moment as Climactic Peak and Sudden Change —— 138
Repeating Uniqueness —— 140
Kairos as a Moment of Present Future —— 141
Fueled by Past and Future: The Utopian Moment —— 143
The Pregnant and Impalpable Moment as American Dream Time —— 144

4.2 The Moment as Tragic End Point and New Beginning: WE ARE MARSHALL —— 145
Recapitulation as Prediction —— 147
A Scenic Complex of Inverted Symmetry —— 149
An Amalgamation of Time: A Prologue of Future Remembrance —— 153
Repetition in Reminiscence —— 156
Suspense, Spectator Reverse Shots and the Decisive Last Pass —— 158
The Invisible Moment of the Crash as Dissolution of Symmetry —— 163
The Slow Occurrence of a Painful Premonition —— 165
The Horror of the Delayed Moment of Recognition —— 169
Historical Experience in a Hall of Mirrors of Affection-Images —— 174
Commemoration as a Movement of Inversion —— 177

5 Dissolutions of/in Time and Images of Communization: Flow in MIRACLE —— 183

5.1 The Montage Sequence as Standard Form and the Flow Experience —— 183
"Even Rocky Had a Montage" —— 184
Flow as a Filmic Modality of Perception —— 186

5.2 Becoming Team as an Image of Flow —— 191
The Shaping of a Group Body —— 191
In Between Fragmentation and Order —— 193

Flow as National Collectivization —— 196
An Audio-Vision of Pure Event as Substrate of
Communal Subjectification —— 198

6 Commemorating Futurity, Projecting Pastness: Never-Ending Endings —— 201

6.1 Immortality as the Multiplication of Immediacy: KNUTE ROCKNE ALL AMERICAN —— 204

A Classical Biopic, Ronald Reagan and a Quote That Made History —— 204
Rockne's Death as Media Discourse and Absent Presence —— 208
Too Late and Too Early: A Mediated Possibility to Say Goodbye —— 211
Staging Invisibility and the Invisible —— 213
A Poetics of Clarity and Control and a Mediated Media Community —— 215
The (Re-)Production of the Exceptional Individual —— 217
A Ghost in an Empty Stadium —— 219
Succession as Exploding Multiplication —— 221
A Nation of Heroes in the Here and Now —— 224

6.2 Cyclical Infinity and Finally Becoming Spectator Again: JIM THORPE – ALL-AMERICAN —— 226

Being Denied and Not Fitting In: Thorpe as Tragic Hero —— 226
Becoming Coach as Final Reconciliation —— 229
Being Out of Time and the (Filmic) Negotiation of Sociality —— 232
The Hero as Isolated Spectator of a Collective Subjectivity —— 234
Spectatorship as Mediated Subjective Collectivity —— 238
Integrating the Individual by Integrating Time —— 241
Becoming Singular Plural as Becoming Spectator —— 244
A Hero's Portrait and the American Dream as Media Imaginary —— 247

7 **Concluding Remarks: The Hill We Climb** —— 255
　The American Dream as an Imaginary of Audiovisual Culture —— 256
　American Dream Time —— 257
　The Hill's Narrow Ridge and Unreachable Peak —— 259
　The Pain of a Momentous Present as Past and Future —— 261
　Delayed Democracy and a Poetic Project of Reimagining —— 262
　A Perfect Union with a Past to Step Into —— 263
　Audiovisual History and Cultural Complexity —— 264

Bibliography —— 267

Filmography —— 281

Table of Figures —— 285

Name Index —— 287

Film Index —— 293

1 Introduction

A Start: Spectator Sports and Media Sports

Sports and film are media that create time. They are temporal not only in the sense that they are defined and regulated by certain temporalities as a result of processes of social negotiation, but also in the sense of modulating and intervening in these processes in the first place. They are determined by multiple temporalities referring to and aligning along perceptual corporeality; but at the same time, they also *produce* time through and along temporalities of bodily expression and perception. Thus, as much as we perceive and understand sports and film by means of our culturally coded conceptions of time, this comprehension is itself already the product or effect of these media's fabrication and modulation of certain imaginations of time. Furthermore, these imaginations come into effect through and along expressing and perceiving bodies, in both film and sports as corporeal and visual cultural techniques: the body of the performing athlete or actress, and that of the spectator watching and sharing in the thrills of the action on the field or the screen.

It is this reciprocal conjunction of involved spectatorship and expressive performance which has not only enabled most sports to be grasped as *spectator sports* in one way or another, but also as *media sports*, producing and at the same time being modulated by means and modes of visual and tonal representation. While the former term is often used, though seldomly applied to audio-visual forms in the media aesthetic manner already hinted at here, the notion of *media sports* has given reason for a whole field of scholarly research assembling a variety of approaches with different subject matters and perspectives. Nonetheless, most of these approaches to the audiovisual representation of competitive athletic action center around (television) broadcasting, thereby putting forward questions of technology, economy and journalism, as well as fandom, race and gender.[1] By dealing with such different topics, most of these

---

[1] For a good overview and a great resource of bibliographic references for further reading (in English *and* in German), see Beck / Bosshart 2003. See for the most prominent approaches the numerous books and articles by Lawrence A. Wenner (for example Wenner 1991, 1998), Rowe 2004 and, for a very ambitious work within the UK context, Whannel 1992. Studies on the culture and history of sports often also include at least one chapter on media representation, see for two of the most renowned representatives Cashmore 2010 and Grundy / Rader 2018 [1983]. For an explicitly global perspective, see for example Maguire 2011, or Rowe 2011. With regard to the research field of sports and Digital/New/Social Media, see Hutchins / Rowe 2012. For an introduction to *Mediensport* in German, see, for example, Schwier 2002.

approaches proceed within theoretical and methodological frameworks that draw from sociology, cultural studies and communication sciences. While these studies generally do not touch upon cinematic forms of screening sports and the fiction film in particular, those which do almost always adopt and implement an understanding of audiovisual representation that ultimately sticks to text-based, semantic models of cultural communication and meaning-making, as well as to a notion of realism as 'truthful depiction,' with a sporting world, a film world and the world of everyday reality as more or less distinct and fixed entities. As such, discussions often evolve first and foremost around narrative content and stylistic convention, thereby ignoring aesthetics: the films' actual and specific audiovisual form, the modalities of expression and perception they produce, and their poetics of affect.[2] I will present a series of examples of this approach especially in chapters 2.1 and 3.1 in order to provide an overview of the research landscape and to demarcate the main interventions of this book.

Central for these interventions, which I will present in detail below, is the conjunction between perceptual spectatorship and expressive performance – with both phenomena characteristic in film as well as sports. It is this conjunction, this interdependency of doing sports and perceiving images, which the very first scene of an early British production, THE ARSENAL STADIUM MYSTERY (T. Dickinson, UK 1939),[3] puts in an audiovisual nutshell: The film starts with (newsreel footage of) a soccer game. After a goal is scored, the moving images turn out to be a 'film within a film,' as the view of the screen is suddenly disturbed by a celebrating man standing up from his seat in a movie theater. It then is revealed that the agitated audience turns out to be the very same team the newsreel they watch is about. Step by step and with the scene switching between shots of the screen presenting mug shots of every single player, and shots of the equivalent moviegoer in his seat reacting to his own image, both film audiences convene in a game of (self) recognition of each player and spectator among his teammates.

Understood as the product of a "poiesis of film-viewing" (Müller / Kappelhoff 2018, 36) later on,[4] it is this dissolution of boundaries between watching and doing sports through cinematic experience and this experience's own double bind structure, its reflexivity, which constitutes the crucial point of departure for this book's object of research: the poetics and politics of time of (what is most often addressed in a rather subsuming way as) the genre of the sports film.

---

[2] See Kappelhoff / Lehmann 2019.
[3] I will specify the country of production of the movies mentioned throughout this book only if it is not an US production.
[4] See further below in this chapter, and also especially the analytical chapters 2.3, 4.2, 5, 6.1 and 6.2.

Perimeters: The US Team Sports Feature Film

This book's line of argument develops ostensibly by means of the analysis of the US team sports feature film – hence by having a closer look at films produced in the United States, whose diegetic world and action evolve around the most popular American team sports (football, baseball, hockey, basketball) and are addressed in a fictional mode of representation. This excludes what Toby Miller in his typology calls films that include sports in the way of a "semi-incidental reference" that "use sport as a component, perhaps to build up the profile of a character, but which traverse a lot of other terrains besides, films which only touch on sport" (Miller 1994, 163–165).[5] In the films analyzed here, sports is a "motif complex," an "object area" and, first and foremost, a "principle of meaning-making" (Waitz 2014, 37–40), which urges us to examine the medial inner logics of sports and film and their productive entanglement.[6] Such examination should not lead us to look at these logics apart from any cultural categories and social conditions but help to understand how the former intervene in the production of the latter. Here, sports serves as a productive practice, form and topic – especially with regard to media representation, as its (filmic) staging produces "metaphors of the social" (King / Leonard 2006, 3) that become significant beyond sports, while sports in its established form nonetheless remains connected with specific values and valuations, thus helping to naturalize certain cultural hierarchies. Similarly, sports provides for a specific sense of realism (by referencing historical events), while at the same time enabling a "magical space" (King / Leonard 2006, 3) to unfold.[7]

It is not least in this sense that the findings of this book should be regarded as by all means applicable to other forms of "screened sport" (Pomerance 2006, 313) and also in regards to movies whose audiovisual and narrative dramaturgy evolves around an individual (and not a team) sport – and here especially to the cycle of the boxing film, which undoubtedly occupies a very important role in

---

[5] Cited after Rowe 2008, 148. Famous examples we can think of here would be STRANGERS ON A TRAIN (A. Hitchcock, 1951), THE NAKED GUN: FROM THE FILES OF POLICE SQUAD! (D. Zucker, 1988), FORREST GUMP (R. Zemeckis, 1994) or MATCH POINT (W. Allen, UK 2005).
[6] Thomas Waitz's article is in German, my translation. In his inspiring take on *The Filmic Productivity of Sports*, Waitz proceeds to describe the audiovisual fabrication of sports in film and the productivity of sports for cinematic techniques. Due to a convention- and rule-based understanding of genre and a more media economic approach, the films' specific expressive structures and modes of experience are not the center of attention for him though.
[7] See Stauff 2008, in German.

regard to the history of film and the filmic mediatization of sports.[8] While the genre-theoretical approach I will put forward in chapters 2.1 and 2.2 not only secures the possibility of including films that were previously excluded, but also marks this possibility as a pivotal operation of historically profound genre analysis, the heuristic exclusion of boxing films here might nonetheless provide for a quite productive reperspectivation in terms of methodology. Namely, as a lot of sports film studies seemingly depart drastically from the paradigm of the boxing film, they exhibit an overly strong tendency to focus on the narrative of the individual (anti-)hero and to prefer questions of cultural context and technology over audiovisual form and the film's politics of aesthetics. Moreover, a lot of very good academic work on the boxing film has been done already, with Stephan May providing the most remarkable account by far (May 2004).[9]

Concerning the restriction of my corpus with regard to nationality: While realizing that there are quite a number of productions that originated outside of the United States[10] and/or in independent, experimental and/or documentary filmmaking contexts,[11] the hegemonic dominance of US/Hollywood production (and) aesthetics in the field is undoubtable. My aim is thus to not only get a better grip on this North American 'core' or 'origin' of the sports film, but to comprehend and define it as a genre by means of its 'Americanness' in the first place.[12]

Furthermore, and following Andrew Miller, whose *Laying Down the Rules: The American Sports Film Genre from 1872 to 1960* provides one of the most valuable reference bases of this work, this book focuses on sports films "that are structured around the display of human athletes" (Miller 2003, 7) and whose narrative as well as audiovisual dramaturgy involves competition. This

---

8 Maybe the most obvious example of this connection between the films I discuss in this book and boxing movies on an aesthetic level is the staging of the football tackle as a moment of impact (see also chapter 4.2).

9 Unfortunately, May's *Faust trifft Auge: Mythologie und Ästhetik des amerikanischen Boxfilms* has not been translated into English yet. For fruitful Anglo-American accounts, see Grindon 2011 or, with a focus on the entanglement of boxing and Early Cinema, Streible 2008, among many others.

10 See especially the large amount and popularity of baseball films in South Korea, or the many sports films produced in India every year.

11 See for rather recent examples ZIDANE – UN PORTRAIT DU 21E SIÈCLE (ZIDANE: A 21ST CENTURY PORTRAIT, D. Gordon / P. Parreno, F/IS 2006), AL DOILEA JOC (THE SECOND GAME, Corneliu Porumboiu, RO 2014), or IN THE REALM OF PERFECTION (J. Faraut, F 2018).

12 See especially chapters 2 and 3. Both Seán Crosson and Andrew Miller use this specific term, although only to describe a semiotic capacity of sports, which the sports film then exploits (see Crosson 2015 and Miller 2003, 304). For the question of how to understand the sports film as an American genre, as well as for a very rare but fruitful binational perspective, see Bonnet 2017.

focus on athletic *agon* excludes for example horse and – as a lately again quite potent genre cycle – automobile racing films.¹³ But as already mentioned before, with an understanding of genre as a dynamic system of cycles and media of expressive and perceptual modalities (as developed in chapter 2.2), I do not aim at any categorical delimitation or exclusion here at all, simply a refined focus at the outset.

Miller himself aspires to "define the sports film within a historical and generic framework that begins with the origins of cinema" (Miller 2003, 6). It is in that sense that his impressive work, which is based on an examination of over three hundred films, constitutes the necessary complement to my work here, as I do not aim at something like a historically comprehensive study at all. With regard to a historical timeline, my film corpus starts with the 1940 production KNUTE ROCKNE ALL AMERICAN (L. Bacon), hence even long after the establishment of the narrative (sports) feature film. This starting point nonetheless coincides with Miller's three-part periodization, as he recognizes "a new era in sporting cinema" (Miller 2003, 10) with the United States entering World War II. He specifies the two prior periods of sports film history as that of early (sports) cinema from about 1896 to 1919,¹⁴ and that from 1920 to 1940, with "the plethora of sports films set on college campuses" (Miller 2003, 10).¹⁵

Intervention I: Aesthetic Analysis and the Poiesis of Film-Viewing

In his article on *The Dramaturgy of Action and Involvement in Sports Film*, Murray Pomerance introduces the notion of "screened sport" by distinguishing it from

---

13 See for example the co-productions FORD V FERRARI (J. Mangold, USA/F 2019), RUSH (R. Howard, UK/GER/USA 2013) and SENNA (A. Kapadia, UK/F/USA 2010), or the NASCAR comedy TALLADEGA NIGHTS: THE BALLAD OF RICKY BOBBY (A. McKay, 2006). There are also a lot of more recent films in a documentary mode, see for example THE 24 HOUR WAR (N. Adams / A. Carolla, 2016) or 1 (P. Crowder, 2013). Historically, the racing feature film reached a peak during the 1960s and 1970s with movies like GREASED LIGHTNING (M. Schultz, 1977), THE LAST AMERICAN HERO (L. Johnson, 1973), LE MANS (L. H. Katzin, 1971), WINNING (J. Goldstone, 1969) and GRAND PRIX (J. Frankenheimer, 1966). Surprisingly, and apart from the ones just mentioned as well as the very popular one DAYS OF THUNDER (T. Scott, 1990), there are not too many NASCAR feature films, given the high popularity of this sport in the US.
14 See especially the many documentary films of (live or restaged) boxing matches, with THE CORBETT-FITZSIMMONS FIGHT (E.J. Rector, 1897) as the most famous representative.
15 See for example THE PINCH HITTER (V. Schertzinger, 1917), COLLEGE (J.W. Horne / B. Keaton, 1927), TOUCHDOWN! (N.Z. McLeod, 1931), HORSE FEATHERS (N. McLeod, 1932), or FIGHTING YOUTH (H. MacFadden, 1935).

what he calls "broadcast sport" (Pomerance 2006, 312–313). Pomerance points out that the latter, by which he seemingly means televised games in particular, cannot simply be understood as a neutral, technological act of transmission, "as a passive response to exertions already in progress as the object of its attention" (Pomerance 2006, 312–313). At the same time, he describes screened sports in contrast to such media coverage as dramaturgically "organized as a *direct* experience for a viewer who would seem to have the good fortune of attending the game being shown onscreen" (Pomerance 2006, 313, [emphasis mine]).

Is it a less direct experience when we perceive images of broadcast sport? What do action and involvement actually mean when we talk about the engagement of a film viewer? Pomerance answers these questions only implicitly, but nonetheless provides very appealing suggestions: first, to grasp broadcast and screened sports as athletic exertion and thus as some kind of sensory performance themselves; and second, to analyze sports film images more according to their formal (shot) construction than to any given cultural context or narrative content (see Pomerance 2006, 311). In that way, Pomerance expresses one of the main points of intervention of this book, while his analytical account at the same time reveals the difference between his approach and what I want to put forward here. Remaining very much inclined to the primacy of narrative function and symbolic meaning-making, the action and involvement of his film viewer is grasped primarily at the level of identificatory and cognitive processes of recognition. In contrast, this book wants to depart from the application of models (of sociology, historiography, communication and cultural studies), which grasp films and their meaning-making by means of predetermined, fixed categories and positions of agency, reality, representation and knowledge. Rather, it will originate from and look more closely at the films' images and sounds – or more precisely, at the dynamics of their audiovisual expressive movement, which, as it is perceived by the recipient, is the actual source of the emergence of their meaning. In this sense, audiovisual meaning-making is to be understood as a dynamic process, as a "process of fictionalization" including "an act of subjectification" (Kappelhoff / Greifenstein 2016, 188) – a process that "is in no way exhausted by reproducing existing cognitive schemata of movement, space, and time" (Kappelhoff / Greifenstein 2016, 191), but modulates such schemata and creates different ones in the first place. Sarah Greifenstein and Hermann Kappelhoff define such processes with regard to audiovisual metaphoricity as follows:

> The processes of fictionalization are carried out as the differentiating, varying, and analogizing of the schemata of everyday perception. That is, film images articulate sense experience that spectators realize as their own bodily perceptual experience, on the one hand, which are comparable to everyday perceptual processes. On the other hand, spectators reflect these as the experience of an outside world, from which they are radically excluded.

> This results in the creation of positioned and differentiated subject positions, which then forms the basic framework within which the cognitive processes of fictionalization are carried out, from which moving images become visual representations in the first place.
> (Kappelhoff / Greifenstein 2016, 184)

Hence, audiovisual meaning-making is to be reconstructed as the dynamics of an affective movement of the audiovisual images, as "movement-images." Such reconstruction – the analytical retracing of visual and tonal constellations, rhythms, progressions, etc. as executed in my analytical chapters – then "give[s] some indication of how diegetic horizons, narrative, and visual representations can emerge from out of audiovisual sense data as they traverse the embodied perceptual sensations of spectators" (Kappelhoff / Greifenstein 2016, 198).

To this effect, Kappelhoff and Cornelia Müller understand "film images as a product of the interaction between viewers and audiovisual images," and this interaction as "a genuine process of creation" (Müller / Kappelhoff 2018, 36). They address this process by referring to Michel de Certeau and with the notion of a "poiesis of film-viewing," which describes "an act of creative production that is to be located in the media consumption itself" (Müller / Kappelhoff 2018, 36). This concept takes up, as Kappelhoff further lays out, a very prominent notion in the history of film theory, namely that of the thinking of filmic images.[16] Gilles Deleuze provides an important impulse for such a notion of cinematic thinking, which grasps the perception of filmic images as a generating force that creatively intervenes in subjective imaginations of a collectively shared reality, as he not only implies a practice of 'thinking in images' with his cinema books,[17] but also defines thinking as the sensation of encountering the new in its becoming and thus precisely not or not only as a capacity of recognition. "Thinking is always experiencing, experimenting, not interpreting but experimenting, and what we experience, experiment with, is always actuality, what's coming into being, what's new, what's taking shape" (Deleuze 1995 [1990], 106).

It is especially in this sense that a specific reading of the Deleuzian concept of the cinematic *movement-image* (Deleuze 2013a [1983]) acquires central importance for Kappelhoff's notion of the *poiesis of film-viewing*. Distinguished from moving images as sheer audiovisual material, it integrates the targeted poetology of filmic thinking as a process of modulating our everyday perception by changing and creating new a priori conditions of our imagination, judgement

---

16 See Kappelhoff 2015 and 2018b, the latter in German.
17 See Deleuze 2013a [1983] and Deleuze 2013b [1985], and especially Deleuze 2013b [1985], 161 et seq. As in the case of most film theorists, he refers especially to Godard and Eisenstein here.

and cognition. From that point of view, films' relation to reality is not one of mirroring an already defined everyday reality, but it is this relation itself being the product of the poiesis of film-viewing, with films as co-producers of this everyday reality.

In that vein, this book aims to avoid the widespread tendency in (sports) film studies to "take the diegetic action as given so that it may be considered in light of prevailing cultural considerations" (Pomerance 2006, 311) and narrative conventions and, rather, to provide insight into how the perceived images and sounds of the team sports feature film intervene as themselves (parts of) an audiovisual discourse within an audiovisual culture in the first place.[18] To be able to recognize this intervention, as well as this discourse and culture, which I develop as a discourse of time as community-building crystallization creating and being embedded in an audiovisual culture of the American Dream as the central image by means of which America addresses itself as an imagined community and in its historicity (see chapters 3.1 and 3.2), it is necessary to reconstruct the cinematic movement-images producing and modulating this discourse by providing not only descriptions of the films' narrative content and cultural context, but aesthetic analysis (see Müller / Kappelhoff 2018, 36).

The confinement to a description of narratives and narrative content inevitably leads to questions of (cinematic) realism and thus (and with regard to the sports film) of the relations between the everyday world, a world of sports or sporting world and a filmic world (of sports). Many sports film scholars touch upon these questions, though not without carrying along a lot of implicit presuppositions – the most prominent one being 'filmic world equals narrative world.' They furthermore very often neglect the mediated disposition of these worlds, and thus how they relate and intertwine through their mutual co-production. While a comprehensive examination of this kind of intertwining surely exceeds the scope of this book, pointing out this imbalance by means of the example of the team sports feature film constitutes an important part of its agenda.

Real and Imagined Sporting Worlds

In his article *Sports History as a Vehicle for Social and Cultural Understanding in American History*, Murry Nelson reminds us of the famous words of historian

---

[18] Discourse being understood here in a Foucauldian sense as a process of the emergence of those truths within which we are forced to reflect our being, with the capacity to produce and structure reality.

Jacques Barzun: "Whoever wants to know the heart and mind of America had better learn baseball, the rules, and reality of the game" (Barzun 1955, 151).[19] Strikingly, and while continuing to talk about the important role of sports in the United States, especially with regard to forming and stabilizing communities, Nelson quite naturally mentions media sports and the sports film HOOSIERS (D. Anspaugh, 1986)[20] – in other words, equating the reality of America with the reality of the game with the reality of the audiovisual imagination of sports. But how can the sports film really be comprehended as a central (sociopolitical) relay of the (imagination of the) United States? In what ways does it become historically effective if we look beyond what it represents as given and toward how it operates aesthetically, producing and modulating the affective and perceptual structures that ground our cognition of what is 'given' in the first place?

By seeking answers to these questions with a focus on the US team sports feature film, I do not want to deny the intertwining of an obviously mediatized world of sports and the no less mediatized world of what is grasped as our everyday life – quite the contrary. What I want to oppose is a hasty understanding of the fictional sports film as a fixed media framework of conventionalized narrative and symbolic techniques, whose capacity is only seen in the mirroring (mis-)representation of preexisting and fixed structures (be them narrative, mythological, social, ideological), or as a media practice that simply exploits and refers to the capacities of sports as social practice and cultural form without modulating it. As David Rowe states, sports on film is as much about the (literal, allegorical, metaphorical, mythological, historical) relation "between real and imagined sports worlds and [...] the intimate or remote subjectivities that are, in turn, stimulated by it," as it is about the relation "between sporting and other worlds" (Rowe 1998, 353, see also 352). While a lot of previous media sports studies tend to focus more on the latter and thereby neglect the fictional sports film's contribution to an audiovisual culture of sports via its expressivity and poetics of affect, the primary task of this work here is to have a closer look at how these imagined sports worlds and the subjectivities they stimulate evolve aesthetically and how this evolution can itself be understood as historically and politically effective and significant.

---

19 This quote is cited from Nelson 2005, 118 who shortens it to: "To understand the heart of America, one must know baseball."
20 As Hoosier is the official demonym for a resident of the state of Indiana, the film's title is already very telling in this regard.

The Sports Film Viewer's Involvement

Bruce Babington recognizes – and I emphatically follow his observation – the focus on the relation of the sporting world and the 'real life' world of social meaning by many studies, which otherwise claim to analyze *images* of sports, as the main reason for the dominant discussion of the sports film "as a regressive site of white masculinism, and racial, sex, gender and class oppression" (Babington 2014, 9). While he acknowledges that such an approach has legitimate reasons and that these accusations must be raised since sports is so fundamentally charged with social significance, he states that for his project, which, similar to my own work, aims at a poetics of the genre of the sports film, "the complex meanings of sports and sports films are not wholly reducible to such questions" (Babington 2014, 9). Instead, such a poetics of genre

> should cover all important aspects of its films, including their narrative forms, their cross–generic interrelations, their formal conventions, their specific investment in spectacle, the histories of particular sports and cinemas, the interconnection of sport, cinema and nation, the positive and negative mythologies they embody, the circle comprising sport, cinema and social context, tradition and change. (Babington 2014, 9)

And even though neither his nor this book here appears to be able to include all of these aspects,[21] Babington continues with a sentence that nonetheless emphasizes an important point of intervention, orienting his as well as my study:

> It [the poetics of the genre of the sports film] should also address – which the most ideologically oriented criticism seldom does – the affirmative pleasures that sport and by extension artistic representations of sport give even in the consumerist and regimen driven world of contemporary sport to both participants and audiences. (Babington 2014, 9)

Following Kappelhoff, who recognizes this pleasure as the Aristotelian core within a (re-)conceptualization of the melodramatic mode and of modern genre poetics as a system of generic modes and "specific expressivities and affect-generating modalities," with "a wide variety of affect-dramaturgical schemata" being endlessly combined and (re-)created "as the sensation of the spectators" (Kappelhoff 2018a, 96),[22] I will put a special focus on the audiovisual expressive movement of the filmic images in my analyses.

---

21 Ultimately, Babington's four film analyses turn out to be rather short, providing quite a lot of (film) historical motivic contextualization but lacking any real engagement with audiovisual form.
22 He refers especially to the work of Christine Gledhill here, while having himself provided such a reconceptualization on fundamental grounds (see Gledhill 2000, 2018, Kappelhoff 2004 and Grotkopp / Kappelhoff 2023, the latter two in German).

Such a focus on "the instrumental engagement of viewers' attention and involvement" (Pomerance 2006, 311) is also what Murray Pomerance demands when putting forth his critique about most sports film studies' tendency to take the diegetic action as a given to be retrospectively classified by cultural categories. Instead of "taking that [narrative] logic more or less for granted and proceeding toward an exceptionally astute discussion of numerous sports narratives that stand upon it," Pomerance's intention is to turn to "specific cinematographic language" (Pomerance 2006, 311), by which he means especially (and almost entirely) camera work and shot length. He identifies three types of shots with crucial importance for the sports film: the panorama, the action, and the character portrait shot (see Pomerance 2006, 318 et seq.).[23] Although his interest lies nonetheless, and more than mine, in "a grammatically meaningful [...] cinematic rendition of sport activity" (Pomerance 2006, 317–318) maintaining authenticity, a make-believe realism, and certain narrative intentions, Pomerance understands screened sport not as a simple act of a (passive, direct, one-to-one) transmission of athletic exertion, but as "a situated exertion in itself" (Pomerance 2006, 312–313).[24] Since it does not just deliver the athletic exertion "to a viewer's distant attention" (Pomerance 2006, 312–313), but aims at "a direct experience for a viewer who would seem to have the good fortune of attending the game being shown onscreen" (Pomerance 2006, 313), the sports film notably evokes questions of involvement and performance, which Pomerance discusses with regard to viewer identification, production techniques and representational realism.

Additionally, he states that "filmmaking is itself a sport and film actors are athletes" (Pomerance 2006, 313), thereby at least implying that such an understanding is aroused in terms of the sports film. This is also an interesting idea insofar as we might grasp the films' audiovisual movement and its embodied perception by the viewer as a kind of athletic exercise itself, and thus not only a sports film's production but also its reception as a creative, meaning-making performance – quite in the sense of a "poiesis of film-viewing" (Müller / Kappelhoff

---

23 For the significance of the latter, see also especially chapter 4.2 of this book. To extract the different manifestations of an audiovisual discourse of the American Dream as the sports film genre's constitutive conflict in my film analyses, I will generally relate to all the different kinds of audiovisual means of expression and staging strategies, while of course identifying certain dominant ones.

24 While Pomerance rightly differentiates between (the production aesthetics of) sports broadcasting and the sports feature film, but then also emphasizes that the latter of course often renders TV and radio aesthetics within its audio-vision, this insight here applies to both realms.

2018, 36) already mentioned above.²⁵ While this notion will be specified by means of my first analytical chapter (2.3) on FIELD OF DREAMS (Phil Alden Robinson, 1989), it also forms an overall theoretical background for this work's subsequent analyses of KNUTE ROCKNE ALL AMERICAN (L. Bacon, 1940), JIM THORPE – ALL-AMERICAN (M. Curtiz, 1951), MIRACLE (G. O'Connor, 2004) and WE ARE MARSHALL (J. 'McG' McGinty Nichol 2006) later on (chapters 4, 5, 6).²⁶

Intervention II: A Different Approach to Genre

The necessary groundwork for grasping the team sports film in this media aesthetic manner in the first place, via its poetics of expression and perception, is a different approach to genre film on the most profound level. The reperspectivation behind it, which I will theoretically develop in detail in chapter 2.1, does not just answer the manifold attempts of how to define the sports film as a genre, but defies the taxonomic procedure usually provided, especially with regard to the sports film. Instead of applying fixed categories to films when grouping them, I will promote the idea of a dynamic genre system of modes of relating to the (fictional) world and modalities of experience, through which processes of creative (re-)appropriation and modulation, as well as a specific, reception and media aesthetically informed notion of cinematic realism take center stage. The implementation of such a genre-theoretical change of perspective will show how the sports film – precisely *because* of its 'unmanageable' heterogeneity frequently brought forward by scholars – presents a more than adequate research subject for elucidating the need and advantage of such a different approach. Namely, an approach that favors the analysis of single films as genre media over practices of classification on the basis of predetermined categories external to these films' forms and movements of perceived expression.²⁷

---

25 Reiner Hildebrandt-Stratmann and Andrea Probst describe poiesis as 'the ability to express subjective feeling and experience through composition,' whereas the poiesis of film-viewing addresses the emergence of this subjective feeling and experience along the dynamics of audiovisual composition, as movement-images (see Hildebrandt-Stratmann / Probst 2006, 184, my translation).
26 For a detailed conceptualization of the "poiesis of film-viewing," which constitutes one of the main focal points of the work having been done at the Center for Advanced Film Studies *Cinepoetics* at *Freie Universität Berlin*, see also Kappelhoff 2018b, 11–37 (in German).
27 As much as every genre film rethinks its genre (see Cavell 1982, 81) and as much as a film is 'made and thought anew' with every new viewing, this work should be understood as one suggestion for thinking the sports film as well as the idea of audiovisual historicity I attribute to it anew, and not as a provision of an in any sense comprehensive account on *the* history of *the* genre of *the* sports film.

The directly following chapter 2.2 will then flesh out such an understanding by means of a comprehensive analysis of FIELD OF DREAMS (P.A. Robinson, 1989) as a sports film that quite explicitly and playfully invokes and combines different Hollywood genre modalities. By rendering what I will, with recourse to a notion of Paul Ricœur, call an experience of deep temporality of the poiesis of sports film-viewing, hence an audiovisually induced experience of film history not as the chronological progression of discreet films, styles and periods, but as a dynamic compound of co-produced time-images reforming in ever new arrangements, this first analytical chapter will open the door to a meta level for defining an audiovisual discourse of communality and temporality in its specific reflexivity – and in that sense as the sports film genre's constitutive conflict. It will thus serve for getting a grip on the sports film as a medium of a shared perception of temporality and "the communal fabrication of a common world" (Kappelhoff 2018a, 99) of American historicity, understanding it in that way as a "genre-as-medium" (Cavell 1982, 79).

With regard to television series and his take on the *comedy of remarriage*, Stanley Cavell contrasts the notion of the "genre-as-medium" with the one of the "genre-as-cycle," recognizing both as different but equally legitimate and not entirely separable approaches to grasp genre (to different ends). While the latter fits the dominant way of how genre is generally and especially with regard to the sports film understood, the former, rather, addresses the change of perspective mentioned above. Hence, instead of executing a categorical top-down process, the single film becomes more the center of attention here, as emerging from and contributing to the genre, but at the same time also always challenging and changing it. This does not imply that the sports film should not be understood as a "genre-as-cycle" at all though, quite the contrary:[28] As should become clear by means of chapters 2.1 and 2.2, the sports film – with its status as what Glen Jones describes as an "invisible genre" (Jones 2008, 117) – reflexively problematizes, as I argue, the concept of genre film itself.

---

28 See also Cavell 1982, 80: "I think, for example, that it is easier to understand movies as some familiar kind of commodity or as entertainments if you take them as participating not in a genre-as-medium but in genres-as-cycles, or if you focus on those movies that *do* participate, without remainder, in genres so conceived." As already implicated above, it might be helpful to distinguish – heuristically and with regard to the specific sport depicted – between certain genres-as-cycle (baseball film, boxing film etc.) of the sports film as genre-as-medium. For a very recent account that seems to proceed in such a way (even though not theorizing it), see Friedman 2020.

The American Dream as Constitutive Conflict

For Cavell, a genre in the sense he develops with the comedy of remarriage (Cavell 1981) evolves along two basic "laws" or "principles": one "internal" and one "external" (Cavell 1982, 81). The latter addresses how a genre can be distinguished or distinguishes itself from other genres by partial negation (leading to new refinement on both ends); the internal principle speaks to "every feature in common" (Cavell 1982, 81) of a genre's members and also to a problem, to which a genre does not necessarily and immediately provide a solution, but around which it forms one by 'working through' it.[29] In the case of the comedy of remarriage, this problem or task involves the legitimation of marriage by means of mutual recognition beyond any religious or economic interest.

Following Kappelhoff referring to Aristotle, I want to grasp this problem as a genre's "constitutive conflict" (Kappelhoff 2018a, 66), which marks its political capacity to participate in the constitution of a (feeling for a) common world by means of the production and modulation of shared sensibilities, and through which it evolves in the first place. Such a constitutive conflict does not primarily address certain (mythological, ideological or sociopsychological) narratives, which represent "clashes of interest existing within a given social, political and cultural order" (Kappelhoff 2018a, 282). Rather, it arises out of the films' perceived audiovisual movement, manufacturing and interrogating "the founding shape of a political community in the sense of an order of sensoriality, a principle antagonism aimed at the communal world itself" (Kappelhoff 2018a, 282).[30] Hence, rather than pointing to the sheer representation of social conflicts, what is meant by this capacity is something more fundamental: a conflict which aims at processing the question of the relation of 'I,' 'We' and 'Them' on the level of expressive and perceptual forms, on the audiovisual poetics of films in their relation to each other and as producers of temporalities and spaces of experience.

Concerning the sports film, this constitutive conflict of competing strategies of subjectification – what is an 'I' in comparison to a 'We,' and vice versa? – is,

---

[29] While Cavell in *Pursuits of Happiness* does not develop a notion of a genre's problem theoretically when describing how films themselves engage in philosophizing, he nonetheless uses the term quite often, and in an at least twofold way that speaks to my conceptualization of it as a genre's constitutive conflict: on the one hand addressing problems 'philosophically' on the level of story and action, but on the other also and especially 'metaphysically' on the level of the medium of film more generally (see Cavell 1981, 54–55, 102, 268). Also cf. Schatz 1981, 35.

[30] One important characteristic of this conflict is, as Kappelhoff emphasizes with regard to the war film which, like the sports film, might also be called an 'American' genre, that it remains or has to remain irresolvable (see Kappelhoff 2018a, 307).

as I argue in chapter 3.2, first and foremost one of the American Dream. Prima facie, such a diagnosis does not seem to be particularly inventive or astute, as the mention of the American Dream comes up quite often within scholarly discussions of the sports film.[31] But these approaches almost always lack philosophically and aesthetically informed engagement with the American Dream, and thus apprehend it mostly as the films' historical or cultural context with which those correspond (affirmingly) via narrative themes or motifs. I want to instead get a grip on its imaginative dimension, capacity and effectiveness and thus discuss it as a cultural fantasy.[32] A cultural fantasy that is first and foremost concerned with a community-building temporality of crystallization, of an idea of time that addresses time not as a culturally codified container of measurement and thus as a linearly expiring juxtaposition of discrete sections or points, but as non-spatialized time in a Deleuzian/Bergsonian sense, as an ever new arranging simultaneity of "a present of the future, a present of the present and a present of the past" (Deleuze 2013b [1985], 105) in the event.[33] Thereby, I attend to an idea of communality defined by the productive tension between individual and collective subjectification, and the processes of exclusion and inclusion, separation and usurpation, which come along with it and are directly intertwined with a certain sense of historicity feeding from this apprehension of time as crystallization. In this light, and thus as a kind of reflexively effective, audiovisually co-produced discourse of imagining collectivity and historicity in the first place, the American Dream addresses the United States as the function of the possibility of becoming an exceptional individual among exceptional individuals *in time* – exactly because time is not a fixed and linear line of distinct instants, but a perpetual reconnection (with) a recapitulation of the past and future in the present.

---

31 See for example Crosson 2014, Farred 2008, Whannel 2008, or also Englert 2011 (in German).
32 For in-depth discussions of the 'Athletic American Dream,' which at least partially go along these lines, see Crosson 2013, and especially Miller 2007. Nonetheless, both accounts eventually rely on an understanding of the American Dream and its representation as narrative/narration. For a description of the American Dream as a cultural fantasy in the sports film context, see Gill 2012 [1999], 122 (citing Grella 1975).
33 According to Deleuze, this splitting or crystallizing of time is being directly expressed by means of the second form of the crystal-image, the time-image of the 'peaks of present' – an image that directly images time in its division (see Deleuze 2013b [1985], 105 et seq.). The first form, the pure time-image of the 'sheets of past,' indicates pure memory as the area of co-existence of (potentially) all images, detached from any present consciousness or recollection (see Deleuze 2013b [1985], 103 et seq. and also Fahle 2002, in German).

It is in this vein that this book will show how the sports film constructively intervenes in a culture that is defined by this community-building imagination of communality and historicity and how it thereby forms itself as a genre. Hence, what I examine more closely by means of detailed film analysis is how we can grasp and talk about a "cinematic sporting culture" (Miller 2007, 117), which – at or as the "intersection of sports and 'Americanness'" (Miller 2003, 304) – incorporates the American Dream and the 'Athletic Dream' to become "the foundation of American self-image" (Miller 2007, 118).[34] How does the cinematic thinking of the sports film – as a poiesis of film-viewing and in this sense as the source of an audiovisual discourse of historicity and communality that also addresses the act of film-viewing itself – intervene in what we could describe as an audiovisual culture of the (Athletic) American Dream?

Corporeal Temporalities and an Audiovisual Discourse of Time as Crystal

The general thesis, from which I want to start to answer this wider question, unfolds as follows: sports feature films, especially those concerned with dominant US team sports, seemingly seek to modulate and relate many temporalities at play in media sports. That is, both those generic, 'disciplined and disciplining' ones applicable to a specific sport as a culturally codified practice – the 'rules of the game,' with all the ambiguity of that term;[35] and those corporeal

---

34 See Lester D. Friedman's book on sports movies, in which he, by referring to Miller, describes the American Dream in this sense as a point where sports and culture merge, especially through the mass medium of film, culminating in what he calls "the ESPNing of America" (Friedman 2020). As already hinted at above, I want to breathe life into such a formulation beyond the assertion of fixed entities (media like TV as technologies of communication on the one side, America as a nation on the other) and a comparison of certain narrative archetypes, stories and somehow represented values. Hence, to remain within the picture, questions this book tries to answer would be: In what way is ESPN American? And in what way is America ESPNesque? How and on what level do they relate and produce each other in the first place? And how exactly can we understand the American Dream as the site and mode of this production?

35 I will not treat this aspect in any systematic way here. However, from the about 70 films I have watched in the course of the preparation of this book, it can be stated that these actual sports temporalities are dramaturgically referred to in an often quite detached manner by (the different cycles of) the sports film, rather orienting itself (themselves) strongly towards what might be recapitulated as Classic Hollywood style in all its historical variation. One very obvious point of this relation to observe is the films' generic dramatization of the decisive moment (see the analysis of WE ARE MARSHALL in chapter 4.2).

ones of performance, expression and perception – of the body onscreen and offscreen, the acting body in front of the camera, the (imagined) athletic body on the field, the character and the spectator body – not discretely, but beset by blurred boundaries and interweaving, especially regarding the latter two.[36] They further appear to modulate and relate to those temporalities associated with the "film's body" (Sobchack 1992, 49), which Vivian Sobchack in her film phenomenology conceptualizes as a perceptive and expressive instance itself, whose productive entanglement with the spectator body through movement guarantees for the cinematic experience in the first place:

> The movement generated in the medium of film images takes on a different, physical reality in the perceiving body of the spectator as the physical, sensory experience of being-affected. The movement of the film image materializes as the physical sensation of the spectators, is embodied by them – spectator perception and film expressivity are directly intertwined in movement.[37] (Kappelhoff 2018b, 113, referring to Sobchack 1992, 5–13)

All of these bodies perform and are performed in time. And each of these bodily temporalities is also the product of a certain media specificity: a picture of quarterback Tom Brady in a sports magazine crafts and shapes something different from a slow motion shot of him on TV. Baseball star pitcher Justin Verlander experiences a play by his team differently than a spectator in the stands of Minute Maid Park in Houston, or a viewer digitally streaming the Astros' game on her laptop in Germany. By incorporating all these aesthetic temporalities, the US team sports feature film co-produces, as I argue, an audiovisual discourse of American Dream time, which reflects time not as a secondary determination of

---

36 Central to the sports film's mise en scène is the staging of a diegetic audience, of bodies, voices and especially faces of characters observing what happens on the field. Most often, these characters are acquaintances of the film's hero(es), or broadcast crew people (a radio commentator, for example). Pomerance emphasizes the role of such characters for the sports film, "treated as a visible adjunct to the game, equally available for filmic dramatization" (Pomerance 2006, 313). For the aesthetic implications of such reflexive inclusion of an additional level of spectatorial perception, see also especially the analysis of WE ARE MARSHALL in chapter 4.2.

37 It is this movement of the filmic images – as the represented bodies in space, but also especially as the audiovisual dynamics of montage, camera movement, framing, color processes etc. – which has to be analyzed as the generative ground of the image space that arises for the film-watching spectator as a perceiving body affecting and being affected. In this sense, "the film image is to be understood as a form of media experience" which "encompasses the movement of bodies in space and the dynamics of the embodying perceptual process of the spectator in the movement of a visual space that unfolds and changes in the time of the film" (Kappelhoff 2018b, 114).

seemingly fixed conscious subjectivity, but as temporality as such, and thus as the condition of subjectification – as the ground of *Dasein*, as the source of possibilities of *being-in-the-world*.[38] Here, time is addressed as the force of an ever new instantaneous contraction of eternity and the infinite proliferation of the moment (as different repetition). It is in this sense that the dimensions of past, present and future, which we are familiar with on the basis of their linear relation with regard to mechanical time, are produced and graspable in their primary interconnectedness.

This discourse is not primarily to be derived or does not primarily derive from (the recognition of) the represented, narrative and narrativized content of sports and the sports-related world but accumulates as a dynamic perceptual-expressive environment of audiovisual and affective manufacture, modulation and relationality. Here, time becomes reflexively graspable in what we could describe with Deleuze as its crystalness (see Deleuze 2013b [1985], chapter 4); not as spatialized clock time but Bergsonian lived time *(durée réelle)*, connecting and splitting the virtual and the actual with a present that is or constantly evolves as a dynamic and ever new interpenetration of past and future. As Deleuze argues, it is the "crystal-image" in which time appears in this sense, as 'time itself.' The sports film, as I claim and will argue for in this book, becomes a genre by (co-)constituting such a crystal-image itself. This crystal-image is the American Dream as audiovisual discourse and social imaginary. While the former is expressively and perceptually generated and structured and assumes time not as a linearly progressing line of distinct points defined by fixed relations, but as an open and changing whole of colliding movements, of bodies as images, by means of which the present is always also the future of a past and the past of a future, the latter becomes culturally effective in this very sense of crystallized and crystallizing temporality. Much in the same manner that they

---

[38] I am aware that while there certainly is a similarity between Heidegger's and Deleuze's philosophical modeling of time, the latter's project of course differs decisively from the former's in rejecting the anthropocentrism of phenomenology, and in getting away from any kind of phenomenological consciousness. Hence, while Heidegger in *Being and Time* thinks through the present of the past, the present of the future and the present of the present by referring to the human individual via memory and what he calls our Being-toward-death as a mode of being of a 'not-yet' (of futural projection, of possibilities), Deleuze, with Bergson and against Husserl, with cinema and his fundamental notion of image as movement, explicitly argues for doing away with the assumption of any privileged natural perception (see the second commentary on Bergson in *Cinema I*, Deleuze 2013a [1983], chapter 4). This is also important to note with regard to my film analyses, as I do not want to give rise to the suspicion that what I address with a certain perception and experience of time has anything to do with the experience of film characters treated as human subjects in a psychological sense.

do not primarily address any individual experience or the projection of a fixed collectivity, this discourse and imaginary of the American Dream cannot and will not be derived from the comprehension of represented narrative content in the first place. Rather, what these notions encircle throughout this book is the product of a filmic thinking through movement-images.

2 The Haunting Question of Genre

2.1 The Shortcomings of Narrative Analysis

Within scholarly work on the fictional sports film, the question of genre is a haunting one. Even when approaching sports movies without a specific genre theoretical question, the matter of whether they form their own genre or belong to another always seems too urgent not to be clarified, or at least addressed.[1] Many of the articles on the sports film include at least a small section in the beginning about whether and how sports films can be understood as a genre – as if this problem can and should be resolved prior to delving into proper research questions and analysis. Very often, these texts approach this question primarily (and often solely) with regard to topic and narrative content. At the same time, and as Andrew Charles Miller, whose impressive study "Laying Down the Rules: The American Sports Film Genre from 1872 to 1960" (Miller 2003) might be the only work touching upon the question of a sports film genre in a historically concrete and comprehensive manner, rightfully observes, it is the other way around when it comes to major works of genre theory: here, the fiction sports film is often not recognized as a proper genre.[2]

On a broader scale, I would like to argue that it is this succumbing to the urge to search for a prior definition that paralyzes and obscures further fruitful elaboration. It demonstrates how deeply a certain rule-based understanding of genre, which particularly triggers operations of mere inclusion and exclusion, is rooted in most genre criticism. Very often, scholarly discussion does not even try to venture beyond soft notions of an everyday understanding, especially with regard to the sports film.

While there is no doubt about the existence of a rather strong coherence of certain cycles of films, the impulse to collect their obvious and manifold affinities as the bedrock of a categorical grouping is preemptive and leads quickly to dead

---

[1] Besides those approaches, which I will discuss shortly here in this chapter, there is another way in which sports sometimes enters the discussion of genre, namely, as a kind of metaphorical meta-category, when (the experience of) genre is grasped more generally as a playful operation or a game-like system of certain rules, but also liberties (see Altman 1999, 157 and Schatz 1981, 691–92, as cited in Crosson 2013, 50).

[2] Miller explicitly mentions Altman 1999 and Neale 2000 (see Miller 2003, 4–5). Both do briefly mention sport specific classification by talking about boxing or baseball films – a method I would dismiss not quite as rigorously as Miller does, but nonetheless value as only partially helpful at most, for example with regard to particular, sport specific cycles by means of which one wants to carve out a certain emphasis (see later in this chapter).

ends. This is especially the case in regard to historical studies that seek, or should seek, to focus on dynamic modulations, but then do not do much more than defining and recognizing a taxonomic set of predetermined and persisting narrative topics and regimes, as well as conditions of production. As I do not want to deny a certain need for some heuristic classification to limit and get a grip on one's object of research, by means of a working hypothesis – for example, in the case of this book: to define a sports film by a plot mainly revolving around competitive athletic exercise of American spectator team sports – such proceedings should not be seen as the decisive step to gain valuable historical insights.

Instead of providing another account on how the sports film could be labeled and categorized, I want to present an approach to genre that genuinely considers its dynamic and transformative logic, thereby showing that the question of genre is always also a question of genre theory.[3] An approach which not only takes the most basic fact about genres seriously – that they are multiple and that they change with every new film – but also claims that the differences resulting from that change are not based on, and cannot be adequately explained as solely deriving from the diversity of certain norms and conventions of making and watching movies, especially in the sense of storytelling functions or the capacity of recognition and tacit knowledge of a somewhat definitive viewer. Rather, these differences must be based on (the description of) the variety and the interdependence of audiovisual structures and spatiotemporal dynamics that are part of ever-evolving *modes of realism*, of modes of mimetically relating to a world, and in this sense form *modalities of expression and perception*, which relate to one another and are to be reconstructed and understood as (a history of) ways of worldmaking.

Before I expand on this perspective, which is heavily oriented towards Hermann Kappelhoff's and Matthias Grotkopp's non-taxonomic approach to genre as a dynamic system of such modes of realism and affective modalities, primarily inspired by a revisiting of Aristotle's conceptualization in *Poetics*, as well as by ideas of Stanley Cavell and Christine Gledhill,[4] let me first expand a bit upon the

---

[3] Tzvetan Todorov's work on the theory of genre includes the idea that historical genres are always theoretical genres, but as it is not the case the other way around, theoretical genres are only somewhat helpful when used heuristically (see Todorov 1976, 162/170 and Todorov 1975 [1970], 21 et seq.).

[4] See Grotkopp / Kappelhoff 2023 (in preparation, in German). For an early version of this concept, see Grotkopp / Kappelhoff 2012. For further elaboration with regard to the specific genre of the Hollywood war film, see especially chapters 2 and 4 of Kappelhoff 2018a. For the theoretical foundations, see especially Cavell 1981 and 1982 and Gledhill 2000 and 2004.

different existing approaches concerning the question of genre in regard to sports films. As will hopefully become clear, the genre-theoretical reperspectivation indicated here and developed later in this chapter immediately implies the necessity of the following chapters. In these, I will first try to analytically implement this conception of genre as a dynamic system of modalities in which expressive and perceptual forms are picked up and modulated within an evolving structure of "generic crossroads" (Altman 1999, 145) by looking closely at the baseball movie FIELD OF DREAMS (P.A. Robinson, 1989). As will be shown, this film not only carries the gesture of syncretic reference to extremes, but renders such structure what I will call a *deep temporality of the poiesis of (sports) film-viewing*:[5] an audiovisually constructed experience of a viewer's passage through Hollywood genre history, which reflexively addresses sports and film as media of the self-imagination of American culture and sociality (chapter 2.2). Here, my project certainly shows strong resemblance with Cavell's take on the comedies of remarriage, at the beginning of which he emphasizes that

> [F]ilms [...] are primary data for what I would like to call the inner agenda of a culture. [...] I.e., the idea of something shared, call it a shared fantasy, apart from which the films under investigation here could not have reached their *public* position.
> (Cavell 1981, 17)

With regard to this idea of American film genres and genre films as not only 'primary data' but – if we understand this data in a dynamic-productive (and by all means Cavellian) sense as modes of realism and modalities of expression and perception – *media* of the creative imagining of American culture, I will then elaborate on such a (or maybe *the*) 'shared fantasy' most relevant when it comes to sports films: the American Dream. Or rather, a specific notion of the American Dream as a cultural fantasy of historicity and communality in whose production the sports film is crucially involved, and which, in that way – as the analysis of FIELD OF DREAMS will have shown by then – figures as what I will develop as its constitutive conflict, rendering it a genre in the first place (chapter 3.2). This conflict does not only take place through a film's narrative action, within its diegetic world or between its characters, but addresses questions of subjectification and belonging in a wider sense, with regard to the poetic construction and perception of a shared world of sensation and feeling. It manifests and becomes graspable as filmic thinking, as an *audiovisual discourse of a*

---

5 I will apply Michael Wedel's specific implementation of Ricœur's notion of "deep temporality" (Ricœur 1984 [1983], 62), and combine it with the concept of a poiesis of film-viewing. For the latter, see Müller / Kappelhoff 2018, 36, and (in German) Kappelhoff 2018b, 11–37.

poiesis of film-viewing, which in the case of the sports film is first and foremost concerned with the (paradox) interdependence of past, present and future, as well as of individual and communal subjectification in view of American exceptionalism. I will then provide exemplary close readings of films through which this audiovisual discourse becomes palpable in (some of) its different facets, being reflexively processed in ever new but relating poetics of time as crystallized time – of the decisive moment as crystallization of past and future (chapter 4), of flow as temporal dissolution (chapter 5) and of endlessness as repetition and circularity (chapter 6).

While one might tend to call these analyses exemplary to the extent that such an ambitious approach to genre would eventually demand a close reading of every single film as well as its impact on the genre as a whole, it is Cavell who argues the other way around when assessing his work on the Hollywood comedy of remarriage, saying that every time one puts together a certain group of films and discusses certain single ones of them, one sketches a new theory of genre (see Cavell 1982, 79). I would nonetheless like to call them exemplary in the sense that we could certainly obtain (variations of) these three poetics (through which the sports film "speaks" its constitutive conflict and forms as a genre) by means of other films, as well as more than these two with the films I analyze.

Sports as Textual Material

The German Reclam book series on film genres dedicates an entire volume to the sports film (Sicks / Stauff 2010). In the introduction, which precedes a collection of analytical sketches of almost sixty feature films, mostly fictional, the formation of the sports film as a genre is situated along the emergence of what is often referred to as classical narrative cinema in the 1910s and 1920s. Even before that time, sports as a cultural practice was strongly entangled with the development of moving images on the levels of technology, communication and entertainment, then remaining as motif and dramatical resource (see Sicks / Stauff 2010, 11).[6] Especially with regard to a more or less consistent cycle of boxing films, Kai Marcel Sicks and Markus Stauff understand the sports film as a genre in which important questions of society and culture become assimilated as topics. At the same time, the sports film is described as some kind of myth machine here. Nonetheless it might share some of these myths produced with

---

[6] This technological or techno-aesthetic connection obviously became stronger again with the later advent of television broadcasting.

other genres, they are particularly shaped through the prism of the motives and narratives of athletic competition (see Sicks / Stauff 2010, 11). Alongside the generational conflict and the story of the successful underdog, Sicks and Stauff mention the reconciliation between outsider and mainstream society as one of those myths. Furthermore, sports films contribute heavily to the imagination of an American identity, as well as to the collective remembrance of significant events in (sports) history – two aspects directly connected and with the latter strikingly dominant in most productions prima facie. All of these claims will become central aspects of this book's overall argument about the poetics of time and historicity of the sports film, making it a genre in the first place, as my thesis goes.

Sicks and Stauff do question the status of the sports film as an actual genre – not only because different kinds of sports provide for different kinds of spaces, dramaturgies and body images, as well as different forms of action and conflict, but also because of the wide range of what people classify as a sports film. This would further complicate the potential genre's handling, since it additionally increases its heterogeneity (see Sicks / Stauff 2010, 13). However, it is important to stress that the heterogeneity claimed here derives, first, from the heterogeneity of the world of sports itself (in the sense of these different kinds of forms and codifications just mentioned) and, second, from (linguistic) attribution – both of which remain external to the filmic form itself.[7] While I would agree that a specific sport to a certain extent implies specific characteristics with regard to its cinematic medialization, I nonetheless want to argue that these specifics can be grasped as different 'faces' and accentuations of a superordinate poetics of time in the sports film.

As for the sport films' audiovisual and affective form, Sicks and Stauff claim that there is neither a dominant emotion stimulated by it nor a consistent visual identity to be recognized through for example specific landscapes, objects or clothes (see Sicks / Stauff 2010, 12–13). The comedy and horror film serve as counterexamples here, as well as the western and the costume drama, on which the authors unfortunately do not expand at all. While many accounts on the sports film at least imply that one could actually talk about certain recurring iconographies, audiovisual dynamics, or even standard scenes, no matter if looking at a football, golf or racing movie,[8] the question of whether a certain

---

[7] With regard to this problem, see also Miller 1990, 52.
[8] See for example Cashmore 2000, who argues along the idea of sub-genre forms, Rowe 1998 and especially Miller 2003. While such understanding is quite naturally often informed by considering more or less national cinematographies, it would of course also be interesting to look into the recursions and interferences of certain aesthetic and poetic patterns transcending national production borders. One striking case in that sense is most certainly the interdependence

genre operates by means of some kind of key emotion implies a rather short-sighted concept of the affective dimension of film-viewing, of filmic expression and perception. Such a concept again rather nurtures an analysis based on processes of adding and subtracting conventions, and blocks the possibility of an analysis of genre genuinely oriented towards dynamics of transformation by means of deviation, but also of progression through repetition, both on a level of the movement-images of a single film and the relationality of various films. I will come back to this point later in this chapter.

To really take account of such dynamics, it is therefore necessary to employ – as I will do in my analytical chapters – a more bottom-up approach which develops along a methodology that starts from close readings of the expressive movement patterns of specific films. While such strategy, of course, should not stop us from systematizing and modeling at some point to get a grip on certain groupings and linkages, it prevents an all too quick taxonomic classification often based on "a body of rules and expectations, shared by filmmaker and audience, which govern[s] its [each genre's] particular generic 'world' and by which any new entrant [is] constructed and operated" (Gledhill 2000, 223). As a result, films are seen as primarily structured by a defined (symbolic) relation to a superimposed 'real world' (to its themes, objects, narratives), and therefore evaluated on the basis of what they show instead of how they show it – content prevailing over actual staging strategies and perceptual structures.

Such an understanding is also highlighted when Sicks and Stauff describe the sports film as particularly determined by the specific and highly differentiated rules of the cultural practice of sports beyond its cinematic treatment (see Sicks / Stauff 2010, 13). This cannot be left unchallenged, as sports films certainly are defined by how they relate to the spheres of the sports they depict – especially with regard to the construction and perception of time and space –, but clearly not on a level of a hierarchical one-to-one reproduction.[9] Even though most accounts do not deny that "genres are not fixed in form or style but rather are constantly evolving [in relay]" (Crosson 2013, 50), they mostly search for those developments and linkages with the help of methods and

---

of Asian (especially Japanese, South Korean and Hong Kong) cinema – with a film like WEEDS ON FIRE (DIAN WU BU, Chi Fat Chan, 2016) for example – and American cinema regarding baseball movies.

9 In terms of hierarchy, mind for example to what extent the form of American football has historically been shaped by the forms of its media depiction, especially with regard to television – a phenomenon which might generally be recognized, but is still today often ignored in favor of describing structures of economic and technological transformation (see for example Whannel 2009).

discourses of production and communication studies, or, at best, with the help of concepts of intertextuality. Often, such positions – in addition to assuming equivalence or unchanged mimetic reproduction (from sports to sports films) – also imply, or at least fail to challenge a somewhat transsubjective viewing experience.

Quite similar to Sicks and Stauff, who define a film as a sports film if the subject matter of sports structurally contributes to its looks or dramaturgy, Garry Whannel immediately turns to narrative analysis when he puts "the concept of respect in relation to identity and individualism" (Whannel 2008, 195) at the center of his approach towards the sports film. Sports as the films' subject matter provides, he continues, "an implicit narrative structure" (Whannel 2008, 197). He explicitly adds that this does not mean that sports is a readymade narrative, but that it rather contains a certain potential for narrativization, especially with regard to what Roland Barthes calls the hermeneutic code as that part of a text which creates enigmas and keeps the reader guessing.[10] In the case of sports, it is the "genuine uncertainty" of who will win, which, as "potential narrativity" (Whannel 2008, 197), can then be exploited by a filmic text.

According to Whannel, the then occurring narratives of competition, which favor individual success over everything else, have to be seen in line with structures of neo-liberal, capitalist ideology, masking lived experience and real circumstances of exploitation (see Whannel 2008, 198–202). As such perspective often combines with a rather narrow, functional understanding of the political with regard to media, it comes as no surprise that Whannel qualifies the world of sports films as mostly depoliticized, in the sense that the films fail to pave the way (represent, narrate) for a "concerted response, discussion or possibility of collective action" (Whannel 2008, 196) and a disruption of conventionalized structures of representation, even if one looks at rather 'critical' films like NORTH DALLAS FORTY (T. Kotcheff, 1979) or A LEAGUE OF THEIR OWN (P. Marshall, 1992).[11]

The potential narrativity also provides for the grouping of sports films, as Whannel adds, even though he on the other hand quite rigorously opposes the idea that they actually constitute a genre: "They do not have a consistent set of themes, images and tropes. They do not have a characteristic style or mise en scène. Sports films do not lend themselves to being understood through concepts

---

10 In his (post-)structuralist theory of textual meaning-making, Barthes distinguishes five different codes of this kind, which are woven into any narrative, the others being the proairetic, the semantic, the symbolic and the cultural code (see Barthes / Bellour 2002 [1970]).

11 For further elaboration on this very common ideology critical stance towards Hollywood and especially sports movies, see chapter 3.1 of this book.

of 'auteur'" (Whannel 2008, 196–197).¹² This is quite surprising and, once again, confirms the exciting and exemplary status of sports films with regard to the paradoxes of a taxonomic understanding of genre deeply rooted in film studies, insofar as Whannel himself continues to develop a model of semantic and narrative structures that implicitly combines certain films via the coherence he denied them just before. It is highly unlikely that Whannel's actual implication here is to entirely separate certain narratives from the 'themes, images and tropes' they produce or are produced by.

While Bruce Babington also points to this incongruency within Whannel's statements (see Babington 2014, 4–5), his own account represents another dead end of the taxonomic-textual model of (the sports film as a) genre. Following his claim that the sports film is especially "open to hybridity as the sports narrative attaches itself to different modes and sub-generic categories," he presents a long list which is basically all over the place, from the "romantic comedy" to "the art film" and "the gay and transsexual affirmation film" (Babington 2014, 12–14). Babington's book is clearly meant as an introductory overview, but nonetheless, such procedure of listing and classifying is poison for any further genre film analysis. Things always seem to be settled and questions of in- and exclusion of narrative elements dominate the discourse, often leading to close readings that remain on the surface of single films, treating them as not much more than examples for categories of motive, narration, type of character – and, sometimes, expressive quality and staging strategy. If touched upon at all, the latter two of those categories are almost exclusively discussed by means of the notion of spectacle as some kind of deployment of a forceful audiovisual rhetoric triggering emotional intensity (see Babington 2014, 49). However, a proper qualification of such rhetoric and perceptual intensity usually remains absent.

Such an understanding of sports as first and foremost textual, content-related material existing to be exploited or duplicated by audiovisual media through specific, predetermined forms, which surprisingly cuts across a lot of the research on the sports film,¹³ also manifests in notions of genre that treat sports simply as a thematic add-on to other genres and types of film. Crosson speaks of "sports-themed films" (Crosson 2013, 51), we read of the sports comedy,

---

12 He furthermore justifies this claim from an economic standpoint, with the assumption of sports film being box office poison (see Whannel 2008, 197). While this argument is quite often put forward (see also for example Crosson 2013, 52), such reasoning clearly has to be questioned, especially with regard to sports films having notoriously subsisted on second window exploitation since the upcoming of TV and home video entertainment.
13 Within the German context, see for example also Florschütz 2005.

the sports melodrama or sports animation (Sicks / Stauff 2010, 14),[14] whereby questions could obviously also immediately be raised about the level on which these 'main' genres themselves can be understood as such. Similarly, the term sub-genre frequently shows up in discussions of the sports film, for example when Glen Jones, with regard to the labeling systems of DVD merchandise, video stores or film websites, grants it the status of a "recognizable sub-genre with distinctive subject matter, style, formulas and iconography but not a genre in [its] own right" (Jones 2008, 121). Ellis Cashmore, in one of the most comprehensive interdisciplinary approaches to sports studies, also identifies three dominant 'sub-genres' of the sports film: the dramatic/biographical, the comedy/fantasy, and the documentary (Cashmore 2000, 132–139). While what seems to me a rather superordinate classification certainly helps to group a large number of productions, it is of limited help when aiming to make more precise statements about specific films and the dynamic web of connections and historical developments they form as a genre.

In his mythological take on the sports film as genre, whose obvious reference to Northrop Fryes theory in *Anatomy of Criticism* (Frye 1957) remains unverbalized, Stephan D. Mosher focusses a certain constitutive narrative dramaturgy and tags four different types of plot corresponding to different audience expectations: comedy, tragedy, romance and satire (Mosher 1983, 15–19). Glen Jones, in turn, considers the sports film an "invisible genre" (Jones 2008, 117), thereby mainly alluding to the fact that these films, despite their regular appearance and wide reception at least on a national level, have not received much academic attention yet. While such statements appear quite regularly and seemingly often function first and foremost as a rhetoric of justification of one's own scholarly work,[15] Jones, in his further remarks, nonetheless tackles an important point concerning the sports film and, more generally, an understanding of genre that goes beyond a poetics of narrative rules, conventions and topics. By describing the convergence of boxing films like BODY AND SOUL (R. Rossen, 1947) and THE SET-UP (R. Wise, 1949) with film noir, he develops the idea of the 1940s sports film as a "hybrid film" (Jones 2008, 118), thus making clear that even if one comprehends genre as a "boundary phenomenon" (Gledhill 2000, 221), this cannot imply clear cut demarcations. Unfortunately, Jones hesitates to generalize this insight in favor of a non-taxonomic and non-narratological understanding of genre. And even though he more than once refers back to Christine Gledhill's famous essay *Rethinking Genre*, which will guide, inter alia, the non-taxonomic model of recursive modes and modalities of expression

---

14 For a worthwhile account on sports and animation, see Wells 2014.
15 See also for example Barbara Englert's and Robert Gugutzer's anthology of the sports film, with its subtitle "on the scholarly discovery of a misjudged genre" (Gugutzer / Englert 2014, in German, my translation).

and perception I will suggest further on in this chapter, he does not go along the theoretical trajectory (the part of "rethinking") inherent in her remarks. The "recurring issue with sport themed films [...] often found categorized in terms of other genres (comedy, drama, science-fiction, etc.) or by the individual sport featured" (Crosson 2013, 55) remains encompassed in a more or less unfruitful discussion.

The Necessity to Cease from Narrative Content as Holy Grail

One of the most common points of departure in terms of genre is a narrative content-related one, often supplemented by a statement about dominance: A sports film is a sports film if its plot and action primarily revolve around athletic exercise and competition. This surely is a good starting point to get a grip on a certain body of films, and thus on what Stanley Cavell calls a "genre-as-cycle" (Cavell 1982, 79), with its "repetitions and recurrences" (Cavell 1982, 81). At the same time, however, we have to be aware that it entails the danger of blundering into the traps and dead ends of a perspective of literal (corresponding, denotative) representation, which often remains uninformed of sensational structures, aesthetic perception and the creative capacity of "genre-as-medium" (Cavell 1982, 79), and instead focuses primarily on thematic reproducibility and textual implementation, resemblance and recognition.

If we instead want to tackle the manifold appearances, historical heterogeneity and socio-political embeddedness of these films by analyzing their movement-images as audio-visual structures of perception and sensation creatively relating to each other, such an understanding cannot provide a stable, let alone sole basis for their examination. Since what often follows then – and remains a problem that is, surprisingly, almost never reflected upon – is a constant referral to and application of external, non-filmic or superficial categories and properties, through which merely stating that something is represented seems to suffice as an analysis of that representation, and hence becomes synonymous with and covers over *how* it is represented. In this vein, genres take shape as a result of taxonomic determination, and genre films as well as their production of meaning come within reach based on not much more than acts of attribution, inclusion and exclusion. What such analysis lacks is specificity and unexpected variation in terms of concrete media forms and perceptual structures. It also misses historical development, at least in the sense of a notion of historicity that feeds from forms of aesthetic experience and temporal relationality, rather than from semantic attribution, linguistic meaning and determination.

What I want to suggest in this chapter is, in a sense, an approach that proceeds inversely: to look at a cycle of films, deduce central conflicts of sociality and forms of experience by looking beyond predetermined iconographies, narrative arcs, character behavior and courses of action; then analyze these forms in more detail and in their variation, thereby recognizing that a genre must always be understood (anew) from the angle of every specific film analyzed (anew). This might not be the ultimate solution to the problem of genre, but one which enables us to understand genre films in their historical variation and citation, as media of ever-new arrangements and regimes of expression, and of "a shared perception of the world" (Kappelhoff 2018a, 285) within an expanding (or at least consolidating) net of perpetual ramifications of such affective arrangements and regimes. It productively circumvents an analysis which all too quickly concentrates on and operates with sociological categories (of agency, of identity, of race etc.) that are formed outside of or prior to the films, and which transfers (discursive, metaphorical) meaning from an everyday world (of sports) to filmic (sports) worlds,[16] thereby often drawing connections between these worlds only on the level of narrative content and form, topics, or contexts of production and distribution.[17]

2.2 A Genre-Theoretical Reperspectivation

Historicizing the Transgression of Convention and the Notion of a Sporting Culture

Still to date, one of the most ambitious and comprehensive works outlining the sports film as genre is Andrew Charles Miller's dissertation *Laying Down the Rules: The American Sports Film Genre from 1872 to 1960*, especially in its aspiration to "define the sports film within a historical and generic framework that begins with the origins of cinema" (Miller 2003, 6). Miller combines the examination of discourses of production, marketing and reception with a genre analysis inspired by Rick Altman's semantic-syntactic approach to provide a "cultural

---

16 Remarkably, the fact that the everyday world of sports has to be distinguished, or strives for distinction from everyday reality is almost always acknowledged and even emphasized. It is hence all the more surprising that such differentiation is often not considered when talking about the world of sports and the world of sports in film.

17 While its authors certainly did never strive for proper historical analysis but rather a statistical overview, the study *Sports Films: Social Dimensions Over Time, 1930–1995* (Pearson et al. 2003) nonetheless points to the prevalent tendency to imprecise, generalized accounts which try to understand the sports film as a genre by making up and applying artificial categorizations (especially with regard to narrative content and form), with no added value in regard to the analysis of specific films and their interconnectedness.

2.2 A Genre-Theoretical Reperspectivation — 31

prism through which to view historically shifting notions of class, masculinity, nation and race as they are constructed on [American sports] film" (Miller 2003, 12).[18] It cannot be underestimated how refreshing Miller's account is for the study of the sports film, especially in its uniqueness of understanding (Hollywood) genre as constantly evolving along the tension between concrete textual structures and cultural semantics, as well as between the ideological force of convention (with regard to those structures and semantics) and the "expressive force" of spectacular images of certain films "that have the power to transgress the genre's convention" (Miller 2003, 13). "I delve into both the suppressive impulse of the conventionalized genre and the expressive force of individual cinematic athletes" (Miller 2003, 13), and, as I would like to add and follow up in my study here, of individual films. As Miller also shows, these tensions always have to be historicized, or rather: it is such historical analysis through which a genre can be described and understood in a productive way in the first place – and even though he emphasizes that the act of defining a genre is the necessary first step, his methodological proceeding implies the more radical thesis of understanding genre first and foremost exactly through (the analysis of) its reflexive modulations and (intermedia) relationships in time (see Miller 2003, 17–18). This also feeds into a much more ambitious notion of sporting culture which makes no immediate, categorical difference between (narratives of) real-life sports and (narratives of) sports film with regard to the extent to which both make up this culture (see Miller 2003, 22–24) – even though Miller relies on primarily textual analysis to explore the "generic conventions that bind together sports, cinema and American culture" (Miller 2003, 7).

---

18 Altman continues to be one of the most important figures with regard to an advanced theory of film genre. As the title of his approach implies, he aims at an understanding and analysis of genre that considers both semantic and syntactic dimensions (see Altman 1984). This allows him, above all, to describe the historical dynamic of genre poetics beyond taxonomic schematism, and to tackle aspects of historical creation and transformation. He does so by furthermore introducing another dialectical pair of terms to describe the processes of a genre's (re-)forming and its effectiveness. Namely that of the ritualistic and the ideological function, with an acting out of wishes, fears and desires at play on the one hand, and the affirmation and manifestation of structures of power on the other (Altman 1999, see also Schatz 1981). Even though Altman stresses the importance of the viewer (especially the viewer's expectations) and the role of the audience by later including a third dimension, which he calls pragmatic, he remains within a first and foremost textual framework that rather ignores aspects of affective structures and aesthetic experience. For a pointed and insightful evaluation of Altmans approach, which stresses the importance of this pragmatic dimension by placing the fact of genre communication at the center of every genre practice and uses HE GOT GAME (S. Lee, 1998) as example, see Richter-Hansen 2014 (in German).

According to Miller, there are two main traditions which define this sporting culture: "the community and [the] blood-sport traditions" (Miller 2003, 24). These are, as I want to argue, central to the analysis of the sports film, as they account for the genre's "constitutive conflict" (Kappelhoff 2018a, 110), a notion Kappelhoff addresses as genre cinema's political capacity to be involved in the constitution of a (feeling for a) common world, by means of the production and modulation of (a community through) shared sensibilities. Therefore, rather than pointing to the sheer representation of social conflicts, what is meant by this capacity is something more fundamental: a conflict which aims at a feeling for a common world, which processes the question of the relation of 'I,' 'We' and 'Them' through and along the films' poetic logic and the viewer experience generated by it.[19] In the case of the sports film, this constitutive conflict of competing strategies of subjectification – what is an 'I' in comparison to a 'We' in comparison to another 'We' and another 'I' – is strongly interwoven, as I claim, with a specific idea of community-building temporality, with a society's reflexive historicity inherently inscribed in and described by what we know or rather what I want to carve out as the American Dream.

While what Miller calls the community tradition is connected to the upcoming of "the professional middle-class" and a "rapidly expanding market of mass-produced fiction" (Miller 2003, 24) from the end of the nineteenth century on, hence addressing the changing role of sports with regard to meritocracy, consumerism and liberal mythology of the ruling class, the blood sport tradition describes the more violent and vigorous, raw and excessive aspect of sports, thereby instead putting forward a certain idea of classlessness and nonconformity. Miller connects these traditions to certain kinds and dimensions of sports: the community tradition to the "respectable" (Miller 2003, 25) team sports like baseball and rowing, especially those situated in the college world, the blood-sport tradition to 'underground' sports like dog- or cockfighting and, first and foremost, boxing. Nonetheless, he also makes clear that this allocation is by no means determined, especially when these traditions become or are understood as defining modes of audiovisual media.[20] As much as college football

---

19 Altman seems to address something at least comparable when presenting a model of spectatorship through what he calls "generic crossroads" and "generic community" during the second half of his genre book (see Altman 1999, 145–165). Already understood as a plurality of competing (re-)groupings by Altman, this idea to a certain extent informs current concepts of 'affective communities' or 'communities of aesthetic judgement and taste' (see Kappelhoff / Lehmann 2019, Kilerci / Lehmann 2018, Kappelhoff 2016, Lehmann 2023 [in preparation]). See also later in this chapter and the directly following analytical chapter.
20 Miller does not talk specifically about these traditions becoming filmic modes, but his analytical proceeding by all means implies such an idea.

also bears characteristics of the blood-sport tradition, there are boxing films in which the "hard work-to-victory narrative" (Miller 2003, 25) of the community sports tradition, with its hero being uplifted and incorporated or accepted into civil society, is dominant.[21]

After a more than compelling exploration of the history of the sports film genre as a "discursive label [...] grounded in historical documentation" (Miller 2003, 88–90) – among other things, he consults a plentitude of film reviews and articles – Miller proceeds with an elaboration of "recurrent textual patterns" (Miller 2003, 89) and "the solidification of conventions of narrative and imagery" (Miller 2003, 92). Again, his explorations exceed such restrained statements, providing much more insight than the usual accounts presented above. Coming from and adding to the aforementioned semantic-syntactic approach to genre by Altman, Miller not only presents a list of recurring scenes, characters and staging strategies (see Miller 2003, 94–95), but constantly situates and deduces them historically – for the most part on the basis of concrete examples, thereby at least considering the sensational qualities of the moving images. When he problematizes the connection of early sports films and Gunning's "cinema of attraction" (Gunning 1986, Gunning 2004 [1993]), it becomes clear, on the other hand, how even Miller has a hard time breaking away from the idea of the primacy of narrative content (Miller 2003, 97–98).

There is of course no doubt about sports films being oriented towards and received through real-world (sports) narratives to a certain extent, but this does not mean that we can leave the films' aesthetic capacity, their images' "interest in speed and motion" (Miller 2003, 97), their formal strategies and affective structures aside analytically. While Miller definitely faces this by asserting a "sports-inflected aesthetic of realism" (Miller 2003, 101), which he sees at work through camera positions mimicking certain viewpoints (of athletes as well as

---

21 Miller puts forward the example of ANY GIVEN SUNDAY (O. Stone, 2000) as a community sports (football) film clearly and heavily drawing on the blood-sport tradition (Miller 2003, 26). As already mentioned in my introduction, there is a quite strong connection between the boxing and the football film. Miller touches upon that aspect and its historical development in chapter 4 of his book (see Miller 2003, 145–224, and also 86). Within the framework of this book, ANY GIVEN SUNDAY is additionally interesting in view of at least three aspects: 1. in its quite obvious relationship to other genres, and here especially to the war film, 2. as an intriguing example when it comes to the question of the sports film's mode(s) of parody, and 3. with regard to its poetics of flow, contraction and 'violent' hypervisibility, audiovisually creating a kind of numbing omnipresence (cf. Pomerance 2006, 216–217). For a focus on ANY GIVEN SUNDAY within a take on the sports film as "reassuring cultural therapy," see McDorman et al. 2006, 209 et seq. For a focus on the film within a take on the role of violence in the sports film, see Florschütz 2005, 97 et seq. (in German).

spectators), images of diegetic audience and real time-alternating montage uncovering "unseen 'reality'" (Miller 2003, 100), I would like to go further and take the idea of images that produce certain temporalities through their movement in time as the basis of an understanding of the sports films as genre, and of genre in general as a system of modalities of experience.

Genre as a System of Modalities of Experience

This idea of a genre system of modes and modalities takes its point of departure from Christine Gledhill's theory of genre and the melodramatic (Gledhill 2018, 2000), as well as from her insights concerning the relation of gender and genre in postmodern times (Gledhill 2004, 2012).[22] For her, an adequate conception of (film) genre in general has to grasp genre as a productive process within the creation of popular culture, focusing less on "bounded representations" of "discrete identities," in favor of "cinematic affect and discursive circulation between society and story, public and imaginary worlds" (Gledhill 2012, 2; see also Gledhill 2004, 200). This implies an understanding of media representations not as the final good of ideologies or certain aesthetic practices, but as unique contributions to processes of cultural production and negotiation.

> From this perspective, which differs from perspectives of socialism, feminism or psychoanalysis, the fictions of media are understood neither as 'mirror images' nor as 'distortions' being offset against a fixed package of primary 'real' circumstances, but as sites of cultural circulation and secondary creative elaboration.[23] (Gledhill 2004, 200)

In this sense, genre is not only defined by the dynamic interaction between cultural discourses and aesthetic experience and fantasy, but to be understood as an ever-evolving system of constantly shifting, interdependent generic forms (see Gledhill 2004, 208).

---

22 Even though often speaking of a (intermedia) genre *system*, most approaches, including this book, finally remain at trying to focus on (the formation of) one specific genre. Intriguing exceptions are, for example, Steve Neale's comprehensive introduction to the study of genre (Neale 2000) and Michael Wedel's study on a modern audiovisual culture of the senses in Germany between 1910 and 1930 (Wedel 2019). Even though it eventually renders the notion of a single genre unsuitable, it is of course nonetheless helpful to understand the historical development and cultural embeddedness of a supposedly single genre by means of such a non-taxonomic approach of a dynamic system of modalities of experience.
23 My translation of this passage, which very clearly gets to the heart of the problem, but seemingly only exists in the cited German text.

To better grasp on such a dynamic arrangement, Gledhill draws "on the concept of modality as the sustaining medium in which the genre system operates" (Gledhill 2000, 223) – a concept she explicitly situates in opposition to taxonomic approaches "seeking to define genres as exclusive categories, the identity of which rested in specific fixed features" (Gledhill 2000, 223). A modality, as Gledhill defines, is a "culturally conditioned mode of perception and aesthetic articulation [...] adaptable across a range of genres, across decades, and across national cultures." It functions in both historically generic and permeable ways, "organiz[ing] the disparate sensory phenomena, experiences, and contradictions of a [...] society in visceral, affective and morally explanatory terms," providing the genre system "with a mechanism of 'double articulation,' capable of generating specific and distinctively different generic formulae in particular historical conjunctures, while also providing a medium of interchange and overlap between genres" (Gledhill 2000, 227–229).

Specifically with regard to film, I suggest to conceptualize modality as a coming-together of the aesthetic construction of the images, on the one hand, as a form of affective expression that correlates with certain narrative constellations and strategies of staging, and, on the other, of aesthetic experience, as a manifestation of these affective forms through the viewer's perception. The point of departure of proper genre analysis within the meaning of such a non-rule-governed approach to a system of modalities (of 'genres-as-media') is what Kappelhoff coins the films' "poetics of affect" (Kappelhoff 2018a, 100).[24] In order to tackle genre films as "media for perceiving the world, through which a political community ensures itself a shared experiential horizon of values,

---

[24] See also Kappelhoff / Lehmann 2019. Deleuze defines affect as the virtual interval between action and perception, and, in the sense of Spinoza's *affectus*, as the passage of constantly changing intensity, as a "kind of melodic line of continous variation" (Deleuze 1978, 4). The film viewer takes part in this passage in the sense of the encounter of (at least) two affected (perceptually being acted upon) and affecting (perceptually acting) bodies – his or hers and that of the film. Deleuze calls this "mixture of bodies" (Deleuze 1978, 5), in correspondence to Spinoza's *affectio*, affection. While this encounter becomes especially graspable by means of the "affection-image" as the close-up shot (of a face) in which expression becomes perception and vice versa, every filmic image can eventually be understood as an affection-image. It is in this sense that I want to understand film-viewing as the meaning-making perception of the expressive movement of audiovisual images, and thus as what can be understood with Deleuze as the "movement-image" (Deleuze 2013a [1983]), according to Kappelhoff. It is this dynamic which I want to describe in my film analyses as affective (as perceived expressive) movement, and, in a wider sense, as a film's poetics of affect. It is important to stress that thereby, the viewer's and also a filmic character's subjective sensation is not understood as a psychological phenomenon, but as itself a mediated aesthetic construction.

relations to the world, belongings, and exclusions," we have to have a close look at their "poetic proposals of ever new spaces of aesthetic experience, in which they refer to themselves as a political community" (Kappelhoff 2018a, 153). This comprehension clearly implies refraining from widespread approaches that think of genre works as artefacts which merely reproduce conventions or/and are part of specific media industrial settings whose sociopolitical meaning is grasped on the level of the non-mediated representation of historical events and social conflicts. Instead,

> [t]he relevance of genre for the experience of social facts and their relation to social reality is decided at the level of the historical transformations of the genre system to be described, of the emerging and transforming poetics of affect in genre cinema in which concrete configurations of modes of aesthetic experience are fixed as positionings of aesthetic enjoyment.
> (Kappelhoff 2018a, 153)

At the core of such a dynamic genre system, which, as an ensemble of interdependent expressive forms and operating modes of representation is "part of a sphere of social communication in which heterogeneous events within social reality are made accessible and become transformed as aesthetic experience of living together" (Kappelhoff 2018a, 153), lies melodrama – at least with regard to film. Melodrama not as a distinct 'genre-as-cycle' (as the 'woman's film' or 'family melodrama'), but as the "fundamental mode of American moving pictures" (Williams 1998, 42), as a "genre-producing machine" (Gledhill 2000, 227) and "the mode of aesthetic experience of modern entertainment per se" (Kappelhoff 2018a, 92), encompassing all modalities, providing them with a mode of experience that draws from the potential of compassion with a victim-hero and whose unfolding spans between pathos and action.[25]

In that respect, the sports film is an ideal example for exploring the intersection of converging modalities of aesthetic experience and expression, especially as sports films' dominant audiovisual and narrative structures rely heavily on

---

[25] See Williams 1998, 83. Kappelhoff describes the melodramatic, especially with regard to the war film, as "a specific pathos of individualized suffering" (Kappelhoff 2018a, 92). See also his comprehensive study on the history of melodrama and the melodramatic (Kappelhoff 2004, in German). While Gledhill is not always clear about the difference between the terms mode and modality (which makes sense to a certain extent, given that 'meta-like' status of the melodramatic), I would suggest to distinguish between certain modes of relating to the world such as the tragic, the lyric, the comic, the documentary, and maybe the fantastic and the satirical mode, and the multitude of modalities of experience serving certain affective structures and sentiments, such as horror, action, crime, romance etc., with quite fluid boundaries of course. I tend to dismiss solely literary/narrative categories like 'biographical' for genre film theory.

this melodramatic unfolding of feeling and action, of sentiment and spectacle – the crush of defeat, the grief of losing, the elation of winning and so on. As existing scholarly work on sports films generally tends to identify genre at the level of (narrative and represented) content and through categories coming not from the world created by filmic images, but from the supposed real world of sports, they neglect these films' creative capacity in terms of the fabrication of a sociopolitical world in the first place, and therefore their *historical* appearance and correlation, especially by not analysing their specific *form*.

In this sense, the semantic and the syntactic dimensions of narrative/mythos as well as the visual 'spectacle' are not two mutually exclusive "generic codes that textually ground the genre" (Miller 2003, 9), but effects of the expressive-sentient movement of filmic images and its embodied imaginary reenactment by the viewer. It is on this level of audiovisual movement and affective expression that we should analyze genre films in their historical specificity and entanglement. Such an understanding might redeem what Seán Crosson points to at the end of the genre chapter in his book *Sport and Film* (see Crosson 2013, 49–65): an understanding less static and categorizing, less based on (narrative) convention and (extra-filmic) classification, but focusing more on change and variation, the "genericity" (Collins 1993) of repetition.[26] Here, Crosson refers to Altman and also cites David Rowe: "to claim that sports film may constitute a genre [...] it would be necessary to establish the existence of some shifting yet patterned relationships within or between subject matter, presentation, narrative, and affect" (Rowe 1998, 351).

The Sports Film's Allegorical Play with Time

Central for Rowe with regard to sports films is their allegorical character, in the sense that "they address the question of the dual existence of the social and sporting world as problematic, and that they are preoccupied with the extent to which (idealized) sports can transcend or are bound by existing (and corrupting) social relations" (Rowe 1998, 351–352). According to Crosson, who basically goes

---

26 With regard to this aspect, see also Steve Neale stating that genres, understood as processes, "may, for sure, be dominated by repetition, but they are also marked fundamentally by difference, variation and change" (Neale 1990, 56), and Jason Mittell, who claims that rather than "identifying the abstract theoretical 'essence' of a genre in idealized form" (Mittell 2004, 4), we have to understand genres as "contingent and transitory, shifting over time and taking on new definitions, meanings, and values within differing contexts" (Mittell 2004, 17).

along with Rowe here, the allegorical role of sports in the (Hollywood) sports film becomes most evident "in its attempt to affirm the American Dream" (Crosson 2013, 60). As will become clear during this and especially the next chapter, I follow Crosson in that the American Dream plays a central role for the sports film genre while also offering a number of slight but significant interventions: for one thing, to understand it not just as a certain ideology whose ideologemes become narrativized, but as an effective social imaginary: as a cultural discourse of community-building and historicity by means of and within which a society makes sense of itself and its coming into being, and which *cannot* be thought of as occurring outside of aesthetics and media practices, especially including the expressive and perceptual structures of audiovisual images and their processing of time. While many scholars acknowledge that there is a sports-inflected American Dream, the aspect of a (sports) film-inflected American Dream is given rather little attention.[27]

On the other hand, I claim it necessary to rethink the level(s) on which the allegorical might come into play here. While sports certainly provide a certain allegorical capacity to the films, I want to claim that the latter also *produce* an audiovisual, non-figurative but figural allegory themselves, an allegory of (experiencing) what we could call 'American Dream time.' Two (inherent) references to Deleuze might need some further explanation here: First, his use of the figural as not based on imitative representation, but sensation (see Deleuze 2003 [1981]). And second, his concept of the time-image, which creates (forms of) time through temporality (of movement), with "time provid[ing] access to thinking, to the very nature of being itself, and the forms it takes and can take, through expression on screen" (Colman 2011, 145).[28]

In another text, Rowe himself points to such an idea of sports films being all about modulating time, to their "freedom to play with time and space in elastic ways" (Rowe 2008, 146), even though he probably would not go as far as to say they produce time. Based on the analysis of two non-Hollywood, (semi-)documentary sports films from 2006, LA GRAN FINAL (G. Olivares, GER/ESP) and ZIDANE, UN PORTRAIT DU 21E SIÈCLE (D. Gordon / P. Parreno, F), Rowe follows his claim of the sports film being, on the one hand, subjected to the power of chronological time, but on the other hand constantly trying to free itself from this dictate in order to produce myth. He thereby also specifies the sports film's tendency to the

---

27 For a kind of rule-proving exception, see Miller 2007.
28 Thus, this 'American Dream time' can be seen in the tradition of other specifying conceptions of the time-image, like, for example, Anna Powell's "horror time" (Powell 2006, chapter 4).

allegorical as "the telling of grand moral tales of mythic proportions," especially in what he calls "prohero periods" (Rowe 2008, 147).[29]

Genre Reflexivity

Additionally, and quite differently than many other sports film scholars, Rowe acknowledges a certain kind of reflexivity of the sports film as an important genre capacity. Circumventing the tendency of many genre-theoretical approaches to use the notion of reflexivity to address genre as a site of negotiation of a society's self-image by means of media aesthetically uninformed models of communication,[30] he writes:

> Despite such variations of film style and the centrality of sport to the film itself, the thread that runs through what can be defined as a bona fide sport film is not just, teleologically, a filmic treatment of sport, but a recognition – if only to be critiqued – that sport is 'special' for practitioner and spectator alike, and that, for all its imperfections, it cannot simply be reduced to economic exploitation or political manipulation. In other words, sport films register the inherited, contradictory dimensions of the institution of sport itself, and the often profound phenomenological ambivalence of those who engage with it. (Rowe 2008, 148)

Such recognition is not to be underestimated, as it helps us to further move away from a taxonomic understanding of genre, and towards what Cavell calls "genre-as-medium," in difference (but not at all in complete opposition) to "genre-as-cycle" (Cavell 1982, 79). Cavell develops these "different principles or procedures of composition" (Cavell 1982, 80) via thinking about the format of television, as well as about his own conceptual 'building' of a genre – that of the Hollywood comedy of remarriage – in his book *Pursuits of Happiness* (Cavell 1981). While an understanding of genre-as-cycle addresses the recognition of a member of a given group as originating from this (descriptive) grouping (and thus, much in the sense of how an episode of a serial relates to this serial), the genre-as-medium principle is concerned with how certain individual works

---

29 Rowe refers to Pearson et al.'s 2003 study trying to provide a perspective on overarching ("general") trends with regard to American sports films between the years 1930 and 1995. Methodologically based on statistical data analysis, the study is especially concerned about thematic schemes and developments, and how these might mirror certain sociopolitical configurations.

30 One exception in this regard is, again, Gledhill, who claims genre's central role for "a process of cultural identity or social imaginary formation in which a range of different agents participate" (Gledhill 2000, 239; see also Neale 1990). Another aspect described as reflexivity is the way every single film of a genre refers to and thereby modulates the genre in general (see for example Grotkopp / Kappelhoff 2012).

"push [one] into sketching a theory of genre" (Cavell 1982, 79), how they produce their own existence as a group and the possibility to grasp them as such in the first place. Crucial here, too, is Cavell's insistence on the "double range of the concept of a medium" (Cavell 1982, 80), hence on identifying various media (genres) with the medium of film (see also Cavell 1979, 68–73). As he points out, both principles of capturing genre are perfectly justified, supporting different research perspectives to different degrees.[31] It is especially with regard to the sports film and how it is grasped in scholarly discourse, that it becomes quite evident that both principles are always at work, even though I particularly want to emphasize and test out its capacity as genre-as-medium in what follows.

In such an understanding, genres are not simply *there* as containers that create output, but only come into being *through* and are shaped *by* their output. At the same time, this output (concrete works, films) comes into existence only when certain forms become meaningful, therein shaping a certain significance in a certain medium. The result is a process of simultaneous preservation and reconsideration of expressive and experiential forms, referencing, modifying, rearranging and transforming each other, and thereby redefining their medium, their genre. Films hence "*are what they are* in view of one another" (Cavell 1981, 29), as Cavell famously puts it, thereby emphasizing that in a way media and genres and genres-as-media are always studies of their own existence and the conditions which led to that existence.

According to Rowe, this reflexivity of genre as the site of negotiation of its own existence and, as such, also the site of negotiation of the culture it is part of (and co-produces in the case of sports and the sports film) proceeds on the level of space and time especially.[32] Sports as "a cultural form that is always preoccupied with temporality" produces "sport time," which is "especially protean when translated into filmic form" (Rowe 2008, 148). What serves Rowe as a telling example here is (an analysis of) the Bollywood cricket film LAGAAN: ONCE UPON A TIME IN INDIA (A. Gowariker, IND 2001): According to Grant Farred, the film shows a "double temporality" of a "future anterior" (see Rowe 2008,

---

31 "I think, for example, that it is easier to understand movies as some familiar kind of commodity or as entertainments if you take them as participating not in a genre-as-medium but in genres-as-cycles, or if you focus on those movies that *do* participate, without remainder, in genres so conceived" (Cavell 1982, 80).

32 Here, Rowe provides an idea of the extinction of space through time. By referencing Paul Virilio and David Harvey, he sutures this claim to an argument of technology and postmodernity. Especially with regard to filmic images, I would rather not go along with such argumentation, as it seems to position space as primary to time. Considering the Bergsonian and Deleuzian philosophy of time providing the backbone of this work, I would rather claim that the opposite is the case (see also Clarke 2002).

148 et seq., and Farred 2004, 99/110), with the sport of cricket and the form of Bollywood cinema rendering "the fantasy of an ideal nation" (Farred 2004, 105) possible by conflating remembrance/nostalgia (of/for the colonial past) and the projection of a (post-colonial) future. It is such crystalline temporality, intrinsically related to questions of (national) community, its origins and its future development, which I want to have a closer look at in the following chapters of this book, and which I would qualify as the core of the sports film genre. Directly connected to it, as Rowe continues, is especially (the emphasis on) the pivotal moment as a point in time, to which sports films always come back, or rather around which they regularly evolve (see chapter 4). Even though Rowe continues with an analysis of a movie which rather "de-familiarize[s]" (Rowe 2008, 149) this temporality, he nonetheless acknowledges it as kind of a genre standard. His apparently strong aversion towards the TV-induced "tyranny of the now" (Rowe 2008, 149) of media sports thereby seems to conceal more than it reveals though, especially with regard to proper formal analysis.

As I claim and further elaborate in the following chapter, it is this 'political' temporality, which defines what we call the American Dream, and which accounts for the "constitutive conflict" (Kappelhoff 2018a, 65/75/234) of the sports film genre. While many scholars frankly suggest that sports films are all about the American Dream, they do so by either reducing it to merely a (mythic) narrative of linear time right from the start, charged with topic or ideologemes of upward social and economic mobility ('from rags to riches,' 'the pursuit of happiness'), or by doing so when analyzing specific films – as if those can be grasped (only) through the stories they tell, and the action of the characters (as well as the psychology derived from this action) they show, or – often even more important – do not show.[33] Such approaches almost always aim for this narrative's capacity to produce and support ideological delusion, to distort or conceal real-life conditions, hence understanding and reading the films as images of a social or discursive reality, whose questions of everyday coexistence they are able to negotiate one-to-one at the level of their plot.

---

[33] See Crosson 2013 or Englert 2011, who present a very informed and comparably extensive elaboration on the entanglement of sports, the Hollywood film industry and US society as well as on the American Dream as the most important national (founding) myth of the United States, but then proceed with very limited analytical chapters consisting of not much more than background information concerning the films' production and subject matter, as well as a retelling of their storylines.

American Dream Time as the Sports Film Genre's Constitutive Conflict

What I want to do instead is to acknowledge the American Dream as a problem, as *the* problem around which the genre of the sports film forms, and which provides its constitutive conflict – a problem of social integration, of subjectification as the fabrication and detection of the relation of an I and a We, and, in that sense, of temporality, of thinking time and history. As Altman claims: "the first step in understanding the functional role of Hollywood genre is to isolate the problems for which the genre provides a symbolic solution" (Altman 1987, 334).[34] In this spirit, I will grasp the American Dream not as mere topic or narrative conflict, but as a conflict of social integration in whose constitution and processing and maybe solution all these filmic images intervene by being viewed.[35] That the films act as producers and processors of this constitutive conflict in the first place, that "they are themselves integrating, disintegrating, excluding or subordinating – in relation to the feeling for a commonly shared world" (Kappelhoff 2018c), and, in the case of the sports film, especially with regard to the temporal capacity of sociality and the social capacity of time.

Kappelhoff attempts to reconstitute Aristotle's *Poetics* as the starting point of a genre theory that does not call for convention and taxonomy,[36] but rather implies, as I have already described above, a genre system of relational modes of relating to the world and modalities of aesthetic expression and experience. He derives this idea of a constitutive conflict of a genre as one of the three aspects – or four, if we include, as Aristotle himself does in the sixth chapter with the example of catharsis, the form of pleasure as poetry's affective force – by which Aristotle distinguishes between different genres, as different ways of

---

34 See also Grindon 1996, 54.
35 Deleuze seems not too far away from what I aim at here when talking about Godard's "reflexive genres" (Deleuze 2013b, 190). Appropriating the term category, which I have opposed so far in this chapter with regard to my critique of taxonomic models of genre criticism, Deleuze speaks of these reflexive genres as "never final answers but categories of problems which introduce reflection into the image itself. They are problematic or propositional functions" (Deleuze 2013b, 191).
36 According to Kappelhoff and Grotkopp, most of the common approaches on film and genre even today are – with regard to their Aristotelian lineage – rather influenced by interpretations of the *Poetics*, especially by those of Horaz and seventeenth century French Classicism. Instead of making the *Poetics* productive for a genre analysis that involves (the relationality and possibility of the new with regard to) affective modulation, aesthetic experience and a politics of feeling, these interpretations rather use it for establishing a concept of genres as distinctive entities, based on fixed rules organizing the correspondence between content and form (see Kappelhoff 2018a, 93 et seq., as well as Grotkopp / Kappelhoff 2012).

mimesis, the latter being understood as a proper mode of thinking and the basis of all poetry.[37] This aspect of *hetera* generally translates as 'subject(s),' 'object(s)' or 'agent(s)' (of imitation). While Aristotle refers to certain characters which he in a way assigns to specific genre forms – the form of tragedy is (has to be) populated by 'good': serious, important and virtuous people, whereas the process of imitation of comedy is concerned with 'bad,' less virtuous people – Kappelhoff interprets this criterion more in the direction of a conflict of belonging in a wider (less representational) sense, thereby pointing to the processes of inclusion and exclusion that define every political community:

> For from my viewpoint, this does not mean the social or cultural conflicts represented; even if they can certainly be considered expressive forms of constitutive conflicts. Instead, the level to be taken into account here will become clear if we look at the object of Greek tragedy. In no way does it consist in the actions represented themselves, but in the horror that these actions give expression to for the audience. They are the horrors of a past on which the becoming of the polis itself is founded, the horrors of the myth. In tragedy, they are brought into the present in a way which gives rise to possibilities of acting – the possibility of politics. [...] The object of poetic making always concerns a field of conflict that is identified in constituting a common world itself. To put it another way: There are always conflicts about the breadth and boundaries of the sense of commonality.
> (Kappelhoff 2018a, 286–287)

With his concept of the sense of commonality as the feeling for the communal, Kappelhoff not only conceptualizes genre cinema's role with regard to the connection of the poetics and politics of audiovisual images, but also points to the level on which this connection can be analyzed fruitfully, on which a genre can be understood in a non-taxonomic, non-textual and non-(solely-)content-related way. Namely: the expressive movement of the filmic images, the films' audiovisual construction, and the aesthetic experience this movement creates as the

---

[37] The others being the employed means and media techniques (*heterois mimeisthai*) and the method or mode (*heterós*) as the way of addressing, of relating to the imitated (a common) world (lyrical, epic, dramatic, or with regard to film: documentary, experimental, essayistic etc.). While Kappelhoff conceives of the former primarily as the media technological base on the part of the production (of a film), and the latter also in the sense of modalities of affective expression (see Kappelhoff 2018a, 286), I would think that these modalities are rather addressed by that first criterion (of the employed means), as Aristotle mentions lógos/language, rhythmós/rhythm and melos/harmonia/melody in this context. Such rather minor details aside, what is important is to understand media/films as not defined by certain predetermined techniques of production, but as techniques that themselves produce certain modes of addressing, expressing and experiencing, which allow for new descriptions of a shared perception of the world – an insight which allows us to understand and analyze genres as historical processes of creating and modulating commonly shared perceptions of the world, interpenetrating through an endless process of combining and thereby generating ever new such modes and modalities (see Kappelhoff 2018a, 287–288).

"spectator's passage through a process of affectation" (Kappelhoff 2018a, 271). Genre films have thus to be grasped through their specific poetics, unfolding as movements of affect embodied by the viewer, and experienced as his or her own emotionality. They are interventions in a mediated economy of affect, producing and modulating certain orders of the sensorial with the help of which the integration of the individual subject into communal life is negotiated again and again,[38] as a media practice in which a society addresses itself as a political community (see Pogodda / Gronmaier 2015, 3). Kappelhoff concludes accordingly:

> Certain genres (if not all) should in fact principally be understood as such dynamic ramifications of affects, in which a generic conflict that concerns the fundamental structure of the political polity, the feeling for the communal gets constantly updated. Affect itself is then addressed as the transcending power that works toward changing the community within its given orders of sensoriality. As the capacity of bodies to affect other bodies and to be affected by them, the dynamic of this change works within the symbolic systems, discursive orders, and institutional formations of a community. That is, affect thwarts the stability of the system with every repeating ramification into symbolic forms, images, and signs, and introduces the possibility of differences and deviations into the ordering structure of a community. The affective ramifications are always more than the feelings of individualized bodies and yet they cannot be conceived without them. They are the forces in which the relation between the 'I,' the 'we,' and 'the others' are configured, the subjectivity effect that the shared forms of thinking and feeling in a community themselves are due to. [...] From this perspective, genre cinema itself can be presented as a network of affect transmissions and allocations organized by media, in which the spectators' bodies themselves are engaged as transmission media. Films are media that relate the technological and organic bodies of different planes of time and separate spaces to one another, figuring them as affective collectivity.
> (Kappelhoff 2018a, 282–283)

In this sense, film-viewing is understood as an activity of poetic making, of *poiesis* as a media practice

> in which the remembrance of individuals is synchronized with the temporality of the community, the contingencies of social and familial relationships, the time of love, of desire, or aging are interconnected with the rhythms of the history of the community. In this sense, genre cinema in general [...] can in fact be seen as a ritual practice aimed at asserting the rhythm of the time of the community into the biographical rhythms of the individual – and vice versa.[39]
> (Kappelhoff 2018a, 271)

---

38 See the concept of Jacques Rancière, who understands politics as "the transformation of the sensory fabric of 'being together'" (Rancière 2009 [2008], 56), thus locating the possibility for social change in moments when "two regimes of sense, two sensory worlds" (Rancière 2009 [2008], 58) collide.

39 This idea of a poiesis of film-viewing also in a way includes actual filmmaking, as the latter can always be understood as an activity of film-viewing itself to a certain extent (see Lehmann 2017).

Kappelhoff comprehensively analyzes this constitutive conflict between (the time of) the collective and (the time of) the individual with regard to the war film as a sensorial field, as a field of affect primarily concerned with the transition of the individual from civilian to military society, which results in this individual's dissolution, historically graspable as necessary, meaningful or senseless sacrifice.

The sports film, as I claim, tackles it in a very much related but nonetheless different way: Here, the focus is less on the individual being torn or crushed between two contending forms of community, but about the possibility as well as the limits of a simultaneity of uniqueness/unique character and a communality/community that (forcefully) delimits this uniqueness, but at the same time depends on it. Accordingly, the constitutive conflict of the sports film is about the assertion of individual subjectification in view of a collective one, and vice versa. It is about the promoting and enclosing interdependence of individual performance and collective effort; it is about the ordinary in extraordinariness and the usual in unusualness. A conflict which Miller also seems to address at least en passant when he talks about the

> contestation between rather safe, community building middle-class images [...] and more violent, sexual, and individualized images [...] that continually plays out in the sports film genre and yet is constantly shifting in reaction to moments of historical specificity.   (Miller 2003, 11)

Or about the sports film genre's consistent and continuous reference of

> the dual sporting traditions represented metaphorically by Frank Merriwell (hard-work-leads-to-team-victory) and John L. Sullivan (violent-prowess-leads-to-personal-glory-and-excess), [...] which tend to align with optimistic and pessimistic representations of the athletic American Dream respectively.[40]   (Miller 2003, 19)

Returning to my perspective, this constitutive conflict of the sports film is characterized by the back and forth between (the excess/violence of) individual empowerment and (the excess/violence of) collective appropriation. It is about the becoming of an 'I' among a 'We' (through distinction) and the 'We' emerging from (the multiplication of) such an 'I.'[41]

---

[40] Even though I would hesitate to associate those types of images with certain types of sports (team sports with the former, boxing with the latter), as Miller does.
[41] It is quite remarkable, and probably not a coincidence how this (in a way paradox) dynamic of belonging and distinction, of becoming part of a community created by the individual, and becoming an individual created by that community, resembles the idea of genre film I tried to outline here.

This dynamic, which might account for the heart of American heroism always in a way addressing a 'society of heroes,' reveals a crystalline temporality on which I will elaborate further in the next chapter, in such a manner that I claim it central to the (production of the) concept of the American Dream. The constitutive conflict of the sports film is thus both the American Dream as a certain idea of subjective communality and communal subjectivity, and the American Dream as a certain idea of time – both aspects are intrinsically linked, as they eventually combine to form a quite specific American notion of politics and/as history.

So I would indeed follow Miller when he claims that "the [sports film] genre's semantics and syntax combine to repeatedly grapple with the central question [...]: Can a man control his own body and by extension his own destiny so as to achieve the American Dream?" (Miller 2003, 94), even though my analyses will concentrate less on the films' narrative action and its characters' behavior, but on the actual disposition of the audiovisual images, of the film as an expressive and perceptual body itself, of the temporalities it is made of and creates through affective movement and its embodiment by the viewer. Thus, I will understand the American Dream in that sense not only as a prefabricated and represented storyline 'unrealistically' praising the possibility of ultimate success for every hard-working individual, but as a constantly evolving discourse on what it means to become an (exceptional) individual within an (exceptional) community *in time,* which makes up the core of the genre of the sports film.

With an analysis of FIELD OF DREAMS (P. A. Robinson, 1989), this audiovisual discourse is reflected in what follows as a specific sports film's capacity to take shape as a 'generic crossroad,' by appropriating a variety of different Hollywood genre modalities. And which in doing so addresses American historicity and communality not only through the represented cultural practice of baseball and a certain essential narrative connected to it, but especially by means of its expressive movement – thereby creating an image space of experience in which a national community is reflexively addressed as a historical community of film-viewing.

In the following chapters, this audiovisual discourse of the American Dream (as the sports film's constitutive conflict) will be, first, conceived of once again theoretically in its historical and epistemological embeddedness, before it is then made productive for the analysis of the genre's more specific generic modalities regarding its poetics of crystallized time.

2.3 Encountering Genre History on the FIELD OF DREAMS

The Field as Mise en Scène and Imaginative Space

The field, rink or court is one of the most integral elements of the sports film. In its audiovisual staging, it offers, on the one hand, a place of action and sentiment: of moving bodies and embodied movement, of mechanical procedures and affective involvement, of immersion and observation, of the fragmentation and reconsolidation of the individual as well as the collective body in celebration or disappointment. Most often, it becomes the focal point of the plot in conjunction with the audiovisually constructed diegetic space surrounding it, resulting in a typical arrangement of doubled spectatorship: the film's viewer not only watches the protagonists on the field, but also watches other protagonists watching those on the field.[42] As a paradigmatic example of the 'classical' action modality, which is marked by (the pleasure in) simultaneously maintaining and losing control, this rather straight forward and stable construction of a 'viewing the viewed/viewing' offers a counterbalance to how the events on the field are presented. Most often, these evolve in a more scattered manner, the kinetic force of expressive movement appearing as less controlled and enclosed, hence involving and exposing the viewer in and to what is happening on the field or court in an intensified and more direct, or at least unpredictable and therefore shock-like, sense.

On the other hand, the field is often also grasped in a more figurative or symbolic manner, as a resource, employed to produce, contest or negotiate certain narrative trajectories and conflicts – as a potential mise en scène, but also as a mise en scène of potentiality, as an imaginative or phantasmatic space through and in which time and place are produced, suspended and get mixed up. "The typical mise en scène [of the sports film] is the sports stadium or games playing site, the 'field of dreams'" (Babington 2014, 4), writes Bruce Babington in his volume on the sports film genre as he sets up his analysis of the 1989 movie of the same name. He claims that "the trope embodied in the baseball film Field of Dreams [...] of the protagonist building a field on which the ghosts of players past can play again, might appeal to the followers of any other sport [...] who would recognise the sentiment involved" (Babington 2014, 9–10). Even though FIELD OF DREAMS (P.A. Robinson, 1989) "exemplif[ies] the genre's dominant classical paradigms," Babington nonetheless assesses it to be contradictory to "the sports film's reputation for formulaic predictability, as interrogative and complicating elements, sometimes explicit, sometimes residing

---

[42] See also chapter 4.2 of this book.

in implicit subtexts, play against the most obvious closure and interpretation" (Babington 2014, 77).

Aside from such distinctions, Babington nevertheless tunes into one of the most widespread analytical findings about the movie, and baseball films in general, especially those of the Reagan Era. The film, he claims, "invoke[s] nostalgia for a better past" by "employ[ing] sport as a synecdoche of larger [...] metaphysical thematics" (Babington 2014, 77).

This vision of longing for a purer and more innocent past – not only as an act of redemption, but as the reconstruction of white male privilege in reaction to the changes within late-capitalist post-modern America – is also what Vivian Sobchack observes with regard to mainstream media as well as to sports, specifically baseball, and thus also to FIELD OF DREAMS (see Sobchack 1997, 179–181).

In what follows, I want to delve deeper into the images and sounds of this specific film to suggest that its "hyperbolic nostalgia" (Sobchack 1997, 179) is of a more historically reflexive kind than we might expect, and should thus maybe rather be grasped in the sense of Svetlana Boym, who contends that nostalgia can function as a critical form of remembering that is not bound to a single version of the past and accordingly enables texts to revisit the past to animate different realities and futures (see Boym 2001). I want to justify this claim by showing, first, that the film's audiovisual poetics aim at a genre experience that very much ponders the impurity of history, or the impossibility of purity with regard to (a linear and stable) historical experience, especially by creatively reproducing (mixing, confronting, relating) a variety of Hollywood genre modalities. And, second, that it thereby makes palpable how historiography, of which media representations such as fiction films are a vital part, is never innocent and never can be, as it is always the product of an address and orientation towards both specific and ever-changing senses of community, and in that way inextricably connected to constant processes of in- and exclusion.

Hermann Kappelhoff makes this connection between the referencing of different genre modalities of aesthetic experience and the dynamics of political pluralism evident by employing Richard Rorty's notion of the sense of community as well as Hannah Arendt's reading of Kant's aesthetic judgement of taste. While the latter is emphasized as an "extra sense [...] that inserts us into a community" (Arendt 1992, 70), the former appears "as a dynamic element of a society [...], which must always configure itself anew as a community," and as a product of "the affective agreement to commonly shared values in concrete cultural practices" (Kappelhoff 2016). Implementing such perspective here will also leave us better equipped for the question of how genre films are actually themselves involved in producing and modulating the cultural norms that many scholars often just apply as seemingly fixed and 'afilmic' context.[43]

Nostalgia for Pure Pasts and the Problem of Agency

If we look at the 'genre-as-cycle' of the baseball film as particularly distinguished by its leaning towards a certain idea of innocent originality within an image of 'Americana': baseball as 'America's pastime' translating into often rural or suburban filmic worlds in which a certain sense of amateurism is still at play and the heterosexual couple and nuclear family often constitutes the plot's center,[44] FIELD OF DREAMS is exemplary. What is especially striking about it is the almost complete absence of professional game, in the sense that league games are played or watched. Rather than being or becoming a player or coach, main protagonist Ray Kinsella (Kevin Costner) is first and foremost a fan/layperson who sets out on an enigmatic quest: to build a ballpark for the return of (the ghost of) 'Shoeless' Joe Jackson (Ray Liotta), the most famous player involved in the actual Black Sox Scandal in 1919, in which the Chicago White Sox conspired to fix the World Series.[45] This quest also comes to involve a search for former African American civil rights activist and his wife Annie's (Amy Madigan) favorite writer, Terence Mann (James Earl Jones), as well as former player Archie 'Moonlight' Graham (played by Burt Lancaster and, for his younger version, by Frank Whaley).

While I will focus on the importance of both these latter characters (as well as the actors playing them) later during this analysis, let us first have a look at Costner's protagonist. Kinsella embodies, in the best way, a 'sideline hero,' the Everyman becoming hero both of the fairy tale, by "achiev[ing] a domestic,

---

[43] This can even be the case for genre-theoretically more informed approaches, as for example Crosson's application of Altman's concept of the generic crossroads (see Crosson 2013, 15–16, and also my remarks in the previous chapter).

[44] In contrast to most football or basketball or hockey films with their 'societies of men.' As a result, the sporting and the private sphere of the filmic world become (even) more (metonymically or metaphorically) interrelated in baseball movies than in other cycles of the sports film genre.

[45] In the course of the Black Sox Scandal, eight players were accused of intentionally losing, acquitted in public trial but then nonetheless permanently banned for life from professional baseball. The incident has been the subject of another movie, which came out only one year before FIELD OF DREAMS: While Robinson's film uses the scandal as a kind of nostalgic trigger/marker to spark its fantasy story of belated redemption, EIGHT MEN OUT (J. Sayles, 1988) presents a multi-character narrative, which results in "a lengthy trail of constant exposition, with any real sense of the characters or their dilemma sacrificed to the unfolding plot" (Jenkins 1989, 205). For a nonfiction literary reconstruction of the scandal, see also Asinof 1963.

microcosmic triumph," and of myth, by achieving "a world-historical, macrocosmic triumph" (Campbell 2008 [1949], 30).[46] At the end of the film, Kinsella's long-dead father, with whom he had a strained relationship, also appears – like the old players – on the completed field and plays a round of catch with him. Thus, the (allegorical) reconciliation between the (post-)war generation and the protagonists of the 1960s counterculture movement climactically intertwines with Kinsella's and the film's redemption of the historical affair of the 1919 conspiracy.[47] By means of a (narrative) gesture of superimposition, private and public (sports cultural) history are connected, providing a nostalgic impetus, which clearly equates *longing for* the past with its *reconciliation* in/with the present.

In her monograph on *Hollywood's Vision of Team Sports*, Deborah Tudor argues that there are at least two pasts "evoked by this field" (Tudor 1997, 169), as "baseball becomes a gateway to innocence, transcendence and an uncomplicated social and personal past for the spectators" (Tudor 1997, 169). While the social past would thereby address "a time of national innocence" (Tudor 1997, 169) and an idea of (the love for) baseball as an unregulated, discreet and non-professional/non-commercial sports, "[t]he personal past evoked by the field will transport spectators back to their childhood years, before the loss of innocence that accompanies adolescence. 'Pure' spectators will watch 'pure' baseball" (Tudor 1997, 169). One could of course argue that the purity of the social past is already called into question in FIELD OF DREAMS by the invocation of the 1919 scandal, even though it will be redeemed through the film's diegetic present. This, on the other hand, makes the 'purity' of the personal past more interesting, since its loss seems to coincide with the recognition of the fallibility of the figures of childhood identification. In this case, the return to and of the past could be understood as both a redemption of history and the resolution of a personal narrative of (mis-)recognition.

While Tudor does not go into further detail about how such (filmic) evocation of (symbolic) 'pure pasts' exactly takes place, she criticizes the way it is linked to the question of race. By reproducing the film's plot and its characters'

---

46 Campbell's conception of the different characteristics of the hero – even though quite strictly derived from psychoanalytical theory, and rather lacking a useful notion of media-produced time and space adequate for analyzing (the perception of) filmic images – directly speaks to my claim about the temporality of the American Dream being the constitutive conflict of the sports film (see chapters 3.2 and 2.1), as the tension between individual subjectivity and (universal) communality. He continues: "Whereas the former [the hero of the fairy tale] – the youngest or despised child who becomes the master of extraordinary powers – prevails over his personal oppressors, the latter brings back from his adventure the means for the regeneration of his society as a whole" (Campbell 2008 [1949], 30).
47 This corresponds with Babington's description of the film as the "apotheosis of the fan film" (Babington 2014, 57).

actions, she observes that the movie "structures the very notion of athletic aspiration, the right to dream, around racial terms" (Tudor 1997, 169). According to Tudor, the problem therefore is not only the misrepresentation or the nonappearance of Black athletes, but first and foremost how the act of dreaming is framed, and how agency – the agency to aspire and to dream – is possessed and distributed among the film's protagonists:

> The film evokes the question of race relations within sports by the way the text limits the conception of the 'dream.' The field fulfills Ray's dream of a reunion with his dead father. Shoeless Joe, the Black Sox and other dead players dream about playing baseball again. Annie and Karen apparently do not have a dream, but the film implies that Ray's dream is theirs by extension. The 'dreams' that the field obligingly fulfills only pertain to white players. (Tudor 1997, 167)

Tudor, like Andrew Miller and many others, thus assigns FIELD OF DREAMS to a series of conservative sports films, especially dominant in the Reagan-influenced 1980s, in which the question of race is "present as structuring absence," which roughly translates into "a striking abundance of sports films during this moment that offer images and narratives of a virtually all-white sporting past" (Miller 2003, 308–309).[48] Based on what each character says and does, which of them is able to dream and what they are able to dream about, Tudor concludes that "*Field of Dreams* ties dreaming to mythos and provides connections between athletic ideology and personal growth, but it [presents] a path severely circumscribed by the dreamer himself" (Tudor 1997, 165), by which she means, especially, the male white hero Ray Kinsella.

While not wanting to deny the problematic racial and also gender politics of FIELD OF DREAMS on the level of representational and narrative content, I nonetheless claim that Tudor's analysis does not do the film justice, especially when we take a closer look at its audiovisual composition and the viewing experience this composition shapes. It is, as the following analysis will show, the film's layering and interweaving of certain forms of staging and modalities of experience that

---

48 See also Miller 2003, 41 et seq./156/180/249/298. Aaron Baker also applies this concept of the structuring absence to the sports film, thereby disclosing it as being borrowed from Robert Ray (see Baker 2003, 14 and also chapter 3.1 of this book). Movies often brought forward in that vein of 'Reaganish' sports (especially, but not only baseball) films dominating the 1980s are, besides FIELD OF DREAMS and EIGHT MEN OUT, THE NATURAL (B. Levinson, 1984), HOOSIERS (D. Anspaugh, 1986), BULL DURHAM (R. Shelton, 1988) and MAJOR LEAGUE (D.S. Ward, 1989). See also Briley 2005 and Cooper 1995. As counterexamples produced in the decades before and after, Miller mentions THE BINGO LONG TRAVELING ALL-STARS & MOTOR KINGS (J. Badham, 1976), and the 1990s productions TALENT FOR THE GAME (R.M. Young, 1991), THE PROGRAM (D.S. Ward, 1993) and HE GOT GAME, among others (see Miller 2003, 309–310).

sets up an audiovisual discourse about American community-building and its constitutive temporality of crystallized time. This occurs not only by rendering an incisive event of sports history in melodramatic fashion, but by also disclosing the historicity of genre film-viewing and sports spectatorship in general, and baseball culture in particular, as a reflexive experience of what I will call the *deep temporality of a poiesis of (sports) film-viewing* here. As an experience that not only reveals relationality as the driving force of genre as a system of bifurcation and creative remodulation as presented in the previous chapter, but also confronts the viewer with and makes him/her part of the processes of inclusion and exclusion at work when communities (re-)form and relate to themselves by media. Hence, as much as FIELD OF DREAMS might provide for a stabilization and reconciliation of certain historical narratives from or in favor of hegemonic perspectives (especially with regard to race and gender), the film quite clearly also *undermines* the notion of 'pure,' 'innocent' and linear history – if not so much by means of its plot and the agency of its characters (treated as if they might simply supersede real-life persons), then by the agency of the film and its viewers themselves.

The Horror of the Voice

Let us have a closer look at the first scene of the movie, which not only introduces us to its pivotal formal device – a disembodied voice through which the hero's "call to adventure" (Campbell 2008 [1949], 42) becomes audiovisually realized in a very literal and at the same time enigmatic sense – but which also, as I claim, immediately makes clear that Ray Kinsella is not at all in control of neither his dreaming nor the film's narrative path. Even though seemingly establishing Kinsella as a kind of master narrative instance in the preceding prologue, during which we see a montage of different (photographic, filmic, historical, historically coded) found footage material and hear Costner's off-screen voice telling the story of Kinsella and his family, the film uses the particular disjuncture of image and sound in this first scene here to establish an expressivity of irruption and threat. Becoming recognizable as a horror genre modality, this expressive movement further evolves through the scene's tonal dramaturgy in particular, as well as through the camera movement and the shot lengths used.

Even before the last image of the prologue has faded from view, the soft piano chord transitions into a deeply growling synthesizer sound (TC 00:03:33).[49]

---

[49] The indicated time codes refer to the German 2003 Universal Studios DVD, played on the VLC media player for macOS X.

2.3 Encountering Genre History on the FIELD OF DREAMS — 53

A cut leads to what seems to be a detail of a clouded, purple colored sky. Very poignantly, we hear birds chirping, and another cut presents a long shot of a landscape: a field and a little forest in the dark below the purple sky. As if slicing through the air of the rural mise en scène, a sharp swirling sound appears and increases the weird and eerie tension.[50] The next shot depicts a corn field, with a farmhouse in the background. The scene becomes visually dynamized for the first time by means of a slowly upward panning crane shot. A two-tone oboe sequence plays repeatedly, slowly pealing out into the next shot which brings us closer to the farmhouse. In an otherwise static composition, there is a micro movement to be detected close to the center of the image: The porch swing goes back and forth, producing a squeaking sound. Is someone sitting on it? Before we are able to see clearly, the scene cuts to another crane shot. While a third sonic motif – a sequence of metallic ringing sounds – is introduced, the camera flies over the dark green corn field rows from almost a bird's eye perspective, then takes a left. A man in a white t-shirt walks through the field and enters the frame. The camera dives down into the field and – in the manner of another horror film coded expressive movement – approaches the protagonist from behind (Figure 1).

Before this movement reaches the point of transforming into what might be called in reference to Pasolini 'indirect subjective shot,' where "we are caught in a correlation between a perception-image and a camera consciousness which transforms it" (Deleuze 2013a [1983], 83),[51] a disembodied, or acousmatic voice[52]

---

[50] With Mark Fisher, who dismisses the (all too individual psychological) notion of the uncanny in favor of the weird and the eerie (as basically two modalities of the strange), I would argue that both of these terms seem to be useful to describe the tension created here and the evolving atmosphere of the overall scene, especially because they also match with the observations immediately following. As the weird is "constituted by a presence [...] of that which does not belong" (Fisher 2017, 61), it seems fitting to grasp not only this 'unnatural' sound, but also the disturbing presence of the camera described on the next page, shattering conventions of filmic enunciation and presumptions about self and other. It also speaks to the disruption of our genre expectation and memory (horror at the beginning of a sports film?). On the other hand, the eerie, as "constituted by a failure of absence or by a failure of presence" (Fisher 2017, 61), seems to be the appropriate term to describe the (effect of the) acousmatic voice appearing shortly after, a voice which is present where there should be none (in the corn field).

[51] For Deleuze, it is important to emphasize not so much the (dissolution of the) distinction between subjective and objective intention and agency, but the oscillation and indistinguishability with regard to the image's perceptual quality.

[52] For the concept of the acousmatic/acousmêtre, see Michel Chion 1999 [1987], 17–29. While Chion argues rather technically about the concept, it is quite often used in more advanced and dynamic ways with regard to its undermining capacity, and especially to the analysis of fantastic and horror film forms (see for example Hills 2011).

Figure 1: Approaching from behind (FIELD OF DREAMS).

provides for the latter's emphasized and enigmatic independence, thereby reinforcing the uncanny effect established so far. "If you build it, he will come," whispers the sharp and slightly reverberating male voice, making Costner's character suddenly stop and look around in bewilderment. In the next shot, Kinsella enters the frame from the right, a telephoto lens shows him surrounded by, or rather 'drowning' in the tall corn stalks, another audiovisual motif of the horror modality, with the forlorn immersion within a possibly dangerous nature, being exposed to an ungraspable threat (Figure 2).[53]

The voice appears again 'from nowhere': "If you build it, he will come." Kinsella's panic-stricken looking around is answered by a fast pan to the left from high above the field, a shot still not (clearly) coded as his point of view. It is not until the next shot that this suturing (of the entity of the camera and that of the character) takes place, accompanied by an immediate easing of the tension built up so far. Still depicted as lost within the vast field, Kinsella calls to his wife in the distance – she is now actually shown sitting on the swing with their daughter – asking if they heard the voice as well.[54] They have not, and

---

[53] There is a wide range of examples of the corn field as horror setting, from the famous crop duster scene in NORTH BY NORTHWEST (A. Hitchcock, 1959) to a film like CHILDREN OF THE CORN (F. Kiersch, 1984). The setting of the corn field often also plays an important role with regard to mystery and/or sci-fi modalities, as for example in SIGNS (M.N. Shyamalan, 2002).

[54] With Kaja Silverman, one could argue that the initial 'horror sound' of the swinging and deserted seat is now, by mapping it onto the women's bodies, domesticated and made 'innocent' again, as it can be linked to a visible female subject (see Silverman 1988).

Figure 2: Drowning in the corn field.

Kinsella exits the frame to the right, while the camera remains on the spot where he had stood just a moment ago. While the frame is completely filled with the green corn stalks, the voice can be heard once again, now appearing simultaneously more (in the sense of the complete absence of any human-like character) and less (in the sense of that the alien 'camera consciousness' gets a voice) acousmatized. Kinsella rushes back into the frame, as the already established sonic motifs of eeriness set in again. Now looking even more confused, he makes sure one more time if his wife and his daughter have not heard what he has (and we have), before walking back to the house.

A Future Vision of the Past

The staging of the (first) appearance of 'the Voice' as an eerie and unsettling threat, which triggers all that follows, is picked up once again shortly thereafter, when Kinsella wakes up at night during a thunderstorm and, lying in bed, hears the sentence again, accompanied by the reappearance of the growling, swirling and ringing sounds (TC 00:05:55). This staging then undergoes significant transformation, especially by means of the alteration of this sonic dimension, and namely when Kinsella, working in the field, hears the voice again the day after (TC 00:08:05). While the Voice previously appeared at dusk and at night, this scene takes place around midday. Instead of the non-melodic 'horror sounds' from before, producing a feeling of threatening strangeness, the Voice now figures in combination with first a melodic ringing and then a smooth piano sequence and subtle strings. Unlike before, where sound and image created an expressive movement of splitting and eerie irruption, the different sounds now seem to merge to form a harmonious, orchestral whole. This movement of merging goes along with Kinsella's apparent, slow realization of what all this might be about as the tonal orchestration runs concurrently with him having some kind of a vision. He is seen standing in the middle of the corn field again – now, however, in the center of the image and with his head above the crops! – as he slowly turns towards the camera. A long shot taking up his point of view presents us with the landscape we know from the first scene: the vast corn field, with the farmhouse next to it. But unlike before, a baseball diamond emerges on the field via a superimposition, clearly recognizable and emphasized by the brightness of its switched-on floodlights, the vivid green of its grass and its typical over-all shape (Figure 3).

Figure 3: Having a vision.

A reverse shot depicts Kinsella repeating the first part of the now well-established conditional sentence, before switching to a medium long shot of the corn field again, on which the baseball field appears once more, though in a slightly different shape. The scene then jumps back for the last time to a close up of the face of Kinsella, who finishes the sentence, emphasizing its subject: "... he will come." While the soundtrack signifies harmonious continuity, the shot directly following this statement comes as a visual disruption. Clearly staged as a contrast to the flashing floodlights and Costner's sweaty and suntanned face, we see the pale Ray Liotta in an old-fashioned baseball outfit looking over his right shoulder into the camera, in slow motion and surrounded by darkness (Figure 4). Unlike before, this shot is not the result of a superimposition, but a snippet of another scene shown later in the movie when Kinsella gets in contact with (the ghost of) 'Shoeless' Joe Jackson as he appears on the field for the first time (TC 00:17:50), even though the shot is then visually inverted (Jackson looks over his left shoulder).

Figure 4: A contrastive first glance.

This audiovisual staging of a split – between light and dark, between Costner's and Liotta's face, between an earlier and a later point in narrative time, between the two parts of the decisive sentence "If you build it, he will come," between 'Shoeless' Joe and Ray's father John as ultimately the mysterious "he" of that sentence – which condenses as a horror modality of irruption in the very first scene of FIELD OF DREAMS, will pervade the whole movie, grounding its audiovisual poetics. It is, as I claim, less bound to the agency of one specific character (of Ray Kinsella) as a dreaming and willfully acting person, but, rather, to the film's constant processing of space and time as phenomena of (dis)limitation, of setting and dissolving boundaries (of communality), both on the level of narrative content and motif, as well as on the level of the perceived audiovisual form. Thereby, the film again and again picks up and productively appropriates different genre modalities of expression and perception, especially with regard to the numerous scenes of men encountering each other (for the first time), of which the one described above – when Ray Kinsella starts hearing the Voice – is only the very first.

Between Strangeness and Intimacy: The First Encounter as Western Duel

Shortly thereafter, Kinsella actually meets (the ghost of) 'Shoeless' Joe Jackson for the first time on the field (TC 00:16:31) – a scene in which the 'dueling' nature of baseball, audiovisually exploited by so many baseball movies, is rendered much in the manner of a Western, bargaining the tension between uncanny alienation on the one hand and intimate familiarity on the other.

While Annie and Ray sort through their paperwork and discuss the financial problems the field causes them, daughter Karin (Gaby Hoffman) interrupts: "There's a man out there in your lawn." Ray turns his head, staring into the void with seemingly mixed feelings of surprise, joy and tension. Kinsella's hesitation when walking up to the window – he makes his daughter stay behind him – as well as the chirping crickets on the audio track add up to the suspenseful mood of the night scene. The image blackens for a second while tracking Kinsella, whose face then appears again, now only dimly lit by a dark blue light coming from the offscreen left, from outside of the window he is looking through.

Simultaneously, a sequence of single low tones sets in – the same heard at the beginning of the first scene, though this time clearly played on a piano and not synthetically produced. Similarly, the sharp swirling sound also returns, immediately evoking the threatening eeriness (of disembodiment) of the first scene. Taking up Kinsella's point of view, the following long shot shows part of the baseball field, seen through the window. In contrast to the initial vision of it, it is now hardly illuminated. In the distance, we discover a tiny white figure, who turns to the left, then seemingly looks in the direction of the camera answering Kinsella's gaze. This movement of detecting and spotting is mirrored in the reverse shot of Kinsella, whom we now see in medium scale from a low angle, standing behind the window. His facial expression is not one of surprise but of solemn tension (he looks like he knows what is coming, but is still skeptical), which is also embodied by the introduction of three sustained and slightly swelling synthesizer major key chords countering the now deeply thundering low tones.

Hereafter, these chords turn out to define the rhythm of an expressive movement of cautious approximation, which evolves between utterances of intimacy and strangeness and feelings of fascinated curiosity and suspicion. At its beginning, this movement comes as rather unbalanced: While Kinsella is presented as quite clearly recognizable in medium close up shots, observing the mysterious athlete on the field from within and around his house, the latter literally remains a ghost for a few more seconds. It is not until five more shots, depicting him as either a faraway white dot or a silhouette in the dark, that the brightly illuminated face of Liotta's character appears for the first (or rather, considering Kinsella's vision earlier, second) time (Figure 5).

His gestures and poses are quite telling: first standing upright and with his legs apart as if confidently awaiting his counterpart or 'opponent,' then kneeling down to check out the condition of the environment (the turf on the field). Then, as if startled by the otherwise clearly heterodiegetic sound, the duelist as ghost, 'Shoeless' Joe Jackson, gets up quickly, and again looks in what seems to be the direction of Kinsella stepping out of his house – the squeaking sound of the fly-screen door relating back to the squeaking of the porch swing in the first scene, and also evoking a common sonic element of suspense in horror and Western films. When the two protagonists are finally positioned against each other by shot reverse shot, the two men not only exchange grave looks,

Figure 5: The appearance of a ghost.

but also reassuring nods: While they seem to know what is coming, the audiovisual expression of the filmic images maintains the tension for a little longer. Additionally rhythmized by deep piano sounds and the thunderous sound from before, Jackson slowly walks backwards into the depth of the field, never losing sight of Kinsella, pounding his baseball glove (a typical move of a player to break in the stiff leather), before ending up in a slightly bent-over position typical for a defensive player awaiting the play and fielding his position (Figure 6).

It is not until now that the tension of the described movement of a cautious approach is broken up, or rather transformed into something else: anticipation, excitement and pleasurable anxiety at the start of a game, especially (and as often in FIELD OF DREAMS) due to character movement within the frame and the comic effect resulting thereof: Kinsella quickly runs to get a bag of balls and a bat, then wants to make a hit for Jackson to catch but misses.

After a couple of successful hits and catches, Jackson runs towards Kinsella and the two men introduce themselves. Especially through a long monologue of Jackson talking about the past, his love for the game of baseball and the impact the 1920 ban had for him back in the day, the expressive movement of a tense and rather static confrontation – also a result of a complete lack of dialogue or spoken language – transforms into one of shared intimacy, with Kinsella and Jackson chatting, as well as the former introducing the latter to his wife and daughter. What is also staged here is how this intimacy is based on or bounded by the proverbial 'fine line,' as it is audiovisually made very explicit that Jackson is not able or does not want to step outside of the field, at least not by passing

Figure 6: Awaiting the play.

over the sideline facing the family's farm.⁵⁵ That this rhetoric of spatial-as-social and -historical boundary of inclusion and exclusion with regard to communality should not be understood as simply a device of the film's fairy-tale diegesis or its textual metaphors, but as the politics of its audiovisual poetics always including the film viewer, will become clear by the end of FIELD OF DREAMS (see later in this chapter). Nevertheless, it already begins to take shape here, especially through a quite telling and very long (over ninety seconds) shot which depicts Jackson confessing his feelings about baseball to Kinsella. Very slowly tracking towards the two men, it is the field's safety fence that – prominently staged – not only constitutes a mechanism of demarcation (between the camera and the actors, between the viewer and the characters, between the magic field and the diegetic everyday reality of rural Iowa), a matrix that evokes spatial enclosure, but also a visual ornament binding the protagonists together (Figure 7). While in Westerns such fragile familiarity and community can often only be achieved (or has to be reestablished) at the expense of another character's death, here it is the sport of baseball, a game of hit and catch, which brings the 'duelists' together and generates and strengthens the community of the film.⁵⁶

---

55 On the other side, the baseball diamond is limited by the remaining corn field, through which the players enter and leave the field, hence through which they travel in time.
56 For a straightforward example with regard to the Western, see SHANE (G. Stevens, 1953), when a group of farmers, after one of them is shot dead, want to give up their land, but are convinced to stay by protagonists Starrett and Shane. At the end of FIELD OF DREAMS, it is Ray's daughter

Figure 7: A safety fence as visual ornament of community.

The Personal Is Public: A PTA Meeting as (Comic) Courtroom Drama

The third (genre) encounter in FIELD OF DREAMS happens as part of a parent-teacher association (PTA) meeting, during which the banning of several books is discussed, especially one of (fictive) author Terence Mann (TC 00:32:45). Since the Kinsellas, especially Annie, are great devotees, a fierce dispute arises between her and another mother, who suggests getting rid of literature such as Mann's. Through its mise en scène, the staging of all the other parents as an anonymous but nonetheless (selectively) very involved mass of spectators, of the teachers as a rather helpless 'jury' and of the argument between the two women as a harsh confrontation of extremist statements and excessive body language, the scene evolves via the pathos of a courtroom drama, which, in addition, is partly suffused with expressions of comic effect – a strategy which more or less pervades the whole movie.[57] It is also the only one of those scenes

---

Karin who almost dies, but is then saved through an act which unites and reconciliates the worlds within and outside of the field. Furthermore, it is important to note that one of the duelists here is actually long dead anyway, as is addressed more than once in the film, even by himself.

57 Playing quite an important role with regard to the sports film, such comic mode always already feeds from a reflexive quality/capacity in terms of genre (modality). Unfortunately, a closer examination in this direction exceeds the framework of this book. For comedy's modes of embodied affective expressivity, especially with regard to the screwball comedy, see Greifenstein / Kappelhoff 2014, and, in German, Greifenstein 2020.

of (confrontational) encounters featuring female protagonists, since Ray is staged as only a dreamy bystander here – which is certainly part of the scene's (slapstick) comedy, although it might also lead to critical questions about the film's representational gender politics. While Tudor does not tackle the question of gender explicitly with regard to FIELD OF DREAMS, her narratological perspective on race and agency, together with her statements on the question of women in sports films in chapter three of her book, enable a reading of Annie Kinsella as a "traditional female character," whose desires are subordinated "to male goals of athletic success" (see Tudor 1997, 85). On the other hand, though, and especially with regard to Madigan's overacting style throughout the whole movie, her character might also be seen as a "more progressive" (Tudor 1997, 136) female sports film character – maybe not so much with regard to narrative action, but on the level of filmic expression.[58]

The scene starts with a hand camera low angle close up shot of the enraged mother shouting into a microphone while waving Mann's book, which she calls "smut and filth." We hear supporting applause on the soundtrack, and the elevating camera reveals a large crowd positioned on both sides behind her, making her the extremely foregrounded center of the image. After Annie Kinsella – with Ray sitting next to her – is visually and audibly introduced as sitting somewhere in the cheering crowd but clearly having a different opinion ("Fascist. I'd

Figure 8: A courtroom setting.

---

58 Furthermore, Tudor reads the PTA meeting scene as marking Ray Kinsella as a character who "avoids political commitment and struggle" (Tudor 1997, 168). This again exposes the

like to ease *her* pain."), the scene depicts the jury (of teachers) positioned in the front against the blustering Mrs. Kessinik and the crowd (Figure 8).

What follows is the staging of some kind of circular dance, as the discussion as well as the images jump back and forth between these three entities, or positions: the one of the accusatory 'prosecutor,' of the jury and of the single spectator within the witnessing crowd. The latter is additionally dynamized, as different people get up from the crowd and shout aggressive one-liners. For a short amount of time then, the dynamic of jumping and the displayed exaggeration are stabilized again by a long shot depicting the whole scene in its strictly symmetrical order, which is enclosed by its framing within another representational space of sports activity: the school's gymnasium, thus mirroring the field as a place for confrontation and potential reconciliation of communality and history in FIELD OF DREAMS (Figure 9). It is the contrastive movement between clearly positioned characters within a very ordered mise en scène, characters which selectively break up this order, and all these characters 'flying off the handle' through their extreme statements and excessive acting which sets up an audiovisual image space in which private and public sphere collide, and in which they are exposed to each other. At the same time and relating thereto, it also provides for the satirical effect of this very courtroom drama-like scene.

Figure 9: Gym and order.

---

constraints and unavoidable contradictions of analyses which concentrate solely on narrative action and character psychology and rather ignore the relation of a film's audiovisual poetics and its politics.

The second part of the scene further condenses this expressive movement of confrontation of orderliness and excessiveness/exaggeration, as well as of personal expression and collective reaction. When Kessinik turns around and starts to address the crowd by saying "You know why he stopped writing books?! Because he masturbates," Annie cannot hold her tongue any longer, standing up and finally confronting the woman already staged as her opponent. A sharp then nasty dispute develops, during which, although presented by means of a rather classic shot reverse shot montage, the public – the people surrounding the two brawlers – remain integrated by sound and image: The audio track is full of collective moaning and laughing, wider shot scales always show Annie and Kessinik surrounded by other bodies (or at least heads), while two interposed shots stage the crowd in a very distinctive way as a collective turning of heads (like the crowd of a tennis match), and in stark contrast to the isolated Ray who, distracted by the question of whose pain he is supposed to ease, does not really pay attention (Figure 10).

Figure 10: A heated dispute, a watching crowd and a distracted man.

In the last part of the scene, and by means of its protagonist Annie Kinsella, the film quite literally appropriates this staged dynamic between punctual and isolated eruption and collective observation. After Kinsella and Kessinik almost get involved in a real fight, the former wants to transform the personal anger and tries to animate the crowd by not only democratizing the dispute, but by also taking its matter to another level of historicity and nationality: "I've got a better idea. Let's put it to a vote, alright?! Who's for Eva Braun here? Who wants to burn books? Who wants to spit on the constitution of the United States of

America, anybody?" Annie's shouting and wild gesticulating is answered by almost complete silence and images of the petrified crowd. "Alright. Now, who's for the Bill of Rights? Who thinks freedom is a pretty darn good thing?" A couple of people start to raise their hands, Annie slaps her still inattentive husband and continues: "Who thinks that we have to stand up to the kind of censorship that they had under Stalin?" More arms go up, and while the scene's previous staging made the viewer a rather distant observer of symmetry and clear lines and positions, one now suddenly feels in the middle of a sea of arms and hands, like Annie, especially because a lot of those fill the whole depth of focus of the image (Figure 11).[59]

Figure 11: A sea of arms for the Bill of Rights.

Before being interrupted by Ray, who forces her to go, Annie finally puts the described movement – from a staged fight between two individuals to an inclusive situation of communal vote – into enthusiastic words, thereby lifting it on the level of nation-building: "Alright, there you go America. I love you, I'm proud of you!"

---

[59] The visual similarity between this shot and the depth-of-focus shots of Hitler being surrounded by a Sieg-Heiling crowd, which we know from Riefenstahl, or even more so from the newsreel footage in HITLER: A CAREER (HITLER: EINE KARRIERE), J. Fest / C. Herrendoerfer, FRG 1977) brings of course yet another ironic twist to this scene.

Time Traveling in Film History

After traversing along modalities of the horror, Western and (comic) courtroom drama film, the fourth and fifth (genre) encounter we have with Kinsella occurs during a journey through what the film just addressed as an image space of dispute, agitation and vote, in which the personal becomes public by means of spectatorship: the United States of America. After the Voice appears again, telling him to "ease his pain," Kinsella presumes that it is actually Terence Mann, a Pulitzer prize winner, leading civil rights activist during the 60s and 70s and also big fan of baseball, who needs his help. After a sequence (TC 00:37:21) that shows Kinsella doing research at a university library and then sharing his findings with Annie, who, as it turns out, had the same dream he did of him and Mann attending a baseball game, one could certainly argue whether this reinforces or undermines the film's narrative gender politics Tudor criticizes. With regard to its audiovisual staging though, the scene develops in the way of the couple literally 'finding a common language' after a long discussion, which Annie, who also starts to talk about the dream first, rather dominates.

Hereafter, Kinsella searches for Mann in Boston and tries to make the now grumpy recluse go to a game at Fenway Park.[60] Again anchored in a comic mode of repetitiveness and miscommunication – with Kinsella repeatedly shown in a VW Vanagon practicing his welcome, then trying to get in contact with the rather unfriendly and suspicious Boston city dwellers and with the funny exploitation of Mann's persistence in trying to get rid of Kinsella, and the latter's persistence in avoiding that outcome – FIELD OF DREAMS starts to invoke a dramaturgy of the crime film here, with Kinsella and Mann becoming a team of private investigators. Attending the game, they both hear the Voice saying "Go the distance" and have some kind of vision, as the name and statistics of Archibald 'Moonlight' Graham, a former baseballer who played only one Major League game and never

---

[60] Fenway Park is one of the most well-known sports venues in the world and, as it opened in 1912, the oldest Major League Baseball stadium currently still in use. It is the home of the Boston Red Sox and a spatially quite 'idiosyncratic' ballpark, with lots of quirky features, the most prominent being the "Green Monster," its left field wall (see for example Shaughnessy 1999 and/ or Mann 1965). Of even stronger allusive quality with regard to Kinsella's field in FIELD OF DREAMS, though, is the other invoked ballpark here, Brooklyn's Ebbets Field. In an interview Kinsella digs out, Mann mentions it in connection with a dream he always had about playing there with the Brooklyn Dodgers' Jackie Robinson, the first African-American baseball player in the modern Major League era. Later, when Kinsella meets Mann, the latter denies ever having said that. Ebbets Field was demolished in 1960, becoming one of the most mythologized sports places in American cultural history up until today (see for example the work of Paul Auster, especially his and Wayne Wang's film BLUE IN THE FACE from 1995, or Don DeLillo's novel *Underworld*).

had a chance to bat,[61] appear on the stadium's video display (TC 00:50:39). Consequently, they travel to Chisholm, Minnesota to search for Graham, only to find out that he had worked as a doctor all those years after his short professional athletic career and died in 1972 (sixteen years before the movie's 1988-time frame). As they dig deeper into Graham's life and fate, the film develops further in the manner of a crime film by also intervening in this genre modality on the level of audiovisual expressivity: While we follow the two men searching for clues in old newspaper articles together with an editor who knew 'Doc' Graham, interviewing other contemporary witnesses in a dive bar, and discussing their findings in a shabby motel room (Figure 12), the rhythmic montage and the mise en scène, especially the setting of multiple confined spaces with their large number of props (magnifier, glasses, notepad, hat, umbrella), as well as the infamous lighting – there are lamps everywhere – are key for the audiovisual experience here.

Figure 12: A mise en scène of investigating.

This expressive movement comes to a head in the next scene (TC 01:01:00) when Kinsella leaves the motel room not only to go for an evening walk, but also, as it turns out, to travel through time to meet Graham in the year 1972 – in quite a film noir-like setting in and through which the film seems to merge the

---

61 While the character of author Terence Mann has no real-life precursor, Archibald Graham was a historical figure. On 29 June 1905, he played his only Major League game as a right fielder at the conclusion of the eighth and the top of the ninth (and final) inning. For a biographical account, see Friedlander / Reising 2009.

(modalities of) horror and crime (and maybe even of the Western) of the previous scenes. Embedded in an expressive movement of visibility and invisibility, of acceleration, deceleration and punctual astonishment, Kinsella as well as the film's viewer – thrown into a dark and deserted street – only slowly realize where, or rather *when* they are. Then, in a quite poignant way, the spotting of a figure that turns out to be the old Graham opens up yet another passage through film history, through the historical experience of filmic images.

The imagery of the scene is dominated by a blue and purple colored darkness which we are familiar with already from the first encounter of Kinsella and 'Shoeless' Joe Jackson on the field at night. The camera follows Kinsella walking through the streets from a lateral and slightly low angle position. He looks around in bewilderment, then suddenly stops as if having detected something. While a cinema billboard in the background remains blurry, the next shot reveals an election poster of Richard Nixon: "4 MORE YEARS – RE-ELECT the PRESIDENT." The next shot returns to Kinsella, who, seriously confused, turns his head to the right, to the billboard which, by a change of the depth of field, becomes readable: "THE GODFATHER – ONE OF THIS YEAR'S TEN BEST." Kinsella repeats the words 'this year's' in disbelief. Accompanied by a sonorous roaring and a kind of heterodiegetic trill which, by always appearing shortly after a new 'sign' is discovered, rhythmizes the first part of the scene, Kinsella looks around again, then approaches a parked car. He kneels down to wipe away some dirt on the car's license plate and the number/year '72' is revealed. Even though not

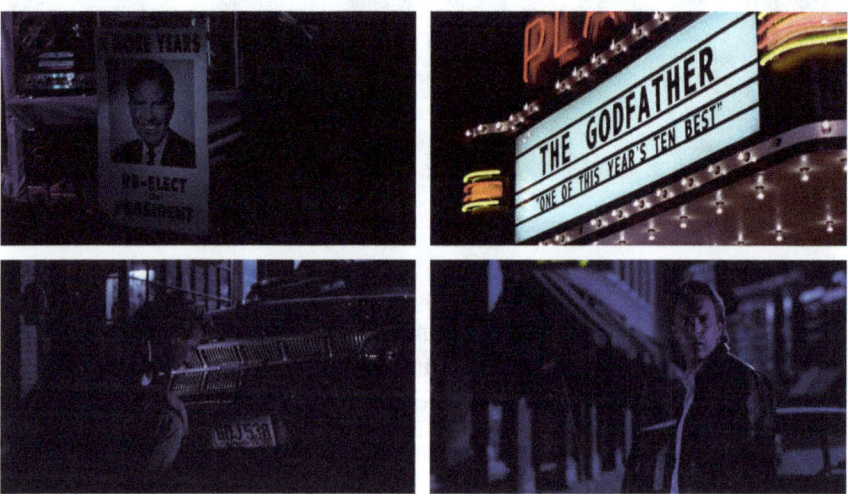

Figure 13: Hints of time travel.

verbalized, it is clear now that Kinsella has traveled back in (narrated) time upon leaving that motel room. He gets up and turns around (Figure 13).

A heavy gong initiates a dynamic shot reverse shot sequence, during which Kinsella spots a dark figure from behind walking under a street light at a misty crossroad on the other side of the street. Through a movement of acceleration, Kinsella is shown following and trying to address the mysterious not so mysterious character: "Dr. Graham?!" A protruding point of view shot as well as the reappearance of that sharp swirling sound from when Kinsella first heard the Voice in the corn field at the beginning of the movie connect the horror of that very first scene with this one.[62] This time though, embedded in an audiovisual movement of gradually dissolving uncertainty and disbelief, Kinsella and the film's viewer are not haunted by the eeriness of a fluid or gaseous perception image and/or a semi-subjective camera consciousness, but by the crystallized and ever again crystallizing time of (film) history itself: by the audiovisual world of FIELD OF DREAMS, which combines and relates genre modalities of horror, crime and film noir; by the presence of (the theatrical release of) THE GODFATHER (F.F. Coppola, 1972) as one of the most popular movies of all time; by the 1973 horror film THE EXORCIST (W. Friedkin), whose famous shot of Father Merrin under a street lamp is clearly evoked here;[63] by the history of film noir, additionally and strongly addressed through the actor who is revealed as playing Doc Graham in the next shot – it is Burt Lancaster, who not only made his first movie appearances in the 1940s in film noirs like CRIS CROSS

---

[62] Which of course could give rise to the question of what really is or incarnates as the horror of the film's beginning: Is it the ever recurring past? The return of the old as the same and (as such) the eerie (un)familiar? A divine instance? In this regard, it should also be noted that the actual owner of the Voice is never revealed, not even in the film's credits, where "The Voice" is listed, but its profilmic equivalent is indicated as "Himself."

[63] There is even more of such referencing going on in the film: While the mentioning of the name "Rosebud" of Mann's childhood bat seems to speak to the film's riddle plot and its general object-centeredness, there are two other occasions where referencing takes place on the expressive level. First, when one of the players imitates the dying Wicked Witch from THE WIZARD OF OZ (V. Fleming, 1939) while going back into the corn field ("I'm melting, I'm melting"). And second, when Kinsella's daughter Karin watches the movie HARVEY (H. Koster, 1950) during breakfast, the morning after Kinsella heard the Voice for the first time. In HARVEY, protagonist Elwood P. Dowd makes friends with some kind of spirit in the form of a big rabbit only he can see and is thus declared mentally ill by his family. As we see and then listen to James Stewart's character retelling the first encounter with the ghost rabbit, Kinsella comes down the stairs, takes the remote control, switches off the TV and then tells his daughter that this "is not funny, the man is sick." See also Babington 2014, 89, who additionally thinks to recognize a (verbal) allusion to KNUTE ROCKNE ALL AMERICAN, which I will analyze in detail in chapter 6.1.

(R. Siodmak, 1949), but also played one of the most iconic roles in sports film history in JIM THORPE – ALL-AMERICAN (M. Curtiz, 1951) (Figure 14).⁶⁴

Figure 14: Traveling through film history (FIELD OF DREAMS, THE EXORCIST, CRIS CROSS).

As another one of the many 'encountering couples' triggering scenes of a two-person dialogue, Kinsella and 'Moonlight' Graham (as 'Doc' Graham as Burt Lancaster as Steve Thompson as Jim Thorpe) then walk together to the latter's office, talking about the past, about that one game Graham played without ever being at-bat, and, in connection to that, about the idea of the (most) significant moment (in life), and about the wish or the chance to experience such a moment (again).⁶⁵

Encountering Genre Film as Time Crystal

So as Kinsella travels back to a diegetic 1972, Graham's last year of life, only to travel back with just this Graham – at least in conversation – to the year 1922,

---

64 For an analysis of Curtiz' film, see chapter 6.2. Lancaster died in 1994, and FIELD OF DREAMS was his last motion picture film, followed only by a handful of TV appearances.
65 For how this idea of that one moment in time is important for the sports film in a wider sense, see chapter 4 of this book.

when, according to the film, the mentioned game occured,⁶⁶ the viewer of FIELD OF DREAMS also travels in time, namely through the history of genre film, experiencing modalities of horror, courtroom drama, crime and the Western through specific forms of expressive movement. The film productively appropriates, relates and modulates these modalities, e.g. with the help of comedy as some kind of reflexive mode breaking up all these modalities, to put forth an audiovisual poetics that not only just cites certain films or refers to predetermined genre categories, but produces what Michael Wedel, in recourse to and extension of Paul Ricœur's considerations, calls a medial deep temporality [mediale Tiefenzeitlichkeit] of the poiesis of film-viewing.⁶⁷ Originally referring to Tom Tykwer's film DREI (GER, 2010), Wedel states:

> What enters the film's fiction here is much more than just a quote of another film. It is the *fiction* of another film, with which the rules of fictionalization itself change: the metaphorical dynamics on which they are based as well as the genre associations they evoke. And last but not least, the historical traces and imprints [Signaturen] with which the film constructs a triangle connecting different points in time [...]. And hence, alongside this construction, installs a form of medial deep temporality, which itself takes shape only through the temporal perception of all the modes of worldmaking multiplying in this way.⁶⁸   (Wedel 2019)

With regard to the affective community the film thereby produces, he continues:

> Just like the referenced historical times are phenomenologically embedded within the time of their referencing, it is at first the perceptual consciousness of the film's viewer

---

66 The real-life Archibald Wright Graham died in 1965. That one major league game he played originally took place in 1905. Furthermore, it was not the last game of the season, as it is (told) in the movie. And last but not least, the real-life Graham continued playing in the minor leagues for another three seasons after that game while already working as a practicing doctor (see Friedlander / Reising 2009).

67 For Ricœur's notion of "deep temporality," which he puts forward in direct reference to Heidegger's study of within-time-ness and his notion of *Zeitlichkeit* (and *Geschichtlichkeit*) at the end of *Being and Time*, see Ricœur 1984 [1983], 62. He writes: "As is well known, Heidegger reserves the term temporality (*Zeitlichkeit*) for the most originary form and the most authentic experience of time, that is, the dialectic of coming to be, having been, and making present. In this dialectic, time is entirely desubstantialized. The words 'future,' 'past,' and 'present' disappear, and time itself figures as the exploded unity of the three temporal extases" (Ricœur 1984 [1983], 61). While this experience, with Heidegger, would ultimately still refer back to a somewhat primary entity of phenomenological consciousness, I want to grasp it (with Deleuze and Wedel) as the product of the modulation of expressive and perceptual image structures effecting such a consciousness in the first place. Besides that, it is important to differentiate such a concept of deep temporality from notions of deep time or deep history, which seem especially popular in anthropology and earth sciences.

68 Wedel stated this in German in the course of a presentation at *Cinepoetics Center for Advanced Films Studies* at *Freie Universität Berlin* (28 January 2019), my translation.

through and within which the expressive movement of the filmic representation – its poetic logic – binds the depicted characters together as an involuntarily instantaneous community of feeling. (Wedel 2019)

This reception-aesthetic and community-building time travel in FIELD OF DREAMS is triggered and secured by the creation of a series of quite distinct and very explicit and saturated image spaces of genre – not only with respect to certain sensual qualities, but also in the way they rely on and emphasize a process of *re*cognition, e.g. with regard to symbolic codes and objects of historical localization like the Vanagon, the cinema billboard, the license plate etc. Seen in such light, this might also speak to the often-made statement about FIELD OF DREAMS being overtly and excessively nostalgic, as the film might not be interested in producing new (in the sense of never experienced before or 'dissident') time-spaces of sensuality, but creates an assemblage of Hollywood genre modalities. It is exactly this assembling that simultaneously makes FIELD OF DREAMS a genre film itself, though, at least if we take the concept of a non-taxonomic genre system of creatively interpenetrating modes and modalities presented in the previous chapter seriously.

Hence, as much as FIELD OF DREAMS might perfectly fit Frederic Jameson's scheme of the 'postmodern nostalgia film,' which, by recycling clichés of the past instead of providing a heightened and authentic consciousness of historical complexity, performs an "omnivorous [...] historicism" (Jameson 1992, 18) and produces 'only' "pastiche" (Jameson 1992, 16) and a "perpetual present" (Jameson 1992, 79) in correspondence to late capitalism, I want to suggest assessing the poetics of appropriation of FIELD OF DREAMS differently.[69] Not – and my usage of the term "assemblage" (Deleuze / Guattari 1987 [1980], 306) instead of pastiche, in combination with the analytical observations before and following, points to that already – as a symptom of an "ahistorical period of history," but as a starting point of "serious historicity" (Deleuze / Guattari 1987 [1980], 296), of the production of history as historical experience, as the experiential manufacturing of time and communality, in the first place. Jameson, for whom the nostalgic films of the 1980s and 1990s are "false realism" because they are films about other films, films "in which the history of aesthetic styles replaces 'real' history" (Jameson 1992, 20), leaves aside in what way such filmic relationality itself can become a reflexive experience of historicity. Taking this one step further, there might even be a bigger historical argument (of nostalgia)

---

[69] While being aware that the term appropriation has a rather negative connotation, especially in an Anglo-American context, I use it nonetheless since it seems to capture the tension between different approaches to genre addressed here quite well.

to be made with regard to the strong tendency of filmic relationality having been so constitutive for New Hollywood in the era before 'Reaganite cinema' and the specific, quite New Hollywood-esque kinds of genre modalities referred to in FIELD OF DREAMS.[70]

A Community of Spectators of and as the Myth of America

After the old Archibald 'Doc' Graham has turned down Kinsella's offer to bring him to a place where his biggest wish of batting against a star pitcher could be fulfilled, Kinsella and Mann leave together for Iowa, back to Kinsella's farm, his family and the field: "we are coming home" (TC 01:07:43). This "We," though, keeps extending as the two men pick up a hitchhiker, who states that he is traveling through the country to find a team to play baseball. This hitchhiker turns out to be the young – and thus even older! – Archibald 'Moonlight' Graham, coming from or sending Kinsella and Mann back to the past. In a certain manner, this scene can also be regarded as an encounter with another genre modality. It is introduced earlier on and, unsurprisingly, binds together the whole string of scenes beginning when Kinsella leaves his farm. It is the modality of the road movie, previously evoked by the 1973 country rock songs *China Grove* by The Doobie Brothers (TC 00:56:00) and The Allman Brothers Band's *Jessica* (TC 00:42:24) in a rather blatant manner, and manifesting by means of a moving vehicle, seemingly never-ending streets, the obvious change of daytimes and light, lots of landscape as well as a long dialogue as an overall experience of 'being on the road.' What is also worth mentioning here is the aspect of generational conflict, especially since this topic finally – with Kinsella telling Mann about the problematic relationship with his father during the road trip – starts to become central for the film's narrative.

The round robin of men being connected (and finally redeemed) through baseball still does not end here though: When Kinsella, Mann and the young Graham arrive back at the farm, there are even more players from the past on the field – the Black Sox, tired of only practicing, invited them to play a game. There is also Annie Kinsella's brother Mark (Timothy Busfield), who is financially involved in the farm and cannot see the players from the past. He therefore thinks

---

[70] For a more detailed reading of Jameson's notion of the nostalgia film, see Lauri-Lucente 2015. For the affect poetics of New Hollywood and a very innovative approach to film history as relationality, see Lehmann 2019. See also DeLanda 2006, who adopts the concept of assemblage for a social theory that speaks to both the genre theory and the constitutive conflict of the team sports film outlined in this book.

the Kinsellas are crazy and urges them to sell, as the farmland has become unprofitable because of the baseball field – the bank will foreclose on it and evict them soon. While this narrative conflict is not presented in any specific classic modality of Hollywood genre, it nonetheless leads to a scene whose audiovisual and affective movement not only variegates a common pathos scene of the sports film, but also puts the movie's poetics of genre assemblage into political and historical perspective. Thereby, the American sports film's central conflict of community formation as a function of celebrated exceptionality and as an audiovisual discourse on time as crystallized or transtemporal time, on, as I argue, history in the sense of the American Dream, are finally merged.[71]

The day after the men's arrival back at the farm and young Graham's participation in a game on Kinsella's diamond, Mark arrives at the farm where Mann, Kinsella, his wife Annie and his daughter Karin watch the players on the field (TC 01:17:05). During a heated discussion between Kinsella and Mark, who is clearly staged as an interruption to the game he cannot see, Karin suddenly states: "We don't have to sell the farm. People will come." And upon request continues that people will come "from all over" and pay them to "watch the game" and to "remember what it was like when they were little kids." Mark intervenes again and hands over the sales contract to Kinsella, before, suddenly, Mann repeats Karin's words, which of course also mirror what the Voice said in the beginning: "People will come."

This extension, from the male individual hero *of the past* to the people who *will* come, epitomizes the circularity of interdependence of the sports film's central conflict, of American communality and (its) historicity: If he will come, they will come, so that we can stay. If Joe Jackson, Terence Mann, Archibald Graham (and in the end and with the last encounter: Kinsella senior) will or have come (from the past), the other players and the people as spectators will come (in the present), so that the Kinsella family is able to stay (in the future). By means of an impassioned appeal by Mann to Kinsella to keep the field, which in a way develops in the manner of a coach's pep talk scene, this interdependence becomes audiovisually tangible. It is staged as a scene of dramatic escalation, in which the characters' speech and movement as well as the camera position and framing, through which specific visual axes and lines of (character) sight are created, become the dominant resources of the audiovisual expressive movement.

---

[71] I dwell on this constitutive conflict in more detail in the chapter 2.2, in chapter 3.2 and also in the following analytical chapters.

2.3 Encountering Genre History on the FIELD OF DREAMS — 75

The scene (TC 01:21:58) develops between Mann, Mark, Kinsella and also the players on the field, even though they, as well as Kinsella, do not say anything. While Mann basically gives a speech, Mark is staged as an interruption to this speech, as intruding even spatially on the developing (pathos-laden) mood of the sensory space, much as he was presented diegetically as an intruder on the field shortly before. Shown in a medium close up shot and sitting across from Kinsella and Mark at the bottom of the stand, Mann repeats the sentence just spoken by Karin, emphasizing every single word: "Ray, people will come, Ray." Another shot of Kinsella turning his head establishes the axis of direction. Mann, who has gazed into the (off) distance (of the field) until now, turns his head as well and continues to speak. The image jumps to a medium long shot of him, imitating Kinsella's point of view. While he starts to lyrically describe how people will turn up at the farm, "not knowing for sure why they are doing it, [...] they'll arrive at your door, as innocent as children longing for the past," the camera approaches him in a slight rotary tracking motion. While in that way breaking away from the strict point of view construction, the expressive movement is further dynamized by the onset of music on the audio track: Gentle (synthetic) strings and a sequence of high bell tones let the audiovision flicker suspensefully, before two deeply rumbling drum beats not only constitute a sonic counterpoint, but also combine with Mann's passionate recitation and vivid description of how the field will have its (paying) spectators in the future.

Consistent with the previous staging, the nascent dynamic is briefly interrupted by Mark telling Kinsella to sign the papers via a shot reverse shot sequence between the two of them. But Kinsella immediately turns his head again as Mann's speech continues. The camera follows the latter while he stands up and walks towards the field. The players in their positions come into sight in the image's background, looking like they can hear Mann and listen to what he has to say. As he walks away from the stand and the camera, but continues his speech to which even the players far out in the field seem to react, the scene's staging opens up an audiovisual space by which Mann's words become part of a rather universal address, as is quite typical for sports films' pep talk scenes. With regard to such scenes, the figure of the coach (here: Mann) does not really speak to one specific character, but to a group which forms or has to be formed due to or by this speech itself. Now, this forming of a group is thereby (and especially here) not solely defined by the depiction and connection of (former) players (on the field) and (future) spectators (in the stands), but unfolds as an expressive movement perceived by the film viewer. It audiovisually points to a sense of community, which clearly exceeds the film's diegetic world and addresses the audience as a forming community of film-viewing, which then also migrates back again into image and sound: The moment Mann turns towards the camera, towards Kinsella and his family, as well as towards the viewer of FIELD OF DREAMS, a horn theme sets in on the audio track and the players start walking up to him in the background. After another quick interruption by Mark, we see Mann in a long shot from a rather high angle standing at the sideline with the field and the players gathering behind him (Figure 15): "People will come, Ray!"

Figure 15: A coming community (FIELD OF DREAMS).

Once again, the camera switches to Mark pleading Kinsella to sign, before Mann is shown again, this time in a medium close up, starting to move himself, the players still doing the same in the background. Mark's urging – "You sell now, or you lose everything." – corresponds with the movement of Mann and the players walking towards Kinsella. The audiovisual dramaturgy, which resembles many encounters throughout the whole movie, is very explicit: A pivotal decision has to be made now! However, because of the scene's sound, this movement of pressurizing does not really have a threatening but rather an uplifting quality. This is also because of Mann's speech, in which he turns from vividly describing the experience of future spectators of the field to praising the significance of baseball in and for American history more generally. It is remarkable how these words correspond to the staged audiovisual expressive movement, and the relation of continuous flow, momentous standstill and repetition as the critical variables of the sports film in general.

"The one constant through all the years, Ray, has been baseball. America has rolled by like an army of steamrollers. It's been erased like a blackboard, rebuilt, and erased again." says Mann while walking with the players. The latter then stop, Mann does the same. "But baseball has marked the time." He turns around smiling and raising his index finger. "This field, this game. It's a part of our past, Ray." Followed by the camera in a circular tracking shot, he starts walking to the right side of the image. "It reminds us of all that once was good, and it could be again." He sits down, having returned to the place where he started his speech and walk two minutes of screen time earlier, and repeats once more: "Oh, people will come, Ray. People will most definitely come." With the onset of another rumbling drum beat, which is now clearly staged as a disturbing contrast to the horn theme and connected to brother-in-law Mark, whose voice we hear one more time while the image slowly approaches Costner's face. His gaze then connects with a medium shot panning along the string of players facing him on the field (Figure 16).

Figure 16: A face-off between past and future.

Everyone becomes a spectator as everyone's existence – in a very material and existential sense – seems to stand on the brink, and as everyone is confronted with the myth of baseball as the myth of the United States of America. But considering what FIELD OF DREAMS has shown us so far, which genre modalities of perceived expressivity have become animated and connected throughout the film's audiovisual poetics, this spectatorship is – if we recognize genre as a system of reference and interpenetration of such modalities – also an experience of American film history.[72]

This experience also densifies once again and in a quite different but no less intriguing manner when looking more closely at the Terence Mann character and especially at the actor embodying him. James Earl Jones became famous for his distinctive, deep voice, which made its most renowned appearance as also a more or less *disembodied* (or acousmatized) voice: Jones lent it Darth Vader in the STAR WARS movies. Furthermore, Jones' acting career started during the time of New Hollywood, the period of film history FIELD OF DREAMS alludes to the most. He had his first leading role in the sports film THE GREAT WHITE HOPE (M. Ritt, 1970), which retells a part of the life story of first black heavyweight boxing champion Jack Johnson becoming the subject of many conflicts and controversies of racial conflict throughout his career. While Jones himself figured as a prominent public voice regarding the history of racial conflict in the United States, he also starred in the sports comedy film THE BINGO LONG TRAVELING ALL-STARS & MOTOR KINGS (J. Badham, 1976), which revolves around a team of African-American ex-Negro League baseball players during the era of racial segregation. In THE MAN (J. Sargent, 1972), Jones plays the first African-American US president, and is more than once shown struggling to find the tone and gravitas as a speaker addressing the nation – the tone and gravitas which he gets across so strongly here at the end of FIELD OF DREAMS.

History as Filmic Experience of Deep Temporality and the Negotiation of Belonging

To come to a conclusion, let us go back to Tudor's claim about FIELD OF DREAMS evoking different pasts, and blending the personal past of an innocent spectator with a social past of national innocence at the beginning of the twentieth century, and thus in the early days of modern professional baseball (Tudor 1997, 169).[73] While I would agree about the constant negotiation of the dependent relationship between the realms of individuality and communality as the (sports) film's central

---

[72] As mentioned earlier, this referencing also pertains to the film's own images, as the scene just described shows once again. Here, Costner's gaze is not only confronted with the panning shot of all the players on the field looking at him, but also with a shot of Jackson pounding his glove and adopting his defense position, which clearly resembles the earlier shot during the first (duel) encounter of the two men.

[73] As became clear after the Black Sox scandal, this "Coming of Age era" (Rader 2008, 91) of modern baseball, which is also often called the dead-ball era, was never as innocent as one might have thought or still thinks. For a comprehensive history of American baseball, see Rader 2008.

concern, I strongly hesitate to frame it simply within an argument of nostalgia in the sense of a wishful longing for a specific – a better, a more innocent – past, which is recognized by the semantics of narrative content and character behavior and speech (the appearance of players from the past, Karin and Terence Mann talking about the good old times, the sport of baseball as nostalgic itself etc.). I would rather like to argue that FIELD OF DREAMS, in its poetic referencing and reflecting of a community-building history of a poiesis of film-viewing, becomes itself involved in an activity that Thomas Elsaesser describes as the typical strategy of New Hollywood cinema initially: "the self-conscious use of old mythologies, genre stereotypes, and the history of the cinema itself" (Elsaesser 1998, 195).

The film, as I claim, does not simply evoke a desirable and better time of the past, a past which seemingly can be equated quite easily with a timespan of actual American (sports) history (the so-called real past), but rather renders history itself as, first, an ever-new experience of what we might understand with Wedel and Ricœur as a form of medial deep temporality, which evolves by means of relating different modalities of audiovisual expression and perception, different chronotopes of genre as interpenetrating vectors and layers of time; and second, as a process of constant inclusion as well as exclusion, which these interpenetrations provoke and are themselves part of. And this not only on a level of representation, by reproducing the (effects of the) practice of segregation in the history of modern baseball during the first half of the twentieth century – Tudor rightfully notes that there is no African-American player turning up on the field, nor is this omission otherwise addressed. But also by staging this process – and this runs contrary to Tudor's claim about the film presenting a kind of hegemonic and self-contained fantasy, with the white and male character of Ray Kinsella having all the agency – as an experience of exactly that, an ongoing inclusion and exclusion, a constant negotiation of who belongs and participates, and who does not. Of responding to certain genre poetics, of knowing about certain aspects of film history, but also of sports and specifically baseball history. Of becoming part of or being excluded from the production of certain genre film communities of taste,[74] or even of/from a transtemporal 'Us' of American history as the history of Hollywood genre film. This viewpoint is not meant to undermine the fact that there are of course certain sovereign structures and perspectives at work here, especially with regard to

---

[74] For a conceptualization of this notion with regard to cinema, see Kilerci / Lehmann 2018. In view of my argument here about FIELD OF DREAMS, this aspect of the formation of communities of taste through and around genre films might also be interesting with regard to the very heterogenous version of such a community that this movie seemingly aims to address. And, in a wider context, how this might illuminate the popular description of the sports film as 'family film.'

the film and its referencing system basically remaining within the cosmos of Hollywood genre filmmaking. It nonetheless seems important to tackle the film's politics of aesthetics the way I propose here, as it not only supports my argument on the team sports film's poetics of historicity, but also provides a vivid example with regard to movies' role in the production of social and political realities, and to the closely interwoven interaction between aesthetic and historical experience, a claim often brought forward but rarely met within the fields of visual culture and visual history studies.[75]

This also counts for the film's narrative: As much as the plot of FIELD OF DREAMS might be dominated by a movement of inclusion, of forming a (trans-temporal) community of baseball enthusiasm, of sharing a certain idea of history, there is also exclusion taking place. There are at least four scenes, or rather scenic situations during the last third of the movie which make this palpable. All of them are connected to the possibility of going back, or rather, going somewhere else in time, thereby subtly tackling questions of generation, of life and death, and of compassion.

There is, first, young 'Moonlight' Graham leaving the field to irreversibly transform into old 'Doc' Graham in order to help Kinsella's almost suffocating daughter, but then cannot go back and join the game anymore (TC 01:23:17, Figure 17).

Figure 17: Leaving the field, transforming in time.

---

75 For an insightful German perspective on this, see Wedel 2018.

There is, second, 'Shoeless' Joe Jackson asking Terence Mann if he wants to accompany the players going back into the corn field (TC 01:27:32) from where they appeared in the first place, even though it remains unclear where this kind of "metaphysical zone of some sort of afterlife" (Babington 2014, 92) leads to.[76] There is, third, the curious Kinsella who wants to go, too, but who is – much to his annoyance – denied the possibility, as Jackson makes clear: "You're not invited" (Figure 18).[77]

---

[76] The following dialogue unfolds between Jackson and Mann: "Come with you?" "Out there." "What is out there?" "Come and find out." In this regard, it is an open question as to which place is actually addressed by the movie's title. Is it the diamond? Is it the corn field next to it? Or is it both? Here, the romantic-fantastic idea of nature as an otherworldly, magic chronotope is combined with sports as a kind of domestication of nature's 'wild forces.' At the same time, there is a religiously loaded discourse resonating throughout the film, as the question about the field being heaven is asked twice, at the beginning by 'Shoeless' Joe Jackson (TC 00:24:36) and in the end by Ray's father John Kinsella (TC 01:35:52), who finally also appears on the field. Both times, Ray answers that it is Iowa, and not heaven, even though the second time he does not seem to be so sure anymore about the two being the same thing, adding "the place dreams come true." This also relates to the status of the players from the past themselves: While the motif of the angel has been quite present throughout the history of the sports film (see for example ANGELS IN THE OUTFIELD, C. Brown / W. Dear 1951/1994, or HEAVEN CAN WAIT, W. Beatty / B. Henry 1978, which is a remake of HERE COMES MR. JORDAN, A. Hall 1941), here it is rather that of the ghost which is frequently addressed and introduced quite early in the film with the help of the film-in-film reference to HARVEY (see footnote 63). Later, Karin asks 'Shoeless' Joe Jackson if he is a ghost, which leads to a short dialogue about the impression of reality (TC 00:23:55): "What do you think?" "You look real to me." "Well, then I guess I'm real." Ghosts also appear in other sports films, for example quite figuratively in KNUTE ROCKNE ALL AMERICAN (L. Bacon / W. K. Howard, 1940), when at the end of the movie the dead protagonist, clearly staged as a ghost, reappears on the field in an empty stadium (see chapter 6.1) or as some kind of 'ghost-image' in TROUBLE WITH THE CURVE (R. Lorenz, 2012), when a flashback montage connected to Clint Eastwood's character Gus takes us (back) to a close-up of the young Clint Eastwood playing Mitchell Gant in the action film FIREFOX (C. Eastwood, 1982), a movie which itself, with Gant as a shell-shocked former Vietnam War pilot, uses a lot of flashback scenes.

[77] Kinsella listens to reason shortly thereafter, as Jackson and Mann make clear to him that he is attached to his family, and that he did not build the field for himself in the first place. Mann also tells him about actually having had the dream about Ebbets Field and Jackie Robinson. After he also claims to write again about what he will discover, the two men say goodbye to each other, and, for quite a long time, we see Mann laughing and acting childishly in excitement before he finally enters the corn field (TC 01:31:07). One could certainly read this scene as a moment of Black empowerment – see for example Babington's analysis, where he qualifies it as "another instance of the film's more liberal inflection of its source's social implications" (Babington 2014, 92).

Figure 18: Inclusion and exclusion.

And there is, fourth, Jackson's earlier comment about (famous and very successful baseball player) Ty Cobb, who also wanted to come and play on the field, but: "None of us could stand the son of a bitch when we were alive, so we told him to stick it," followed by Ray Liotta's loud and nasty laughter (TC 01:13:35).

These staged moments of exclusion might be interpreted as marginal compared to a story that some would qualify as rather superficial and all too homogenous and uncontested, as "archaic, pastoral, and idyllic in tone and location" (Sobchack 1997, 179), but they nonetheless resonate with my analysis of the entire film as a viewer's (sensory) passage through the history of American genre film. Especially as it becomes clear that even though FIELD OF DREAMS invokes what we might call 'classic' (Post New) Hollywood genres, such invocation can never aim at an idea of (the repetition of) something pure or completely unprecedented: By referring and appropriating a genre modality, by mixing it with other modalities, this modality never stays the same (again). It becomes something new by means of how it is connected and embedded, and of how it therefore changes everything that was before and will come after.[78] With regard to this passage, the history of American genre film can thus only be understood and become graspable as one of dynamic interdependence and ramification, as a web of permanent movements of overlap and distinction, of coalescence and separation, as traveling through the times, thereby interrelating duration and timeliness, flow and stoppage, uniqueness and universality to produce ever new temporal communities of history.

By means of its poetics of construction, juxtaposition and transition being at work on different levels in the film,[79] FIELD OF DREAMS to a certain extent

---

[78] For a related idea, see also Cavell 1979, 73.
[79] One could, for example, also look more closely at the film's symbolism or expand on its regimes of sight and visibility.

counters the "quest for purity" (Butterworth 2010, 57) that many scholars assume the film to be about, most often with regard to baseball films in general. In "its ability to integrate a variety of periods in American history" (Gill 1999, 122), which, as I have shown, can also be understood as the ability to integrate a variety of historical modalities of experience of American genre film, FIELD OF DREAMS balances different values and therefore "reflects the struggle of a society trying to come to terms with the relatively extreme value tensions of the previous two decades" (Gill 1999, 122) of the 1960s and 1970s. It does so not only by creating a completely balanced vision of America as a perfect world (see Gill 1999, 114–115), but by making palpable that this perfect world is a cultural fantasy, by all means in necessity of and provoking conflict, impurity and exclusion; that American cultural history is not only a question of "opposing values of individualism and community," for which FIELD OF DREAMS "creates a place [...] of constant balancing" (see Gill 1999, 114–115.) via its plot and characters, but also by addressing and making the (history of the) film's viewer experience a crucial part of this tension and the constructive force of this history in the first place, via its forms of audiovisual movement and within a genre-as-media system of interpenetrating modalities of filmic expression and perception.

3 Becoming What We Were and Will Be Again: The American Dream

3.1 The Shortcomings of the American Dream as Narrative and Narrativized Ideologeme

The notorious question of what a certain cycle of films is all about rarely provokes a firmer, more homogeneous, and, at the same time, more encoded answer than in the case of sports feature films. Everyone seems to know: these films are all about the American Dream. Sometimes, this is even directly verbalized in the films, like, for example, in THE JACKIE ROBINSON STORY (A.E. Green, 1950), when a voice-over tells us right at the very beginning that "this is the story of a boy and his dream, but more than that, it is the story of an American boy and a dream that is truly American." The film ends on a blatant cross-fade of its main protagonist and the Statue of Liberty.[1]

This impression of the American Dream's importance strengthens when looking into research literature on the sports film, as most books and articles within the field at least mention the term, or notions connected to it. While I will dwell on some of these studies in more detail in what follows, one general observation imposes itself at the outset: A proper conceptualization of the American Dream, how it can be framed and put in perspective for a culturally and historically informed analysis of (filmic) images and media reception, is basically always absent here, even when its role is regarded as central or important for the sports film.

Does this result in approaches that try to think of the production and modulation of the American Dream more or less strictly from (within) the films themselves? Do these approaches try to touch upon the aesthetic dimensions and imaginative capacity of the American Dream as national ethos and "cultural fantasy" (Grella 1975, 550)?[2] Not at all, as the focus is almost always one of rudimentary ideology critique, with a quite restrictive and narrow orientation towards a mythological dimension, and hence towards an analysis that renders the American Dream first and foremost a universal and – with regard to real life social conditions as a fixed reference system – a *false* narrative of upward social and economic mobility, often referred to as the Horatio Alger myth.[3] It is

---

[1] For a more in-depth analysis and historical classification of the film, especially with regard to the American Dream, see Crosson 2013, 72 et seq.
[2] As cited in Gill 1999, 122.
[3] See for example Farred 2008 or Whannel 2008.

this myth that lies at the heart of the understanding of the American Dream as a certain narrative. Its name goes back to a corpus of more than a hundred novels published by the author Horatio Alger during the second half of the nineteenth century. The books mainly deal with stories of young men, who are born into poverty and transcend their social and economic situation through hard work and persistence. The Horatio Alger myth thus describes a storyline and character development repeatedly picked up by Hollywood films in general. Quite similar to sports films, Alger's novels have often been object of sharp criticism in regard to their propagandistic or socially destructive ignorance towards socio-economic constraints existing beyond an individual's power and control, especially towards race.[4]

To this effect, examinations of what Andrew Miller calls "the cinematic construction of the Athletic American Dream" (Miller 2007) most often do not comprise much more than the recognition and retracing of certain narrative structures and procedures by looking at a film's story and its characters', especially its hero's, actions. The question about the way and extent of the sports film's intervention with regard to the American Dream is thereby always a question about realistic equivalence, framed (and in that way also already answered) by the idea of misrepresentation from the very beginning. The films evolve around a certain, but obviously highly unspecific tragic plot structure, which goes something like this: an isolated hero faces obstacles, succeeds in overcoming them by individual will power and for the greater good, which then translates into moral elevation often accompanied by social and/or economic elevation as well. Thus, every film feeds the myth, becoming the 'accomplice of false testimony' that it was already suspected to be. At the same time, this myth is grasped as not much more than exactly this false narrative, distorting or concealing the truth of real-life conditions. The ways sports, film and the American Dream might function as mutually interdependent media (practices), which produce, share and dynamically modulate an aesthetically structured and imaginatively functioning environment of affective temporalities and experiential spaces, is suppressed and precluded by static models of realistic equivalence.

Apart from treating the American Dream as a self-explanatory notion – it always seems to be clear what the American Dream is, what it naturally signifies or alludes to – the role it plays for or within the sports film is primarily discussed on the level of narration, and of ideology as *false* narration, i.e. as the (re-)production of untruthful narratives, with the actual social conditions as (a prior, apparently unmediated) reference system. Hence, at the center of these

---

[4] See for example Dalton 1995, 127 et seq.

approaches, there is often a critique of the genre's and/or a specific movie's shortcomings and inadequacies with regard to the 'proper' representation of real-life circumstances: the American Dream, itself eventually understood as nothing but a deceptive belief system of false or unrealistic narrative, joining forces with the mainstream movie's gesture of narrative concealment and masking of a reality that is not only somewhat metaphysical, but also supposedly accessible in a pure, unmediated way.

Accordingly, sports – itself often already understood as an activity of escapism within the cultural industry of a capitalist system – and (blockbuster) film appear as affirming (media) comrades of and within a constellation of delusion. Thereby, the "Athletic American Dream is produced, packaged and sold by mass media so successfully that one could argue that it becomes the most dominant vision of the American Dream by the end of the twentieth century" (Miller 2007, 104). Most of the time, the reasons for this success and efficacy can be traced back to an ideology of "self-determination and of [...] a level playing field," put forward by "underdog-to-champion, hard-work-leads-to-victory narratives" (Miller 2007, 103–104).

In the following, I will introduce two approaches proceeding in the manner just described as exemplary cases, before then taking a step back to develop a philosophically as well as media aesthetically and media culturally informed understanding of the American Dream – one that, first, acknowledges it as an aesthetic and social imaginary by emphasizing its manifestation as a specific, historio-culturally embedded as well as socially effective and reflexive conception of historicity and communality. And that, second, takes up the disposition this conception shares with Benedict Anderson's reflexive 'image of communion' of the American nation as an "imagined political community" (Anderson 2006 [1983], 6), with sports, film and sports film-viewing as media of and within the imagining of this image.[5] The productive intervention of the filmic audiovisualities of sports in this imagining, which eventually also marks the social, political and historical effectiveness of the sports film as an 'American' genre, has to be grasped on the level of a filmic thinking that is self-reflexively concerned with a specific idea of time. As will become clear by means of this book's analytical chapters, this thinking relates an idea of communality – as a conflict of inclusion and exclusion, as the mutual dependence of and tension between

---

[5] Anderson writes about this community: "It is *imagined* because the members of even the smallest nation will never know most of their fellow-members, meet them, or even hear of them, yet in the minds of each lives the image of their communion" (Anderson 2006 [1983], 6). Of course, something similar can be said about the community of moviegoers, whose practice of imagining is most obviously a media practice (see Gaertner 2022, in German).

exceptionality and collectivity – and a distinct understanding of historical becoming, of thinking the present (moment) as an ongoing crystallization of (a present of the) past and (a present of the) future, through which this communality can take effect and be grasped in the first place.

As I will show by means of an exegesis of the historical text of the Declaration of Independence, along with a consultation of a variety of philosophical takes on the American Dream and the intrinsic idea of communality as the interdependency of individual and communal subjectification in the following chapter, it is this notion of time as the interconnection of past, present and future that constitutes the core of the American Dream as the imagination of a new historical community of becoming. A community that forms initially because it addresses and thinks of itself as a community in constant transition, always at the same time both antecedent and yet to come, and in that way facilitating the possibility of (speaking, thinking, reflecting about) history in the first place. In this sense and with regard to the audiovisual images of the sports film, the American Dream should be understood not only as a social, but as a media cultural imaginary that enables a (audiovisually structured and effective) discourse of reflexive historicity through which US society can refer to itself as a political community (constantly renewing itself).[6] Of course, this social and (media) cultural imaginary, which draws its power precisely from sustaining a process of perpetual renewal, has to be understood as itself historical.[7]

In correspondence to what Garry Whannel does in a condensed form in his text on narratives of identity in sports films, where he outlines the American Dream as an ensemble of different ideological elements such as the frontier myth or the Protestant work ethic (see Whannel 2008, 198–199), I understand and develop the idea of the American Dream as something which historically evolved much before James Truslow Adams coined the term in 1931.[8] While Whannel acknowledges that "concepts of community, of team work and of collectivism have always existed in tension with individualism" (Whannel 2008, 199) as the dominant narrative of the American Dream, he eventually sees them

---

6 For this idea, see Vogl 1994 (in German).

7 Both these aspects of constant renewal and historicity are key insights of Winfried Fluck's engagement with the cultural imaginary of the US, which he develops with such refreshing richness along the history of the American novel of the late eighteenth and the nineteenth century (Fluck 1997). In what ways Fluck's extensive study might open up an interdisciplinary and intermedial perspective on my idea of an American Dream culture must remain subject to future inquiries for now.

8 See also Lawrence R. Samuel's great account on the cultural history of the American Dream, in which he stresses that "the roots of the phrase go back centuries, its origins to be found well before the nation was a nation" (Samuel 2012, 3).

as "ideologically compromised concept[s]" (Whannel 2008, 200) within a neoliberal society. But rather than looking more closely at the changing of forms of subjectification and the changing means and forms of media affecting this subjectification, he only points to counter culture movements of the 1960s and 1970s and their "stressing [of] forms of collectivity" (Whannel 2008, 200) in a quite unspecific way. With what follows in the second part of this chapter, I want to underline that the idea of communality which the American Dream contains is first of all not so much about historically concrete forms of collectivity, but about the possibility of communal subjectivity, and thus about the suspenseful correlation of singularity and communality.

With regard to the following analytical chapters, it is, I claim, this understanding of the American Dream as a specific imaginative mode of (the interdependence of) historicity and communality that serves as the constitutive conflict around which the genre of the team sports film emerges, forms and processes, and through which certain movies coalesce (in difference) and can thus themselves be grasped in their specific historicity. Thereby, the idea of temporality of the American Dream, its politics of crystallized time – in which a historical society happens to never be anything else than a society of an endless Future Perfect Progressive, a society that, in every and ever new present moment(s) of its existence, will become and has been becoming – should not only be addressed as a general topic of the genre, but as something each film creates and works on by means of its affective poetics, of its concrete temporal forms of audiovisual expression and perception. In the course of this, the aim will also be to put the idea of film-viewing as a possibility of thinking time through movement, of creating audiovisual image spaces through which a society is able to think itself as historical in more concrete terms.

Middlemen of Prescribed Meaning

Very often, the validity and appropriateness of the American Dream is strongly questioned by simply dismissing it as an outdated historical concept or doctrine, and/or by weighing it against real life sociopolitical conditions. Primarily, such rejection or critique follows a hypothesis of delusion with regard to consumer capitalism and the media representation within, and arguably in favor of, it. Hence, sports films, as the broader argument goes, present the American Dream as and through an idealistic narrative of (the affirmation of) individual opportunity and success, thereby fulfilling a compensatory function by offering a whitewashed, and therefore incomplete and/or distorted understanding of social reality. They offer magical resolutions, utopian outcomes in which contradictions seem to be healed, tensions erased. [...] Barriers can be broken down, and obstacles overcome, but in the process, awkward and unmanageable tensions, such as those associated with sexualities [or race or identity], are often rendered marginal, invisible or irrelevant. (Whannel 2008, 202)

In doing so, the films – or rather, the institutionalized power structures accounting for their production – in a way provide for the deception and sedation of the audience in respect to actual societal circumstances, past and present, exactly by manipulating those very circumstances as historical facts, especially with regard to the exclusion and marginalization of non-white and non-male people. Besides broader, more monographic accounts on the sports film including such perspective in varying ways and degrees and to varied fruitfulness,[9] there exists a very large number of individual papers, which nonetheless and even though they apply different methodological approaches and are concerned with various films and topics almost always turn out to be already primed by this vantage point of a media aesthetically uninformed ideological critique, with its paradigm of faithful representation interfering analytical efforts.[10]

Even though the continuing pervasiveness of this dominant vantage point might come as a surprise to a certain extent, it has its roots in a strong tradition of ideology critique and textual analysis within the fields of film and media studies (which necessarily include literary and communication studies, as well as social science, all three fields in which most sports film scholars are trained in). Here, one of the guiding impulses is to treat movies, and especially Hollywood movies, first and foremost as products and representations of a hegemonic, self-confirming class and its institutionalization (in the form of the studio system industry or the television networks system), thereby helping to mask and support structures of power and oppression. While I do not want to condemn such perspectives, which are all somewhat rooted in the Marxist notion of "false consciousness" (Engels 1893)[11] and rightfully pledge for historical and sociological contextualization, it is nonetheless – and especially with regard to scholarship on the staging of sports in film – important to point out and

---

9 See Baker 2003, Crosson 2013, Rader 1990, Tudor 1997.
10 For a nuanced account on the sports film as historical film, which recognizes its importance and "power for shaping historical consciousness" by considering its "significant ideological work," but then again remains on the level of represented content and narrative structure when it comes to actual film analysis, see Schultz 2014. For a sociological perspective on the connection of sports and the American Dream, see especially Nixon 1984. For the political capacity of sports as a diversion of the public from real problems, see Allison 1986.
11 Engels uses the term (in German: "falsches Bewußtsein") in a letter to fellow politician, journalist and historian Franz Mehring. While for Marx and Engels, the notion of false consciousness is inextricably linked to that of ideology, and applied almost solely to the class of

counterbalance the often very restricted notion of media aesthetics going along with them, resulting in the neglect of genuinely analyzing audiovisual and affective form, as well as the perceptual modalities and experiential qualities from it and becoming politically effective.

In what follows, I will first more closely look at the conditions and implications of this all too dominant paradigm within sports film scholarship just described above in a more general sense. Often then, the examination of the sports film appears as bifurcated: as an examination of 'sports *and* film' (or also 'sports *in* film'), parallelizing them on both structural and functional levels as distinct cultural practices and social phenomena, which are nonetheless understood as being shaped and proceeding similarly; which, as could be said with Althusser, reproduce along different tracks of the same cultural Ideological State Apparatus (ISA). It seems as if this ISA in sports film scholarship often runs under the label of 'entertainment.'[12] Althusser himself includes sports under the umbrella term of entertainment when he talks about the institutions and organizations corresponding to the cultural ISA (see Althusser 2014 [1971], 76). Shortly after, he mentions sports as a practice or an activity supporting or being part of ISAs more generally (see Althusser 2014 [1971], 77–79). Since Althusser seems to understand sports mainly as educational sports though, and therefore first and foremost as a practice of physical exercise and not as one of media perception and expression (see Althusser 2014 [1971], 77), it becomes clearer where the shortcomings of such approaches I criticize here derive from and how these shortcomings are rather to be understood as an effect of a methodological impossibility to understand sports and media as aesthetically intertwined (with regard to a social and cultural imaginary).[13] Although there seems to be no doubt about the generic entanglement of the new medium of film and, with the increase of rural-urban migration and leisure, the accompanying rise of (professional) sports at the beginning of the twentieth century, most of the given studies until today nonetheless treat sports and film as rather separate domains (just) utilizing each other's capacities and qualities.

One important exception is a series of approaches within the (primarily UK- and Germany-based) field of what is often called Media Sports or Mediensport, which are equipped with methodical tools of communication studies, media

---

the bourgeoisie, that changes with the later development of these concepts by Antonio Gramsci and others. For a more detailed discussion, see Eyerman 1981.
12 See for example the beacon studies of Seán Crosson and Aaron Baker, which I will discuss in more detail on the following pages.
13 For a more comprehensive account on sports as an ISA, which is critical about the "myth of educative sport" (v) though, see Brohm 1978.

economics and/or cultural sociology and conduct studies in view of what is often referred to as 'media sports complex' or a 'media sports reality.'[14] Such studies often place their main focus on ideas and questions of production, consumption and mediatization, especially with regard to TV and radio coverage, as well as phenomena and processes of fandom, lately also in relation to the use of New or Social Media.[15] While really acknowledging the intertwining of sports and media with regard to the production of reality as an ineluctable media sports world, these accounts, besides only seldomly looking at fictional feature films in general, most of the time favor methods of textual, sociological, technological and/or institutional over aesthetic analysis.

Most of the approaches actually concerned with cinematic forms of sports representation proceed as short-sighted as already hinted at above though: Instead of recognizing sports and film as generically interlinked media of audiovisual display, which always already interact in view of the production of modes and technologies of perception, social sensibilities and ideological stances, they rather confront them as producers and participants of two quite distinct worlds – worlds that (only) correlate with each other by their tendency or capacity to exploit certain predetermined tropes and narratives, e.g. of competitive play and upward social mobility. Such an understanding fails to acknowledge sports as a profound field of practice in modern western society,[16] and film as one of the dominant media technologies of this society and directly connected with the practice of sports from the onset.[17]

Deemed as agents of what might be called a culture of distraction, sports and film provide for the covering and blurring of the real-life circumstances of the historical incidents the sports film pretends to depict, as well as of the world of the addressed spectators themselves. Manipulating people as viewers in the name of dominant power structures, sports in film and filmed sports can, according to this view, never be more than middlemen of prescribed and situated textual significations, metaphors and narratives of the American Dream. Consequently, these tropes and narratives are then often understood more as extra-worldly than as generic with regard to the mechanisms and manifestations of social order.

---

14 See the extensive works of David Rowe, Lawrence Wenner and Garry Whannel, especially Rowe 2004 and 2011, Whannel 2005 [1992], Wenner 1989 and 1998; for a first overview within the German context, see Schierl 2007 and Schwier / Schauerte 2008.
15 See for example Hutchins / Rowe 2012 and 2014.
16 See Gruneau 2017.
17 See Crosson 2013, chapter 2.

A Community-Building Idea of Lived Time

What goes missing when we grasp sports movies as always already narratively masking and thus whitewashing the circumstances of a given, pre-filmic social reality, as glossing over the social inequalities present in the real world by means of American Dream-like stories of individual opportunity and perseverance as well as upward social and economic mobility and success? What remains untouched when we assume that film and sports share in exploitative (narrative) structures of an entertainment industry, reproducing a blurred and seemingly strictly sociological and non-aesthetic idea of the American Dream, while it does not even seem very clear what either this idea or its blurring is really about? It is, for one thing, the matter of to what extent those stories as ideological narratives are themselves produced and shaped by audiovisual media and the affective temporalities, perceptual modalities and experiential qualities these media create; of how certain ways of expression and perception produce an audiovisual culture in which these ways, modes and technologies of sports and film generically interact, in which they intertwine in shaping each other and in this sense create this audiovisual culture in the first place. An audiovisual culture we might then call the audiovisual culture of the American Dream – with the idea of the American Dream thereby itself much more than a linear narrative (structure) and a myth to be reproduced as ideologeme, but rather a social and media cultural imaginary. At the core of which lies the community-building apprehension of lived time as an ongoing crystallization of past, present and future, as an always dynamic stratification of a present of the past and a present of the future in the (absent) presence of a present.[18]

So, while it certainly would be foolish to claim that the American Dream and its role in regard to sports films has nothing to do with myth-based ideological structures, whose narratives do not map onto real-life courses of individual destiny, I want to broaden the perspective by looking at where and how the (mediated) American Dream can be understood as more than that – namely, as the manifestation of a discourse of community-building (and) history, which is intrinsically formed by traditions of a philosophy of pragmatist communitarisation, as well as (re-)created by and as an audiovisual culture. This manifestation proceeds not primarily by means of a relatable, *primary* narrative, but

---

18 In phenomenology, this stratification is understood as one of the key microstructures of lived experience, through which people as temporal beings "constitute their 'reality' in a meaningful way" and "interact with their worlds in these ways over time" (Wyllie 2005, 174, citing Matthews 2002, 60). The other microstructures are, according to Wyllie, embodiment, lived space, and intersubjectivity.

rather through specific modulations of expressive and perceptual structures allowing for the possibility of aesthetic experience as the basis of fictional worldbuilding, and thus for the *possibility* of such a narrative (which we then might finally call the self-referential meta-narrative of American society again). But before coming back to this thought in greater detail in the second part of this chapter, let us first recapitulate how what Miller calls the "Athletic American Dream" (Miller 2007) is discussed within sports film scholarship.

Exploiting Utopian Sensibility and Distracting from Social Reality

Seán Crosson describes sports as the "prime material" (Crosson 2013, 31) for the new medium of film at the turn of the century and, furthermore, as a trigger for the "changeover from film as a medium of scientific study to a medium of entertainment" (Crosson 2013, 32). He cites Luke McKernan, who reminds us that the early boxing films were "the very birth of American cinema realism and drama" (see McKernan 1996, 109–110). What is inherent in Crosson's take on the role of sports for the medium of film is one of Tom Gunning's claims with regard to what he has conceptualized as "cinema of attractions" (Gunning 1986): namely, that the power of and fascination for very early films did not primarily originate from their own (new) mediality, but from the popular appeal of what they displayed – for example, and especially, sports.

In their ability to entertain, both sports and (Hollywood) film provide, as Crosson states with reference to Richard Dyer, an "utopian sensibility," which he explicitly describes as a seductive quality (see Crosson 2013, 6–7). Now, in the case of the sports film as a primarily "North American" genre, this utopian sensibility is strongly connected to the American Dream, the "central ideology in American life" (Crosson 2013, 67). While he does not elaborate on the specificity of this sensibility in regard to film in general – one might think of the topos of worldbuilding within film theory, as well as certain genres like science fiction, where this sensibility can become a pivotal stimulus – Crosson does so in terms of sports. One of his main reasons for examining the social role of sports itself before turning to its representation in film seems to be his mythological approach to genre film, which builds on Thomas Schatz' understanding of film genre as "social ritual" (Schatz 1981, 31), and the idea of genre films as a means of social control, as brought forward by various approaches to genre based on perspectives of ideology critique. Hence, in finding the 'functional role' of the sports film, which he defines with Rick Altman as the provision of a symbolic solution to ('real' world) problems, Crosson points to sports' utopian sensibility (see Crosson 2013, 66).[19]

Sports, understood as entertainment in the sense of Dyer, "offers an image of 'something better' to escape into, or something we want deeply that our day-to-day lives don't provide" (Dyer 1977, 373; cited in Crosson 2013, 7). The crucial point for Dyer, who does not touch upon sports in a more comprehensive way, is that this "image of 'something better'" is not produced by and communicated through the creation of specific "models of utopian worlds," but through "the feelings it embodies" (Crosson 2013, 7). Hence, sports utopianism according to Crosson's elaboration of Dyer's idea does not arise primarily from an instalment of some kind of autonomous otherworld that is (thought of as) alternative or 'still to come.'[20] It rather lies within (the restructuring of) an actual sensual domain as the potentiality of affective experience. Now, this potential "visceral intensity" (Crosson 2013, 7), is, as Crosson continues, "exploited readily by directors of sports films" (Crosson 2013, 7), especially in scenes depicting the final fight or game or play move, thereby sending viewers into a state of ecstasy and letting them experience intense emotions. In describing film (and TV) as a "seductive and powerfully influential form" that "provide[s] powerful tools for exploiting sport's utopian sensibilities" (Crosson 2013, 8), Crosson reveals an aesthetically quite limited stance towards audiovisual media. While I would agree with describing film as a "significant mediator of social relations," the claim that this mediation proceeds as a "naturalization of cultural norms" (Crosson 2013, 10) has to be contested, in the sense that audiovisual forms significantly partake in creating and shaping these cultural norms in the first place as recursive patterns of perception and experience through which we relate to the world and thereby create it. In this case, the limitations arise out of a truncated notion of experience. Here, experience is, on the one hand, understood as something given that appears regardless of the dynamics of affective and perceptual structures, and thus as self-contained units of sensibilities, which can be taken up and used by films,

---

19 For a critique of the ritual-ideological myth model of genre in regard to the sports or, more specifically, the boxing film, see Grindon 2011, 5–6. My own approach to the question of genre stems from Hermann Kappelhoff's and Matthias Grotkopp's findings, which, by explicitly distancing themselves from still dominant conceptions based on poetics of rule and convention (especially in the tradition of seventeenth century French classicism) and referring especially to Cavell and Gledhill, propose a dynamic and non-taxonomic model of modes of realism (of relating to the world) and modalities of experience (see Grotkopp / Kappelhoff 2012 and Kappelhoff 2018a). For a detailed discussion of the question of genre with regard to the sports film, see chapters 2.1 and 2.2 of this book.
20 As in the case of science fiction for example: a world achieved and at the same time feared, familiar but also alien.

but originate from somewhere else, from a 'real,' supposedly non-mediated everyday world, in which the world of sports itself is then often understood as some kind of detached refuge.[21] On the other hand, the description of the deployment of theses sensibilities then seems to be limited to a quantifying, but not qualifying recognition of an (expression of an) excessive intensity. Sometimes, this excessiveness becomes a sports film's kernel (and thereby often subject of a mode of parody), like in ANY GIVEN SUNDAY (O. Stone, 1999). Nonetheless, it does not seem sufficient to describe the audiovisual expressiveness of moving images only on the basis of a notion of perceptual excess. To what such a perspective translates, in terms of the actual examination of certain films, can be observed by means of Crosson's analytical proceeding, which frequently favors content over form, plot and character psychology over expressive strategies of audiovisual staging.

At the same time, following Crosson, such an ideology-critical stance seems to be almost inevitable in the case of the sports film, especially because it is already the utopian sensibility of sports itself that "may ultimately obscure and mislead audiences regarding the issues touched upon within the films themselves" (Crosson 2013, 66). David Rowe integrates or confirms such thinking when he talks about the mythologies of sports that form its filmic treatment, describing sports as a somehow magical "cultural practice transcendent of everyday life and realpolitik" that keeps its "distance both from a real, material struggle and from triumphalist and xenophobic extrapolations" (Rowe 1998, 252).

The visceral intensity of sports and its exploitation by the medium of film, which relies itself on somatic stimulation, thus make for a double distraction from social reality, especially in regard to race, class and gender.[22]

> In these films, poverty, deprivation and marginalization in American society are often acknowledged; however, there is little attempt in the mainstream sports film to engage with the reasons for, or indeed, realistic means for most people to overcome them. Rather, sports films suggest that through sport and individual effort the American Dream of upward social

---

21 For the concept of the world of sports as "a world with its own internal coherence," see Whannel 1984.

22 Besides the topics of nationalism and heroism, most of the studies published on the subject of the Hollywood sports film are involved with at least one of those three categories of identity politics (see, for example, Kusz 2008 and Tudor 1997 or with regard to a growing number of studies concerned with non-American films, Hill 2015 and Ransom 2014). All too often, these categories remain nothing more than subject matters by being related to discussions about narratively represented content, which seemingly could be conducted without taking any note of how certain films are actually staged. For studies which examine identity in sports media, and thereby also look beyond the feature film, see, for example, Hundley / Billings 2010 and Baker / Boyd 1997.

> mobility and success can be achieved. It is a double lie, a lie made all the more convincing through the impressive and seductive medium of film. (Crosson 2013, 65)

With regard to the film SPACE JAM (J. Pytka, 1996), Crosson fleshes out this finding:

> Space Jam provides a seductive depiction of African American masculinity and family life. However, this utopian portrayal relies on conventional constructions of race, gender, and the family that disguises the reality for many Black families and may, in line with the American Dream itself, contribute to the perception of the marginalised and underprivileged as deviant. (Crosson 2014, 13)

Crosson's critical conclusion reveals not only a seemingly functionalist understanding of film and ideology – in the sense that both are supposed to provide solutions for social problems – but also, and this is directly intertwined with such an understanding, a quite rigorous, but limited conception of fiction and realism in a highly mediatized world. While acknowledging that sports films sometimes actually show societal issues like racism, Crosson states that they eventually only do so by affirming, or to reinforce the myth of the American Dream, whose fallacy in real life is obvious, but which still is a powerful ideological device when rendered through sports (see Crosson 2013, 66 et seq.). And even if one film is critically intervening, this intervention has to be seen within the wider context of the ideological agenda of the film or the genre as a whole. "Indeed, the inclusions of references to racism are present arguably to make the subtly racist message all the more convincing" (Crosson 2013, 71).

While there is more to be addressed with regard to, as the latter's, I will also focus a little more on the consequences such an enclosing perspective has for the analysis of (the sports) film as a myth-exploiting medium of deceptiveness in view of an allegedly clear-cut and independent reality.

Films as Secondary Containers of (Un-)Faithful Correspondence

Such a mythological take on the American Dream like Crosson's seems incapable of refraining from thinking of the American Dream apart from its non-fulfillment in real social life. What goes missing or is not taken seriously enough is the insight that the American Dream's "not being real […] ultimately turns out to be the most significant finding about it" (Samuel 2012, 1). And that it hence has to be understood as generating and stabilizing a sense of community exactly *because* of its fictional status and the imaginative force enabled by it. While it is certainly not wrong or superfluous to try to transfer aspects of social theory (with its categories of agency and representation) towards media fictions, it nonetheless cannot support or supersede an analysis that tries to describe the concrete ways in which these fictions intervene and are structured as referring connections between the real and the imaginary, between materials of reality and rather vague but nonetheless effective inventories of fantasy (see Fluck 1997, 12–13). I will provide such an analysis that tries to understand films as filmic images, which are produced, perceived, and circulated; which are part of and intervene in the actual world from their very inception, namely by producing and modulating (and arising themselves as) expressive and perceptual structures out of which this world is generically built. In this sense, films do not generate some kind of separated, concluded sphere, which relates or is then related to a so-called real world. They are rather, as Wolfgang Iser said about literary texts, "made up of a world that is yet to be identified" (Iser 1989, 250), that cannot be represented but comes into being when expressed and perceived.

This is one of the central points where this study intervenes, especially because the limited understanding of film and its sociohistorical role and embeddedness leads to quite unsatisfactory analyses, which I am trying to point to with Crosson as exemplary for the field of sports film studies. These analyses all too often remain within a simplified model of (textual and psychological) representation, thereby failing to take into account the films' actual aesthetics, and neglecting the expressive and perceptual forms that create and determine this representation in the first place. Moreover, these analyses identify the sports film as the fantasy of a fantasy without ever delving into the audiovisual and affective realm in which this supposed double lie takes shape and is modulated. Instead, such an understanding marks the characters and their actions within a movie as ready-made entities, and relates them to a real, profilmic world, which supposedly works in the same manner, and functions under equal rules – thus at least implicitly suggesting a corrective of a 'more realistic' sports film that would show the real problems of real life. Again, such an analysis of a film then tends to be more concerned about the creation of ideal archetypes than about the description of actual images and sounds, proceeding as a process of classification and valuation especially oriented towards what is and what is not shown, said or done within the diegetic world. Understood as not much more than cohesive agents of a faithful transmission of predetermined structures and meanings, the films then have to be constantly checked against what goes on in 'the real world' or, to be more precise, what is *alleged* to go on in it.

With regard to the American Dream as an ideologeme, a belief system or a social and/or cultural imaginary, an analysis based on such an idea of more or less direct and unmediated referentiality cannot reach beyond descriptions of story and plot, of the presence or non-presence of certain objects, protagonists, actions and symbolic imagery, as well as of (psychologically attributed) behavior of characters. In such a perspective, films can – strictly speaking – only reproduce what is already a designated part of the 'outside' world. Rather than placing the emphasis on how their expressive and perceptual dimensions, their sounds and images are relevant to this world in a constitutive sense, e.g. by inducing modes of relating to it, films are understood in a functionalist sense from the very beginning, as a kind of tool which operates and is being operated simply by the fact of what is shown and seen.

In this model, 'living' the American Dream becomes possible through watching movies as a compensatory act, as a kind of *Ersatzhandlung* (an activity of redirection) forced upon a supposedly passive and naive spectator.[23] The need for and amount of compensation thereby stems from and is defined by the differences between the real-life situation, context and possibilities of action of the audience, and those of the character ensemble in the film. The evaluation of film's capacity for societal representation – a constant and important discourse throughout the history of film studies – tends to become a figurative relation between two quantities, through which each element of one quantity is related to and exactly measured against one element of the other.

The Mediated Sporting Star and Film as Sugar on the Ideology Pill

Although the assertion of such a system of direct and explicit reference and impact certainly provides for a cover-up of the films' actual aesthetics (their audiovisual expressive movement and fabricated perceptive qualities), it might actually be helpful to make such robust historical statements to a certain extent, especially with respect to the period of early (sports) film as born out of a documentary mode of representation. As many early film scholars like Noël Burch or Janet Staiger describe, the aspect of (real life) familiarity plays an important role for the production as well as the reception of audiovisual imagery on many different levels in the very early period of film (see Burch 1986 and Staiger 1992). With regard to sports – while certainly a very popular subject matter – it seems that this familiarity as one feature of the documentary mode was nonetheless very much generated and structured by a media star system owing a lot to journalistic media forms. Crosson mentions, for example, the establishment of the first newspaper sports section in 1895 (Crosson 2014, 3). With their obsession for newspaper articles, radio commentators etc., a lot of

---

[23] For the notion of the naive spectator, in contrast to the ironic one, see Ray 1985. The addressing of a viewer as both, which Ray describes with regard to New Hollywood, seems of importance for the genre of the sports film and its penchant for self-parody.

later movies show that these cross-media circuitries continue to be an important element for the sports film genre.

Crosson, for example, mentions early prize fight pictures, which, by including Black athletes, popularized the sport of boxing within the African-American community, strengthening its belief in the possibility of upward (social) mobility during a time when boxing was "a means [...] of maintaining the superiority and cultural hegemony of White America" (Crosson 2014, 67). Aaron Baker, despite having a much more distinct film analytical impetus, follows a similar path when he looks at how basketball films of the 1980s and 1990s "use an African American athletic aesthetic to reaffirm an individualist notion of success best represented by Michael Jordan" (Baker 2003, 2).

Central to such ideas of filmic representations of sports as a (substitutive) mean for living the American Dream is the sports star, in both its profilmic and its diegetic appearance as (fictional) hero. In this light, it is not only the success story shown on screen that is supposed to lead viewers to believe in the promises of the American Dream of prosperity and affluence, but especially the metonymic capacity of the actual biography of sports stars like Michael Jordan, Knute Rockne or Babe Ruth. Their real lives – undoubtedly already only available as speculatively and mythically entangled projections – become models with exemplary function, charging the films' capability to (re-)affirm the Horatio Alger myth with its famous trope 'from rags to riches.' These sports stars' 'real lives' are then an implicit undergirding of the film's fiction to begin with. The argument in regard to (early) sports film, in its recourse to a profilmic reality, stays structurally the same then: the real sports star provides just an additional utopian sensibility, which a film can then utilize to deliver its ideological message, in this case especially the story of uniqueness and performance of an individual coming from a humble background. At the same time, the film itself can function as further evidence of a figure having 'made it' through his or her sporting achievements.[24]

---

[24] The relation between the celebrity existence of a sports star and his or her mediatization has of course to be described as one of interpenetration. As much as a film relies on the fame of a star, the popularity of the star draws on his or her media representation. While often being discussed as an economic relation, the point of reference being the seek for 'attention' within a 'market' (see Crosson 2014, 7–8), it would of course also be fruitful to examine this mutual dependency with regard to aesthetic structures and strategies, and with every single sports film that features a real-life sports star anew. As Crosson's explanations regarding early sports cinema make clear, this relation must always be historicized. For the cultural politics of sporting celebrity, see Andrews / Jackson 2001. For more on the media production of the (male) sports star, see Whannel 2002.

Crosson presents Babe Ruth, who is considered by many the best baseball player of all time and whose career spanned from 1914 to 1935, as one of the paradigmatic examples with regard to this 'rags to riches' trajectory of the American Dream and its media reification.[25] As Ruth – similar to quite a lot of (especially baseball) players at that time – starred in several movie productions like HEADIN' HOME (L. C. Windom, 1920), BABE COMES HOME (T. Wilde, 1927), or SPEEDY (T. Wilde, 1928),[26] "these works exploited Babe's iconic status for their appeal while contributing to his 'ruthian' image and affirming the American Dream of success in the process" (Crosson 2014, 6). Seemingly an expert not only in baseball but also in self-marketing, Ruth was "an ideal figure to promote American consumer culture" (Crosson 2014, 6). Having had a rather difficult childhood – he spent a couple of years in a reformatory school – and able to "project multiple images of brute power, the natural uninhibited man and the fulfilment of the American success dream" (Rader 2008, 130), he and his star persona perfectly fit in with the 'ordinary but special' rhetoric the sports film drew and still draws its power from according to Crosson:

> This theme of the seeming simpleton with limited apparent ability overcoming the odds and turning out to be a gifted athlete would be a recurring trope of many subsequent productions [...]. It provides a powerful affirmation again of the American Dream ideology suggesting that even for those of seeming limited intelligence the dream remains a possibility, particularly if they show a talent for sport. (Crosson 2013, 35)

In this case, the role of the American Dream is grasped as the central part of a consumerist cultural ideology, which conventionalizes recipients of popular culture as, above all, immature customers being blinded, and in which filmic image becomes sort of a communication tool in favor of this delusion – something that often arises from and leads to problematic ways of analyzing media artifacts of entertainment culture, as Dyer identifies quite clearly when pointing to the connection between all too often shortened conceptions of entertainment and the discussion of ideology. As he writes, the latter "tends to treat entertainment as a sugar on the pill of ideological messages, either condemning it as a disguise for world views of which the writer disapproves or else commending it as a strategy for promoting those of which she or he does approve" (Dyer 2002 [1992], 1). It is no surprise that Dyer immediately continues by stressing the

---

25 The biopic THE BABE (A. Hiller, 1992), whose German subtitle is "Ein amerikanischer Traum" ("An American Dream"), fictionalizes Ruth's turbulent life story and his charismatic personality. For a written biographical account, see Montville 2006.
26 Babe Ruth also starred in a whole string of short films written and directed by Benjamin Stoloff and Lou Breslow.

importance of (his method of) analyzing the "formal properties and affects" (Dyer 2002 [1992], 1) of works of entertainment, as well as the world views going along with them. In such a way, and while emphasizing that entertainment media should not at all be immune from ideological criticism, he suggests a different, more bottom-up approach, which "refuse[s] the in fact valuable evaluative connotations of art and ideology and only [...] consider[s] the way form, affect and world view constitute the enjoyment that an entertainment proposes" (Dyer 2002 [1992], 1).

A Seemingly Stable and Transparent Reality as Ineluctable Template

Dyer's diagnosis gets to the heart of my criticism of most of sports film scholarship presented here, and marks the point of intervention of this study. This calls for a move away from matching predetermined standards, judgments and analytical categories born out of (our criticism of) the real world (of sports) against what and whom is depicted (or not) in films in the sense of a naive realism of duplication. Instead, we have to look more closely at the media and mediated forms of expression and perception that films use to create worlds – worlds through which these films then not only relate to one another by producing audiovisual discourses of filmic reality, but are also always involved in the coproduction of a reality that so many approaches deem to be their ineluctable template of analysis.

The immediate conflation or superimposition of a filmic world and a seemingly transparent reality as an undistorted reference point, as well as the detection of non- or misrepresentation along with it, often proceeds at the level of narrative content, with topics, tropes, constellations and motifs as already given categories in a commercialized world of sports. In that way, a sports film's plot is either related to socioeconomic milieus and conditions of a world whose structures it supposedly does not reveal, or which it affirms in wrongful ways; or it is traced back to biographical narratives, which can themselves be accused of representing a wrong image of society, as they are always already mythologically charged stories of stark individuality.

The 'real problems,' whose recognition serves as the measurement for adequate historical analysis, can only be detected through the reconstruction of what is negated or not dealt with in terms of story and subject matter, in reference to the profilmic world. The audiovisual image is exposed to moral judgement from the very beginning and therefore rarely examined in its own right in terms of its forms of expressivity and perceptual structures. Crosson, however, provides one of the few instances of actual image analysis within the field of sports film studies when confronting the 'classic' American sports film, with its "recurring failure to provide either a social or historical context for the events depicted" (Crosson 2014, 15), with the French production ZIDANE, UN PORTRAIT DU 21E SIÈCLE (2006), made by video and performance artists Douglas Gordon and Philippe Parreno. While Crosson sees the affirmative rhetoric of uniqueness and individual performance of the former put into effect through an aesthetic of intimacy created especially through close-up shots, it is – quite tellingly – only the latter which, according to him, provides a critical intervention in regard to ideas of privacy and publicness, and thus problematizes the (im)possibility of objectifying subjective individuality, as well as what it means to historicize (see Crosson 2014, 15).

Through what follows in this chapter and what I have already indicated with the previous one and will show with the following film analyses, I want to make clear that this problematization of individual exceptionality, which both demands and triggers the forces of exclusion and (re-)integration of a community, is not at all simply an accomplishment of a European experimental documentary about a sports star, but lies at the very center of the sports film genre (and genre cinema) in general.[27] This also implies a turn away from perspectives grasping the way media feeds into ideological structures only on a level of (the negation of) faithful representation and unmediated storytelling, and toward the aesthetic modulation of cinematic forms of experience; toward the production of an audiovisual image space that "emerges from the temporal arrangement of the percepts, affects, and actions that guide the dynamic of perceiving, feeling, and thinking that the spectators join in the process of viewing films" (Kappelhoff 2018a, 40).

The Structuring Absences of Historical Complexity

With regard to the intertwining of the sports film and American Dream ideology, Aaron Baker makes quite similar observations as Crosson, but leads them in a different direction: especially in view of the sports film's relation, or rather, obsession with 'real history,' which often expresses itself in the most straightforward way through the frequent occurrence of the introductory claim 'based on a true story' in all its variants, through the increased usage of filmic and photographic found footage material, as well as through a general interest for events

---

[27] As should become clear in chapter 6.2 with my analysis of the ending of JIM THORPE – ALL-AMERICAN (M. Curtiz, 1951), an increased number of close-up shots does not at all rule out such an aesthetics of the social that Crosson suggests here.

and dramatis personae of the past. Working on the affirmation of "American beliefs in individualism," the central concern of these films, according to Baker, is the presentation of the success of the individual performance, wrapping up "the utopian promise of sport" in a melodramatically contained message that says: "once the contest begins, success depends primarily on one's determination and effort" and "history is made by individuals" (Baker 2003, 10–11). Sports films can or should thus be considered as a "historical proof of the American Dream" (Baker 2003, 8) showing the possibility of individual chance and upward social mobility. Following Baker, this message is then charged with historical significance and meaningfulness in sports films. However, this happens at the cost of the "historical complexity" (Baker 2003, 8) having been effective during the real events, by which he supposedly means those events the films pretend (but fail) to depict.[28] As it were, sports films become ideological agents/tools because of their poor performance in historical materialism, by which Baker means that the particular (often problematic) socioeconomic circumstances surrounding the hard working and (un)successful individuals within their stories are kept in the dark. So again, what Baker accuses the sports films of refers back to an understanding of film as a medium of (only) illustrative representation, triggering problems of (seemingly unmediated) inclusion and selective emphasis. Quite similar to Crosson, Baker suggests that a central part of creating and maintaining such a "single explanation" form is the exploitation of "an emotional resonance that undermine[s] critical scrutiny" (Baker 2003, 8). Unfortunately, this emotional resonance is then not further examined.

While Baker joins the ranks of most sports film scholarship with such a boiled down stance of ideology critique eventually based on a concept of not only realistic but also *faithful* representation, he nonetheless prevents himself from slipping into a solely negativistic perspective, which would ultimately deny any analytically productive view on the actual audiovisual images with regard to his special interest in socially constructed identity. He does so by deploying a dialectical strategy when introducing his notion of historical complexity. This historical complexity – by means of which he seemingly addresses the real circumstances, structures and forces at play at a certain time in history, and beyond an assumed narrative simplification – is not, as he states, completely lost in sports films. It is rather, in a way, secondarily communicated: We are able to

---

28 It is remarkable how most of sports film scholarship still today withholds from an idea of film itself as historical event, or from film itself "doing history" (Rosenstone 1995, 172), as Rosenstone calls it but nonetheless seemingly never grasps it as a real capacity of the perceived filmic images themselves. For a description of how such historical complexity can nonetheless appear on the 'narrative surface' of sports films, see Philpott 1998, 176 et seq.

reconstruct it by looking at what is *not* shown and told in a film. Hence, Baker suggests concentrating on those "voices distorted or drowned out" (Stam 1991, 256, cited in Baker 2003, 13), which nonetheless shape what Baker calls a filmic text. In a way, Baker follows Crosson here, as both are aiming to 'counterbalance' the ideology of sports via implicitly constructing a kind of 'phantom film,' which would show things as they 'really are,' while at the same time pointing to the fact that sports, as a cultural artefact, is already mired in and supportive of dominant ideologies.

Borrowing from Robert Ray's notion of 'structuring absences' of Hollywood movies and the concept of dialogism introduced by Bakhtin, Baker is able to offer in his analysis "a more contextualized understanding of history and identity" (Baker 2003, 14), thereby targeting at the discourses and institutions that shape the destiny of the individual hero, especially in regards to gender, race and social class. While Ray claims that to "a great extent, American history's major crises appear in American movies only as 'structuring absences'" (Ray 1985, 31), Bakhtin himself develops his conception of dialogism (as opposed to monologism, and in strong resonance to his notion of heteroglossia), inter alia, on the basis of the polyphony in the work of Dostoevsky, especially with regard to the equality and simultaneity of the voices and perspectives of different characters (see Bakhtin 1981 [1975]). Hence, doubts remain on whether Bakhtin's understanding, which emphasizes coexistence and interactive incompatibility and thereby in a way distances itself from any dialectical understanding of synthesis and (transcendental) unity, really fits with Baker's aim to enrich his analysis with what is not told by, or shown in a film.

Baker, again like Crosson, consults Dyer's remarks on utopian entertainment, describing it in its capacity to "not only avoid suggesting specific ways to change the current social reality," but also "ignore [...] how social identities such as race, class, gender, and sexuality complicate self-definition" (Baker 2003, 13). And this even though Dyer makes it clear from the very beginning that it is virtually impossible to understand media of entertainment in any sense outside of ideological structures of social reality, and that his intervention thus rather concerns the constitutive role these media play with regard to such structures, with their specific expressive design and poetics of affect, with their "feelings and forms" (Dyer 2002 [1992], see also above).

While Baker does not at all deny that sports films, especially with regard to their narrative trajectory of an individual hero, have a strong tendency to perform such omission and concealment in order to create and endorse a message of individual performance and self-reliance – the message that he and others often reduce the American Dream to – he nonetheless suggests another way to look at those movies analytically. That is, by treating them as historical films in the sense that they are witnesses of the real-life social contexts of their time of production, assuming that it is possible to derive insights about an actual life-world at a certain time from a diegetic world, even though the latter functions as some kind of negative of the former.

Although Baker not only encounters, but also deduces this point of view from a claim about sports films' "need for verisimilitude" (Baker 2003, 13), thereby maintaining the implementation of a strong distinction between the non-filmic and the filmic in terms of realism and truth value, hence implying that the filmic image is to be taken as less truthful and realistic than the actual world, and thus needs to cleave to it to attain veracity, Baker makes a contribution to the field of sports film studies that should not be underestimated. To a certain extent, he grants the films themselves the potential and power to play an immanent part in creating and modulating the social world, instead of only (faithfully) representing it. So, whereas Crosson describes a kind of doubling down of ideological deception, Baker seems to be arguing for a kind of filmic beautification of reality. Thereby, he nonetheless recognizes the feedback loop between film and world with regard to the creation and modulation of an audiovisual culture, in which social and ideological structures are constantly negotiated in the first place – even though he seemingly can only do so at the cost of a more phenomenological approach towards the actual images and sounds, focusing, instead, on their own history of creation.

At the same time, Baker is one of the few who not only talks about the narrative trajectories of sports films, but looks at how these are dramaturgically generated, modified, and contradicted. Nonetheless, his analyses remain primarily on a level of narrative content focusing first and foremost on protagonists: their actions and (assumed) psychological behavior, specific character constellations etc. As much as such a perspective might suggest itself, given Baker's interest in the question of identity building, it is remarkable how the films' concrete poetics, their audiovisual fabrication of an image space, as well as their construction of a perceiving viewer by generating modalities of perception and qualities of experience are – again and as so often is the case – sidelined here.

As I want to argue, this is one of the reasons why a complex, mythically pervaded and media culturally structured and operating imaginary like the American Dream has become identified as a pre-determined idea and topic, transmitted and thereby affirmed through a specific storyline, that goes something like this: an individual, equipped with rather meagre resources, overcomes obstacles and is finally successful and rich in material as well as immaterial goods (if not in the former, then definitely in the latter). What goes along with such an understanding is basically a denial of any idea of the American Dream as something which film, through its audiovisual form and the specific affective experience this form generates and absorbs, can *itself* create, intervene and reflect, or of which it can be a constitutive part.

Film as the Sensory Constitution of Audiovisual Space

In summary, one can claim that what Hermann Kappelhoff states in regard to war film genre scholarship seems to apply for the field of sports film studies to an even greater extent, and becomes especially evident when taking a closer look at the latter's dealing with the subject of the American Dream. That is, most of the approaches understand and read their filmic objects of research as texts which represent thoughts, things, actions and persons, hence putting especially argumentative structures and represented content into the center of their investigations. But, as Kappelhoff claims,

> [t]he reduction to the represented contents always already disguises the essential characteristic of the film document – the particular aesthetic structure in every media presentation that allows the viewer to establish a specific relation to what is represented in the first place. (Kappelhoff 2018a, 262)

Ultimately, such studies reconstruct textual contents (topics, actions, behavior, sites, events), which could just as well be perceived and communicated through other media, formats and/or configurations of spectatorship. The *form* of presentation – the modes of staging, the visual imagery and the affective movement it performs and elicits, etc. – are thereby treated as nothing more than an accidental ingredient, as stylistic or rhetoric means that add an expressive coloring or valuation to what is represented, but in the end remain external to it (see Kappelhoff 2018a, 70). This is all the more surprising when one considers that no one in the field (of war and war film as well as sports and sports film studies) denies the decisive role of media technologies when it comes to sports or warfare. But instead of taking a closer look at the specific forms these technologies produce, the discussions very often remain "indifferent to the concrete cultural practice in which media are comprehensible in the first place as concrete forms of perception, that is, as concrete ways of using media technologies" (Kappelhoff 2018a, 262).[29]

Kappelhoff, opposing especially the dominant strand of cognitive film theory and its strong tendency to subordinate analytical observation to the function of 'realistic' representation and narration, emphasizes that one cannot separate what is shown from *how* it is shown through the contents from the dramatic and emotive forms of cinema – the latter, in turn, themselves not detachable from the specific coupling of the projected moving images and the viewer's activity while watching them. This very coupling defines what we call the cinematographic

---

29 This indifference becomes even more apparent when we look at the huge amount of research being done on sports media from a more communication-studies-oriented angle.

movement-image, as a concept of the dynamic interaction of technically animated moving images and (their) embodied perception.[30]

Hence, film cannot be analyzed in the same way we analyze text. Its processes of meaning-making take place as performative acts of embodiment, and they are therefore neither textual nor can they be understood textually.

> Only in the medium of the spectators' bodies does the visual space that we call film emerge from the projection of moving images. In the succession of its projections it causes a world to emerge that is due to the sensoriality of our bodies alone, and that has no reality outside this sensorial resonance of constantly being affected by what one has heard and seen. (Kappelhoff 2018a, 213)

Film thus not only takes place within and as a carnal and sensual process, it is to a pivotal extent *produced* by it in the first place, as a "perception that realizes the expressive dimensions of audiovisual moving images directly as a process of bodily sensation, directly as a psychic, mental, physical activity of the spectator" (see Kappelhoff 2018a, 70). Kappelhoff therefore

> view[s] neither the spectator's emotional process nor the modalities of film expression as accidental aspects of stylistic, formal, or aesthetic additions to a given narration or representation, but as a foundation that precedes all embodying constitution of meaning in the film as mode of experience. The processes of meaning making cannot be detached from the affecting power of the forms of cinematic expressivity. Film analyses that refer directly to the actions, characters, or contents represented mask exactly the temporal structures of viewing films that representation, as a product of this process, is based on in the first place: the constitution of a visual space in which things, bodies, and powers are positioned in relation to one another and react with each other in a way that is fundamentally different from what we assume as the shared everyday world. (Kappelhoff 2018a, 116–117)

3.2 The American Dream as Time-Image of Community-Building Historicity

Hence, when contextualizing the analysis of sports films with and within a cultural fantasy, social imaginary and/or national ethos like the American Dream, as a complex system of ideas, values, myths and beliefs, it is helpful to elaborate in a framework in which the films have something to say *as films*, in which they can and have to be analyzed as a constitutive part of an audiovisual culture of the American Dream in which they create, shape and reflect it. This

---

30 Kappelhoff develops this concept by following especially Eisenstein and Deleuze. See also my remarks in the introduction and in chapter 2. For a more detailed discussion about the shortcomings of cognitive film theory, see Kappelhoff / Müller 2011 and especially Kappelhoff 2018b (in German).

offers a counter to the reduction of the latter to a mere narrative trajectory, which is then, as a filmic plot, either set against and assessed on the basis of its shortcomings in regard to a so-called social reality, or entirely cut off from that social reality by nodding to notions of escapism or 'mere' entertainment.

While I absolutely agree that the American Dream is of central concern for the American sports films, I still want to claim that this relation is nowhere near as adequately spelled out theoretically as it is analytically. At least and especially, that is, in a way that considers the ideas of temporality and communality coming along with a historical and philosophical perspective of the American Dream on the one hand, and how these films actually think the American Dream and its poetic and political structures through their capability of generating and modulating time through movement on the other. In understanding sports films as media of affective movement that – by means of this movement – engage with the production and modulation of an audiovisual culture, in which the American Dream becomes graspable and socio-historically significant as a social and cultural imaginary, with an idea and image of time as the endlessly repeated crystallization of past and future in a significant, but never subsumable moment at its core, I hope to provide a perspective through which these films can be analyzed in what we might call their poetics of crystallized time or historicity (which is then again itself subject to historical development and referencing). This is a poetics which I have described as an experience and an audiovisual discourse of the deep temporality of a poiesis of genre/sports film-viewing on a meta level in the previous chapter, and which I will further develop in the following analytical chapters by focusing on more specific facets of that sensory discourse, especially with regard to poetic constructions of the momentary, of flow, of repetition and of endlessness.[31]

But before proceeding in that way, it is necessary to map out what I mean when talking about the American Dream as more than an ideological narrative of a political myth, but as a time-image that is nothing less than the sports film's constitutive conflict, through which it *takes* shape as a genre, and which it (re-)shapes with every single film.[32] At the core of this conflict lies an understanding of historical time as an ongoing crystallization of past and future in an overfull present, and, relating thereto, or rather emerging from this, an idea of communality defined by the tension between the extraordinariness of individuality and the containment of this extraordinariness by collectivity, the latter at

---

[31] Each of these facets will be fleshed out with the help of close readings of paradigmatic examples of films. These are but a few examples to be developed in this study though more can be found in regards to this genre theory.
[32] For the genre theoretical ideas behind such an understanding, see chapter 2.2 of this book.

3.2 The American Dream as Time-Image of Community-Building Historicity

the same time being in need of the former though, in order to form a (extraordinary) community in the first place. The time-image of the American Dream as the sports film's constitutive conflict thus puts forward what I want to call the two paradoxes of being as becoming. First, the concomitance of having been and going to be, the constant meeting of a being of a past and a being of a future in the present; and second, what Jean-Luc Nancy addresses with his notion of 'being singular plural' (see Nancy 2000 [1996]).[33] That is, an understanding of existence as essentially co-existence, which, while not assuming any original and stable collective formations, does not prioritize or demand the dissolution of either an 'I' nor a 'We,' and forms and reforms through mediated processes of permanent exposure, distinction and enclosure. These processes are oriented towards an *imagining* of community – with a medium like film as "the condition of possibility of [this] imagining" (Anderson 1983, 25), providing "a space where a particular apprehension of time can be exercised, an apprehension that is analogous to the constitution of the imagined community" (Vermeulen 2009, 102). Pieter Vermeulen grasps the relation between Nancy's notion of the "inoperative community" (Nancy 1991 [1983]) and Benedict Anderson's notion of the "imagined community" (Anderson 1983) as complementary. While he searches for this complementarity especially on the level of how the community-building role of death and loss is reflected in both concepts, what is important for me is that he thereby also emphasizes how both Nancy and Anderson acknowledge "the enabling role" (Vermeulen 2009, 101) of media for this imagining of community as a process of aesthetic figuration and experience. Even though referring primarily to literature and not film, these media do not represent a particular, existing community, but are able to provide, with Nancy, a vision (of another community) that can also be effective in a non-mythical way (see especially Vermeulen 2009, 106–108).

This particular (imagined) apprehension of time is – as Vermeulen continues to point out with regard to Anderson's statements about the genre of the novel, and as I want to adopt it with regard to my claims about the genre of the sports film here – simultaneity, the figuration of "a 'noncontemporaneous contemporaneity'" (Vermeulen 2009, 103, citing Harootunian 2007, 475). A figuration that is, as Vermeulen (with Jonathan Culler) also notes, not to be found in, or at least exceeds particular narrative structures and thematic representations (see Vermeulen 2009, 102).

Thus, the task of the following part of this chapter is to sketch out in what way this imagining of a noncontemporaneous contemporaneity – as

---

[33] See also chapter 6.2 of this book.

the imagining of community – can be understood in its specifically American form, as the American Dream time of a new community as nation.

A Matter of the Imaginary

To get away from the common approach of describing the sports film's concern with the American Dream as solely a matter of plot, topic and cultural context, I want to breathe more life into this notion from a philosophical perspective. This will lead to a better understanding of it as a central dimension of the United States' social imaginary, which the sports film not only co-produces, but along which it evolves as a genre in the first place. The level of this entanglement of mutual intervention is one of cultural fantasy, becoming graspable as an imaginatively structured and proceeding discourse of history, as a thinking of community-building time and time-creating community. Instead of addressing the American Dream as a mere 'unrealistic,' and therefore ideologically exploited, narrative of self-conquest through hard work, of individual chance and success, of upward social, economic and moral mobility etc., which conceals and distracts from factual circumstances, this chapter will sound out its development and status as a socially reflexive and effective image or audiovisual thinking of historicity. This thinking draws its power from ideas of transition and incompleteness, from openness and fictionality rather than from any notion of prescribed, stable, linear and concluded entities.

At the heart of this thinking lies an idea of time and community as a crystal: an entanglement of past, present and future, and the interdependency of individual and collective subjectification directly connected to this entanglement. It is in this sense that I suggest understanding the American Dream as a kind of formative self-imagining of a coming community torn between tradition and emancipation, remembrance and projection, as well as, accordingly, between communitization and separation, generalization and uniqueness. Furthermore, these tensions – we might speak of them as dialectical modes of subjectification – account for, as I claim, the constitutive conflict of the genre of the sports film. This is not only in the sense that sports movies representationally convey a certain narrative and/or message, but that they are a constructive and intervening part of this imagining themselves – by means of the expressive movement of their images and sounds, and the audiovisual thinking and feeling that evolves when these images and sounds are perceived by the viewer. It is *this* level of the American Dream as a community-building imaginative discourse of temporality and communality (and thus: of historicity) on which sports movies relate the media of sports and film, and thereby relate to each other and form as a genre in the first place.

While I will further develop this notion of the American Dream as the sports film genre's constitutive conflict with the help of three detailed and exemplary analyses in the chapters following this one, the insight I want to put forward can also be addressed and underpinned philosophically.

A Dream Is a Dream

One first, seemingly simple but decisive point leading towards this notion is the acknowledgement of the word 'dream.' It seems that this term is often overlooked, or only seriously examined when discussing the American Dream within a socio-economic and/or ideological critical context as an instrument of delusion, thereby setting it – as a false story – against predetermined real-life conditions (see previous chapter). As much as one might criticize the American Dream as such a constitutive and bolstering part of what Max Horkheimer and Theodor W. Adorno so famously coined "Verblendungszusammenhang" (Horkheimer / Adorno 2006 [1944], 48),[34] one at the same time has to admit to its – by all means real – meaning and power as a constitutive force of societal self-imagination. This is an imagination which cannot be reduced, as most sports film scholars do, to mythological narrativization, within which the American Dream remains a narrative template, exploited by (media) technologies and operations of distraction and delusion, and thus evaluated as deviant against the backdrop of an alleged, narratively structured reality of fixed real-life circumstances, of which it (the American Dream as narrative) is supposedly not a part, but which sets the standards for the assessment of its deviancy.

Obviously, there is a popular and many-voiced meaning of the American Dream as first and foremost designating materialistic success and monetary social advancement in the name of a (neoliberal) economic system that dominates all areas of everyday life. "Even when the phrase isn't being used to describe the accumulation of great wealth, it's frequently deployed to denote extreme success of some kind or other" (Kamp 2009). As he "shows how the American Dream came to mean fame and fortune, instead of the promise that shaped a nation" (Kamp 2009), David Kamp, in an article for *Vanity Fair,* performs a quite similar argumentative move to the one I aim at here – namely to emphasize or rediscover

---

[34] Andreas Huyssen translates this term as "universal manipulation and delusion," see Huyssen 1975, 11.

the Dream's speculative political kernel by looking more closely at its historical roots, and safeguard it against an all too hasty realist appropriation in the name of modern market economy. While the latter effectively reduces the American Dream to a mere linear and causal narrative of upward social mobility, what is instead on the agenda here is to penetrate and carve out the specific sense of community and history inherently connected to it from the very beginning of the United States' history. It is an idea of being singular plural through and within a temporality of crystallization, which makes the Dream "central [...] to the American idea and experience [...], rather than just a powerful philosophy or ideology" (Samuel 2012, 2).

Therefore, instead of addressing the sociopolitical effectiveness of the American Dream by means of a superimposition of real-world social structures and media produced narrative structures, I try to show on the following pages how the American Dream can rather – and especially with regard to the sports film – be understood as of central concern for the self-imaging of (American) society. Here it serves as the focal point of a discursive sphere, in and through which a specific idea of time and communality is propagated and circulated, thus providing for a community's opportunity to reflexively describe and experience itself as a collective. This sphere is a collective which puts forth outstanding individuality, but is at the same time – as an outstanding community – constituted *by* this individuality in the first place. It is this paradoxical dynamic of an egalitarianism of individual uniqueness addressing the communality in individuality and the individuality in communality, which the American Dream (community) renders the effect of a certain idea of crystallized time. An idea of time which is Deleuzian or Bergsonian insofar as it recognizes (the divisive conjunction of) a presence of the past and future in an overfull and never subsumable present (of the moment), and which thinks repetition not on the level of the (opposing or analogous) resemblance of fixed identities and characteristics, but as "difference without a concept" (Deleuze 2014 [1968], xiii), and thus as primary to the process of individuation, as a medium of becoming.[35]

---

[35] According to Deleuze's conceptualization in *Difference and Repetition*, the (passive, connective) synthesis of the living present as a contraction of the past and the future would be the first of the three interdependent syntheses around which time is constructed. The two others are the (passive, conjunctive) synthesis of the pure past and memory as all of the pasts coexisting with the present as virtuality, and the (passive, disjunctive) synthesis of the future as the (Nietzsche's) eternal return of difference, with the present and the past as dimensions of the future (see Deleuze 2014 [1968], 93 et seq.). While the first synthesis relates to our general, everyday understanding and encounter of time, it is the third synthesis which provides the decisive, extraordinary twist in Deleuze's theory of novelty and becoming, with time as the between-time of the event or instant (see also chapter 4.1).

In this sense, the American Dream paradoxically addresses a society *yet to come* and at the same time *already having been*, imagining a world defined in no small part by its future, and, consequently, by its past as well, a world which comes into being because this being is (understood as) becoming, as a mode of historicity apprehending the present as the past of its future and the future of its past.

The American Dream as a Romantic Mode and a Sense of Crystallized Time

From this perspective, it is not too farfetched to claim that the American Dream can be understood as a romantic mode in Frye's genre critical sense, hence operating as "a *wishfulfillment* or *Utopian fantasy*, which aims at the *transfiguration* of the world of everyday life in such a way as to restore the conditions of some lost Eden, or to *anticipate a future realm* from which the old mortality and imperfections *will have been* effaced" (Jameson 1981, 110, [all emphases mine]).[36] Fredric Jameson, who refers to Frye's genre theory[37] in his *Magical Narratives* essay, rightly stresses the 'inclusive,' non-binary idea of realism at play here, where it is not about an everyday world being substituted with an ideal, entirely alternative one, but rather about a "process of transforming" (Jameson 1981, 110), where one both contains and modulates the other. In that regard, the American Dream is not to be understood as a pathway of escape into some kind of separated idyll, which detracts (or is used to detract) from so-called real life, but rather as an expression of the incompleteness of and the possibility for change within exactly this life.

It is quite fitting when Jameson continues his take on Frye by problematizing the notion of 'world' as a perceptible entity in its own right, consequently recognizing romance as a "form in which the *worldness of world* reveals or manifests itself" (Jameson 1981, 111), and, subsequently, once again denying the existence of a mode of perception or imagery more 'natural' (and thus, less socially and historically specific) than any other. This speaks by all means to my claim about the American Dream being an audio-visual-affective discourse through which the temporality of American (historical) time and communality manifests and reveals itself, through which the community (of the American nation) deals with its own constitutive historicity, with its 'becoming community' in and through a specific sense of time as crystallization.

---

36 For the romance of the American Dream, see also Rowland 2007.
37 See Frye 1957.

On another, but nonetheless directly related note, Jameson's criticism about the tendency to understand (character) subjectivity as a pre-determined and naturalized entity within (Frye's) genre theory follows my claims about genre, and the sports film as a genre. As I argue, genre cinema is fundamentally concerned with the production of subjectivity and, interdependently, of communality in the first place, by (re-)creating, connecting and modulating ever-new forms of expression and perception (see chapter 2). Now, this argument receives additional emphasis with regard to the American sports film in particular, given that sports itself is extremely inclined towards this generic dynamic of communal subjectivity and subjective communality, and the temporality and idea of historical time do not only go along with it, but produce it. It is this idea which, as I want to explain in more detail now, makes up a decisive part of the American Dream as an imaginatively and sensorially structured and effective discourse of community-building historicity: as a reflexive mode of imagining and imaging time, by means of which a community forms because it is able to grasp itself as a community in time.

Deleuze on Melville: The American Dream as Becoming-We as Fractal Unity

Gilles Deleuze himself talks rather briefly about the American Dream in *Cinema 1: The Movement-Image*, seemingly defending it in a quite similar way and against the same encroachments as I do here: "One cannot criticize the American dream for being only a dream: this is what it wants to be, drawing all its power from the fact that it is a dream" (Deleuze 2013a [1983], 152). To find a more detailed elaboration of the American Dream, especially as an idea of social relationship and with regard to how works of art (here: literary works) productively intervene in and as the structures, types and processes of what is often – and in explicit connection to Deleuze – entitled "human flourishing" (see for example Tampio 2015, 69), we have to look elsewhere and consult two essays by the French philosopher on Walt Whitman and Herman Melville. In the text on Melville (Deleuze 1998b), which is for the most part about *Bartleby, the Scrivener*,[38] Deleuze provides insight into, or rather, provokes thinking on, the intertwined formation of communal subjectivity and subjective communality central to American community-building as a function of time, where becoming and the fragmentary beat out any thought of totality or fixed ratio. He

---

38 It builds up to widen its perspective in the end towards Moby-Dick and Billy Budd as well.

advances towards this dynamic by analyzing specific literary features such as the disposition of language and of certain characters and their language.

In what follows, I will not touch upon Deleuze's conceptualization in full, but rather present that part of his deduction of Bartleby's famous formula "I would prefer not do," which seems important for the idea of the American Dream as an idea of community-building and history as simultaneity, and in this sense for the idea of the American Dream as the constitutive conflict of the sports film.[39]

In regards to the American Dream, Deleuze's Whitman text (Deleuze 1998a) plays with the idea that the American experience – the American nation and society as well as its literature – is of spontaneous, fragmentary and convulsive character (see Deleuze 1998a, 56–57),[40] and that its central object therefore is a poetics of relation and interchange rather than one of totalization. On the other hand, the much longer and more elaborate essay on Melville introduces us to a metaphysics that originates from Bartleby and his formula based on the differentiation between (an order of) "primary Nature" and (an order of) "secondary Nature" (Deleuze 1998b, 79). Quite typically for him, Deleuze introduces this differentiation rather suddenly and randomly, just after having projected his detailed (psychologically impregnated) characterization of Bartleby (as well as of Captain

---

39 One other fitting aspect is certainly Deleuze's distinction between different types of (Melville) characters, as eventually two "poles" which are opposed but finally "haunt one and the same world" and are thus "perhaps the same creature – primary, original, stubborn, seized from both sides, marked merely with a 'plus' or a 'minus' sign": the Monomaniacs or demons, which are "driven by the will to nothingness" (like Ahab or Claggart), and the Hypochondriacs or angels as "creatures of innocence and purity," with "no will at all, a nothingness of the will rather than a will to nothingness," like Billy Budd and Bartleby (Deleuze 1998b, 79–80). It appears to me that many of the main protagonists of sports films are presented as such characters torn between those poles, the most apparent one being Jim Thorpe in JIM THORPE – ALL-AMERICAN (M. Curtiz, 1951). For my analysis of the film, see chapter 6.2 of this book. It might be interesting to further follow this line of thinking with regard to a more general theory of the Hollywood movie hero as Bartleby as "the man without references, without possessions, without properties, without qualities, without particularities: he is too smooth for anyone to be able to hang any particularity on him. Without past or future, he is instantaneous" (Deleuze 1998b, 74).

40 In contrast to the European one, which is defined by "an innate sense of organic totality, or composition, [having] to acquire the sense of the fragment, and can do so only through a tragic reflection or an experience of disaster" (Deleuze 1998a, 56), Deleuze claims that there nonetheless exists an idea of a whole when it comes to Whitman's/American literature, but that this is more of an "assembly" (Deleuze 1998a, 59), a non-totalizing whole which "comes after the fragments and leaves them intact" (Deleuze 1998a, 58). See also Herzogenrath 2010, 171–207.

Ahab and Billy Budd) onto broader concepts of the American experience/Dream as "no longer a question of Mimesis, but of becoming" (Deleuze 1998b, 78).[41]

While the "secondary Nature" is "sensible" and "governed by the Law (or laws)," thereby designating or grounding a universe of reason and norm, the "primary Nature" is lawless, "supersensible," "original and oceanic" and "irrational" (Deleuze 1998b, 78). Analogous to his description of the overall movement of Melville's novels going from "*à l'anglaise*" – the language of the Englishman – to "*à l'américaine*" (Deleuze 1998b, 77) – the language of American fragmentation (of Whitman, Melville, Bartleby etc.) – Deleuze allocates certain forms of communal subjectivity to the Old and the New World. While the former, belonging or constituting to the order of secondary Nature, is characterized by the "paternal function" (Deleuze 1998b, 77) of a society ruled by the father figure, the latter puts forth a "society of brothers" (Deleuze 1998b, 85) functioning through camaraderie.[42] It is with regard to this society that "alliance replaces filiation […], drawing its members into an unlimited becoming" (Deleuze 1998b, 84). Hence, in Deleuze's perspective, the idea of American society is to get rid of the Oedipal phantasm, to break with "the image of the father" (Deleuze 1998b, 77) and instead rely on the "fraternal relation pure and simple" (Deleuze 1998b, 84). One becomes the other and everyone else not by giving up her or his eccentric singularity, but by embracing it up to the form of its maximum humanistic base, to the point where there are no "particularities" anymore, only "proprieties of a 'democratic dignity'" (Deleuze 1998b, 85).

Therefore this idea of 'becoming-we as a fractal unity' (see Herzogenrath 2010, 194–195) in regard to the formation of society in the New World offers not only a different perspective on community-building, but points to the significance and scope of this community-building itself, given that it refers back to the humanistic grounding of the very idea of community in the first place. This is characterized by the belief in the potential of living a better life through (and in) democratic solidarity and dignity – an insight brought to the fore by Richard Rorty as well, as I will describe later in this chapter. Deleuze leads us to such

---

41 While referencing Sade here only in passing, this connection can be traced back to his essay *Coldness and Cruelty*, where he also further elaborates the two Natures of Sade and Masoch, even though it seems to me that this conception is not fully compatible to what Deleuze is on to here (see Deleuze 1991 [1967], 27–28, and also Bogue 2003, 17–19).
42 As a matter of course, Deleuze equally addresses a society of sisters, even though his statements remain quite male-centered (for example when mentioning the homosexual aspect within his conceptualization). For further examinations on the relation of Deleuze's philosophy and questions of sex and gender, see Colebrook / Weinstein 2008, Cull 2009, Marrati 2006, and Nigianni / Storr 2009.

3.2 The American Dream as Time-Image of Community-Building Historicity

insight, and by that to the final step of rendering his (anti-)psychoanalytically drenched literary analysis a socio-historical theory, by asking questions:

> How can this community be realized? [...] But is it not already resolved, by itself, precisely because it is not a personal problem, but a historical, geographic, or political one? It is not an individual or particular affair, but a collective one, the affair of a people, or rather, of all peoples. It is not an Oedipal phantasm but a political program. (Deleuze 1998b, 85)

He continues by summarizing once again what it is that characterizes the American Dream as an idea of a historically self-referential community of fragmentation and relation, and its inherent idea of crystallized time, of the present moment (or what he in *Difference and Repetition* with regard to the first synthesis of time calls "living present") as the synthesis of past and future, as including "temporally two different instants: the past which 'retains' in the contraction, and the future which 'anticipates' in the same contraction" (Rastovic 2011, 51):

> The American is one who is freed from the English paternal function, the son of a crumbled father, the son of all nations. Even before their independence, Americans were thinking about the combination of States, the State-form most compatible with their vocation. But their vocation was not to reconstitute an "old State secret," a nation, a family, a heritage, or a father. It was above all to constitute a universe, a society of brothers, a federation of men and goods, a community of anarchist individuals, inspired by Jefferson, by Thoreau, by Melville. Such is the declaration in Moby-Dick (chapter 26): if man is the brother of his fellow man, if he is worthy of trust or "confidence," it is not because he belongs to a nation or because he is a proprietor or shareholder, but only insofar as he is Man, when he has lost those characteristics that constitute his "violence," his "idiocy," his "villainy," when he has no consciousness of himself apart from the proprieties of a "democratic dignity" that considers all particularities as so many ignominious stains that arouse anguish or pity. America is the potential of the man without particularities, the Original Man.[43] (Deleuze 1998b, 85)

As the detailed analysis of especially Bartleby's formula before points to, this idea of communal subjectivity is of course also intrinsically linked to questions of expression and representation for Deleuze. He makes that clear shortly before in the text, thereby also explicitly using the notion of the American Dream,

---

[43] In this perspective, Thoreau's *Walden*, as one of the central literary reference points or interpretations of the American Dream, stands out a little bit, insofar as the tension between individuality and communality seems to be dissolved in a rather unilateral way, with its reclusive protagonist immersing himself in nature. But then again, this reclusion can be interpreted as a deliberate way of regaining a sense of communality – with, for example, the chapter on "Visitors" as a very interesting part in this regard (see Thoreau 1997 [1854], 127). Also, Deleuze's reading of (the dying) Bartleby as 'becoming-mineral/stone,' as becoming "an Original, in relation to a first inhumane nature" (Pombo Nabais 2019) clearly relates to Thoreau's conceptualization. For a discussion of Bartleby being (identified/interpreted as) Thoreau, see McCall 1989, 70–78.

to which he attributes three characteristics, "which together make up the new identification, the New World: the [formless] Trait [of expression], the Zone [of indistinction], and the Function [of universal fraternity]" (Deleuze 1998b, 78).[44] So, while for Deleuze American community-building is still based on an identificatory process, this process runs more in a formless, non-directional and non-conditioned manner, free of any already given entity and identity (in Deleuze's words: rather schizophrenic than neurotic, rather free than closed, see Deleuze 1998b, 78). Its mode of expression is therefore characterized by opposing the traditional model of mimetic representation and its procedures of matching, complying and adapting.

> Rather, a zone of indistinction, of indiscernibility, or of ambiguity seems to be established between two terms, as if they had reached the point immediately preceding [sic] their respective differentiation: not a similitude, but a slippage, an extreme proximity, an absolute contiguity; not a natural filiation, but an unnatural alliance. [...] It is no longer a question of Mimesis, but of becoming.[45] (Deleuze 1998b, 78)

In both of the two essays, the one on Whitman and the one on Melville, Deleuze finally finds a telling image for his concept of the American Dream and of American politics: a wall. This wall, however, is not a soundly built structure but rather "a wall of loose, uncemented stones, where every element has a value in itself but also in relation to others" (Deleuze 1998b, 86).[46] In *Whitman*, he furthermore writes about America/American literature:

> It is [...] created by the people, by the "average bulk", [...] and not by "great individuals". And from this point of view, the Self [Moi] of the Anglo-Saxons, always splintered, fragmentary, and relative, is opposed to the substantial, total, and solipsistic I [Je] of the Europeans. The world as a collection of heterogenous parts: an infinite patchwork, or an endless wall of dry stones (a cemented wall, or the pieces of a puzzle, would reconstitute a totality). The world as a sampling: the samples ("specimens") are singularities, remarkable and nontotalizable parts extracted from a series of ordinary parts. (Deleuze 1998a, 57)

---

44 Additions in the brackets based on Deleuze's further explanations on the same page.
45 'Term' here clearly transcends its colloquial (merely linguistic) meaning (as spoken or written word).
46 According to Jacques Rancière, who commented on Deleuze's Bartleby (see Rancière 2004 [1998]), it is in this image of a wall of free, uncemented stones where one should search for Deleuzian politics, if at all, as in his opinion Deleuze's philosophy rather "erects an impasse for politics" (Wolfe 2006). For a very impressive approach dismantling Rancière's reservations towards Deleuze and relating the 'Politics of Aesthetics' of both thinkers via Kant (via locating the foundation of Rancière's conceptualization in the *Critique of Pure Reason*, and via her own and Deleuze's reading of the *Critique of Judgement*), see Katherine Wolfe's article *From Aesthetics to Politics: Rancière, Kant and Deleuze*.

3.2 The American Dream as Time-Image of Community-Building Historicity — 119

What seems to be decisive with regard to his metaphor, moreover, is that this wall is always unfinished: Deleuze's American Dream wall is a (fragmented/unformed) arrangement of (fragmented/unformed) singularities,[47] which bears the possibility to arrange anew anytime through any minor rearrangement of its parts, with these parts also only being partial by means of the also always 'only' partial whole they are part of.

Furthermore, and with regard to the sports film and the 'common man' as individual hero – something the former obviously celebrate – is that Deleuze's model by all means seems to include individualities in that very sense (of 'great individuals,' of heroes). What he addresses is not a democratic community of egalitarianism and/or ultimate tolerance and universality, where finally nothing and no one stands out, where all friction and tilting is seemingly balanced (see Beaulieu 2009, 213), but of the singularity of the common man in relation to every other 'common man' bearing the potential of becoming singular, of becoming hero.

In this sense, America for Deleuze seems to be also what Giorgio Agamben calls a "coming community" (Agamben 2007 [1993]), in an essay which in part also builds on an interpretation of Melville's *Bartleby, the Scrivener*.[48] What becomes clearer with Agamben is the ambiguity that comes with the idea of (non-)particularity being integrated in such an understanding of community as always a new community to come, and thus defined by potentiality rather than given laws of lineage, belonging, reason and/or identity. Especially because he – with his notion of the 'whatever' [*qualunque*][49] – emphasizes that it is not the idea of

---

47 Deleuze states that the characters which he typifies as angels or hypochondriacs (like Bartleby) "can only survive by becoming stone" (Deleuze 1998b, 80). See also LaRocca 2017, 205. This again resonates quite well with the sports film and its many heroes becoming angels (HEAVEN CAN WAIT, W. Beatty / B.Henry, 1978) and/or possessing continued (post-mortem) presence on and as sculptures (WE ARE MARSHALL, J. 'McG' McGinty Nichol, 2006), engravings and gravestones (REMEMBER THE TITANS, B. Yakin, 2000), or even buildings (KNUTE ROCKNE ALL AMERICAN, L Bacon, 1940).

48 Agamben also published another essay solely dedicated to Melville's *Bartleby, the Scrivener* (see Agamben 1999).

49 The French word is 'quelconque,' which in Deleuze is translated as 'whatsoever.' For the English translations bearing different and sometimes confusing connotations, see Agamben 2007 [1993], 106. The Italian circumnavigates this linguistic confusion by adhering to the Latin expression 'quodlibet.' With regard to cinema, Deleuze picks up the concept of 'any space what(so)ever' [l'espace quelconque] from Pascal Augé, but instead of understanding it as a homogenous and de-singularizing (non-)space, he interprets it – in close proximity of his notion of the time-image – as the very condition for singularity to emerge, for the possibility of unique identity being constituted or questioned, in films such as those of German Expressionism, of Antonioni, Bresson, Dreyer, and Marker (see chapter 7 of Deleuze 2013a [1983], and chapter 1 of Deleuze 2013b [1985], and also, in German/French, Bensmaia 1999).

indifference ("being, it does not matter which"), but the capacity of self-sufficient being ("being such that it always matters") by means of which the interdependency of individual and communal subjectification should be conceived. Because more than only addressing a spiritual art of living in rejectionist solitude (as in Thoreau's *Walden*) or an idea of society as an entirely transcendent, single, homogenous mass, the coming community of the American Dream is rather about being singular plural, about the ineluctable constitutive relation to individual and communal subjectification. Agamben writes:

> The Whatever in question here relates to singularity not in its indifference with respect to a common property (to a concept, for example: being red, being French, being Muslim), but only in its being such as it is. Singularity is thus freed from the false dilemma that obliges knowledge to choose between the ineffability of the individual and the intelligibility of the universal. The intelligible [...] is neither a universal nor an individual included in a series, but rather "singularity insofar as it is whatever singularity." In this conception, such-and-such being is reclaimed from its having this or that property, which identifies it as belonging to this or that set, to this or that class (the reds, the French, the Muslims) – and it is reclaimed not for another class nor for the simple generic absence of any belonging, but for its being-such, for belonging itself.   (Agamben 2007 [1993], 1)

Agamben's as well as Deleuze's coming community is thus not to be simply understood as a future community soon to be realized because of a somewhat predetermined form, but as a community which forms as it forms, which crystallizes in the moment, and in its uniqueness as a multitude of integral but fractal uniqueness.

In View of a Past and a Future: The Declaration of Independence

Let us now build off of this idea of a communality of uniqueness being central to the American Dream as some kind of productive-reflexive discourse of a coming community of singularities by carving out the modes, discourses and ideas of time and temporality which the American Dream not only addresses and through which it is addressed, but also from which it historically accrued.

As James Truslow Adams, who coined the term 'American Dream' as late as 1931 in his book *The Epic of America*,[50] makes clear, this brings us back to the act

---

[50] Concerning this, Cullen mentions that Adams' book, which he describes as a "history of the United States for the general reader" (Cullen 2003, 4), should initially have been titled *The American Dream*. See also the introduction to the Transaction edition of the book by Howard Schneiderman: "One might wonder if Adams invented the American dream, or if he discovered it. If he invented it, he married the strange with the familiar. If he discovered it, he merely gave a new and compelling name to a preexisting social force majeure" (Adams 2017 [1931], XV).

of founding the United States of America. In 1776, thirteen Anglo-American settler-states by means of the Declaration of Independence set up this new nation and a new form of community.[51] This act is, as we know, explicated as a procedure of "separation," of a splitting-off from an old world out of the necessity "to dissolve the political bands" with the latter, as stated in the first paragraph of the Declaration.[52] Although this detachment was supposed to be, as is expressed in the concluding paragraph, one of a rather total dissolution – in the sense of a new order realized through the somehow singular event of voting for and signing a document – the Declaration of Independence, as an act as well as through its content, does not bear the temporality of a beginning in the sense of a definitive, punctual split-off, of an absolute new (that would go along with the nonexistence of a before). Furthermore, it is less about any current state of existence or reality, but rather an explication of the new: of a new era, of a new form of community and a new us in clear view of and connected to a past as well as a future.[53] It is about a process of dealing with what happened in the past – the biggest part of the text itself is a list of indictments towards King George and his "repeated inju-

---

[51] See the first chapters of Adams 2001 [1931], and also the first two chapters of Cullen 2003. In terms of the Declaration of Independence itself: There continues to much discussion about the history of this document up until this day, especially about its different versions and its legal status. See for example the numerous publications of Julian P. Boyd (for example Boyd 1945, Boyd 1976), John Phillip Reid's *The Irrelevance of the Declaration* (1981) or Gary Wills' *Inventing America: Jefferson's Declaration of Independence* (2002). The drafting and signing of the Declaration of Independence is of course only one part of the United States' road to independence, which also included Great Britain's enforcement of tax and administrative reforms in their colonies in the 1760s, the outbreak of the American Revolutionary War in 1775, the Peace of Paris in 1783–1784, the ratification of the United States Constitution in 1788 and the swearing-in of the first US president George Washington. For an extensive overview of the historical events, see for example Robert Middlekauff's *The Glorious Cause* (2007).

[52] You can find the full text of the Declaration of Independence on archives.gov, as a transcription of what is known as the Stone Engraving, an 1823 copperplate engraving by printer William J. Stone, commissioned by Secretary of State John Quincy Adams in 1820, when the original parchment already showed signs of age. The Stone Engraving is the most frequently reproduced version of the Declaration (https://www.archives.gov/founding-docs/declaration-transcript, accessed 9 February 2020). Wikipedia provides an annotated version of the text: https://en.wikipedia.org/wiki/United_States_Declaration_of_Independence#Annotated_text_of_the_engrossed_declaration (accessed 9 February 2020).

[53] John Winthrop, an English Puritan lawyer and leading figure in the second major settlement in New England, captures this claim in his 1630 treatise *A Model of Christian Charity* with the famous spatial trope of the "City upon a Hill" (which originally dates back to the parable of Salt and Light in Jesus's Sermon on the Mount, Matthew 5:14).

ries and usurpations" of the American states – to be able to venture towards a renewal as a point in time that is to a great extent defined by what it is supposed to trigger: the possibility of futurity.

For Hannah Arendt, this double bind is of decisive importance for the American Revolution, and, moreover, for revolutions in general. In her effort to analytically define the notion of revolution in its proper sense, she contrasts it with a coup or revolt: While such events share (the use) of violence with a revolution, they primarily take place as procedures of change which do not include an act of a new beginning. A proper revolution though is about both change *and* (the experience of) a new beginning as well as liberation *and* (the founding of) freedom (Arendt 1990 [1963], 29 et seg.).[54] Its meaning lies in the (violence of the) moment, through which a separation from the past takes place, but which also functions as a starting point of a new future. In that way, "revolutions are the only political events which confront us directly and inevitably with the problem of beginning" (Arendt 1990 [1963], 21). This could be said about sports films, too, especially when we look at how many of them immediately – right with their first images and sounds – establish their worlds as 'secondary' worlds, by means of textual and aesthetic referencing (through the use of found footage or intertitles), and/or by means of an audiovisual poetics of immediacy, repetition or new beginnings.[55]

In the written document of the Declaration of Independence, this dimension of a simultaneous orientation towards a past and a future becomes especially evident when at its end the text speaks of the "Representatives of the united [sic] States of America" which "mutually pledge to each other [their] Lives, [their] Fortunes and [their] sacred honor" on the basis of "a firm reliance on the protection of divine Providence" (all concluding paragraph).

To refer to and rely on something that is yet to come, while this relying is part of the founding of a new formation (through exactly this formation!) in a present moment formed out of a (immediate) past, which here is the American Revolutionary War is to comprehend time as a temporality of crystallization which reveals the American Dream, or at least the notion of the American Dream, that I foreground here with regard to the sports film. That is, it is a kind of a Deleuzian time-image becoming socially effective: a perception by means

---

54 It is important to note Arendt's quite special notion of freedom and politics here. For her, both go hand in hand and are not to be thought of as separated from each other: If one talks about politics as 'taking action' in the public sphere, one already also talks about freedom.
55 For very telling but differing examples to this effect, see the intros of BLUE CHIPS (W. Friedkin, 1994), NORTH DALLAS FORTY (T. Kotcheff, 1979), and JIM THORPE – ALL-AMERICAN (M. Curtiz, 1951). I will analyze the latter in more detail, and especially from its ending, in chapter 6.2.

of which time becomes graspable as duration or lived time, as a force of becoming and actualization in a system of immanence where the possibility for the new is ubiquitous as a question of change and of intervention, not of invention. Where time is not just simply a representation of something that is 'here/there,' but where it creates and produces, in the sense of unfolding: time, life, reality; individuality as singularities, social collectivity. In that way, the American Dream can be understood as a vital activity, enabling us to reflexively relate to reality as a *"reality which is making itself in a reality which is unmaking itself"* (Bergson 1998 [1911], 248, emphasis in the original, see also Grosz 2007).

Lived Time and a Reality Making Itself in a Reality Unmaking Itself

Underlying such understanding is a philosophy of time which grasps past, present and future not as measured segments of a single line of chronological successiveness, thus as representative parts of what Bergson calls "clock" or "mathematical time," but as functions of each other; as ongoing (and always indirect and incomplete) actualizations aligning with each other within "duration," within the indivisible whole in and through which time does not exist as a spatialized and measurable series, but in and through which it appears again and again as "layered, simultaneous moments" (Wasserman 1985, 229). As lived time, which "moves by 'reciprocal interpenetration' into the present" (Wasserman 1985, 229), in a world where "vital difference is the very machinery of the real" (Grosz 2007, 2), and where life flourishes along "a continuous, never ceasing relation of change" (Grosz 2007, 14). The force of this contingent flourishing is what Bergson calls the *élan vital* (vital force), which itself consists of endless "forces of self-organization" (Grosz 2007, 17), in turn, and which provides for "all forms of life [sharing] this protraction of the past into present [and the present into future], and the retroaction of the present on the past [and the future on the present]" (Grosz 2007, 17.).

It is this lived time, which not only divides the present into a present of the past and a present of the future, but along and by means of which community (as a life form) takes shape as both a collective of related individualities and an individual collectivity, as it (time as duration as indivisible whole) knows no final or absolute independence or distinct individuality, but only relations and encounters – 'singularities,' as Deleuze calls them, constituting the virtual proper of things without acting neither entirely autonomous nor as predetermined and fixed entities.[56]

Duration, or lived time, remains intangible, it is not representable as a whole, but only shows itself, according to Bergson, in images, or rather: in the perception of images as image. But what does that mean? In order to push his intervention forward, Bergson uses the image to bridge the gap between mind and matter, between the material world and consciousness – for him, there is nothing *outside* of images, and nothing *in* consciousness. Hence, matter for him is "an aggregate of 'images'" (Bergson 1991 [1896], 9) already, an (unconscious) perception of images. Bodies, too, are all compositions of images among images. Thus, as Temenuga Trifonova very rightfully states:

> Bergson's account of perception as the birth of consciousness [...] does not, however, suggest that we should expect to find in Bergson's work a visual bias. Throughout his works, he consistently argues that images do not express duration since they are on the side of spatiality, rationality. [...] The image, then, is important since it reveals the origin of consciousness as conscious perception, but insofar as conscious perception differs only in degree from unconscious perception. The image does not reveal the qualitative difference between matter and mind, which consists of the mind's capacity to preserve images, in its capacity for memory. (Trifonova 2003, 81)

As such, Bergson uses the notion of image for matter and not only for visual representations or mental images. At the same time, memory for him is of imaginative nature, opening up possible (new) connections of images/things/bodies by preserving them (in a non-pure way as pure memory). It is this idea of 'existence in potentia' (see Trifonova 2003, 95), of imaginatively producing something yet to come out of something that (already) has been that I want to carve out as the essential idea here. I want to focus on it not only as an idea of a specific anti-substantialist philosophy of time, which Deleuze later picks up for his notion of the filmic image, but also as important for understanding the American Dream as a socially effective imaginary; as a community-building apprehension of time as lived time. In other words, as a discourse of temporality that recognizes time not "as indirect representation or number of movement," (Deleuze 2013b, 36) which

---

56 See Levi R. Bryant's explanation concerning the role of singularities for individuation, with becoming as the central force: "Individuation refers to those processes by which an individual is produced. Singularities are central actors in that process of individuation. They are not something outside of things – they are strictly immanent in things – but neither are they the qualities (such as color, texture, taste, etc) or shape of things. Rather, they are that within a thing that will generate qualities and shape when a thing enters into a particular field of forces. Other fields of forces would lead to the genesis of other qualities and shapes" (Bryant 2012). See also Simondon 1992.

proceeds linearly, but as an "experience where time is given to me as a perception" (Deleuze 2013b, 37); and (therefore) not determined by events, things and subjectivities (as primary composites, or as privileged images in Bergson's sense), by *the* past and *the* future, but as the ever new actualization of a past and future within an overfull, impalpable present, "as a continuous forking into incompossible presents and not necessarily true pasts" (Trifonova 2004, 134).[57]

Understood in this sense of discursive perceptual imaginary, the American Dream is not about a prefabricated idea or image forming a world, which, as a fixed entity, can be related and contrasted to other worlds on the basis of conventionalized representation, in whatever manner. It is rather about world-*building*, addressing reality as first and foremost virtuality, as a (not yet becoming) part of the real, as a potentiality which is no less effective than when it becomes actualized – a *"reality which is making itself in a reality which is unmaking itself"* (Bergson 1998 [1911], 248).

This brings us back to the Declaration of Independence and the act of founding a new nation out of the new world (the 'discovered' America) as the old world which it describes (the America as colonies). This is memorialized through a document, while at the same time is also executed or performed *through* it, then and ever anew. The idea of the American Dream originates here, as an idea of time as constant becoming, and in that way – the preceding remarks here have already indicated that – of community, and thus history, as constantly in the process of becoming. The group known as the Committee of Five, who drafted the Declaration and presented it to Congress, and the fifty-six representatives, who finally signed it, quite literally embody a 'community that is making itself in (or maybe rather as) a community unmaking itself,' a community that manifests only through constant new manifestations, through having been and continuing to become.

The American Dream as an Aesthetic Regime of Becoming Community

With regard to the Declaration of Independence, this becoming of (historical) community figures is addressed as an act of separation from the past, or rather, in Deleuzian/Bergsonian terminology, as an act of 'becoming different.' It includes the acknowledgement of this past (as pure, virtual, and universal) through the

---

[57] Trifonova reminds us that Bergson develops this idea of duration as "the contemporaneousness of perception and memory" (Trifonova 2004, 134) along an analysis of the phenomenologically paradox phenomenon of the déjà vu, where we feel reminded of an experience of the past, but at the same time cannot really trace it back on the plane of our own past.

acknowledgement of the (immanent) pastness of the present moment, as well as of the force of change of a future for which this past/present moment is the starting point, and through which it thus takes shape.[58] The Declaration is about the creation of a new community, which simultaneously constitutes and proceeds from its very futurity, its 'will be,' but also from its 'having been' (in the moment of recognition, which is then post-facto repeated, and simultaneous with its enunciation). This community defines itself not through any final determination, stable condition, or claim of originality, but through its potentiality; the possibility for change as an ongoing modulation of what was and what will be. In this regard, it is telling that in the fourth paragraph of the Declaration of Independence, the text speaks of an alteration of "the former Systems of Government" in reaction to the transgressions of King George (and not, for example, of an abandonment).

In a letter to Henry Lee in 1825, Thomas Jefferson emphasizes this aspect, thereby hinting to the temporal paradox of the moment in time, which always already *was*, but at the same time still *will be* (again), and to its importance for the dynamic formation of collective subjectivity:

> This was the object of the Declaration of Independence. Not to find out new principles, or new arguments, never before thought of, not merely to say things which had never been said before; but to place before mankind the common sense of the subject, in terms so plain and firm as to command their assent, and to justify ourselves in the independent stand we are compelled to take. *Neither aiming at originality of principle or sentiment, nor yet copied from any particular and previous writing*, it was intended to be an *expression* of the American mind, and to give to that expression the proper tone and spirit called for by the occasion.[59] (Jefferson 1984, 1500, [emphasies mine])

Besides describing the historical moment as an act of 'bundling forces,' Jefferson brings something else into play, which should not be underestimated with regard to this book's aim – namely, to join certain temporalities addressed within political thought or philosophical conceptualizations of society with the autonomous aesthetic times [*ästhetische Eigenzeiten*] of media artifacts (like a film), as well as

---

[58] One could also think about this separation in the sense as presented by Claude Lefort as part of the constitutive difference of a (national) community recognizing itself (its subjectivity) through the founding of a governmental body, separate from the 'body' of the people, at once preceding it (and thus giving it meaning) and proceeding from the community's identification with it (Lefort 1988). Slavoj Žižek also talks about this as a time-paradox and the 'stain' of the originary moment in *For They Know Not What They Do* in a Kantian sense (Žižek 2008 [1991], especially part III).

[59] While such "common sense of the subject" might obviously be described as an ideologically shaped object in the first place, Jefferson nonetheless seem to address it as a product of aesthetic negotiation here.

the temporal structures and relations through which these artifacts are formed.⁶⁰ With the assertion of such entanglement comes the recognition that politics is always already media aesthetic politics, and that texts and images and sounds, as much as they might absorb certain dynamics of social life, also prepare the ground for such dynamics (of perception, of thought, of belief) in the first place. In this sense, and with Jacques Rancière, who states that "there never has been any 'aestheticization' of politics in the modern age because politics is aesthetic in principle," the American Dream should also be understood as an expressive-perceptive regime that

> first free[s] up the norms of representation, and second, constitute[s] a kind of community of sense experience that works on the world of assumption, of the *as if* that includes those who are not included by revealing a mode of existence of sense experience that has eluded the allocation of parties and lots.⁶¹ (Rancière 1999, 58)

That, as I argue, has eluded the allocation of time as chronologically 'spatialized' time, as clearly identifiable and separable on a linearly progressing/expiring line. Against this backdrop of the American Dream as an aesthetic regime, constituting a perceptually operational, speculative and community-addressing mode of existence, I regard its essence as the twisted temporality of the ungraspable present (moment), as the both not yet and already gone, as a present of the past and a present of the future described above – as Bergson's and Deleuze's 'Time of Aion'

---

60 For the idea of form as an organization of time, see Seel 2007 (in German). The DFG Priority Program *Aesthetische Eigenzeiten. Zeit und Darstellung in der polychronen Moderne* puts this idea at the center of its research focus, pointing out in a wide variety of studies concerned with the analysis of concrete artifacts (first and foremost of literature, theater, dance, and the fine arts) how specific temporalities become tangible through their temporal disposition, and thus how the 'non-propositional/-semantical sphere of the cultural knowledge of time' comes to expression (see for example Gamper and Hühn 2014 and Gamper et al. 2016, in German). By conceptualizing film and its perception as the relation of at least two temporalities – a dramaturgical one which the viewer undergoes while watching, and one concerned with the construction of time relations through audiovisual form – Kappelhoff and Lehmann do something similar for the medium of film (see Kappelhoff / Lehmann 2021, in German).

61 With defining the political as "the very possibility of dissensus, of redistributing and reassembling the sensible, of evicting the alleged ideological line between appearance and reality" (Vihalem 2018, 5), Rancière sees democracy not as a political regime that arranges subjectivities by superimposing an essentialist set of principles, but as "the very regime of politics itself" (Rancière 2010, 31), as an "aesthetic regime where the nature of the politics is essentially non-grounded" (Vihalem 2018, 5). With Richard Rorty, this line of thought could also count towards the American Dream, thereby disclosing it as a medium of the political, so to speak (see later on in this chapter).

or time of the pure event.⁶² It is in this light that the American Dream is the constitutive conflict through and around which the genre of the sports film develops, and which is not merely addressed in the text of the Declaration of Independence, but, as Jacques Derrida argues, in the very historical act it describes and from which it is born.

The Paradox of the Declaration of Independence as Constative and Performative Act

Derrida elaborates on this act's temporal twist, using the signing of the Declaration of Independence as an example for his critique of structuralism in his lecture/text *Otobiographies: L'enseignement de Nietzsche et la politique du nom propre* (Derrida 2005 [1984]).⁶³ He examines the different representative authorities and temporal shifts at play when a new state is founded through a signature, which declares the freedom of the people, thereby identifying a paradoxical feedback structure, as the Declaration is at the same time a constative and a performative act:

> The "we" of the declaration speaks "in the name of the people". But this people does not exist. They do *not* exist as an entity, it does *not* exist, *before* this declaration, not *as such*. If it gives birth to itself, as free and independent subject, as possible signer, this can hold only in the act of the signature. The signature invents the signer. This signer can only authorize him- or herself to sign once he or she has come to the end [*parvenu au vout*], if one can say this, of his or her own signature, in a sort of fabulous retroactivity.   (Derrida 1986, 10)

With regard to this point, Daniel Matthews analyzes as follows:

> The sort-after [sic]⁶⁴ effect of the declaration lies in the instability, or undecidability [sic], between the performative and constative. [...] Derrida leaves us with an aporia: the representatives sign on behalf of the people but "the people" does not exist before the signature. The representative's [sic] can only be thought to represent something after the

---

62 See Deleuze 1990 [1969], 63: "The agonizing aspect of the pure event is that it is always and at the same time something which has just happened and something about to happen." Brian Massumi calls this "the virtual" and "lived paradox" (2002, 30), which for him is always both empty and 'overfull' in a way, a "crowded void" (1992, 53). As opposed to the 'Time of Aion' this would be the (mathematical, measured) 'Time of Chronos.'
63 Strangely enough, the parts most interesting for the line of argument here cannot be found in an English version of this text bearing the exact same title: "Otobiographies – The Teaching of Nietzsche and the Politics of the Proper Name" (Derrida 1985, 1–38). But, luckily, they have been translated into English and published as a stand-alone text with the title "Declarations of Independence" (Derrida 1986). See Derrida 2000 for the extended German version.
64 Matthews certainly means sought-after here, a word Derrida uses himself in his text.

> signature itself. Everything happens *post factum*. The authority of the people is conjured through a retroactive affirmation and so the people as guarantor of the constitution is caught in temporal flux. [...] [T]he people, at the moment they are supposedly present in the declaration, necessarily infer their radical absence; they are only able to persist as a spectral trace of a future affirmation. (Matthews 2013)

The 'expression of the American mind' addresses a communal subject that is "radically unstable" (Matthews 2013), and radically empty in the present moment. There is no and can never be 'the people' as a stable and present collectivity, which makes, as Matthews continues, "the meaning and effect of such a declaration [...] not closed or unified but radically and necessarily open" (Matthews 2013). The idea of the American nation, the American Dream, is thus not about a specific telos at the end of a stable, mapped out mythos (in its initial meaning as story), but about an ever-new founding of a presence that is both compressed and split into past and future; and, further, about a dynamic of communality conditioned on and only functionally thought through crystallized time. The power of this communality does not come from the (pre-)existence of a reproducible 'We' as a fixed entity, but from the fact that there is "no political 'we' that is ever present to itself, no 'people' that is without differences, omissions and elisions" (Matthews 2013). According to and/or derived from the Declaration of Independence as both performative act and medium of address, the 'We' of the American nation – as "a creation of the collective imagination" (Cullen 2003, 6)[65] – is not based on a 'We' that can simply and clearly be located, (re-)told, or represented. Rather, it is always a 'We' of a becoming community, a 'We' envisioned and strived for, even though or exactly because it might never be achievable in the sense of a final, fixed entity or end point.[66] It is a promise of a 'We' according to which a 'We' forms in the first place, a promise whose effectiveness relies on a 'We's' belief and trust in itself as futurity, grown out of the historical act of repeated definition of a new future in the present,[67] by both detaching from and pointing to the past.

---

[65] See also Bonzel 2020, 81. In her newest monograph, Katharina Bonzel seems to tackle quite similar issues as this book here does. Furthermore, she also published on the connection of the American Dream and the world of sports in film (see Bonzel 2011).
[66] In a sense, there are then only two future possibilities: the immortal continuation of the 'We' (the survival for the community), or its dissolution.
[67] Jim Cullen also addresses this aspect of the repetition of defining anew: "And it is a nation that has been re-created as a deliberate act of conscious choice every time a person has landed on these shores" (Cullen 2003, 6).

Utopia America: Fractal Unity and an Endless Process of Poetic Redescription

Both this trust and this ever-forming but never finally formed 'We' play a decisive role in Richard Rorty's understanding of the American Dream, which underlies his proposition of a politics of pragmatism in his critical analysis of the development of the American Left in the twentieth century. Quite similar to James Truslow Adams, who in *The Epic of America* speaks of the American Dream as "not a logical concept of thought" but a "religious emotion, a great act of faith" (Adams 2001 [1931], 182), Rorty understands the idea of "America as a country of promise" (Rorty 1998, 101), and as a kind of social order of possibility and recognition. For him, the ideals of the American Dream are democracy and (the possibility of) a classless society,[68] which – as partially described above – are not only born out of the country's history, but are also already existent and effective, *precisely*, but not necessarily *only* as promises (see Rorty 1998, 8). In an essay called *Truth Without Correspondence to Reality*, which precedes his seminal book *Achieving Our Country*, Rorty addresses the temporality I try to carve out here quite directly within his description of an American self-conception: "America has always been a future-oriented country, a country which delights in the fact that it invented itself in the relatively recent past" (Rorty 1999b, 24).

Rorty's statements occasionally seem to hint at or can be understood as propagating a very determined notion of community, in the sense of a rather settled entity of the American nation – especially with regard to his emphasis on the necessity of national patriotism.[69] Yet the "idea of the political that is at core an idea of political community" (Kappelhoff 2018a, v) lurking behind his request to revitalize the concept of American liberalism, is worth highlighting with regard to the political temporality and the notion of historicity at play in what I describe as the American Dream here.

For Rorty, the pivotal feature of the American project is the creation of solidarity through constant redescription – in order to increase freedom and reduce

---

[68] Rorty actually uses this Marxist formula of the classless society – for example in his essay *Back to Class Politics* – as "the goal that matters most" (Rorty 1999a, 261).
[69] Michael Liegl quite clearly maps out the ambiguities within Rorty's considerations, especially with regard to the different vectors at play when it comes to the notion of democracy, which he seemingly tends to naturalize as a representational, culturally and nationalistically charged life form of a definite (an 'achieved') American nation from time to time. While this in a way contradicts his (Deweyan) understanding of democracy as an experiment with ever self-critical potential, such contradictions should at the same time, as Liegl points out, be assessed as arising from Rorty's 'anti-theoretical coquetry' and problematic self-positioning (between philosopher and politician), which is, in turn, itself a product of rhetorical strategy in regard to inner- (or inter-)disciplinary controversies (see Liegl 2000, in German, especially 106–109).

3.2 The American Dream as Time-Image of Community-Building Historicity — 131

pain – through an overall poetization of culture and the acknowledgment of the significant creative force of forms of cultural life over any kind of given, dictating rationality or natural order:

> We need a redescription of liberalism as the hope that culture as a whole can be "poeticized" rather than as the Enlightenment hope that it can be "rationalized" or "scientized." That is, we need to substitute the hope that chances for fulfillment of idiosyncratic fantasies will be equalized for the hope that everyone will replace "passion" or fantasy with "reason." (Rorty 1989, 53)

Rorty stresses the fundamental role played by futurity in this liberal utopia, which is distinguished by the recognition of hope and belief, fantasy and imagination. Human solidarity is not seen as simply there, but "as a goal to be achieved," as something that "is not discovered by reflection but created" (Rorty 1989, xvi). This creation of solidarity is embedded in a constant process of experimental self-creation through redescription, of oneself and of unfamiliar others, who then become less alien.[70] This reduction of unfamiliarity is hence achieved by an increased sensitivity towards what is alien to us. And here, media comes into play as,

> [t]his process of coming to see other human beings as "one of us" rather than as "them" is a matter of detailed description of what unfamiliar people are like and of redescription of what we ourselves are like. This is a task not for theory but for genres such as ethnography, the journalist's report, the comic book, the docudrama, and, especially, the novel. Fiction like that of Dickens, Olive Schreiner, or Richard Wright gives us the details about kinds of suffering being endured by people to whom we had previously not attended. Fiction like that of Choderlos de Laclos, Henry James, or Nabokov gives us the details about what sorts of cruelty we ourselves are capable of, and thereby lets us redescribe ourselves. That is why the novel, the movie, and the TV program have, gradually but steadily, replaced the sermon and the treatise as the principal vehicles of moral change and progress.[71] (Rorty 1989, xvi)

---

70 With regard to such a conception of poetic selfhood, Rorty initially refers to Freud (see the second chapter of Rorty 1989, and also Malachowski 2020).

71 Even though Rorty mentions movies and TV here, he nonetheless provides a strictly linguistic perspective throughout his considerations, basically addressing solely written articulation and providing semantic analysis. Kappelhoff addresses this shortcoming and implements an expansion towards moving images via, first, a concept of expressive movement and poetics of affect (primarily based on Eisenstein, Balázs, Deleuze, and Sobchack, see Müller / Kappelhoff 2011, Greifenstein, Kappelhoff, and Scherer 2014), and second, Arendt's highlighting of the aspects of taste and subjective commonality in her reading of Kant's conception of the aesthetic judgement (see Kappelhoff 2017, 2018a). Accordingly, Grotkopp demands to introduce the corporeal, sensory and affective dimension (of media artefacts such as audiovisual images) into this discussion about the (re)constitution of a sense of community (see Grotkopp 2021, 61).

Here, Rorty not only provides a strong argument for the elementary sociopolitical role of (narrative) media, through which a community forms as distinct from other communities in the first place. He also renders the American Dream a specific and more concrete idea of political temporality, an idea in which the thinking of historical time coalesces with a specific understanding of the formation of a liberal society.

If we take Rorty's claim and his demand to "aestheticise society" (Rorty 1986, 14) seriously, there is no community that exists outside of specific narratives and mimetic expressions[72] triggering consent (or refusal) and hence leading to the production of solidarity as the maximum concordance of miscellaneous, private and eccentric self-designs. Such conception lets go of the implication of any kind of a pre-existent, suprahistorical 'We' arising from reasonable or so-called natural necessities, or from the application of predetermined norms and policies, or from historically and/or metaphysically ultimate justifications in the sense of Enlightenment rationalism. According to Rorty, a community is rather always historically contingent (see Rorty 1989, chapter 3, and Rorty 1986): never predetermined, concluded, exclusive or solitary; only existing and forming in relation to itself and in competition to other communities, on the level of descriptive expressions (through artifacts, media, etc.), which produce and address a sensibility seeking for members' agreement in view of a best possible future. A moment of maximum concordance of miscellaneous, private and eccentric self-designs, where the individual – as not just a temporally inflected, aestheticized body, but also an affected one – fits in through its sensational judgement, through complying with what Kappelhoff – by directly relating to Rorty – terms a "sense of commonality, [...] the feeling for the communal" (Kappelhoff 2018a, 30).[73]

The American political community as well as (its) history are thus to be understood as a permanent, imaginative work-in-progress, which is crucially determined by (a sense of) a contingent present, by openness and futurity, but also by its reference to a past, with the American Dream as the reflexive discursive space of becoming. Despite emphasizing trust and hope as the cohesive forces of this community, Rorty makes clear that the liberal utopia of America emerges from and invokes a history, even though this history is obviously in

---

Similar to Grotkopp, I want to pull in this dimension especially through detailed film analysis, and thus through the thinking of the images and sounds themselves (see chapter 2.2, 4, 5 and 6 of this work).

72 Mimesis understood here not as a process of reproducing a reality, but of creatively redescribing, and thus of fabricating realities and subjectivities in their emergence (see Doran 2012, 223–225).

73 See also the following pages of Kappelhoff's book, as well as Rorty 1998, 101.

large part also one of cruelty, violence and injustice. In this way, it functions at most as a reference point of comforting self-assurance, of an always more or less unstable community in the present, rather than as a template for projection of conformity, of a stabilized and confident community standing the test of time. Rorty sees this cruelty described in Nabokov and in Orwell's *Animal Farm* and *1984* for example, and claims that this kind of "sensitizing an audience to cases of cruelty and humiliation which they had not noticed" should not be understood "as a matter of stripping away appearance and revealing reality," but rather as another "redescription of what may happen or has been happening – to be compared, not with reality, but with alternative descriptions of the same events" (Rorty 1989, 173). This speaks to the sports film, and to team sports film scholarship in interesting ways. For one thing, sports films most often seem to avoid the depiction of all too explicit cruelty, or immediately 'package' it within reassuring pathos, with some sports films of the 1970s – like THE LONGEST YARD (R. Aldrich, 1974) and SLAP SHOT (G.R. Hill, 1977) – forming a noticeable exception. On the other hand, such an understanding of media realism seems to rebut a lot of the criticism of sports films that come from perspectives that apply a very narrow notion of fictionality.

The liberal utopia of America functioning at most as a reference point of comforting self-assurance rather than a template for projection of conformity and a stabilized community comprises an idea of realism which is not based on content-centered sameness, but on a temporality of change, of the possibility of 'founding/beginning anew,' making the present moment, in a way both a point of supreme, crystalline intensity and one of vacuity, of overfull duration and timelessness – both times *creating* and *absorbing* past and future. As Rorty puts it:

> A historicist and nominalist culture of the sort I envisage would settle instead [of an encompassing theoretical metavocabulary] for narratives which connect the present with the past, on the one hand, and with utopian futures, on the other. More important, it would regard the realization of utopias, and the envisaging of still further utopias, as an endless process – an endless, proliferating realization of Freedom, rather than a convergence toward an already existing Truth. (Rorty 1989, xvi)

This idea of historicity as folded time and repetition resonates quite clearly with what Adams describes in 1931 as the nation-making American Dream and the ever-ongoing struggle to save that dream, which "lies *just ahead* of us at *this present time* – not a struggle of revolutionists against the established order, but of the ordinary man to hold fast to 'life, liberty, and the pursuit of happiness' which were vouchsafed to us *in the past in vision* [...]" (Adams 2001 [1931], viii, [emphasis mine]).[74]

It is interesting to see that Adams, when employing multiple comparisons and metaphors with regard to the American Dream and its temporal disposition, talks about the connection to the past of the Old World more often than one might expect, thereby qualifying the American Dream both as an idea long predating the Declaration of Independence (which then put it into practice), and as an idea which draws its consolidating power (for the American nation) from remaining never fully realized.[75] Furthermore, Adams in this way also describes – as many others have done before him – the spatial dimensions of this open-/endlessness, resulting in the well-known mythologization of the American frontier.[76] Similar to what Rorty claims, or rather wants to see restored more than sixty years later, the basis of this temporality of endless redescription and (re-)creation that makes for American identity, of "the long-delayed but always expected something that we live for," as described by playwright Tennessee Williams (Williams 2009 [1944], 5), is "explicit allegiance, not involuntary inheritance" (Cullen 2003, 6).

In this sense, there is no (national, American) community born out of or justified by a definite history – it is rather the permanent (self-reflective, self-justifying) reformation and reaffirmation of this community – itself, in turn, comprised and part of multiple micro- and macro-communities constantly intersecting and relating, "a nation swarming with nations" (Deleuze 1998, 57) – which *makes for* history. This, via the poiesis of media forms, lets us perceive and think of history as a time-crystal, a constantly reforming and slipping present pervaded and infused by past and future, and thereby position ourselves as part of a communal subjectivity and subjective communality in the first place.[77] As "not a dream of motor cars and high wages merely, but a dream of a social order" (Adams 2001 [1931], 404), as a

---

[74] For a historical breakdown and contextualization of (Thomas Jefferson's introduction of) the expression "pursuit of happiness" in the Declaration of Independence, see Shannon 2016.
[75] See for example Adams 2001 [1931], 119, where he talks of "the new America as the child of 'Ol' Man river" and Adams 2001 [1931], 91/375.
[76] For instance, in 1774, the Royal Governor of Virginia, John Murray, the fourth Earl of Dunmore noted in a letter, that the Americans "for ever imagine the Lands further off are still better than those upon which they are already settled [...] if they attained Paradise, they would move on if they heard of a better place farther west" (Miller 1959, 77). The obviously religious aspect of this idea of endlessness, with America being equipped with divine providence for endless expansion, clearly shows here.
[77] For an inspiring attempt to cross-fertilize Deleuze and Kant in order to articulate a model of collective (human) subjectivities and social history via the former's concept of the time-crystals, see Olivier 2016.

3.2 The American Dream as Time-Image of Community-Building Historicity — 135

time-image of 'becoming-We' (as 'becoming-America'),[78] the American Dream puts forward the idea that individual existence means always both being ineluctably part of and differentiating oneself from temporary and rather precarious amalgamations of other individuals, and, at the same time, merging into and exposing oneself again as part of a communal formation. It is an idea of both history and of community as a dynamic and open system of 'fractal unity,' making clear that they cannot be understood as separated, static entities only concerned with seemingly fixed, predetermined things and events of an enclosed, unchanging past and a separated, not-yet-efficacious future.

---

[78] In his Deleuze-infused take on *An American Body|Politic*, Bernd Herzogenrath attributes Whitman's prose to the production and composition of "a paratactic 'fractal unity' [never to be reached, impossible to attain as a 'closed system', but 'to be made' in terms of an 'open system']" (Herzogenrath 2010, 195). Furthermore, he grasps the poet's 'I' as a Deleuzian multiplicity and minority, and thus as always already a 'becoming-we,' and in this case more specifically a 'becoming-America' (see Herzogenrath 2010, 194). Differing from my argument here, Herzogenrath suggests that this 'I as we' of (Whitman's) America should perhaps be seen in contrast to the 'we the people' of the Declaration of Independence though, as the latter "by dint of various embedded representations reduces the complexity of America to one homogeneous block" (Herzogenrath 2010, 194).

4 Still to Come and Having Already Happened: The Moment as Crystal

4.1 Time-Philosophical Considerations

The One Moment in Time as Time-Giving and Time-Consuming

"One moment in time, when I'm racing with destiny, then, in that one moment of time, I will feel eternity." With regard to both story and audiovisual orchestration, sports films are obsessed with that "one moment in time" that Whitney Houston sings about in her song of the same name, which became the anthem of the 1988 Summer Olympics in Seoul.[1] In one of its most famous lines, Houston addresses this moment's capacity to mark and distinguish, but at the same time to dissolve the perception of temporality. It points to the paradox of time as both primordial temporality, what Martin Heidegger qualifies as the actual time of *Dasein* which is temporal because it is temporality, and discursive time, which is always a derivative (of the prior) and is temporal because of certain concepts and techniques of temporal interpretation, such as, for example, measurement. On the one hand, and especially with regard to sports, this moment becomes significant by virtue of punctuality and its being the one distinct and decisive point in time. On the other hand, and in this distinctiveness, the moment also reveals itself as prone to infinite extension, 'de-temporalizing' time, creating a black hole that swallows it and leaves a sense of timelessness, a feeling of temporality's dissolution into forever. As the following time-philosophical considerations and my next film analysis, as well as the conclusions they suggest, will make clear, it is this temporality of the moment playing hide and seek as a time-emphasizing and time-consuming moment of (non-)presence that is central for the sports film's poetics of crystallized time, for its constitutive conflict of the American Dream, and thus for how it audiovisually reflects communality and historicity. Thereby, it also figures as a generic link between this poetics or filmic thinking and the

---

[1] Houston's song appeared on the compilation *1988 Summer Olympics Album: One Moment in Time*. Despite not being the official theme song – that was *Hand in Hand*, produced by Giorgio Moroder / Tom Whitlock and performed by South Korean band Koreana – the song became very popular worldwide, especially due to its heavy usage with regard to TV coverage of the Games. For many years afterwards, the song kept on being a popular choice especially in the production of sports video clips. The original music video is an over five minutes long compilation of found footage snippets of performing and cheering athletes in slow motion – a seemingly endless search for that one moment in time among hundreds of them.

practice of sports and (sports) film-viewing, as Murray Pomerance emphasizes: "The individual athletic moment and the viewer's personal perception of such a moment are both critical to a viewer's engagement with filmed sports action" (Pomerance 2006, 319).

In German, the term moment can be addressed with the word *Augenblick* in a visual metaphor as (the duration of) a quick glance, as the 'view of the eyes.'[2] Heidegger, in turn, uses the same notion and contrasts it with the notion of the *Gegenwärtigen*, thereby describing exactly the paradoxical tension of the moment that fuels the sports film genre and its constitutive conflict of historicity and communality, as I addressed in the previous chapter. He designates *Augenblick* as the present proper, as the present that lies within actual, primordial temporality, and that therefore cannot be grasped by means of a Now, since it provides for this Now as a temporal phenomenon in the first place, or even is this Now that provides for (present-at-hand as well as ready-to-hand) things to even be in time. In contrast, the *Gegenwärtigen* is allocated to the present improper, or 'currentness' (in opposition to something like 'occurrentness' for the *Augenblick*). While the *Gegenwärtigen* becomes significant by means of a temporal interpretation as the realization of its expiration, hence by a certain kind of retrospection or resentfulness, *Augenblick* occurs reversely: not through a movement of referring back, but through one of anticipation, coming from future proper.[3] The *Gegenwärtigen* is there to expire, the *Augenblick* caters for the

---

2 While, strictly speaking, the word does not designate a specifically short duration, it is generally understood as pointing to a rather brief time interval, even though this remains a relative dimension of course. In contrast, the term moment (Latin: momentum/momenta), as a medieval time unit in use before the introduction of the mechanical clock and the sexagesimal system, has, or once had, a quite specific length of about ninety seconds on average, since one solar hour in the cosmological system covered forty moments/momenta. This time length still appears today as a defined unit in the imperial and US customary measurement systems. In applied mechanics, the term moment defines how a physical quantity, seen from a fixed reference point, is located or arranged, thus multiplied by a distance (for example torque as a product of force and distance). The term momentum is the product of the mass and velocity of an object in Newtonian mechanics. With regard to sports, it is often used when the course of play changes in favor of a previously inferior athlete or team.

3 See Heidegger 1976 [1927], 338 (in the German original): "Die in der eigentlichen Zeitlichkeit gehaltene, mithin *eigentliche Gegenwart* nennen wir den *Augenblick*. Dieser Terminus muß im aktiven Sinne als Ekstase verstanden werden. Er meint die entschlossene, aber in der Entschlossenheit *gehaltene* Entrückung des Daseins an das, was in der Situation an besorgbaren Möglichkeiten, Umständen begegnet. Das Phänomen des Augenblicks kann grundsätzlich nicht aus dem jetzt aufgeklärt werden. Das Jetzt ist ein zeitliches Phänomen, das der Zeit als Innerzeitigkeit zugehört: das Jetzt, 'in dem' etwas entsteht, vergeht oder vorhanden ist. 'Im Augenblick' kann nichts Vorkommen, sondern als eigentliche Gegenwart

possibility to expire, and therefore in a way creates time. The sports film exploits both these dimensions for its poetics of the moment as time-giving, time-consuming, and even time-travelling.

The Decisive Moment as Climactic Peak and Sudden Change

While the original video for Houston's song, which consists of found footage clips of various Olympic ceremonies, is quite prominently concerned with a very specific, iconic and highly ritualized moment in sports culture itself: the lighting of the Olympic flame, the team sports feature film often employs the possibilities of its audio-vision to stage the moment as an instant point in time in a variety of ways. The genre-typical referencing of historic moments of the real past, often apprehended as such exactly because of their (prior) mediatization, frequently builds into an audiovisual poetics that itself draws upon emphasized instants and therefore produces the decisive moment at the center of the sports film dramaturgy. Thereby, this decisive moment most often marks or, rather, appears as an interruption, a condensation, a discharge and/or a dilatation, triggered by a more or less sudden change within a film's expressive movement – a change of color, of rhythm, of tone etc. Embedded within the flow of the moving images and sounds, such a change – signifying the moment as an emphasized point in time – can serve different kinds of dramaturgical progression and perceptual effects. It can lead to a surprise and shock – as an unexpected point in time, embodying an unforeseen interruption and/or a beginning of a new dynamic passage; or expectation – or to a sudden, but more anticipated (end) point in time, when either a condensation or a discharge takes place. In any case, the moment figures as a temporal paradox, as continuity and discontinuity, as being both discreet and unfolding, as simultaneously not yet and no longer there.

By audiovisually staging (decisive) moments, sports films often take up temporalities of instantaneity already to be found within the performances and

---

läßt er erst begegnen, was als Zuhandenes oder Vorhandenes 'in einer Zeit' sein kann. Im Unterschied vom Augenblick als eigentlicher Gegenwart nennen wir die uneigentliche das *Gegenwärtigen*. Formal verstanden ist jede Gegenwart gegenwärtigend, aber nicht jede 'augenblicklich'. Wenn wir den Ausdruck Gegenwärtigen ohne Zusatz gebrauchen, ist immer das uneigentliche, augenblicklos-unentschlossene gemeint. Das Gegenwärtigen wird erst aus der zeitlichen Interpretation des Verfallens an die besorgte 'Welt' deutlich werden, das in ihm seinen existenzialen Sinn hat. Sofern aber das uneigentliche Verstehen das Seinkönnen aus dem Besorgbaren entwirft, heißt das, es zeitigt sich aus dem Gegenwärtigen. Dagegen zeitigt sich der Augenblick umgekehrt aus der eigentlichen Zukunft."

procedures of the depicted sport itself, such as the moment a football is caught or a baseball is hit, a player tackled or an opponent punched. Often, the films highlight such decisive moments not only with the help of an orchestrated punctual emphasis provided by certain filmic techniques such as cutting, slow motion or fast forward, but also by making these moments take center stage in regard to their overall audiovisual as well as narrative dramaturgy (the latter being first and foremost the outcome of the former). In a way, these staged moments therefore become centers of gravity, around which the rest of the images and sounds are arranged or positioned. As a consequence, the dramatic structure of the decisive moment, produced by and connected to the sports scenes on screen, often also 'contaminates' the narrated action, otherwise not directly concerned with the actual athletic performance on the field. As already noted above, this goes hand in hand with the sports film's general interest in decisive events; the tendency of these movies to touch upon and epitomize an event-like spectacularity, which focuses on (and produces) what we might call occurrences of uniqueness: a remarkable game (FOR LOVE OF THE GAME, 1999), an outstanding performance of a team and/or an individual (REMEMBER THE TITANS, 2000 or JIM THORPE – ALL-AMERICAN, 1951), the injury or (upcoming) death of a player (THE STRATTON STORY, 1949 or BANG THE DRUM SLOWLY, 1973), or other tragic incidents such as the crash of a college football team's plane (WE ARE MARSHALL, 2006) or a (natural) catastrophe like Hurricane Katrina (HURRICANE SEASON, 2009).[4]

The fact that these events often originate from prior real-life predecessors underlines the kind of historical discourse from which these films emanate and the idea of historicity to which they are all too often hastily related to in critical and scholarly treatises. At the core of this idea lies an understanding of history or the historical as (a linear chain of) singular, unprecedented and therefore exceptional points in time. It is especially put forward by scholarship that is exclusively concerned with questions of subject matter and plot and that thereby remains within a perspective of replicating representation. It is this book's aim

---

4 What stands out here is that sports films of the last type, dealing with major real-life catastrophes, have become far more common after the September 11 attacks. At the same time, the biographical form of the sports film, very dominant and popular during the time of what is often referred to as the Classical Hollywood era, has made a comeback, too, even though contemporary biopics like MIRACLE (G. O'Connor, 2004), THE EXPRESS (G. Fleder, 2008), 42 (B. Helgeland, 2013) or MY ALL-AMERICAN (A. Pizzo, 2015) clearly treat the relation of individual heroism and communality (in light of a shaken and unsettled real-life communality) differently. For the analysis of JIM THORPE – ALL-AMERICAN and KNUTE ROCKNE ALL AMERICAN (L. Bacon, 1940), two other genre-defining team sports feature films of the classic biographical form, see chapter 6.

to show that sports films themselves constantly contest and complicate such an understanding. They do so by means of their poetics of affect and audiovisual discourse created by their expressive movements, one of which manifests, as one of the driving forces of the sports film genre, in the effort to repeat what can never be repeated – not merely as some kind of narrative desire, but as an aesthetic reflexiveness. This further marks these films' reference to each other as films, binding them together as a "genre-as-cycle" (Cavell 1982: 79 et seq.).[5]

Repeating Uniqueness

Repeating what can never be repeated – the sports film meets this task by not only focusing on but *creating* (decisive) instants again and again. As already indicated above, these moments appear as a result of specific audiovisual movements and therefore take different shapes and have different rhetorical purposes and narrative effects. Nonetheless, the different shaping of those specific points "where the magic happens: those decisive instants in which the world suddenly changes" (Anderson 2015),[6] generally arises from, or is embedded within two different affect-poetic strategies: one of abruptness and surprise, and one of upsurge and projection. While the former is often defined by a sudden change within the audiovisual orchestration, expressing itself as a shock-like intensity of unexpected punctuality, as a point which disrupts a line and creates a gap or a deviation in relation to its progression, the latter contrarily performs as the (expected) punctual culmination and/or release of a process of intensification, as a resulting, anticipated point *on* that line.

As such, the filmic moment can be the outcome of a continuous accumulation, a climactic peak of a preceding audiovisual movement, its culmination, escalation, or discharge; or a point of (successive) change/transition, which might introduce a new expressive movement and affective quality by still relating strongly to what directly precedes it.

---

5 See also chapter 2.2.
6 In his think piece for the New York Times, Sam Anderson contemplates the role of the moment in contemporary society and in the wake of the then starting 2016 US presidential election campaign. His conclusion, which considers labelling and remembering the moment *as* a moment the most pivotal procedure – "the declaration of the moment turns out to have been the moment itself" (Anderson 2015) – certainly speaks to the sports film and the temporality of the American Dream as described in the previous chapter.

Kairos as a Moment of Present Future

We might apprehend such an instant of condensation and transition in the sense of Kairos as the critical and opportune moment. The concept of Kairos was introduced by the ancient Greeks in opposition to the quantitative and sequential time of Chronos. Since then, it has been implemented and discussed in a variety of approaches situated in classic and modern rhetoric and Christian theology as well as the philosophy of time and the theory of history.[7] Hanno Berger develops and applies the (temporality of the) Kairos moment to film when analyzing the affect-poetic logic of movies and TV series about the American, French and Russian revolutions (see Berger 2022). While I do not want to stress a particularly close connection between revolutionary and sports films here, the time-philosophical considerations concerning the Kairos moment of revolutionary processes Berger draws on – especially with regard to Hannah Arendt, Walter Benjamin and Slavoj Žižek – are quite productive when it comes to the temporality of sports films and their audiovisual creation of 'intense' moments. Furthermore, the overarching argument about the American revolution, lacking exactly this Kairos moment, which for Berger has crucial consequences for this revolution's audiovisual representation in films, seems to speak quite heavily to the sports film's political dimension as a distinctly American/Hollywood genre – a genre that is virtually obsessed with the (re-)creation of Kairos-like instants, in conjunction with the representation of sports, but also beyond it.

Berger recognizes that thinking about Kairos is embedded within, or at least closely connected to thinking about utopia. This not only emphasizes the former's proximity to fictional and imaginative media forms, but also once again singles out the political quality of specific ideas of temporality – in this case, a certain kind of timelessness as well as a future-orientation in the form of a 'not yet' – and how these play a decisive role regarding the formation and self-conception of a community. While Arendt describes Kairos rather negatively as a condensed moment characterized by a loss of control (which has to be brought back under control for a proper revolution), Žižek sees that "magic moment of universal solidarity, when 'everything seems possible'" (Žižek 2002, 7) in the light of what he calls "the enacted utopia" (Žižek 2002, 259). Central to this kind

---

7 For a good overview beyond prosaic lexicon entries, see the essay collection Sipiora / Baumlin 2002; see also Theunissen 2000 (in German), who, with regard to the Ancient Greek poet Pindar, discusses Kairos as both a reality and a poetic principle. With regard to sports, it might not be a coincidence that the only traditionally testified cult of Kairos as the deity of the opportune moment relates to an altar located right in front of the stadium at Olympia, where the ancient Olympic Games took place (see Sauer 1894, 897).

of utopia is a certain timelessness, caused by a contraction of the temporalities of present and future.⁸ He writes:

> In a genuine revolutionary breakthrough, the utopian future is neither simply fully realized, present, nor simply evoked as a distant promise which justifies present violence – it is rather as if, in a unique suspension of temporality, in the short circuit between the present and the future, we are [...] briefly allowed to act as if the utopian future is (not yet fully here, but) already at hand, there to be seized.⁹ (Žižek 2002, 259)

Hence, the Kairos moment undermines the linear-chronological cause and effect chain, with which we usually make sense of our own and others' being in the world. As Žižek continues, the experience of hardship – an experience not only of pivotal importance for the revolutionary process, but also for this process of sense-making with regard to community building in a more general sense – is not one we have to get through in order to then afterwards achieve a different mode of being or experiential state or status (here, for example, happiness and freedom). Rather, those experiences, modes, and statuses are always already mutually mapped onto each other in the decisive moment of (revolutionary) Kairos: "In it, we are already free even as we fight for freedom; we are already happy, even as we fight for happiness, no matter how difficult the circumstances" (Žižek 2002, 259). Thus, Kairos not only invokes the moment or event as something which suddenly interrupts, shocks and "emerges seemingly out of nowhere" (Žižek 2014, 2), but also accounts for this moment's or event's future in the present: its present future, and thereby, with regard to Gilles Deleuze's conception of repetition as something that "interiorizes and thereby reverses itself" (Deleuze 2014 [1968], 2), also for its past in the present: its present past.¹⁰

---

8 For the relation of film and the notion of utopia, see for example Fitting 1993, who provides an introductory overview to Richard Dyer's article *Entertainment and Utopia* (Dyer 1977), which figures as a seminal reference point until today. For a discussion about the relation of sports or game-playing and utopia, see Suits / Hurka 2005 [1978], McLaughlin 2008 and López Frías 2016. For the relation of sports film and utopia, see Baker 2003, who also refers to Dyer. For the temporality of the utopia of the American Dream, which, as I claim, accounts for the constitutive conflict of the sports film genre and its audiovisual thinking of (American) community-building and historicity, see chapter 3.2 of this work.
9 See also Berger 2022, 145–146.
10 In *Difference and Repetition*, Deleuze refers to the specific conception of the event and its repetition in Charles Péguy's philosophy of history. The decisive twist with Péguy is, according to Deleuze, that he does not conceive of repetition – and, in a wider sense, of historical course – from an (end) point which marks and is marked by equivalence and an act of back reference. Instead, repetition is thought of the other way around, as something that one could call a 'forward recollection' with Kierkegaard: It is exactly the past event or moment, which in its uniqueness triggers its own repetition in the first place, which already contains all its

Fueled by Past and Future: The Utopian Moment

Although the sports film may not be depicting revolutions themselves, the audiovisual staging of Kairos, as both a decisive moment within its course of action and a poetic modulation of a prior historic event to which it refers, often takes center stage. By this means, sports films reference and reflect Kairos as the temporality of a present moment, which on the one hand is fueled by its past, and in that way emerges as an act of remembrance itself; and, on the other hand, driven by its future, it appears as a moment to be remembered – to be repeated with difference, as we could say with Deleuze. Thus, the moment-like event in sports films is always treated as both moment and momentum: as its own actual occurrence and as an impulse that determines its future, its difference-repetition, its remembrance. In that sense, it also relates back to its past, claiming that it is itself a difference-repetition in the present. To this effect, utopia appears not in the form of a promise into a faraway future more or less cut-off from a Now and, even more so, from a Back Then; but, rather, as a (sensually produced) idea of time, which might be well described in terms of the Future Perfect Progressive tense: it will have been happening. Perhaps more exactly, it appears in terms of the concurrence of the Present Perfect Progressive and the Future Perfect: the moment as a present event that is both happening at once and will have happened at the same time. This quite obviously also has a religious aspect to it, as this temporal structure can also be grasped as one of belief. It speaks to the topos of religiousness being omnipresent in media sports and in sports films in particular.

Žižek, in the same vein, speaks of a "unique suspension of temporality," of a state of being "in the short circuit between the present and the future" (Žižek 2002, 259 et seq.). Hence, the utopian moment is not so much understood as something (unrealistic) to strive or wish for, but as something that was and will be and that has to be actualized again and again – the "urge of the moment is the true utopia" (Žižek 2002, 5).

It is important to note that this urge, in accordance to what I have explained so far, and probably in contrast to the notion of utopia Žižek has in mind when talking about a Leninist idea of revolution, describes a double movement, which

---

possible repetitions. Deleuze puts up two examples here that Péguy mentions in *Clio. Dialogue de l'histoire et de l'âme païenne* (Péguy 1932): Monet's Water Lilies series as well as the storming of the Bastille, which he sees as actually the first Bastille day holiday. In such an understanding, the historical event or moment does not only always already refer to its future, but – by concurrently exposing itself as being itself the outcome of such a forward recollection – also to its past (see Deleuze 2014 [1968], 2/26/248–249, and also Schmidgen 2014, 16 et seq.).

marks the Kairos moment as a mode of historicity – in the sense of what we could call nostalgic futurity, or an act of remembering to be remembered: directed towards a future, but (thereby) always also shifting to a foretime, repeating the past (differently) into the future. This understanding of the moment as a crystallizing circuit of past and future, which renders the present an ultimate but never graspable presence, a present always lost, an intangible and therefore all the more desirable present, also speaks to Lessing's *Laocoon*, where Kairos is a pregnant moment of synthetization: "A moment that is chosen because it best captures a narrative trajectory and implies prior and future movement" (Pollmann 2018, 67), even though and with regard to my understanding of (filmic) images as first of all (embodied) affective movement, I would not qualify such a trajectory of expressive movement as immediately narrative.

The Pregnant and Impalpable Moment as American Dream Time

In what follows, I want to explore the sports film's audiovisual orchestration of the moment on the basis of one exemplary film. In WE ARE MARSHALL (J. 'McG' McGinty Nichol, 2006), the sports film genre's occupation with the decisive and historic moment not only experiences one of its most striking configurations, but also – not least as one of the most recent agents of the body of films taken into consideration for this work – very pointedly reflects this occupation in line with the time-philosophical considerations brought forward.[11] It thus allows us to quite easily draw conclusions regarding the American Dream as an imaginative discourse of a community-building temporality of crystallization, around which it forms in a more general sense, and which makes up the sports film genre's constitutive conflict (as developed in the previous chapters).

This section will ask: how do sports films stage (decisive) moments and how do these become perceivable as a viewer experience? Further, what does that tell us about the genre's idea of historical and political time – not only with regard to the films' storytelling and reference to real historic events, but also, and more importantly, to the form of their expressive and perceptual movement, which constitutes this storytelling and referencing, and which, as the specific processing and modulation of discursive temporality, is key to what we might call an audiovisual culture of the American Dream by way of the media of sports and film?

---

11 Another very instructive example here (yet in a completely different way) would be FOR LOVE OF THE GAME (S. Raimi, 1999), in which the moments of the baseball pitch and hit become the center of a poetics of eternal circularity of life and love.

4.2 The Moment as Tragic End Point and New Beginning: WE ARE MARSHALL

With a view to these questions, the subsequent analysis will account for both the fleshing out of the sports film's specific audiovisual thinking of crystallized or 'de-temporalized' time, which becomes describable, inter alia, as a poetics of the moment (with WE ARE MARSHALL in this chapter), of flow (with MIRACLE in the following chapter) and of endlessness as multiplicated immediacy and repetitive circularity (with KNUTE ROCKNE ALL AMERICAN and JIM THORPE – ALL-AMERICAN in the chapter thereafter);[12] as well as attempting to historicize the specific film of WE ARE MARSHALL in regard to this thinking, which is of course always modulated anew by each specific film – a fact that renders the film analyses of this study, in their small number as well as in their exhaustiveness, at the same time historically necessary (in the sense of a historical phenomenology) and speculative (in a historiographical sense). While in the first analytical chapter using the film FIELD OF DREAMS, I tried to show how the team sports film becomes (describable as) a genre by means of its permeable disposition towards film history, as a reference system of certain modes of world-building and modalities of affective experience, the analyses of this and the following chapter(s) will rather try to make palpable the more idiosyncratic aspect of the team sports film's generic capacity via the specific modes and modalities which it produces and through which it primarily produces itself. With Cavell, we might call that the 'internal law or principle' of the "genre-as-medium" (see Cavell 1982, 81). Of course, the internal principle (understood as a force of higher originality) and the external principle (addressing the capability of permeability and appropriation) never act independent from each other and can thus never be fully distinguished.

4.2 The Moment as Tragic End Point and New Beginning: WE ARE MARSHALL

WE ARE MARSHALL is a football film directed by Joseph 'McG' McGinty Nichol, which hit US theaters in December 2006.[13] The film's plot picks up with the

---

[12] There is at least one more major mode this poetics unfolds into: repetitive circularity as a problem of absolute beginning, which I touch upon briefly in chapter 6.2.
[13] The film's only theatrical release outside of the US was in Brazil a few weeks later. This is a quite unusual phenomenon in the sense that US football films are normally not very profitable outside of their domestic market, even if they happen to have an internationally known star behind or in front of the camera (as is the case with regard to REMEMBER THE TITANS, 2000 for example). The situation is different with films about those sports also popular in other countries, which is especially the case for baseball and boxing movies, the former generating quite

events around the tragic plane crash of the Southern Airways Flight 932 in November 1970, when nearly the whole Marshall University college football team – along with fans, staff and flight crew members (all in all 75 people) – were killed. After an opening prologue setting the scene, which should not be passed over but rather has to be seen as central for the film's audiovisual discourse on the moment as a tragic end point and this end point's commemorative repetition as a point of new beginning, the film dramatizes the events leading up to the tragic crash during the first ten minutes.[14]

After that, another ten minutes of screen time are spent capturing the crash (which nonetheless remains, as we will see, a kind of blank space) and its immediate aftermath: the arrival of the fire department at the sight of the crash, together with some relatives and team members not present on the flight; a mourning ceremony in the stadium; the funeral service. The remainder of the film then deals with how the University's football program nonetheless continues under the guidance of coach Jack Lengyel (Matthew McConaughey), who, besides having to build up an almost completely new team, faces the impact the disaster has on the community in the small city of Huntington, West Virginia.

McConaughey's protagonist, instead of functioning as a hero constituting a new order by virtue of his individual power and ability to lead and act in exemplary fashion, rather embodies a kind of prismatic outsider figure, through which the tragedy and conflicts of the community are neither canalized nor resolved or covered up, but to a certain extent leveled off and deflected. Much of what contributes to the development of this figure is McConaughey's specific style of method acting. While I develop my analytical arguments in what follows primarily along the first twenty minutes of WE ARE MARSHALL, these arguments could easily be further retraced throughout the rest of the film. Furthermore, with WE ARE MARSHALL as a very acute case of the team sports film's time philosophy of the moment, my analysis speaks to the genre as a (ungraspable) whole.

WE ARE MARSHALL not only refers to one of the most tragic and memorable events in US sports history, but also transforms this event into and embeds it

---

high revenue in Australia, Japan, Mexico and South Korea, the latter especially in France, Italy and the UK.
14 The real crash was caused by an erroneous approach procedure towards Tri-State Airport three miles south of Huntington, West Virginia, during which the airplane descended too much and outside of the approach corridor, and as a result collided with the tops of trees on a hillside just a little west of the runway, dipped nose-first into the ground and burst into flames. For a detailed look at what happened as well as the conclusions drawn from the crash that led to the implementation of technical improvements shortly thereafter, see the Aircraft Accident Report drafted by the National Transportation Safety Board at the time (National Transportation Safety Board 1972).

within an audiovisual poetics of the moment as a crystallizing point in time. The latter is created by and effects opposing expressive movements of anticipation and retrospection, of fluidity and abrupt interruption, of presence and absence – especially when it comes to the representation of the actual tragic moment of the plane crashing. Constituting images of shock and sorrow on the one hand, as well as of invigoration, optimism and euphoria on the other, these movements provide for the film's overall constant back and forth between a poetics of discontinuation and disintegration with its pathos of loss and grief, and one of departure and (re-)congregation with its pathos of communality and self-assuring pride and optimism. Both of these complexes of audiovisually generated expressive movement and pathos interlink and account for WE ARE MARSHALL's discourse on remembrance as a process of both obstruction and creation, and as a feeling of separation and connection, idiosyncrasy and communality.

Thereby, the film's center of gravity is the tragically charged moment in time, emphatically established and addressed during the first quarter of the film both as a sudden rupture within an affective movement of surprise and shock, in what I would like to call a moment of impact, and as a (end) point of controlled projection and repetition, forming and being formed by an affective movement of dismayed but, in a way, uplifting commemoration.

Recapitulation as Prediction

Let us have a closer look at the images and sounds introducing the film. How is the event of the plane crash as a historic national disaster initially addressed, or, to be more precise, audiovisually created as a tragic moment? Although often and for no particular reason disregarded in analyses of WE ARE MARSHALL,[15] I want to start with what can be described as the film's very beginning, its prologue (TC 00:00:29).[16] Raymond Bellour emphasizes the importance of (analyzing) the very beginning of a film when connecting Daniel Stern's concept of "vitality affects" (Stern 1985, 54) to film reception: Every time, with the first appearance of image and sound, a new world comes into being, and because the film as well as its

---

15 See for example an article by Amanda Kehrberg, in which she puts forward a very compelling argument about the contemporary US sports film and its aesthetics of spectacle having absorbed the syntax and cultural functions of the classic Hollywood musical, but totally ignores the first two minutes of WE ARE MARSHALL when she calls the first game scene "the opening" (Kehrberg 2011, 56) of the film.
16 The indicated time codes refer to the German 2007 Warner Home Video DVD, played on VLC media player for macOS X.

viewer are not yet entangled with what he calls 'narrative passion,' we are more sensitive to tonal and temporal forms, structures and intensities.[17] This perspective also connects more generally with this book's aim to grasp and reconstruct such temporal forms, structures and intensities as being at the heart of filmic perception and viewer experience, as a film's poetics of affect, reflexively actualized by means of a poiesis of film-viewing.[18]

The prologue of WE ARE MARSHALL functions as a typical introductory gesture of localization, as an act of audiovisual mapping, which quite literally brings its viewer to the site of action of the movie: the city of Huntington, West Virginia. Yet, while not showing any athletic activities at all, the prologue establishes, as I argue, a (first) audiovisual idea of the historic moment of tragedy as an incisive end point. By means of the sequence's expressive movement and cinematic metaphorizing, this end point is presented as something to be remembered, as something that, in its closure, is worthy of collective memory, and through its 're-membranceness,' opens up (to) a 'new time' and provides for futurity. In the directly following sequence, which is staged in stark contrast to the opening of the film, this futurity then turns out as game and as the spectacle of (watching) sports.

Though it is not directly shown nor explicitly addressed during this introductory sequence, the moment of the plane crash nonetheless takes center stage here already. What will be presented to us as a sudden, unforeseen but not to be seen impact and horrible shock about fifteen minutes of screen time later, takes place as a rather smooth audiovisual expressive movement: spatially fabricated as a downward movement 'from sky to earth,' the camera descends from above the city to the ground, literally flying into the fountain that was actually put up on Marshall University's Huntington campus to commemorate the tragic event.[19] Rhythmically and tonally figuring as a self-perpetuating

---

[17] See Bellour 2005, especially 51 and 76 (in German). With regard to Stern, see also Køppe et al. 2008: "The concept [of Stern] in fact covers an attempt to maintain the idea that subjectivity is constituted through vitality affects. It is the movement, dynamics, and temporal progression that imprint meaning onto the experience of a feeling, a succession of memories, or any mental process. They are the activity itself from which the type of activity is abstracted or extracted. [...] Vitality affects denote the passage of time and the way in which the single elements in a feeling process or any other mental processes are connected together" (169).
[18] See Müller / Kappelhoff 2018, 33, and Wedel 2019, 7/134.
[19] The fountain was created by sculptor Harry Bertoia and dedicated by Marshall University president John G. Barker on 12 November 1972. It received repairs and was rededicated in 2008. Each year on November 14, there is a memorial service, during which the fountain is silenced and turned off until the following spring. Its symbolic capacity with regard to what I call the temporality of remembering (society) into the future also becomes apparent when comparing how Bertoia imagined the fountain's function as to "commemorate the living –

flow coming to a stop, the images of this sequence combine with a fitting, pathos-driven voice-over: "... and in this moment, once every year, throughout the town, throughout the school – time stands still."

When looking at the sequence's narrative position and function, the opening's (and the whole film's) occupation with entangled temporalities already becomes obvious. We might call this entry a cold prolepsis: the presented world (the town, the campus with the Memorial Fountain) is set in the future of what we will later witness, but because it is positioned at the very beginning of the movie it lacks any temporal reference – the future of remembrance is set as the Now of perception, which at the same time 'predictably recapitulates' the tragic historical event to which the film refers and around which it constructs its audio-vision. The central questions that WE ARE MARSHALL evokes by making them affectively palpable are already addressed here with this opening: How does memory puncture (linear) time? How can remembrance be also prophecy and vice versa? How can a moment as a point of arrested time be both an end and a new beginning? And ultimately, how do we make sense of the past and the future as ever new arrangements of interpenetration?

A Scenic Complex of Inverted Symmetry

Let me come back to the more macrocosmic structure one more time, as the prologue is the first part of four segments into which I would like to divide the first twenty minutes of the movie. These segments, which I will now describe only briefly before coming back to every single one of them in much more detail afterwards, strongly relate to each other. They form, I argue, a complex figure of symmetries, inversions and chiasmi, especially in regard to the affect-dramaturgical course of the audiovisual expressive movement in each of the segments: from the unhindered flow of a controlled descent in the prologue, to a rhythmic splitting and splicing in the following game scene, to a dynamic of obstruction, when people try to rush to the site of the crash, to one of pathetic elevation in connection with the memorial service, with a movement of symmetry suddenly disrupted in the middle (Figure 19).

---

rather than death – on the waters of life, rising, receding, surging so as to express upward growth, immortality and eternality," and what the actual inscription on the plaque attached to the fountain says: "They shall live on in the hearts of their families and friends forever, and this memorial records their loss to the university and to the community." (See the website of Marshall University: https://www.marshall.edu/history-and-traditions/sample-page/historic-buildings-and-monuments/memorial-fountain, accessed 14 February 2020.)

150 — 4 Still to Come and Having Already Happened: The Moment as Crystal

Figure 19: A scenic complex of symmetries (WE ARE MARSHALL).

4.2 The Moment as Tragic End Point and New Beginning: WE ARE MARSHALL — 151

After the prologue has introduced us to a fluid and steady downward movement/flight, which establishes an imagery of controlled and elegiac pride, before it then quite awkwardly ends in a gesture of spatial constriction and temporal punctualization, a game scene takes up and heavily rhythmizes this motion path as a suspense structure of stretch and delay (TC 00:01:42). This time, it is framed by the temporal dramaturgy of the flight of a football during a Hail Mary pass, with the outcome literally being 'in the air' for quite some time.[20]

This following game scene, or rather its audiovisual gesture of spatial dissolution and temporal proliferation in contrast to the fluidity and clarity of the scene before, is shortly thereafter mirrored by the next but one part of the scenic complex, which depicts the immediate events after the plane crash, once again taking up an audiovisual poetics of chaotic delay to employ an audiovisual dramaturgy of a dilated shock slowly beginning to take effect (TC 00:11:28). This part could also be read as the dark, existential version of the prior game scene, implementing the defeat on the field as a 'real' loss in the filmic world. The staging of this loss couples the protagonists that were not onboard the plane and therefore survived with the film's viewer through the (reflexive) experience of a Future Perfect temporality: an arising realization of a certainty, as the growing awareness of a recognition of an event that has already happened, referred to as (the perspectivation of) the tragic event which *will have happened*. This Future Perfect manifests as a feeling of anticipating and anticipated despair.

The moment of the crash itself is depicted as a sudden interference (of, literally, image and sound) into the nothingness of a silent black screen at the end of a short that is nonetheless an important transition scene connecting the worlds of the homebound supporters and the homecoming team, as well as marking approximately the middle of this scenic complex and orchestrating its symmetry (TC 00:05:25). This is additionally emphasized by images bearing a strongly symmetrical composition themselves, especially when depicting the protagonists in the locker room, at the airport or within the plane after the game (see the middle section of Figure 1). While, at this point, the shock effect is realized first and foremost as a strongly induced feeling on the part of the

---

20 A Hail Mary pass is a play in American football mostly used at the very end of a game. It basically is an emergency solution created out of desperation, and consists of a very long forward pass of an attacking team, which is lagging behind when time is running out, or already ran out. As in American Football, the ongoing last play continues even when the game clock has expired, as is the case here in WE ARE MARSHALL. For a detailed account on the history of the Hail Mary, see the corresponding entry on Peter J. Brown's *Early Sports and Pop Culture History Blog* (Brown 2018).

film viewer, the two following scenes – of people rushing to the site of the crash and the memorial service – both in contrast rely heavily on the integration of the characters watching: diegetic spectators, affected but powerless. This integration is first and foremost achieved by means of montage, through what I will describe in more detail as spectator reverse shots later on.

The fourth segment, into which the third smoothly (and especially through the soundtrack) transitions, consists of a comparably long grief and commemoration scene (TC 00:16:27). This scene not only shows the mourning people of Huntington at a funeral ceremony, but clearly readopts the temporalities and spatial configurations of the expressive movement established during the prologue scene. Witnessing the horror of the burning airplane wreck just before, this scene picks up the expressive movement of the very first scene but reverses it. The downward movement of approximation and constriction in the prologue, with its punctual stop within the dwindling Memorial Fountain as a moment of (repeatedly) arrested but overfull time, is turned around into an upward movement, which takes us back into the stadium and on the playing field, capturing the commemoration of the catastrophe and its victims by means of an audiovisual metaphor of the game of football, specifically of a kind of kickoff as a play of 'starting anew.' In this sense, which I will address further on, one could also construe the movement of the prologue as an audiovisual metaphor of a precisely executed pass, thus anticipating (an ideal course of) the game sequence which comes right after.[21]

But back to this last segment: within the mentioned imitation of a kickoff, the arrested moment, when "time stands still," as the voice-over told us before, is not only marked or readjusted as an absolute low and a new starting point, but also as the critical point of the concurrence of halted and progressing time as the fundamental temporality (paradox) of the feeling of grief. It is expressed by exactly such a (painful) state of disunity between an impression of or a desire for arrested time on the one hand, and time that relentlessly keeps on running on the other: "Clocks ticked, but time did not pass." Here, the scenic complex of the first twenty minutes of WE ARE MARSHALL comes to a conclusion, finally completing the audiovisual exegesis of the historic tragedy as a non-linearly entangled transformation of immediate shock and grief into melancholic commemoration and remembering pride. In the center of this transformation, which rather presents itself and

---

21 In my understanding of an audiovisual metaphor, I want to follow Cornelia Müller and Hermann Kappelhoff's concept of Cinematic Metaphor, which, in its critique of cognitive theories in the field, comprehend metaphor as a performative action of meaning-making, grounded in the dynamics of a viewer's experience with a film by means of the embodiment of its expressive movement (Müller / Kappelhoff 2018).

4.2 The Moment as Tragic End Point and New Beginning: WE ARE MARSHALL — 153

hence is to be understood as an endless cycle or loop, lies a poetics of the moment as ending *and* beginning, as a point in time between recognition and speculation, shock and hope, from which we (want to) distance ourselves and at the same time hold on to. In what follows, I will retrace the expressive movement and audiovisual rhetoric, which form the core of this poetics and thus the film's cinematic thinking.

An Amalgamation of Time: A Prologue of Future Remembrance

WE ARE MARSHALL starts with the appearance of the genre's formulaic "this is a true story" opening in white letters on black. In her text on the Hollywood historical epic, Vivian Sobchack rightfully states that such narrative device like an inserted text plate or a voice-over narrator at the beginning of a film not only calls reflexive attention to a film's existence as a representation, but also indicates its capacity to render history by means of what she calls with Pierre Sorlin the historical film's "'double exposure of time, with the superimposition of symbolic time on other forms of time,'" and, with Janet Staiger, the "'history effect'" resulting thereof (Sobchack 1990, 34). I argue that this applies to the sports film, too, and that this book's aim could be understood as a specification of such temporal superimposition and history effect.

Following the text plate is a long helicopter tracking shot. It is only disrupted by two dissolving cuts, which nonetheless maintain the fluidity of the movement. After a slight acceleration in form of yet another eerie allusion towards the circumstances of the real plane crash, we fly at constant speed just above a piece of woodlands, a river and a couple of buildings that appear to be part of the industrial area of a small city in a rather rural area.[22] A slow and melancholic toned piano sequence on the soundtrack anticipates the motion of rise and descent more than once, thereby perverting the ostentation and lightheartedness of the visual movement into a more subdued, elegiac mood. A female voice-over describes what we glide along and see step by step: the city, the river running through it, then the steel mill located next to the river, and finally the school. After another cross-fade, the motion stops for a short period of time, the frame almost entirely dominated by a brick building (Figure 20).

---

[22] Throughout the history of the sports feature film, the rural, working class setting is omnipresent. Kehrberg connects it to a kind of blue-collar aesthetics, functioning "to make 'safe' the new objectification of the male form," (Kehrberg 2011, 52) at least with regard to film productions from the 1990s onwards and their connection to fashion campaigns around that time. See also Tudor 1997, 152 et seq.

Figure 20: Flying over the city.

The precedent steady camera movement is taken up again after another cross-fade, this time proceeding to the side, thereby circling around a water fountain. The voice-over continues: "In the middle of this school, there is a fountain" and the solemn pathos is intensified by strings setting in. "Each year, on the exact same day, at the exact same hour, the water to this fountain is turned off. And in this moment ..." Another cross-fade leads to the (repeated) replacement of the lateral movement by a movement into depth: A slightly accelerated tracking shot executes a falling motion into the fountain. For the first time, we hear some slight diegetic sound (of the water) in the background while listening to the continuing voice-over: "... once every year, throughout the town, throughout the school ..." The movement of the camera stops, the water stops bubbling: "... time stands still." The image fades into black, the piano sequence ends in a resolving chord (Figure 21).

Figure 21: Diving into the Memorial Fountain.

4.2 The Moment as Tragic End Point and New Beginning: WE ARE MARSHALL — 155

By directly relating space and time in this last sentence, the voice-over addresses the audiovisual composition and development of this whole sequence itself: The punctual stop as the decisive moment, of whose 'deeper' meaning with regard to the real-life event the viewer might know or sense already, but will not learn more about before another ten minutes later into the movie,[23] is produced by a movement of approximation, which goes along with a drastic narrowing of the image space. This converging constriction is quite adequately represented in the funnel-like form of the fountain, which itself, as the Memorial Fountain built and "dedicated to the memory of the plane crash victims" on Marshall's Huntington campus in 1972, already points beyond the diegetic world of WE ARE MARSHALL, and to the manifestation of a temporality of collective mourning. But, nonetheless, even if the viewer is not able to keep up with this specific historical relation through personal/collective/media memory and knowledge, the sequence shows the plane crash in 'fictional remembrance' as a smooth and light landing, or, in a spatial sense and considering the similarity between the arc of flight of the disembodied camera and the parabola of a football pass,[24] as exactly such a precisely executed pass. A pass that flies across the whole field, across the campus, across the whole city of Huntington, West Virginia, whose entire community seems to gather on this campus shortly thereafter, as a shot later in the film makes us believe. What is thereby established is an imagery of control, security and steadiness (in the sense of defined trajectory). In this way, this last sequence of the film's scenic complex of the first twenty minutes elicits a feeling of elegiac pride, thereby revealing the ambiguity of (an American way of) historical (media) remembrance, which can never rid itself of an amalgamation of a processed past, a punctual present and an anticipated future.[25]

---

[23] Most sports films, and especially those 'based on a true story,' certainly refer to something like an American (sports-cultural) memory in a similar way. Nonetheless, such a discursive sphere of knowledge has of course itself to be understood as a highly dynamic, constantly evolving and branching media construct. This calls all the more for an analysis of the specific modes of audiovisual staging and affective experience by means of which each film relates to and thereby modulates this dynamic construct.
[24] This convention of the camera as ball can of course also be identified in many other sports films. See for example the ending of JIM THORPE – ALL-AMERICAN, which I analyze in chapter 6.2.
[25] This also includes – in pointing to the steel mill and rural American – the establishment of a kind of geographical cultural elegy of 'old world' American values, pointing to an industrialized way of life that is fading out of existence by the time of this film's production at the latest. This old world, its mise en scène and motifs, are often central to older films, especially with regard to a dramaturgy of 'breaking out and making it.' See for example ALL THE RIGHT MOVES (M. Chapman, 1983).

Repetition in Reminiscence

While we encounter the timeliness of the actual moment of the crash about ten minutes later as a sudden and surprising strike, the sequence which immediately follows this prologue picks up the temporality of flow and sudden stop. It does so by taking the dilated temporality of the moment that 'lasts forever' and resituating it within a continuous rhythm of initiation and arrest.

During this sequence, which depicts the dramatic end of a football game of the 'Thundering Herd' of Marshall University, the steady motion and clear spatiality from before is fragmented and dissolved as the expressive movement evolves and builds up a cyclical tension. This movement ends in an image of disappointed relief which also triggers, or at least marks, the immediate transition from the playing field as the place of action to the 'everyday life' of the film's various protagonists introduced here: the star player (who surprisingly is a receiver and not the quarterback), the two coaches, the clearly singled out cheerleader at the sidelines and the supporters as well as the (injured) players who stayed back home. This gives the seemingly unpopulated site of the town in the prologue before even more significance as explicitly not a diegetic everyday world but rather an audiovisual chronotope of transtemporal, collective remembrance to which the then following scenes refer back.[26] With this in mind, the descent into the fountain becomes a gateway between the mythical time of communal and community-building remembrance, the determined sports or game time and the melodramatic time of the film's embodied affective movement. In the short and moment-like temporality of its depiction, the dark inside of the fountain (Figure 3) figures as the first of three prominently presented black screens, and thus as a perceptual image space that produces and interrelates these time domains with regard to the film's poetics of omission. Already referring to the plane crash, which we will (not) see shortly thereafter, this poetics grasps the moment as an overfull and at the same time empty point in time, decisive but also highly volatile.

While the screen is still black, emerging sounds of a cheering crowd blend in (TC 00:01:40). A text overlay hints at the fact that what we will soon see is a historically game: "Marshall / vs / East Carolina / November 14, 1970." The specific singularity of this temporal determination seems exemplary in regard to the prologue's addressing of a cyclical temporality of repetition. The melodrama of the action on the field is superimposed with the foreshadowing melodrama of the tragic historical event. The latter is, as I have described above, audiovisually

---

[26] For the concept of the chronotope, see Bakhtin 1981 [1975].

4.2 The Moment as Tragic End Point and New Beginning: WE ARE MARSHALL — 157

produced and addressed as a temporal-affective form of remembrance, but still not specifically contextualized. So far, its historicity stems from the affective course of the film's movement-images and this course's (verbal) reconstruction, sensually signifying the moment as a contingent point in time that only becomes graspable as a crucial instant due to the synthesis of future retrospection and past anticipation. Hence, as Deleuze reasons, not (or at least not yet) due to or as memory or reflection, but due to/as "imagination [...] as a contractile power," which forms a "synthesis of time" and in that way constitutes the "lived, or living present" (Deleuze 2014 [1968], 94). In the context of a media aesthetically and affect theoretically oriented film studies, this definition of imagination might be fruitful for further development of the notion of cinematic thinking.[27]

Now this lived, or living present, understood as the product of the embodied perception of the audio-vision's perceived affective movement, becomes especially exposed in the way that these first scenes of WE ARE MARSHALL clearly refer to the film's historical context, but do so not by explicitly mentioning this context in any way, but first and foremost by means of its audiovisual poetics

---

[27] Deleuze writes with regard to Hume: "The imagination is defined here as a contractile power: like a sensitive plate, it retains one case when the other appears. It contracts cases, elements, agitations or homogenous instants and grounds these in an internal qualitative impression endowed with a certain weight. When A appears, we expect B with a force corresponding to the qualitative impression of all the contracted ABs. This is by no means a memory, nor indeed an operation of the understanding: contraction is not a matter of reflection. Properly speaking, it forms a synthesis of time. A succession of instants does not constitute time any more than it causes it to disappear; it indicates only its constantly aborted moment of birth. Time is constituted only in the originary synthesis which operates on the repetition of instants. This synthesis contracts the successive independent instants into one another, thereby constituting the lived, or living, present. It is in this present that time is deployed. To it belongs both the past and the future: the past in so far as the preceding instants are retained in the contraction; the future because its expectation is anticipated in this same contraction. The past and the future do not designate instants distinct from a supposed present instant, but rather the dimensions of the present itself in so far as it is a contraction of instants" (Deleuze 2014 [1968], 94). This passive synthesis is not carried out by the mind, as Deleuze makes clear, and occurs prior to what he calls the "active syntheses of memory and understanding," which "are superimposed upon and supported by the passive synthesis of the imagination" (Deleuze 2014 [1968], 95). In my opinion, it is not too far-fetched to relate this passive synthesis of the imagination with what we might call cinematic thinking with regard to Deleuze's affect-centered theory of film. In such a perspective, filmic cognition – as the process through which the "past of retention" and the "immediate future of anticipation" of the passive synthesis become the "reflexive past of representation" and the "reflexive future of prediction" (Deleuze 2014 [1968], 95) of the second synthesis – would not primarily be understood as a process of recognizing given content and comprehending its narrative configuration, but as a process of the viewer embodying the affective movement of a film's audio-vision.

of the moment as crystal and thus by means of a poetology of historicity. Even if not knowing about or remembering the real-life tragedy, the viewer experiences the historical moment as a crucial point in time to be remembered, as the "repetition in reminiscence" (Deleuze 2014 [1968], 115), synthesizing past and future, grief and hope, remembrance and optimism.

This repetition in reminiscence resonates of course with the idea of play as a practiced and then punctually retrieved move in sports. WE ARE MARSHALL follows this line not only by showing a game scene, but by presenting this game scene as a movement of 'restarting,' of beginning anew, which is not only typical for most sports films' overall dramaturgy, but also the central temporality when it comes to the actual game of football, with the down – as the temporal period during which a play transpires – at its center.[28] In this way, the scene evolves as a double arc of suspense, of which the second part figures as a countdown sequence, relating to the actual countdown of the plot on the field: We see a catch resulting in a new first down for the Thundering Herd; the time is almost up, so only one more play is possible and it has to be a game-winning touchdown.

Suspense, Spectator Reverse Shots and the Decisive Last Pass

With the onset of heavy and rhythmically fast paced drum sounds, the first image after the text overlay shows a football flying through the air, followed by a quick shot, which, in its quick, lateral movement, depicts a couple of players running along the field, supposedly after the ball. The view is partly blocked by players standing at the sideline, while we see parts of the stadium stands filled with spectators in the background – already, the images establish a typical viewing-viewed situation of a sports film's game scene: We watch athletes being watched.

---

28 The attacking/offensive team respectively has a maximum of four downs (in Canadian football three) to gain at least 10 yards towards the opponent's goal line. A down starts with a snap or a kick, and ends when the ball or the player in possession of the ball is declared down (for example due to a tackle) or out, or when a team scores – hence when there is no more possibility to advance the ball further down the field. A down usually does not last for more than a few seconds. This makes football a sport whose actual playtime is stopped a lot. For temporal statistics about an average NFL football game, see for example David Biderman's breakdown of a respective study by the Wall Street Journal, which showed, among other things, that "the average amount of time the ball is in play on the field during an NFL game is about 11 minutes" (2010). It also shows how teams have the opportunity to play with and use all that 'dead' time in their favor. Not surprisingly, a study like this is almost always conducted to eventually analyze football as a heavily televised sport, filling this dead time with replays, expert statements, atmospheric shots and, obviously, commercials.

4.2 The Moment as Tragic End Point and New Beginning: WE ARE MARSHALL

After a cut back to the ball flying through the air – now clearly shown in slow motion – the film starts to introduce its protagonists by means of what I would like to call *spectator reverse shots*. What I mean by this is (close-up) shots of the often very expressive faces of characters watching and, especially in the case of WE ARE MARSHALL, also listening to the action on the field: fans, coaches, commentators, team owners, other players, etc. (Figure 22).

Figure 22: Spectator/listener reverse shots.

These shots can be described as affection-images, which are not only characterized by the "ability to affect and be affected" (Massumi 2002, 212–213), but which also, through this ability, function as a kind of relay, connecting the diegetic action on and off the field, the expressive qualities of the image space and the film viewer's perception of these in a very pointed way. By establishing a constellation in which the film viewer sees someone who sees and reacts to the game, these spectator reverse shots simultaneously prime, anticipate and absorb an emotional response created by the interaction of the affective movement of image and sound with the viewer's perception. They interrupt or suspend the flow of the audiovisual expressive movement of the athletic action – of the "movement [that] has become expressive movement" (Deleuze 2013a [1983], 87). At the same time, in their role as a "reflecting unit" (Deleuze 2013a [1983], 88), they also condense the many single shots, which present very fragmented elements of this action, thereby creating an impression of unity and joint spectatorship. Through and within this impression of unified, collective spectatorship, the film's viewer also becomes a diegetic spectator and the diegetic spectator is implicitly invoked as the viewer of a film – not in a (psychological) sense as a mimetic doubling or mirroring of human emotion, but as an interactive manufacturing of the expressive and perceptive media bodies of the viewer, the actor or actress, the filmic character and the filmic image itself.

By contrasting the action images of the game with this different type or quality of expressiveness, the spectator reverse shots also help building up the suspenseful structure and the sequence's composition of interruption and delay. They provide a counterbalance with regard to the fast cutting and pronounced (especially horizontal) movement within the frame during the rest of the shots, which destabilize space and time, creating an expression of hectic forward movement, repeatedly interrupted by means of slow motion, sudden stops of movement within the frame and/or elevated disruptions on the soundtrack, as well as a feeling of disorientation.

We see one of the cheerleaders, who we already know from her voice through the voice-over and later learn to be the receiver and soon-to-die star player Chris Griffen's fiancé Annie Cantrell (Kate Mara) – in a close-up shot, staring into the upper off, spellbound, her eyes and mouth wide open (TC 00:01:51). A similar shot follows showing assistant coach Red Dawson (Matthew Fox), who will later trade his plane seat for a car ride as a favor to a colleague and thus survive the night. The visual slow motion of these shots appears in stark contrast to the fast rolling drums on the audio track and the short length of the shots themselves. The resulting expression of stretched but simultaneously accelerated and heavily rhythmized time produces a strong tension. It briefly dissolves for the first time in the next shot, when the camera returns to the action on the field and Griffen (Wes Brown) makes the anticipated catch. The emphasized sound of the player going hard and painfully down to the ground immediately releases images of, once again, vertical and horizontal movement within the frame: the cheerleaders cheer, the coaches and players at the sideline move along the space just gained on the field by the players.

While the fast-paced editing continues – we see two teammates helping the seemingly shaken Griffin to get up again, the worried gaze of Cantrell, then for the first time a person, who is not a live spectator but radio listener to the game – a radio host explains the dramatic game situation: The Marshall team is out of time-outs, thus cannot stop the game clock, but still needs a scoring play to turn the game around. To listen to the radio host, whose face we do not see until late into the scene, provides us with an interesting *acoustic* counter-shot: We see someone hearing the game as we hear it announced and then also see the announcer, who is of course watching the game and providing a play-by-play commentary. By all means and similar to what I described before with the spectators reverse shots, short, rapid bursts of speech flow together into a continuous narration here, generating an imagined, simultaneous community of acoustic 'spectators,' which also envelopes the film viewer or listener.

4.2 The Moment as Tragic End Point and New Beginning: WE ARE MARSHALL — 161

A score board shows us that they are three points behind, with only twenty-five seconds to go: "The clock is now ticking." In the following seconds, the audio-vision settles down a bit: For the first time, there is a shot lasting longer than three seconds (head coach Rick Tolley, played by Robert Patrick, shouting at Dawson to keep Griffen in the game), followed by a pause of the drum roll on the audio track, during which more snippets of the people listening to the game at home via radio are intercut with the stadium action. A close-up of the game clock initiates the movement towards a further start – the last start of the game for the very last play.

The now fourteen seconds of narrated time displayed on the score board (the period which is completely used up before the Marshall team snaps the ball one last time) are split into seventeen single shots hereafter, with a total length of thirty seconds of narrative time. This narratological stretching of time manifests by means of an expressive movement of an unredeemed swelling, seemingly signalling an imminent outburst, but then instead leading up to another swelling. This movement of a 'feinted' instant of discharge on the level of staging is primarily produced by the soundtrack and repeated multiple times. Again and again, the audio-vision seems to condense and accelerate, then stop and dilate. The point of maximum delay is reached when a couple of strong screams – by the coaches, the spectators and finally, by the injured player Nate Ruffin, who stayed at home but will later try to lead the new team after the crash – cut through the images. These images have come to a rest through slow motion and slightly longer shots, as well as through the quietness produced by the brief suspension of the otherwise omnipresent drum roll. Then, at the very last moment possible, the ball is snapped, and the (last) play starts.

As the drums begin to roll again, the frame is filled by a great deal of especially horizontal movement: players chasing and tackling each other. The quarterback manages to escape the threatening chaos of these opposing, mobile forces and sets up a final Hail Mary pass: The camera follows the ball flying high up in the air, the huge crowd of spectators visible in the background. A clash of cymbals marks the moment when the ball leaves the quarterback's hand, while the higher-pitched drums suddenly stop. Only the base drums continue to beat, thereby creating an expression of slight acceleration and vectored tension through an increasing stroke rate. The ball is shown in the air for about six seconds and depicted in slow motion. Similar to the previous expressive movement of dilation, the audio-vision seems to irrevocably head toward the decisive point in time, which then finally occurs: The hands of two players, of the Marshall receiver and the defender of the opposing team enter the frame from below, reaching for the incoming ball – the former to catch it, the latter to prevent such a potential catch. Accompanied by another clash of cymbals, the ball touches the receiver's hands, but, unlike one and a half minutes before, it is not caught: The game is lost.

The image and motif of the football flying high through the air, which functions as a kind of parenthesis in this sequence, also similarly frames the whole movie: Its story within a story ends with the Marshall team's first win after the Southern Airways Flight 932 crash, accomplished by another last-second pass, this time leading to a touchdown (TC 01:50:22).[29] This last pass at the very end of the movie is clearly embedded within what we might call the sister scene of the scene I just described, although it differs in that not only do we see the spellbound faces of the coaches, players and spectators watching the trajectory of the ball, but also moment-like snippets of scenes we have already seen over the course of the film. This interwoven flashback sequence emphasizes the motif of the decisive (moment of the last) pass and its structuring function for the plot, and also once again stresses the sports film's typical superimposition of different domains of time and its poetics of a conciliatory confrontation of seemingly opposed vectors of temporality. This becomes even more graspable when we have a closer look at the differences of these two scenes with regard to their sound design, with the one in the end picking up the leitmotif of remembrance introduced during the film's prologue and fully executed during the commemoration scene, in contrast to the fast paced, 'forward-oriented' drum sounds just described.[30]

But let us return to the last moment of that game at the beginning of WE ARE MARSHALL, the last game before the plane crash, which we will finally witness shortly after. As the ball could not be caught, the dominant horizontal movement

---

[29] The game the film refers to was the second of the 1971 season on 25 September, the Thundering Herd's first home game. After they had suffered a clear defeat on the road against Morehead State University, the Marshall team, which for the most part was put together of sophomore players, freshmen with a special permission to play and athletes from other sports programs at Marshall University, beat the Musketeers of Xavier University 15–13. It was not until thirteen years later though, that the team had a winning season, and seventeen years later, that it won its first conference title (since 1937).

[30] For further remarks on the question of temporality and historicity in regard to the (narrative) endings of sports films, see the analyses of KNUTE ROCKNE ALL AMERICAN (L. Bacon, 1940) and JIM THORPE – ALL-AMERICAN (M. Curtiz, 1951) in chapter 6. While the staging of a football being thrown also plays a central role at the end of the latter and of many other football films (see for example also the last images of NORTH DALLAS FORTY, T. Kotcheff, 1979), the final scene of the former heavily dwells on the motif of endlessness, which is also very prominent at the end of WE ARE MARSHALL, both on the level of plot, with the fans not wanting to leave the stadium after the winning game, and on the viewer's side with a whole series of potential 'final image' sequences.

of the depicted characters transforms into a motion of emphasized verticality: The fall of the two opposing athletes in the foreground exposes the coaches, players and cheerleaders of the Marshall team at the sideline, in slow motion and right in the moment when disappointment sets in. The downward movement of the easing tension is taken up in the next slow motion shot, when we see coach Tolley's head lowering in a close-up from behind, this movement immediately countered through the opposite vertical movement beer of the cheering opponent team, which is unveiled in the same shot through a strong shift of the depth of field – the image literally contains the momentous simultaneity of victorious joy and great disenchantement. The following shots once again show the film's main protagonists watching/listening to the game. Their bodies and faces almost do not move at all, but are nonetheless gestures and postures of disappointment, in which the affective-expressive (downward) movement of the images (before) has inscribed itself (Figure 23).

Figure 23: Movements of disappointment.

The Invisible Moment of the Crash as Dissolution of Symmetry

After a sequence of post-game, everyday life scenes of those who stayed behind or had to stay at home during the game and a first (cold) introduction of future coach and the later central character Jack Lengyel (Matthew McConaughey), WE ARE MARSHALL returns to the football team starting its trip home from the away game (TC 00:07:35). The team and staff arrive at the airport, welcomed and at the same time sent off by the marching band, cheerleaders and supporters. Throughout four scenic vignettes, the film continues to draw on the melodramatic capacity of spatial separation and media (here: telephonic) connection: One of the players calls his friend in Huntington to get beer for his return home, but gets caught by the head coach; lovestruck Annie and Chris have to say goodbye for a couple of hours, given that he takes the flight, while she travels home by car; coach Dawson gives his aircraft seat to his colleague Hutch Davis at the very last minute, so that he can be home in time for his granddaughter's piano concert; Dawson then calls his neighbor to tell his wife, who happens not to be at home, that his travels will take longer – she will forget to deliver this message though.[31]

An 'impossible' exchange of glances between Annie in the car and Chris high up in the air, which is realized by means of an elaborate cross-fade, finally leads us into the airplane, where head coach Tolley walks through the center aisle. The camera follows from the front, first framing Tolley's head, then descending to depict only his moving torso and the excitedly murmuring players in the seats, before ascending again. With this movement, the chaotic crowd calms down bit by bit and aligns itself in orientation towards the coach's (as well as the camera's) body. This concludes in an image of strict group symmetry, which we already encountered shortly before, during the coach's postgame locker room speech, and with which we are generally confronted very often in most team sports films (Figure 24). With WE ARE MARSHALL being a very distinct example in this regard, one could follow these shots as one side of a poetic strategy going back and forth between creating ordered clarity and providing for this clarity's dissolution throughout the whole film.

After Tolley has sworn in the crowd once again ("We are ..." "Marshall!" "Almost home."), he sits down, becoming himself part of the symmetric, ornamental image composition. For a short moment of time, the overall stillness and clearness of the image provides for a greater presence of a visually and sonically recognizable phenomenon, already there but so far unnoticed: bad weather. We hear thunder, lightning illuminates the inside of the airplane. The captain makes an announcement, giving notice of the prompt landing. But instead of a cut (to a long shot of the airplane landing for example), the audio-vision is shattered: A sudden and hardly perceptible dissolution of the image through distortion and overexposure in combination with a very loud and blunt crack stages the actual moment of the crash as a kind of explosion or lightning strike hitting the airplane. Seven seconds of a black and silent screen follow – we have finally encountered the moment at which time stood, stands and will continue to stand still.

---

[31] A quite comparable audiovisual dramaturgy is brought about at the end of KNUTE ROCKNE ALL AMERICAN (L. Bacon, 1940), when its main protagonist dies in a plane crash. Here, the melodramatic medium is not the telephone though, but a letter, and then – again similar to WE ARE MARSHALL – the newspaper (see chapter 6.1 of this book).

4.2 The Moment as Tragic End Point and New Beginning: WE ARE MARSHALL — 165

Figure 24: Group symmetry.

Although, or maybe exactly because the actual crash is not shown and cannot really be comprehended in the sense of a movement-image, the violence of the audiovisual expression is very effective and strikes hard. The shock to the filmic image and its characters is embodied in the fright of the film's viewer. At the same time, we are transported back to the fountain of the prologue, the blackness of the image letting us travel back and forth in filmic and historical time. As described before, this is prepared and intensified through the contrast of a very clear spatial order established before, especially through the striking dominance of symmetrical image compositions up to that point.

The Slow Occurrence of a Painful Premonition

While the actual crash is staged as a sudden and surprising moment of impact, which to a certain extent denies its visibility, the realization of this impact as well as its consequences within the diegetic world are presented in what follows. First, as an audiovisual movement of delay and elongation in which we follow different peers of the team in a multi-parallel sequence of calm everyday situations shortly before the news of the crash make the rounds through all different kinds of media: a radio at a gas station, a car radio, a telephone, a TV ticker; followed, second, by an accelerating and confusing motion, when the news about the plane crash finally reaches the city and the protagonists who stayed home rush in droves to the nearby site of the catastrophe; then, third, culminating in an expression of prolonged shock, with a spectatorship-like situation at its center, during which these protagonists stand on the edge of the crater-like crash site looking down in horror at the burning remains of the plane.

In this way, this scene picks up the audiovisual movement of the prologue and the following game scene described above: the expressive course from calm clarity to overwhelming confusion now also culminates in an image of disappointment, although this disappointment has a very different quality and intensity, for both the film's protagonists and viewer. While in the game scene earlier, the audiovisual staging and rhythm fabricated a feeling of disappointment in the manner of a punctual release of tension as a rather sudden turnover of/change from a feeling of hope maintained until literally the last second, it is now the rather slow occurrence of a painful premonition, which the film's expressive movement creates. As the abrupt and violent distortion and discontinuation of the audio-vision leaves no doubt that something terrible has happened, the following scene, which can, as I would argue, also be read as a darker version of the game scene before, makes the foreshadowing of an unfulfilled hope, or the slow occurrence of a painful premonition, evident. In quite a similar way to the game scene, this scene works on a temporal de- and reconstruction, as well as on spatial disposition that then turns into a clarity (of spectatorship) and a more stringent temporality of suspense, this time, though, ending not on images of disappointment but on an intensified form of upset: shock. But let us have a closer look at the scene's actual composition, which creates this quite complex and reflexive affect dramaturgy in the first place.

From the clear break of a long standing black and silent screen, which follows the crash, the film fades to the calm night scenery of a desolate gas station (TC 00:11:28). A country song plays on the audio track, seemingly coming from a radio at the station. A car approaches from the left side of the frame, we see the moving headlights and hear the sound of the engine. A cut brings us closer to the gas station, with the attendant sitting in front of it, getting up while the car we just saw and heard enters the image and stops. It is Dawson, who leaves the car, triggering a short dialogue. The camera starts to follow him, as he walks towards a stall where the gas station attendant sells boiled peanuts. The country song is still very present, and, as a small radio can now clearly be seen sitting on the stall, has also become 'de-acousmatized': The sound has been allocated to a source visible in the image frame.[32] While Dawson grabs himself a bag of peanuts, the song is interrupted for a special announcement: A distorted voice follows a ringing noise, but because the dialogue between Dawson and the attendant about the peanuts continues, it is hard to tell what is being said at first. Then, in-between the spoken words of the two men, a short extract can clearly be heard: "Incredibly, there has been another plane crash."[33] Dawson does not react immediately, but begins to ask about the spiciness of the peanuts, before his smiling face drops and he turns around in the direction of the radio. A deep grumbling, clearly non-diegetic sound sets in, literally haunting the innocent and in that way horror genre-related scenery staged here up to that point. Facing the camera again, Dawson asks with eyes wide open in despair and a trembling voice: "What did he just say?"

What then follows are four variations of this scene, each depicting the moment when the horrible news of the crash reaches the surviving protagonists. Remarkably, they all stage everyday situations of media consumerism and communication: The group of cheerleaders also listen to the radio (announcement) in their car; Nate Ruffin and Tom Bogdan (Brian Geraghty), two injured players who stayed at home, are at the movies and watch the 1970 World War II movie KELLY'S HEROES (B.G. Hutton, 1970), when the screening is interrupted and a woman comes up on stage to deliver the bad news; the family of Marshall's sports radio commentator watches TV at home, when a teletext at the bottom of the screen announces what has happened; the owner of the city's diner, in which, among others, Dawson's wife Carole and Paul Griffen, the committed father of Chris Griffen, spend the evening, picks up the phone to receive the terrible news (Figure 25).

Strikingly, the news itself is not verbally expressed by any of the characters – the scene in the movie theater even cuts away before the woman on stage really starts to inform the audience about the incident, and we neither hear what is said on the phone in the diner, nor does this scene run long enough to provide an answer to Carole's question "What's happened?" By using the tremendous

---

[32] Michel Chion in his seminal studies on film sound introduces the acousmatic as the "sound one hears without seeing its source" (Chion 1994 [1990], 221). In my opinion, the concept becomes most interesting when 'set in motion' and used to describe certain sonic dynamics.
[33] The film refers to another crash of an aircraft carrying the college football team of Wichita State University only about seven weeks prior to the Southern Airways Flight 932 crash.

Figure 25: Media transmission of bad news.

capacity of the not so uncertain uncertainty – the film's viewer knows of course what happened, even though the scenes remain fragmented and no one in the film talks about it yet – and by combining an elliptical dramaturgy with the creation of a very present and graspable feeling of (the paradox construction of) the occurrence of a premonition in the orchestration of those vignette-like scenes here, the film creates a very suspenseful audiovisual poetics of the tragic moment as crystallizing temporality. This poetics of what I have already addressed earlier in this chapter as one of Future Perfect Progressive, makes itself tangible by means of (de-)synchronizing and interrelating different layers of temporal progressions within and beyond WE ARE MARSHALL's diegetic world, thereby splitting the historical event of the tragic plane crash into a series of decisive points within the time of the film's audiovisual dramaturgy.

The first of these four decisive points is the moment of repeated remembrance at the end of the prologue, as the end point of a downward movement into the Memorial fountain, which functions as both a gesture of proclamation and of retrospection with regard to the tragic event at its historical and narrative core. It addresses the future commemoration of the plane crash, while at the same time anticipates the crash as an event still to come – not only through symbolic and linguistic referencing, but as a concrete, audiovisually produced affective movement. The second decisive point that follows is the moment of the missed catch, which marks not only the end of the last game before the crash and therefore connects the historical and the filmic time with that of sports, but of an audiovisual structure of suspense, that relies, as I described above, on the integration of the film's viewer and the diegetic spectators through what I call *spectator reverse shots*. At its end, after the game is decided, this structure leads to an image of disappointment. The third decisive point is the actual moment of impact, the moment the plane crashes. It is staged as a sudden breakdown of the image and the irruption of a then long held black screen. What was shown as a slow and steady movement from a controlled clearness and overview to the black 'nothingness' inside the fountain and the 'moment of silence' of the stoppage of its water on the anniversary during the prologue is now condensed and staged as an abrupt dissolution and strike. Similar to how the prologue and the post-game/crash sequence correspond on the level of their expressive movement, the sequence which follows the crash, and which also stages a decisive point in time – the fourth one, which I would call the moment of recognition – seems to connect with the game scene.

The Horror of the Delayed Moment of Recognition

After the news has hit the city, the camera follows the two players Ruffin and Bogdan, who could not play and instead stayed at home and went to the movies. After they have left the theater, a close-up shot frames the two young men as they watch fire trucks rapidly passing by on the main street with sirens blaring (TC 00:13:00). Ruffin stops a pickup truck and they hop on. The camera follows the car for a short moment, then frames freshman player Reggie Oliver watching it while holding the requested box of beer on his shoulder.

A cut to a long shot of a piece of woodlands – is it the one we flew over during the prologue? – takes us to the site of the incident. The image space is dominated by darkness, only the red sirens of the ambulance and fire trucks slightly illuminate the scenery, while on the right side of the image a group of trees in front of what seems to be the glow of a fire is recognizable. The expressive mode now changes dramatically, sharply contrasting the calm mood and the orderly scenery from before. As Ruffin and Bogdan try to make their way through the crowd of people who also rush to where the plane supposedly crashed, and past the firemen who try to stop them, the two execute a quite similar obstacle course as the players on the field. A frantic and close to the action hand camera follows them on their way to the site of the crash. The dark mise en scène and the many uncontrolled and arhythmic swish pans create an image of confusion, which is additionally enhanced by lots of lateral movements (of people) within the frame and the babble of screaming voices on the audio track. More than once, Ruffin and Bogdan manage to pass firemen and police officers trying to stop them from making their way to the site of the crash. In this way, and even though it lacks the rather strict tonal rhythm, the sequence relates itself to the expressive movement of the game scene at the beginning of the film. This becomes even more evident when this movement of confusion and interruption is slowed down for the first time as the two young men, together with a couple of other people, finally arrive at the burning remains of the plane. In a relatively long close-up shot from below, we see them looking down in shock, the flickering glow of the flames being mirrored on their faces. An upward moving camera reveals what the two young men see in a reverse shot: the burning remains of an airplane at the bottom of a wooded hillside (Figure 26).

Figure 26: The horror of being spectator.

The alternation between the shots of the faces of people arriving at the scene of the crash, which clearly echo the spectator reverse shots from the game scene before (it is also the same people), and ongoing segments of hectic movement and spatial dissolution, with people rushing down the embankment and 'chaotic' depictions of the conflagration, reinforces not only the highly rhythmized Go-Stop-Go movement we have already encountered during the game scene before, but also sets up a quite familiar spatial configuration of the mise en scène:

4.2 The Moment as Tragic End Point and New Beginning: WE ARE MARSHALL — 171

a kind of a (stadium) bowl, with viewers on the perimeter watching the events down 'on the field.' By means of a relay of gazes, which connects the community of survivors to the burning plane and the firemen trying to fight the flames, the scene develops further along this spatial configuration.

The scene continues to exploit its poetics of a somewhat confirmed, but still occuring premonition by further delaying the suturing of the rupture between the knowledge of the film's characters and the knowledge of the film's viewer, between plot/diegetic dialogue and the (perceived) expressive quality of its audiovisual movement: Ruffin comes up to one of the firemen, boisterously asking him to tell him the name of the airline in order to find out if it is the plane with his teammates on board that crashed here. After he gets the answer that such an immediate identification is not possible anymore because of the high degree of destruction, the camera rushes up the hill again and stops to frame the arriving Paul Griffen and Carole Dawson, the wife of assistant coach Red Dawson, who still thinks that her husband also took the plane to get home. Griffen screams desperately: "This our boys' plane? This our boys' plane?" The menacing horns and strings on the soundtrack, which started right when we arrived at the crash site and which accompanied the hectic images in the manner of a slow swelling, are very present now.

Then, even though we remain at the crash site, the scene undergoes a clear change in terms of its audio-vision. With a cut to a medium close up and rear view shot of one of the firefighters standing next to the burning wreck, the ambient noises (the clutter of screams, the thunderous sound of the fire) almost completely fade out. So do the dramatic horns and strings, which are replaced by a solo piano and a female voice singing a gentle and sad melody. This 'angelic singing' immediately coalesces with the reduced speed of image movement, which is almost simultaneously initiated and will go on for a little more than a minute of screen time. The moment of recognition, the decisive point which will finally suture the rupture between WE ARE MARSHALL's expressive movement of shattered safety and order on the one hand, and its audiovisual suspense structure as a poetics of occurring certainty and *re*assurance on the other, has finally come.[34] But its eventuation is once more delayed, or rather extended, through the deployment of an aesthetics of excessive slow motion, and of masking: A fireman, looking down, seems to have picked up something, which we as viewers do not see.

---

[34] For suspense as a mode of affectivity with regard to the poetics of New Hollywood, see Lehmann 2019.

He then looks up and turns his head, exposing his shocked face to the camera and, as the next shot discloses, to his nearby colleague. This relay of gazes, which started with Griffen screaming at Ruffin positioned below him, now finds its way back up the hill, triggered by the found object remaining unknown to the viewer. The fireman walks up to his colleague and shows him what he has found but still remains concealed by the characters' bodies and the film frame. They both look down, then at each other. A transfer takes place, not only of the found object, but of a (facial) expression of sad realization. Dismayed, they both look back over their shoulders, up to the people waiting on the edge of the slope. The older one then starts walking up the hill, up to Dawson and Griffen, in a shot reverse shot sequence.

Hence, the sad news, the final confirmation that it is the plane of the Marshall team that crashed here, is delivered twice, through a proper chain of expressive faces/affection-images of sad realization, consternation and shock, as well as through the character movement of the two firemen delivering the found object that continues to remain hidden to the viewer until almost the very end of this scene (Figure 27). Quite similar to the spectator reverse shots during the game scene before, these affection-images function as both an integral part of the scene's expressive movement and as points of rupture to that movement. As such, they relate the perception of the diegetic spectators and of the sports film's viewer within the spectatorial arrangement of the film's arena-like mise en scène, thereby not only reflecting this specific configuration on a representational level, but creating it as a doubled viewing experience in the first place.

Figure 27: Affection-Images of sad realization.

4.2 The Moment as Tragic End Point and New Beginning: WE ARE MARSHALL — 173

Using this established configuration to further dramatize the moment of *reassurance*, the second walk up to Dawson and Griffen is staged as a very focused and stretched final delay. Completely shown in slow motion, the roundabout twelve steps of the fireman take up about twenty-five seconds of screen time – one is able to count those steps quite easily due to the fact that they are tonally emphasized. The continuing extra-diegetic, female singing is blended with only a few and very isolated noises, above all those clearly highlighted footsteps, and the flickering of the flames of the burning wreck and the trees around it. The speed of this last audio track seems to be slowed down, too, creating a couple of dramatic swoosh sounds, which often coincide with heavy panning of the camera.

After another exchange of consternated gazes between the fireman, Griffen and Dawson, the sad message is 'finally delivered' in form of the burned Marshall playbook – probably one of the most important artifacts with regard to a football team.[35] We were already made familiar with this playbook, albeit seemingly incidentally, during the scene before in the plane (Figure 28). Together with the memorial fountain and the flying football, it aligns into a triad of highly charged symbolic objects, which are not only shown here as representations connecting the world of sports with the world outside of sports, as well as the filmic world of WE ARE MARSHALL with the world of a historical past, but which are (re-)created by the described expressive movement of the film as cinematic objects of temporal mediation. These objects are able or make it possible to 'travel' in time: to stretch and to condense, as well as to connect and interrelate different layers of time. And this not only on the level of narrative and narrated time, but also on a reflexive level of the temporality of this very expressive movement itself, and of the viewer's experience when perceptually retracing it. One could even think about including the camera itself into this group of cinematic objects as time machines, especially with regard to the prologue, in which it becomes quite graspable as an object-like presence, (p)reenacting the flight of the ball or even the fall/crash of the airplane. More generally, sports films are full of such objects, which, when we look more closely at how they are actually staged, become often more than just represented things of symbolic capacity.

---

35 The playbook is a team-specific document, which not only includes notes and drawings of all the different moves, routes and coverages to execute, but which in addition might deal with a lot more information (for example team policies or stats), as Johnson 2019 shows.

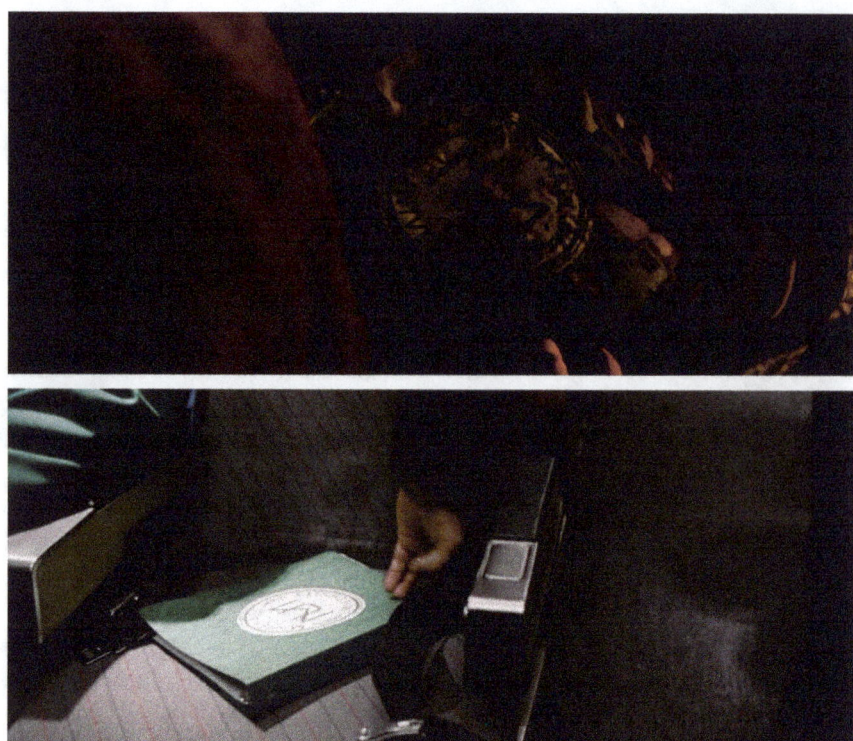

Figure 28: A cinematic object of temporal mediation.

Historical Experience in a Hall of Mirrors of Affection-Images

The film's audiovisual processing of the "worst sports related air tragedy in U. S. history" (Wilson 2006) during its first twenty minutes as an event of crystallized time, which audiovisually takes shape as always both the occurrence of something that is about to or will happen, and the occurrence of something that has happened already, then slowly merges into the last part of the symmetrically arranged scenic complex, which I described at the beginning of this chapter, and which evolves around the tragic moment of the plane crash. Especially reinforced by the audio track, on which a violin takes on the sad melody of the singing from before, the audio-vision smoothly merges from Griffen's dismayed gaze into the fire of the burning wreck at the site of the crash to a couple of scenic vignettes in a church, at the Dawsons' house, and in a dorm room (TC 00:16:28). They then further lead to a climactic scene of commemoration in the stadium and a finally conclusive scene at the cemetery. While, on the one hand, the affection-image of shock and grief starts to get further multiplied in the many faces of the town's community, it is on the other hand the melodramatic timing that strikes one more time.

It arises, first, out of a certain "knowledge *discrepancy*" as well as a (seemingly) "temporal *irreversibility*" (Gaines 2018, 325) on a narrative level, thereby dialectically conflating a 'too late' and a 'too early': Freshman player Reggie Oliver sits down with the box of beer that will never be drunk by his teammates who ordered it in the first place; Carol has been crying too soon in sorrow of her husband, who, without her knowing, did not take the plane and now, surprisingly for her, arrives at home late, but alive. And second, out of an audiovisual dramaturgy which significantly makes the experience of grief and remembrance palpable as an interplay of permeable media temporalities, and which again and again connects individual destiny with the experience of a sense of community. This "feeling for the history of the community" (Kappelhoff 2018a, 280), emerging from the perceived expressive movement of WE ARE MARSHALL and extending beyond the film's diegetic world, is additionally made explicit here by means of the interweaving of found footage images and sounds into the audiovisual orchestration.

Condensed into not even ninety seconds of screen time, and after another completely black screen – the third after the camera's flight into the fountain at the end of the prologue and the long break after the plane was struck, and again one which rather functions as an integral part of the scene rather than an interruption or a device of division – WE ARE MARSHALL creates an audiovisual space of experience by means of which the image of shock-induced paralysis and pain from before is mobilized again and transforms into one of joint commemoration and grief. It connects the perception of the 'survivors' (Dawson, Oliver, as well as the granddaughter of Davis, the man to whom Dawson gave his seat), which is itself on display as image perception, with the historical time of the public media perception of the tragedy: We see anchor John Chancellor reporting on the plane crash in a snippet of *NBC Nightly News*, then Dawson looking at a newspaper article which shows a picture of him as one of the passengers of the flight and proclaims him presumably dead. After another found footage snippet, which shows the removal of a dead body at the real site of the crash, the sequence jumps to Oliver sitting in a dorm room with the box of beer. Then, it once more jumps back to the news snippet showing an official giving a statement about the "tragedy that is beyond all comprehension." By means of a series of crossfaded close-ups of faces, which appear as a kind of hall of mirrors of affection-images, this rigorous interweaving then culminates in a gesture of blending together the living and the dead of the film's diegetic world, as well as the media expression and perception of past and present film/TV viewing constituting this world in the first place (Figure 29).

Figure 29: Images of images as historical experience.

WE ARE MARSHALL hereby addresses a feeling of grief that transcends any clear distinction between the historical event and its media representation, between individual and collective destiny, between a bygone experience and its recollection, and creates an image space through which a national community of mourners addresses itself and forms in the first place. Dawson as film character and newspaper image, the appalled Oliver, the interviewee in the NBC snippet grasping for words, a picture of Davis on the piano his granddaughter now seemingly plays along the film's soundtrack, the experience of film-viewing itself – all this becomes perceptible as part of a "poiesis of film-viewing" (Müller / Kappelhoff 2018, 36), which "addresses an act of creative production that is to be located in the media consumption itself" (Müller / Kappelhoff 2018, 36). And that, as this scene makes very evident, transforms and (re-)creates different materials and modes of such media consumption as cinematic movement-images, enabling WE ARE MARSHALL to reflexively produce an ever-new image space of historical experience, and a world always already consisting of images of images as acts of creation.[36]

Commemoration as a Movement of Inversion

The staging of the historic tragedy of the plane crash as an event of past, present and future via a twofold loosing of clear order and rhythm – from the consistent flow of the prologue to the chaos on the playing field, as well as from the post-game clearness and symmetry to the uncontrolled havoc at the crash site – finally ends with a commemoration scene in the stadium and at the cemetery (TC 00:18:41). The act of remembrance, addressed as a repeated moment in time that transcends time at the beginning of the film ("… and in this moment, once every year, time stands still"), is now executed, once again and in reverse: With regard to the audiovisual expressive movement presented before, and especially in respect of the distinct falling motion of the prologue, which now in a sense finds its symmetrical complement, WE ARE MARSHALL retrieves an image of controlled order again.[37] By readopting the temporality and spatial configuration established during the prologue, and in this way reacting to the poetics of

---

[36] The following gives further contextualization of Kappelhoff's approach, towards which this study is strongly oriented: "[T]he powers of affection in film images can neither be traced back to the event represented nor to a power of the images themselves. The affective intertwining of the spectator in the world represented cannot be detached from the unfolding of the structures of representation staged in the media. Referring to the real persons, places, events, and documents […] does not verify or 'authenticate' the representation of genre films. It is quite the opposite: the genre itself becomes the medium of an affect event that branches out dynamically in the film images, with which the film material becomes the a priori object of a feeling for the history of the community. Only in the restaging of the genre does it become a historical document in this sense. Historicity is itself still an effect, produced by the media structures and staging strategies in which films relate to 'a past event as history.' In historical film material, the events of the past are not present for us by themselves; but a possibility is retained for us to allow the sense world of a different audience to become present in our own aesthetic sensations in the act of viewing films" (Kappelhoff 2018a, 280).
[37] For an overview of the complete symmetrical construction of WE ARE MARSHALL's first twenty minutes, see again Figure 19 on page 150.

suspenseful masking, non-visibility and circling immobilization in which the viewer took part just before (the black screen, the hiding of the playbook, the series of affection-images create a tactile rather than an action space etc.), this scene here not only shows mourning people at a memorial ceremony, but remobilizes the moment of tragic epiphany as the starting point of an uplifting movement. The feelings of shock and grief, realized as the dissolution and shattering of a clear image space, transform into one of remembrance as the retrieval/re-beginning of order and safety (in motion).

Already during the last, sophisticated mirror shot of the just described transition sequence, blending Dawson and the picture of Davis into each other (see the last two screenshots of Figure 11), solemn horns set in on the audio track. We enter the stadium by means of a medium shot of a boy, who was introduced to us as the son of the radio commentator we saw and heard during the game scene before and presumably also died in the plane crash. Sitting in the shade of one of the tunnels leading to the stadium stands, the boy holds a pocket radio in his hands and seemingly listens to what we also hear on the audio track: probably a recording of a priest's speech on the occasion of the actual ceremony.[38] "No one of us will ever enter this stadium without thoughts of them. And so, our Lord, grant them eternal rest and peace, which enables them at this very moment to look upon us here, and smile, and be with us. This is our faith, this is our hope. Amen." While these words once again not only address a community of the living and the dead, but emphasize the conditionality of the idea of the moment as a present point in time and that of eternity making for the forming and stability of this community, WE ARE MARSHALL returns to the football field, depicting the mass of mourning athletes and spectators, its images expressing a strong symmetrical order again (Figure 30).

Angelo Bartlett Giamatti, former president of Yale University and the National League, has described this (imagined) community of grief that forms around the moment as temporal crystal in sports:

> Very soon the crowd is no crowd at all but a community, a small town of people sharing neither work nor pain nor deprivation nor anger but the common experience of being released to enjoy the moment, even those moments of intense disappointment or defeat,

---

38 As the film's credits only provide sources in form of the institutions from which material was acquired, it remains unclear what kind of specific recording can be heard here. The assumption that sonic found footage might be involved stems from how the film really accumulates historical material more generally at this point and how this speech snippet is actually staged here, because when shortly after we still hear the voice and even see a priest in the background, the place in front of the microphone from which one would suspect such a speech to be given, remains unoccupied.

Figure 30: Mourning athletes and spectators.

> moments made better, after all, precisely because our fan is part of a large family of those similarly affected, part of a city of grievers.
> (Giamatti 1989, 32)

Especially with regard to WE ARE MARSHALL and its time of production, one cataclysmic event comes of course immediately to mind here and basically pervades the whole film: 9/11.

Reestablished by means of a public ritual, the described order and the following expressive movement at the same time strongly throw the film viewer back upon herself. This is not so much because of the depiction of a memorial service, but through a 'rehearsed' affective movement as cinematic experience, oscillating between the private and public acts of mourning.

For a short time, the film picks up the distinctly lateral movement from the game scene at the beginning: Striding towards the center of the field, Nate Ruffin passes his remaining teammates and coach Dawson, thereby creating another symmetrical formation for a quick moment. This lateral movement, as well as the priest's words, then end with the placement of the football on a kicking tee in the middle of the field, presented in a close-up shot. From this in a spatial and quite literal sense lowest mark of the film's diegetic world, which at the same time represents the symbolic center of the athletic world within it, the camera rises high up into the air, inverting the downward movement from the prologue and reclaiming a clear overview of the mourners in the stadium and then, by means of a second upward movement, of the mourners at the funeral of Chris Griffen (Figure 31).[39]

---

39 The orchestrated correlation of the playing field and the graveyard is of course not at all innocent. While it is common that US sports stadiums and facilities honor the dead (their heroes of the past) with the help of a variety of plaques, inscriptions, sculptures etc., some of them are more or

180 —— 4 Still to Come and Having Already Happened: The Moment as Crystal

Figure 31: A community of grievers.

This upward movement is then repeated two more times on a micro level, as the camera pans along the heavily crying Annie and the still consternated Nate

---

less actual graveyards: The college football team of the Clemson Tigers symbolically buries its ranked opponents after on the road wins at the entrance of their practice field (see https://clemson tigers.com/the-graveyard/, accessed 14 February 2020), while some teams have actually buried deceased mascot animals, the most prominent example being the Bulldogs of the University of Georgia (see https://en.wikipedia.org/wiki/Uga_(mascot), accessed 14 February 2020). Another cemetery can be found next to the practice fields of the Florida State football team. Here, patches of grass from other stadiums, which were collected after surprise wins or successful bowl and championship games, are buried (see Bishop 2014). A sports film in which the site of a cemetery plays a very crucial role, is REMEMBER THE TITANS (B. Yakin, 2000). The film is not only framed by a scene which depicts a group of players and coaches attending a funeral, but also includes that famous scene in which Coach Boone (Denzel Washington) forces his team, which is heavily affected by interracial conflicts, to go for an early morning run to the Gettysburg cemetery, where he then delivers a speech. The film is another impressive example of the sports film's occupation with a poetics and politics of future remembrance and remembering futurity.

4.2 The Moment as Tragic End Point and New Beginning: WE ARE MARSHALL

from waist to face. The voice over from the prologue – it is Annie's now – resumes, and as before, the expressive movement seems to directly go along with it: "Clocks ticked, but time did not pass" is followed by a series of images with very little movement, which, in combination with Annie's voice setting in again and again and also the gloomy singing from before returning on the audio track, create a rhythm and mood of sad monotony, of circular or even frozen time. Nonetheless, and even though the figurative spoken words invoke rather apocalyptic images,[40] the staging leaves not much doubt that this is not the end or a moment of stoppage of any kind. It is rather a turnaround, a change of vectors, a restart: from falling into the darkness deep inside the memorial fountain to elevating high up into the air, with the center of the football field as point of departure.

This inversion of vertical movement is addressed once again in the second to last shot during the funeral, which distinctively plays with it: We see a detail of the coffin, along which – similar to the two micro-movements before – the camera seemingly pans upwards. As soon as the background becomes visible, this turns out to be an optical illusion though, as it is not the camera but the coffin that is moving downwards into the grave. Exposing its own relativity, this movement is then immediately absorbed into the faces of Griffen's fiancé and his dad, who show quite different reactions (Figure 32): the former lowering her head and bursting into tears, the latter immediately turning around with serious demeanor and leaving the scene of action, as if wanting to prevent any kind of emotional duration – only to then, after another black screen, seemingly find it amidst the fire of the furnaces in the steel plant where he works. This fire of course takes us immediately back to the burning plane wreck from before, but at the same time leads us into the next part of the movie depicting the slow and tough process of reestablishing a new team, as well as a new community of remembrance.

In summary: Realized by means of a poetics of the moment as a single, but ultimately unavailable, inaccessible, or maybe even nonexistent point in time, WE ARE MARSHALL, in these first twenty minutes, presents the historical event of the tragic plane crash as an event of crystallized time, which audiovisually takes shape as both the occurrence of something that is about to or will happen, and the occurrence of something that has happened already. The four sequences described here in detail thereby not only form a symmetrical figure with regard to the form of their audiovisual movement, but in their interplay become a kind of a crystal-image themselves. As "the indivisible unity of the virtual image and the actual image," this crystal-image not only "fuses the pastness of the recorded event with

---

40 "Sun rose, and the sun set, but the shadows remained. When once there was sound, now there was silence. What once was whole, now was shattered."

Figure 32: Differences in movement.

the presentness of its viewing," but also "splits the present into [at least] two heterogeneous directions, 'one of which is launched towards the future while the other falls into the past'" (Totaro 1999, citing Deleuze 2013b [1985], 84). This idea of a splitting of the present into vectors of past and future, or – thought of in the other (constructivist) way – of the condensation of past and future as the present moment also speaks to, as I argue, a specific way of thinking history, which I address in chapter 3.2 as the audiovisual discourse of historicity of the American Dream, along which the sports film evolves and can be grasped as a genre. And which, as I further argue by means of this film analysis here and the ones in the next chapters, makes up the core of the genre of the (team) sports film.

It is in this sense that we can understand sports movies as 'historicity films,' making history palpable as 'crystal-imaging,' as audiovisually and affectively producing the tension between selective presentness, recurrent pastness and always already effective futurity. As WE ARE MARSHALL very pointedly shows, this tension translates into an audiovisual discourse on commemoration as a movement of temporal superimposition and inversion.

5 Dissolutions of/in Time and Images of Communization: Flow in MIRACLE

5.1 The Montage Sequence as Standard Form and the Flow Experience

The film THE PROGRAM (D.S. Ward, 1993) unfolds during a fictitious college football team's season; chronicling the destinies of the players, who – after a good half an hour into the film – get together the night before the season kick-off to assure each other of their love of the game. Joe Kane (Craig Sheffer), the promising, gutsy and yet secretly self-doubting quarterback of the team of coach Sam Winters (James Caan), which is under a lot of pressure after two athletically disappointing years, points out the following: "The great thing about football is that you can lose yourself in it. There is no time to think or to worry, you just move and react. Hell, everything else fades away," (TC 00:36:34).[1]

While this statement can be read psychologically with regard to the character and within the context of the genre-typical topos of (overcoming) class affiliation, which the film points out again and again, it also invokes the concept of flow experience put forward and also discussed in the context of sports by psychologist Mihály Csíkszentmihályi. Csíkszentmihályi, who subsequently reevaluated and reread the concept of flow with several co-authors in his decade-long work and also discussed it in the context of sports (Jackson / Csíkszentmihályi 1999), stresses flow as a "state in which people are so involved in an activity that nothing else seems to matter" (Csíkszentmihályi 2008, 4). It is the basis of an "optimal experience" (Csíkszentmihályi 2008, 3), which is characterized by a feeling of involvement and control and can be reached through consciously increased awareness. While Csíkszentmihályi is invested in an anthropological and psychological understanding of experience as (the succession of) willfully controllable and changeable "states," I intend to rather read and apply the phenomenon of flow in the sense of a media aesthetic (film) experience in what follows. Here, emotion is understood as *medial* emotion occurring as the embodied implementation of (filmic) expressivity and less as an effect of intentionality and cognitive understanding, with perceptual structures and affective dynamics becoming the center of interest.[2]

---

[1] The given timecode refers to the American DVD edition of Buena Vista Home Entertainment from 2002, played on VLC Player for macOS X.
[2] See Bakels / Kappelhoff 2011 (in German) and Bakels / Greifenstein / Kappelhoff 2023 (in preparation, in German), who develop such an understanding as well as the methodology

In this reading, it will not only be possible to relate the activities of doing sports and viewing film to one another, but also to further understand and historicize the sports film as genre, via another facet of its poetics of historicity.[3] The analytical focus of this chapter as such is a standard form of the sports film's audiovisual orchestration: the montage sequence, in English literature often referred to as just *montage*. It is, first and foremost, defined by a high number of cuts and the rapid succession of fragmentary shots, leading it to serve as a device of condensation of (narrated) time and (action) space in support of narrative economy. Here, I would like to focus on the montage sequence's expressive movement and perceptual form and dynamics. In this way, the montage sequence should be understood – next to its function to perpetuate the plot and to provide for a denser mediation of information – as the culmination of an audiovisual dramaturgy typical for the sports film and as an integral part of the spectacle of audiovisual media sports in a broader sense.[4]

"Even Rocky Had a Montage"

By means of a media reflexive gesture within the last third of its runtime, the satirical puppet film TEAM AMERICA: WORLD POLICE (T. Parker, 2004) shows just how much the form of the montage sequence is intertwined with the genre of the sports film. When preparing for his mission to infiltrate Kim Jong-il's palace and free the members of the title giving paramilitary team in order to prevent the destructive plans of the villain, the movie's hero Gary Johnston is told he needs to become a "complete soldier in very little time" (TC 01:07:39).[5] When Johnston asks about how this challenge is to be mastered, the film answers via a montage that spotlights Johnston doing different physical activities, such as running on a treadmill, doing a karate class and weightlifting. These activities

---

interrelated with it along (the history of) the notion of *expressive movement* and its role with regard to early and modern film theory.

3 See chapters 2.2 and 2.3, in which I discuss to what extent the US (team) sports film can be understood as genre precisely by means of its historicity as the deep temporality of a poiesis of film-viewing.

4 One especially thinks of the form of (TV or online) game recaps in sports journalism. Here, a very telling example for how summarizing montage sequences come into focus not so much because of their information content but because of their audiovisual expressivity would be the game recap and Top 10 videos produced by nba.com and starring Beau Estes as narrator, with Estes' pronunciation and rhythm of speech taking center stage.

5 The given timecode refers to the American DVD-edition of Buena Vista Home Entertainment from 2002, played on VLC Player for macOS X.

are highlighted through short excerpts in rapid succession. In the manner of a musical,⁶ these excerpts are accompanied by a new wave song, whose lyrics reflexively address what is shown as film specific or, rather, as a problem of time that can (only) be resolved by filmic means, including a direct reference to one of the most famous figures in sports film history: Rocky.⁷

The lyrics appear to be some sort of instruction for the making of a (sports film) montage sequence. While ostensibly providing for narratological advice, the performed text also makes the blurring of the boundaries between the filmic images' production, their reception and the world of action they represented a subject of discussion: "The hours approaching to give it your best / You've got to reach your prime / That's when you need to put yourself to the test / And show us a passage of time / We're gonna need a montage / Uh, it takes a montage." The scarcity of time and the ideal of giving one's best are addressed as the hero's purpose for action here. At the same time, the sung words address this hero as a simultaneously sportive competitor ('against' time) and creator of his own (filmic) staging, which, in turn, is implicated by means of the We of spectators (being in need of the montage sequence to become this We in the first place).⁸

The second verse then once again puts forward a narratological definition of the montage sequence's form by means of addressing, first, the relation of narrative time and narrated time; second, the represented content and the knowledge thereof; and, third, a rhetoric of improvement regarding the athletic body on screen.⁹ Its last three lines, charged with parody as a result of the clumsy movement of the puppets, then refers back to the statement of Joe Kane

---

6 In recent years, research concerning the interface of music and media sports has increased. See for example the already mentioned article by Kehrberg (Kehrberg 2011).
7 The song is performed by *DVDA*, the band of director Trey Parker and screenwriter Matt Stone. It partly resembles Paul Engemann's song *Scarface (Push It to the Limit)*, which appears in the famous montage sequence in SCARFACE (B. De Palma, 1983) showing Tony Montana's rise in Miami's cocaine business. The *DVDA* song already pops up in as an earlier version in *Asspen* (T. Parker, 2002), the second episode of the sixth season of SOUTH PARK (USA 1997–) in which Stan, Kyle, Kenny and Eric travel to Aspen (Colorado) to learn how to ski and Stan challenges cocky Tad McKowski to a race. The last line of the first verse says: "A sports training montage" (TC 00:16:33).
8 The "you" can in this case rather be understood as personal pronoun (of the second person's singular) than as impersonal pronoun, as the prior dialogue implicates that these lines are said/sung by Johnston's supervisor Spottswoode to Johnston.
9 "Show a lot of things happening at once / Remind everyone of what's going on / And with every shot you show a little improvement / To show it all would take too long / That's called a montage / Uh, we want a montage."

in THE PROGRAM (see above): "[...] you can lose yourself in it. [...] Hell, everything else fades away," (see above). Here in TEAM AMERICA: WORLD POLICE, this process of full immersion and fading out that Kane reaches when playing football is addressed not as a mental activity or an emotional state, but as a filmic staging strategy that changes our experience of time: "Always fade out in a montage / If you fade out, it seems like more time has passed in a montage."

Flow as a Filmic Modality of Perception

What connects these two descriptions, of which one addresses a perceptual dimension of physical activity and the other an experience of filmic images, is the experience of flow as described by Susan A. Jackson, who follows and adds to the theory of Csíkszentmihályi specifically with regard to sports (see Jackson / Csíkszentmihályi 1999). Starting from descriptions of emotional states that athletes brought forward during conducted interviews and mirroring them with a concept called "challenge-skills balance" (Jackson / Csíkszentmihályi 1999, 6), the central terms of Jackson's and Csíkszentmihályi's study are those of "focus," "intense" or "total involvement" or "absorption" and "enjoyment" (Jackson / Csíkszentmihályi 1999, 5/10).[10] The terms seemingly function both as synonyms (with regard to the notion of flow) and descriptions (concerning the related procedures taking place). While the former describes the (intentional) mental activity necessary and the second the mental state that then occurs, the latter captures a (self-)feeling of intensity, merging and homogeneity setting in:

> More than just focus, however, flow is a harmonious experience where mind and body are working together effortlessly, leaving the person feeling that something special has just occurred. [...] [F]low offers something more than just a successful outcome. This is because flow lifts experience from the ordinary to the optimal, and it is in those moments that we feel truly alive and in tune with what we are doing.
> (Jackson / Csíkszentmihályi 1999, 5)

Altogether, they describe nine dimensions or components of flow as "a psychological state [...] one can achieve [...] through control of the mind – or attention" (Jackson / Csíkszentmihályi 1999, 16). With regard to flow as media aesthetic experience and movement-image, which manifests and becomes especially tangible

---

[10] Another important term is the already mentioned "optimal experience" (Jackson / Csíkszentmihályi 1999, 11), which, with its judgmental connotation', seemingly owes much to Jackson's and Csíkszentmihályi's approach being quite strongly rooted in cognitive and behavioral science. From a phenomenological and aesthetic standpoint, I suggest to rather refrain from it.

in/with the sports film's montage sequences, six of these dimensions become instructive, especially as they can be related to key points of the (historical) discussions on the aesthetics of film images.

First, there is the "action-awareness merging" (Jackson / Csíkszentmihályi 1999, 19), through which Jackson and Csíkszentmihályi not only seem to describe a wholeness of physical and mental movement ("oneness with movement," Jackson / Csíkszentmihályi 1999, 19), but also (and with the example of a professional cyclist) a fusion of human being and machine, of active body and technical apparatus. In the state of flow, physical exercise is sensual activity and technical process (and vice versa), practice is perception and perception a process, a system of kinetic procedures interacting mutually producing one another. Reading Jackson's and Csíkszentmihály's statements like this, obvious parallels to conceptualizations of film reception and the cinematographic dispositive of perception come up. This is especially the case when the filmic movement-image is understood "not as object, but as a product of the manufacturing of audiovisual images on the part of the viewer," and as "temporal form [...], which needs to be situated in between media techniques of the production of audiovisual moving images and the media practice of recipients who experience, feel and think [...]" (Kappelhoff 2018b, 69).[11] Hermann Kappelhoff calls such a conceptualization a "poiesis of film-viewing," with which he subsumes "the interaction of the recipients with the audiovisual images as a production process very similar to the artistic production of filmmaking" (Kappelhoff 2018b, 68). Vice versa, Kappelhoff understands film-making as the product or continuation of this poiesis of film-viewing. The outcome of this process is the "thinking of filmic images" (Kappelhoff 2018b, 69), which has to be analytically reconstructed again and again. This thinking does not derive from represented facts, linguistic structures nor a recognition of these facts and structures that is rooted *beyond* the filmic images, but rather refers to the conditions and dynamics of the modulation of sensations and perceptions, as well as to the (fictitious and reflexive) production of a "collectively shared reality of experience" (Kappelhoff 2018b, 70).

However, it does not seem like Jackson and Csíkszentmihályi in *Flow in Sports* aim at such a degree of complexity when it comes to such media aesthetic consideration. Still, thinking the former through the latter appears to be quite productive from at least two different angles. On the one hand, there is the time of Csíkszentmihályi's early academic career, by means of which it is possible to find a theoretical bridge between his psychological concept of flow and a more aesthetic approach, as he occupied himself thoroughly with artists and ("professional")

---

11 Kappelhoff's book is in German, these and the following are my translations.

aesthetic experience back then.¹² In this early work, Csíkszentmihályi understands the process of artistic production as well as the process of the sensual experience of artworks (by trained museum staff for example) as correlating with the flow experience. Understood like this, there is always a dimension of creativity connected to flow, as can be seen when Csíkszentmihályi considers statements of a painter and a composer for example. On the other hand, there are more components of the flow experience, which can function as points of reference and help to understand flow as a filmic modality of experience – and one that has special significance with regard to the sports film, especially by means of the medial form of the montage sequence and as a viewer experience not limited to the retracing of a film's narrative action.

When talking about the condition of a strong focus ("concentration on the task at hand," Jackson / Csíkszentmihályi 1999, 23), what is attributed to the flow experience is a high degree of presence and the potency of 'making present,' respectively – a topic having often been brought forward when discussing the experience of film and sports, too.¹³ At the same time, this penchant for and sense of presentness somehow comes along with the notion of an immediate experience as/and aesthetic thinking: "In flow there is no room for any thoughts other than what you are doing and feeling right at the moment, the 'now'" (Jackson / Csíkszentmihályi 1999, 25). Furthermore, and again by analogy to film experience and here especially to the mode of the action film in between ecstatic omnipotence and the powerlessness of being overwhelmed,¹⁴ Jackson's and Csíkszentmihályi's flow experience combines a "sense of control" (the third element, Jackson / Csíkszentmihályi 1999, 26) and a concurrent "loss of self-consciousness" in the sense of a psychosocial I (the fourth element, Jackson / Csíkszentmihályi 1999, 27, see also 67). It is within the synthesis of these paradoxical dimensions of feelings, which

---

12 See Csíkszentmihályi / Getzels 1976, Csíkszentmihályi et al. 1984 and Csíkszentmihályi / Robinson 1990.
13 Vanessa Aab puts forth this aspect of film as an experience of presentness within a Deleuzian discussion (Aab 2014, 162 et seq.), while Vivian Sobchak refers to it from an early film-phenomenological perspective (Sobchack 1988). Providing a perspective on and from early film theory and film critic Jean Epstein, Margrit Tröhler develops the term of filmic thinking (Tröhler 2007, in German). Regarding the relationship between spectator sport and the production and experience of presence, it is essential to look at Hans Ulrich Gumbrecht's work, who also touches upon the states of being emotionally affected, "lost in focused intensity" (Gumbrecht 2006, 50) and "immerse[d] in the realm of presence" Gumbrecht 2006, 214).
14 Kappelhoff describes this mode of action cinema as a decisive element of the war film genre, next to the melodramatic mode (Kappelhoff 2018a, 130 et seq.). It is characterized by a dynamic processing of the viewer's space of perception, which is also typical for the training and game sequences of the sports film.

can otherwise also be described with ludologist Roger Caillois' terminology,[15] where the feeling of being merged (into something bigger when performing), which was mentioned earlier, and the sense of unity of body and mind in motion ("sense of oneness," Jackson / Csíkszentmihályi 1999, 72) can or have to be located. Furthermore, and as the fifth component, Jackson and Csíkszentmihályi qualify the flow experience as an "autotelic experience" (Jackson / Csíkszentmihályi 1999, 30),[16] hence as an experience of intrinsic gratification and indulgence as an end in itself. It is striking how the two authors explicitly talk about autotelic *experience*, while not using the more common term of autotelic action (that then leads to or causes an experience) at all.[17] This makes it much easier or more interesting to consider this idea in the context of a discussion on the experience of filmic images as an act of reflexive embodiment, medially composed effects of subjectification and hence sensory self-awareness, as Kappelhoff understands it in his conceptualization of the expressive movement image. Here, a "feeling for the whole" (Kappelhoff 2018b, 140) plays an equally important role, while at the same time, a difference between aesthetic theory and Csíkszentmihályi's psychological approach becomes evident: While the former often tries to refrain from defining feeling as a physical reaction or state and understands it rather as a "reflexive sentiment of the relation between bodies" (Kappelhoff 2018b, 166), as well as 'the whole' as a "fictitious coherence" (Kappelhoff 2018b, 164) that is (re-)experienced as embodied perception time and again, the latter comprehends inwardness less as a dynamic construct of medially and intersubjectively structured effects of subjectification but more as an absolute entity that is to be understood along cognitive patterns.

Of course, I do not mean to accuse Jackson and Csíkszentmihályi of not or only barely treating the flow experience as a medial mode of perception. Rather, what this rereading hopefully helps to illustrate is how the practices of doing sports, watching sports and watching sports films have always already been intertwined as sensualistic culture of sports, in which athletic activity itself is already an integral part of spectator and media sports and in which, the other way

---

[15] Roger Caillois differentiates between four different forms of play: *agon, alea, illinx* and *mimicry* (Caillois 1962 [1958]). They can principally be described as four different types of pathos. *Agon* signifies the demonstration and enforcement of strength, *alea* a state of being at mercy. *Illinx*, in contrast, refers to the ecstatic, which is also of central concern for the flow sequences of sports films, as will become clear during my analysis later on. *Mimicry*, on the other hand, rather has to be connected to the reflexivity of the melodramatic mode.
[16] See also Jackson / Csíkszentmihályi 1999, 142 et seq.
[17] The term autotelic is usually being used in the context of action theory. However, it also plays a role in theories of aesthetic perception, especially following Immanuel Kant and Friedrich Schiller.

around, the activity of these spectators can be understood as some kind of athletic exercise.[18] Such an assumption seems especially self-evident when one captures filmic reception as the embodied retracing of an affective *parcours*, of time modulated through movement, as it is done with regard to the mentioned concept of expressive movement images. Once again, a connection can be made to *Flow in Sports* here, as, according to Jackson and Csíkszentmihályi, flow, sixthly, comes along with a change of time, or rather a change of the sense of time (with regard to the 'time of the clocks'):

> [O]ne of the characteristics of being in flow is having a transformed sense of the way time proceeds. Generally what is experienced in flow is a shortening of time, so that hours pass by like minutes, or minutes like seconds. The reverse can also occur, with minutes seeming to stretch into luxurious longer periods, providing the perception of having all the time in the world [...]. (Jackson and Csíkszentmihályi 1999, 28 et seq.)

These lines could also work as a description of filmic temporality as well – a temporality that is not simply to be understood as represented time but as made up of at least two different but intertwined components: One that concerns "the time that is experienced by the spectators, that is the *dramaturgy of affect* of a film: a succession of intensities that refers to a concrete *duration*" (Kappelhoff / Lehmann 2021, 536),[19] and the other that "means the establishing of temporal relations, the process of fictionalizing the filmic image: the construction of a filmic world" (Kappelhoff / Lehmann 2021, 536). Understood as an image space which is produced by means of the process and in the time of the film viewer viewing, such a filmic world is made up of "an orchestration of sensual references" (Heller 2010, 47), of a dynamic net of modalities of expression and perception, whose reconstruction is the problem of a historical poetics of (genre) film.

Hereafter, flow shall be understood as such a modality of the sports film, which figures especially in and through the montage sequences typical for the genre and as mimicked by TEAM AMERICA: WORLD POLICE.[20] It will be analytically sketched out with regard to its modes of staging, its affect dramaturgical

---

18 Such a perspective should then also widen an aesthetics of sports, which develops around spectator perception but then puts the media reception of sports as secondary or deducible from that perception.
19 Kappelhoff's and Lehmann's article is in German, my translation.
20 This should not exclude that this modality may be connected to other dramaturgical patterns or that it can even be grasped as a more fundamental element of genre film experience. In the book just cited, Franziska Heller puts forward an inspiring approach towards a film aesthetics of the fluid by developing a phenomenological narratology and provides a closer look at the auteur film especially. Heller's book is in German, my translation.

formations, as well as with regard to the perceptual world-building and political function resulting thereof. Thereby, my leading thesis of a sports film aesthetic perspective goes as follows: flow is not only a visualization of a subjective and individual state of mind, but can be understood as a phenomenon of communal subjectification, which plays an important role in cultural theories of play and sports[21] and can at the same time be reflexively related to cinematic experience. At the center of such an understanding is the notion of interaction or team play – on the level of plot, of the bodies and characters represented, but also in the sense of media technique, perceptual structures and staging strategies, as the interplay of multiple elements of the mise en scène (according to a holistic notion of montage), of moving image and movement, of audiovisual corporeality and the spectators' bodies. This interplay culminates in an image of a fluid coming together.

5.2 Becoming Team as an Image of Flow

The Shaping of a Group Body

The idea of flow as filmic modality of experience becomes paradigmatically vivid in the film MIRACLE (G. O'Connor, 2004). The film fictionalizes the surprising triumph of the United States men's ice hockey team at the 1980 Winter Olympics in Lake Placid, New York over the actually superior and heavily favored Soviet team.[22] The sports story is narrated against the background of the Cold War, specifically the Soviet invasion of Afghanistan, which started seven weeks before the Olympic games took place, and the Second Oil Crisis. The presence of this background is obtained by the repeated use of TV footage of the time.

Coach Herb Brooks (Kurt Russell), the central and very peculiar main figure of the plot, tries to form a promising team out of a roster of amateur athletes

---

[21] See Huizinga 2016 [1938] as certainly the central source until today. Robert Gugutzer provides a perspective of phenomenology and sociology of the body, see for example Gugutzer 2004 (in German).

[22] The four Olympic ice hockey tournaments before 1980 had all been won by the Soviet Union. The reason for this dominance was a system of centralized professionalization. In contrast to the US Olympic teams, which usually consisted of college amateur athletes selected shortly before the Games, the Soviet players practiced and played together for many years as 'amateurs of state' (in the army team of ZSKA Moscow). This imbalance also existed regarding other team sports, as the opening sequence of MIRACLE hints at by mentioning the scandalous basketball finale of the 1972 Olympic Games.

from many different colleges. His coaching style is characterized by relentless meticulousness, an iron fist and (finally not so) unorthodox training methods. His aloofness and doggedness and the private struggle coming along with it is prominently staged from the very beginning and connected to the 'personal trauma' of having been the last player cut from the Olympic roster twenty years earlier. This backstory does not only fuel crucial motifs of the sports film (like, for example, the two-sidedness of toughness) and its constitutive conflict of the tragic necessity and (im)possibility of (dis)integrating the exceptional individual as outsider, but also connects to the narrated present of the MIRACLE.

During the try-outs shown at the beginning of the movie, Brooks selects the full preliminary roster of twenty-six players on the first day, even though the try-outs were supposed to last one week. Before the start of Olympics, he needs to cut this roster to twenty. Since he does not automatically take the biggest stars into consideration but searches for players with fitting skills and especially the 'right' set of values, Brooks upsets the powerful establishment of hockey officials. However, he persuades them that he acts out of everyone's main interest of building a team with the best possible chemistry.

This forming of a group body beyond civil life, with which sports films often start, is elementary throughout MIRACLE and is strikingly detailed when it comes to the film's audiovisual dramaturgy.[23] The first hour of the film is interwoven with several short parts of a training montage sequence. The whole sequence culminates in an image of the formation of a new, national family, marking the completion of a process of collectivization as a dynamic of separation and connection, exclusion and inclusion. This culmination includes at least three scenes or scenic vignettes: After a farewell scene between one of the players being sent off to camp and his father, there follows a short scene that captures the protest of a group of players against coach Brooks' last minute decision to nominate another player who was not previously on the roster. Their argument: "We're a family!" (TC 00:58:28).[24] Then there is the team's Christmas

---

[23] Hermann Kappelhoff describes this formation especially in relation to the war film genre (Kappelhoff 2018a, 129). While in the war film the merging of the sacrificing/sacrificed individual into the body of the military corps obviously has a more existential quality to it and civil life only becomes present there very selectively (in a mode of flaring remembrance), the separation between the worlds on and off the field are a lot less absolute and basically always shown to be directly interwoven when it comes to the sports film. Here, doing sports does not prohibit or disintegrate civil life, but rather triggers (the chance of) social advancement within civil life. Nonetheless, there is a similar or even stronger nationalist imagery to be found in the sports film, as can be seen in MIRACLE as well.

[24] The given time code refers to the German DVD edition of Buena Vista Home Entertainment from 2004, played on VLC Player for macOS X.

party, which fades into a parallel montage audiovisually connecting the players' communality (culminating in pick-up football game in the snow) with the lingering separation of coach Brooks and Jimmy Carter's televised *Crisis of Confidence* speech of 1979.

Within "the ecstasy of the medial transgression of space, time, bodies, and objects in the kinesthesia of montage and of the intensification of movement" (Kappelhoff 2018a, 125), the generally very dynamic training montage sequences are in stark contrast to the rather statically staged scenes of dialogue, which makes the former emerge rather eruptively.[25] At the same time, and within the duration of the perception of the filmic images, they form a quite coherent expressive movement, which can be described as an image of getting into a flow. What coincides in and through this image is, first, Brook's idea of team play as a form of constant movement and passing;[26] second, the concept of montage as interaction of different elements to form a perceptual unity of movement; and, third, the feeling of communality that correlates with this audiovisual manufacturing of a group body. Eventually, it is not only the fictional characters but also the film's spectators as sensual bodies that are constitutively involved in these dynamics of exclusion and inclusion.

In Between Fragmentation and Order

On the level of representation, all parts of this sequence capture the proceedings on the ice. At the same time, they are continuously embedded in a medial configuration of a viewing-viewed, which is typical for the genre of the sports film and lets the action on the field appear to be always already sutured with an audience of the spectators in and of the film, connecting and being connected by affection-images (see also especially chapter 4.2).[27] The first part of the (divided) montage sequence shows the first try-out practice of all candidates from across the country. It is also the last, since Brooks has already

---

[25] Csíkszentmihályi also talks about such an ecstasy with regard to the flow experience as a "step towards a different reality" apart from the reality of everyday life (Csíkszentmihályi 2004). For Kappelhoff, this ecstasy stands for the "energetic exceeding of ordinary perception in the phantasms of the action movie" (2018a, 125).
[26] This concept is usually called *motion* or *flow offense*, especially in basketball. With regard to soccer, a comparable style of playing called *tiki-taka* became popular during the first two decades of the twentieth century.
[27] I hereby primarily refer to Gilles Deleuze's description of the close-up of a face as affection-image (2013a [1983], 97 et seq.).

made-up his mind. What can be seen and heard here (and then especially again in the last part) corresponds with the typical audiovisual disposition of such flow montage sequences in sports films. The most basic staging strategy is, on the one hand, a very dominant audio track, which makes for continuity of movement, most often in form of a vividly pushing, orchestral music and a background noise rhythmically intertwining with it. This background noise consists of (exaggerated) breathing sounds, screaming voices and sounds of movement and especially collision.[28] On the other hand, there is a certain emphasis on the athletic body in movement, which cannot, however, be described in the sense of an individual body of a certain athlete character as a represented whole, since it keeps on being highly fragmented and rhythmized. It can rather be understood as a cinematic body emerging to the time of the film's expressive and perceptual movement. The temporality of this affect dramaturgy often takes place via movements of augmentation, acceleration and repetition, with the latter being especially prominent in MIRACLE.

Following the dialogue of two players in the locker room that already hints at a hostile imbalance within the team soon to escalate, we hear a sequence of string instruments (TC 00:10:19). After the blow of a whistle, the setting changes into the hockey arena and onto the rink. The camera follows the run of a player from beyond the ice via lateral medium tracking shot. As part of the exercise, the player is checked into the rinks repeatedly by several of his teammates. The string instruments' hitting spiccato intertwines with the impacts of the colliding bodies. The rhythmic linearity of this movement is carried even further by the music and leads – by means of the repetition of an ever the same sequence in an increasing tone pitch – to an expression of rhythmic tension and of culmination at the same time. On the visual level, however, things become literally confusing, even though what we see are a couple of players carrying out the same exercise one after the other. By means of a lot of movements entering/within the image, a camera that by seemingly taking up these movements and reacting to them often suddenly and quickly pans vertically, as well as primarily (medium) close-up shots with little depth of field, the training session shows as an image of energetic chaos here. This confusion is additionally enforced by repeatedly and erratically changing and jumping camera viewpoints, as well as by a multitude of different noises typical of hockey: hitting, screaming and sliding. It is not before the mise en scène returns to the officials and coaches watching and judging the players from the stands that an image of calmness and clarity is possible again.

---

28 Sometimes, there is (also) an explicitly homodiegetic voice of a TV or radio commentator that causes this continuity, like in WE ARE MARSHALL, which I analyze in chapter 4.2.

A reverse shot of these officials and short dialogue between two coaches make clear that all of this is about getting this 'wild pack' of players under control and in order. The hectic and hitting sequence of string instruments fades away to be replaced by a slow legato, the movement of the camera and the movement on screen come to an almost complete standstill.

With the following return to the exercising players on ice, the calmness and clarity once again though very briefly give way to the expressivity of tense restlessness and chaos experienced shortly before. This time though, it is immediately caught by a more stable perspective connected to the figure of the goalkeeper, Jim Craig (Eddie Cahill). Via a slow pan shot, a change in depth of focus and very symmetrical shots, the audiovisual orchestration changes from an extreme close up of Craig's face to Brooks, who watches the action on the ice from a very exposed position in his box seat (Figure 33).

Figure 33: Establishing clarity under the eyes of coach Brooks (MIRACLE).

This dramaturgy of delimiting verticality seems to capture coach Brooks' overall approach, which he himself summarizes by stating "I'll be your coach, I won't be your friend" during his first address to the players of the preliminary squad shortly thereafter (TC 00:15:00). Remarkably, he is also staged as coming from above and looking down to the players in the beginning here. This dramaturgy can be witnessed again in the montage sequence's last part, when it is set into motion, with Brooks becoming the center of the fluid actions on the ice by means of an upward camera movement. At the same time, it marks the core of the poetics of affect of the sports film more generally, especially when put into effect as a contradictive audiovisual dramaturgy between images of chaotic fragmentation and those of balanced clarity and overview. The former thereby captures the dissolving of individual corporeality and a feeling of being overwhelmed by movement as a loss of spatial and temporal coordinates of everyday perception, while the latter captures the merging into a unified whole, which goes along with the retrieval of a feeling of control.[29]

Flow as National Collectivization

This main conflict of forming a unified whole through fragmentation and reassembly as a temporality of getting into an unbroken flow, which does not only contain the action, but first and foremost the filmic orchestration and experience, is also to be found in Brooks' idea of the game. After a long-standing dispute flares up in the form of an excessive foul during the first practice, he says: "We move forward starting right now. We start becoming a team right now! Skating, passing, flow and creativity. That is what this team is all about, gentlemen. Not old rivalries," (TC 00:21:31).

Flow in this case not only signifies a style of playing, according to which every player is always in motion and the puck constantly circulating, but also refers to a process of communal subjectification, which relies on procedures of inclusion and exclusion, and which is then again rendered tangible in an affect poetical way by MIRACLE itself. The film's trick then is that this dialectic of communitization intertwines and culminates with the peculiar character of the head coach, who, as already mentioned earlier, was himself the last player to be cut from an Olympics hockey team many years earlier. The scene of the team's Christmas party stands as a striking example for this culmination and rendering of time as present past and past future. Here, Brooks is shown as both outcast and – by means of the integration of images and sounds of the historical and televised speech of President Carter – national hero of an American media memory tied to the history and medium of spectator sports.[30]

This audiovisual reflection of national communality is fleshed out on several levels in MIRACLE, for example when Brooks, after having evoked the future team spirit, introduces a game to get to know each other better. This game is the topic of several of the following sequences and requires every player to introduce himself with name, place of origin and the name of the team for which he plays. While the viewer witnesses a team sports film-typical sequence of faces in the time of montage and perception, this dynamic culminates in a

---

[29] This contradiction is illustrated right at the beginning of WE ARE MARSHALL.
[30] A similar audiovisual rhetoric of media heroism is to be found in JIM THORPE – ALL-AMERICAN and KNUTE ROCKNE ALL AMERICAN (see my analyses in chapter 6), but also in non-biographical/-historical sports films like FOR LOVE OF THE GAME.

scene in which Brooks makes the team perform a drill exercise after a bad test match. He pushes his players to the point of complete exhaustion and only stops the exercise when one of the players – barely illuminated and only to be seen as silhouette – does not name the team of his college anymore, but screams: "I play for the United States of America!" (TC 00:44:26) (Figure 34).

Figure 34: Faces of a forming community.

The drill exercise, also named *Bag Skate* or even *Herbies* (after Brooks), is the central topic and structuring element of the second part of the training montage sequence, in which the previously staged image of chaotic confusion undergoes order and directionality so that it can literally enable the formation of the group body as flow.

The sequence is introduced by a short speech by Brooks, who explains to the team how important the soon following strength and cardio exercise will be if they want to stand a chance against the also physically very strong team of the Soviet Union (00:31:30). While clear image structures dominate the visual expressivity, with the camera moving more linearly and less hectically to capture the entire row of players (Figure 35), the repeatedly transposed string sequence, which is especially characterized by its rhythm, becomes part of a more polyphonic, fugue-like constructed symphony on the audio track.

The dynamic of a choreography of coming together and a wave-like flow is further strengthened by the drill-defining movement of the Bag Skate itself and how the camera captures this movement by means of close-up shots that 'dance' with the players' legs. Where there was before an expressivity of constriction, fragmentation and chaos, there is now an image of unification and arriving order. It ends with a smoothly executed offensive play by three players, on which an impressed Coach Brooks comments: "Run that again."

Figure 35: Together as a team.

It is this "again" as a call to repetition, which subsequently becomes the anchor of the audiovisual orchestration, for example when Brooks calls for the already mentioned punitive training, during which the Bag Skate drill becomes an instrument for physical punishment in some kind of a suspense scene. Here, the modeled group body once again experiences a sort of (visual) obliteration – some players collapse or leave the formation, the arena lights are literally turned off – before it then reassembles with the vocal declaration of national pathos: "I play for the United States of America!" During the Christmas party scene, which basically constitutes the completion of this national communitization, it is also this "again," which is picked up ironically by the players.

An Audio-Vision of Pure Event as Substrate of Communal Subjectification

The last part of the training montage sequence, which spans across the first half of the movie, gets close to the 'classic' form that TEAM AMERICA: WORLD POLICE referred to in its parody. After another pep talk by Brooks following a video practice session, MIRACLE presents us with several training situations over a time span of more than three minutes (TC 00:48:55). Again, the basic elements of the audiovisual orchestration are the audio track, which this time strikes by means of sudden changes in volume, range and tempo, and the group choreography of players skating back and forth. The scenes on ice are accompanied by spotlight-like images of the catacombs, while the viewer witnesses how, on the one hand, the group body is strengthened by being put in formation and how, on the other hand, this formation depends on a process of (the brutality of) exclusion, with names being crossed out on a list and removed from lockers in extremely detailed close-ups. This eradication of individual names corresponds with the already mentioned audiovisual rhetoric of formation dramatically culminating in the punitive training scene, when Brooks yells at his players: "The name on the front is a hell of a lot more important than the one on the back! Get that through your head!" This scene here now offers yet another image of that formation, of that getting into the flow, when it again shows extreme close-ups of the faces of the players, who previously were hesitant to say their names and who are now bound together in an easy-going, polyphonic dialogue about game strategies.

Altogether, what emerges is a spiral-like movement of repetition and progression, through and during which it is not only the represented bodies but the expressive and perceptual elements and developments that come together and combine as an image of flow seemingly oblivious to linear time. One of these developments especially marks this expressive movement as an image of improvement: that of the progress of goalkeeper Craig being staged in several short episodes, which move from his anger about a missed shot in a dry run, to an exercise of him training his reactions with a tennis ball, to the depiction of multiple saves and a shot of him juggling three tennis balls at the same time as yet another update of the image of interweaving flow.

In MIRACLE specifically and in the sports film more generally, flow is not just a way of playing that one can read off and analyze from the images and the actions they show anymore. It is neither just a tactic, which a character speaks of or another one wants to reach or internalize, nor is it just the representation of a subjective state of focussing, which, as Jackson and Csíkszentmihályi describe, comes along with an impression of wholeness and detemporalization (see Jackson and Csíkszentmihályi 1999, 19, 28, 72). Flow is rather a filmic modality of experience that can be related to Gilles Deleuze's time-image, in which sensomotoric action dissolves into "pure optical and sound situations" (Deleuze 2013b [1985], 12). In that vein, wholeness and detemporalization do not refer to subjective experience in a psychological sense, but to the visibility and visualization of "pure time" (Ott 2011, 116) as never-ending processuality and reconstellation of movement. This (non-successive, non-causal) temporality that is not yet understood spatially (in spatial metaphors) constitutes the ground for processes of embodied subjectification and also, as one could understand Martin Seel, for an aesthetics of sports: "Watching sports as well as doing sports are about the experience of a physical activity, which is performed under more difficult conditions, as pure event" (Seel 1993, 91).[31] Accruing from the 'clusters

---

31 Ott's and Seel's articles are in German, my translation.

of movement,' from the audio-visions of pure happening of the flow sequences in sports films, are ever new time-images, which become especially interesting for a historiography of the sports film genre with regard to their sensual reflection (as a film's audiovisual thinking) of communal subjectification. In MIRACLE, this (always precarious and double-edged) subjectification is eventually bound to the anti-heroic hero figure of the coach. Last but not least, this is made clear by the statue-like staging of Brooks in the last training montage sequence, in which he is the center of a movement of effortless and seemingly never-ending sliding and passing. This movement emerges as embodied expression and the viewer's perception. Interestingly enough, it is also this subjectivity, by means of which, and against all odds with regard to an US sports film fictionalizing the time of the Cold War, one might discover a modestly respectful devotion towards the historical, systemic enemy throughout MIRACLE's further course of action.

6 Commemorating Futurity, Projecting Pastness: Never-Ending Endings

After describing the sports film genre's constitutive conflict and its production of an audiovisual discourse of a community-building temporality of crystallization through a poetology of cinematic thinking particularly concerned with the moment as crystallization of past, present and future in the previous chapter, I will now present yet another perspective on this conflict and thus yet another specific realization of this poetology. In order to demonstrate how my approach has developed throughout this book and how to understand the genre in its historical variation and thus through the reshaping and repositioning of this audiovisual discourse of communality and historicity, I will carry out a comparative analysis of two sports films in this last analytical chapter. The first one will be KNUTE ROCKNE ALL AMERICAN (L. Bacon, 1940),[1] the second JIM THORPE – ALL-AMERICAN (M. Curtiz, 1951). The selection of both these movies is of course not arbitrary: The former was produced right before the United States entered World War II and presents the earliest production of the American team sports film examined here.[2] The latter was produced shortly after the war, in a time when the beginning of the Cold War not only provided for a prospering economy but also brought lines of harsh domestic conflicts to light. Though the historical distance between these two productions is quite short, it is a very decisive and telling one.

But let us for one short moment step back from the movies and the history in which they are not only embedded, but which they, as we have seen, co-create, and take a detour to the notion of futurity as omnipresent in sports culture more generally. It manifests itself again and again in numerous sayings, slogans and ideas, all circling around topoi of continuation and infinity and most often being interconnected with or embedded in motifs of bodily and spiritual improvement, endurance and obsession. This goes from a figurative idiom like 'going the extra mile,' whose origins can be traced back to the New Testament,[3] to the ubiquitous

---

[1] William K. Howard was replaced by Lloyd Bacon as director during the shooting of the film. Howard is not mentioned in the movie's credits.
[2] Even though the genre theory developed in chapter 2 clearly works against the idea of clear cuts regarding historical periodization, one has to start somewhere. For the plausibility of KNUTE ROCKNE ALL AMERICAN as some kind of starting point, see again Andrew Miller, who proclaims "a new era in sporting cinema" (Miller 2003, 10) with the United States entering World War II. The position of this analysis at the end of this book, in a last chapter concerned with this film's ending in particular and the sports film's issue with the (im)possibility of ending in general, of course epitomizes in itself the topic of this book.
[3] See Matthew 5,41: "If anyone forces you to go one mile, go with them two miles."

dictum of 'trying harder.' Even when reaching peaks of ultimate success – an apex that is, to a certain extent, always illusory – the idea of continuity, of an 'on and on,' the impulse to 'never stop' or 'keep on fighting' persists.[4] The decisive moment as a contraction of time, as an overfull, impregnated present triggering a sense of timelessness or detemporalization, gets embedded (again) into a temporal rhetoric of sequential succession and progress.

This process of embedding can take different shapes in view of directionality, interval, qualification and vectoriality. The emphasis may be on the potential for reversal, in the sense of a recovery or improvement in the face of a negative event or experience like a defeat or a dissatisfying performance, provoking a rhetoric of turnaround and/or enhancement. Or, the other way around, it might hint at the potential for maintaining and repeating a good performance, hence resulting in a rhetoric of retention and repetition. Furthermore, it is worth considering the manner in which this process of embedding and transforming the moment *out of* time or, rather, the moment *through* time (as discussed in chapter 4) into a moment *in (sequential) time* is itself temporally addressed. Is the emphasis placed on the moment's becoming part of a past or a future sequence of events? In the first case, the moment becomes aligned with something prior, whereby in the second case it becomes that something towards which something still to come orients itself. While in the former case, the antecedent character comes to the fore and leads to a rhetoric of remembrance and tradition, the latter emphasizes the yet to come and is thus more inclined to constructions of projection and matters of hope, faith and destiny.

In the detailed analysis that follows in this and in the next chapter, I present and compare two very distinct and, especially in their variance, quite fruitful examples to show how the constitutive conflict of the sports film genre figures and becomes describable as yet another poetics. It emphasizes a different facet of the sports film's cinematic thinking of a community-building temporality of crystallization, namely that of endlessness. Both movies bring forward and exploit such a poetics of endlessness in a related, but then also decisively different, form: in the case of KNUTE ROCKNE ALL AMERICAN, the earlier film, it comes as an expressive

---

4 Surely, one of the most blatant incarnations of it is the former German goalkeeper Oliver Kahn. After his team Bayern München won the national title very dramatically in the fourth minute of extra time in the last game of the season of 2000/01, Kahn became famous for his words "Weiter, immer weiter!", which he shouted at his coach and teammates after the final whistle. Seemingly out of place at that moment, his words would gain in meaning and importance when four days later Bayern München proceeded to also win the Champions League title. Kahn saved the decisive penalty.

movement of multiplication and intensifying immediacy; with JIM THORPE – ALL-AMERICAN, the poetics is one of repetitive circularity. How do the films cinematically think of the crystallized moment as a point within a never-ending sequence? How do they audiovisually implement an idea of the moment as both an end (to a series) and a beginning (of a new series or the continuation of an ongoing one), hence as simultaneously producing a past and a future by cutting open the continuous flow of time?

For obvious reasons, this audiovisual discourse of endlessness (of the moment as crystal, see chapter 4) becomes especially critical and thus interesting to analyze when the respective films have to deal with absolute endings, both on the level of plot – usually in the sense of a protagonist's death – and of narrative time at a film's actual ending.[5]

In regard to KNUTE ROCKNE ALL AMERICAN and JIM THORPE – ALL-AMERICAN, these two levels coincide as the actual or symbolical death of their heroes and the films' actual endings go hand in hand. Nevertheless: coming to a (narrative) end in no way means that events and actions chronicled in the films are definitely terminated and everything is settled. On the contrary: Sports films' endings often open up and evoke a sense of sudden presentness (*Gegenwärtigkeit*) and (im)mobilization, thereby creating images of a 'futurity in the Now,' which solidify as stories and audiovisual metaphors of endlessness and immortality. This is often achieved or bolstered by text insertions, the presentation of still images or photographs or the frequent use of a final freeze frame.[6] As already mentioned, in the case of KNUTE ROCKNE ALL AMERICAN, this opening up is staged as an explosive multiplication and heightened sense of immediacy, while in JIM THORPE – ALL-AMERICAN, it is embedded in an expressive movement of cyclical repetition triggering an audiovisual rhetoric of a reintegration through spectatorship. Both films thereby capture the tragic moment (of death) as both discontinuation and standstill, as the beginning of a process of departure/awakening/uprising and 'productive' remembrance in the realm of legacy and tradition.

---

5 This moment, when narrative time cracks open as an illusion of endless chronology is of course also important in regard to the films' beginnings, which, accordingly, quite often figure as rebeginnings in a variety of ways.

6 For the latter, see for example BRIAN'S SONG (B. Kulik, 1971), MAJOR LEAGUE (D.S. Ward, 1989) and ALL THE RIGHT MOVES (M. Chapman, 1983).

6.1 Immortality as the Multiplication of Immediacy:
KNUTE ROCKNE ALL AMERICAN

A Classical Biopic, Ronald Reagan and a Quote That Made History

KNUTE ROCKNE ALL AMERICAN tells the life story of the famous football player and legendary coach Knute Rockne.[7] An immigrant from Norway, Rockne went to Notre Dame University, where he also played on the college football team. After graduating with a degree in pharmacy and working as a laboratory assistant at the university for a short period of time, he was offered a coaching job for the Notre Dame team. By developing and utilizing a great number of new tactical schemes and realizing the possibilities of the commercialization of the sport, Rockne had a great impact on the rise of Notre Dame college football to one of the most successful and prestigious programs in the country, as well as on the evolution of modern collegiate football in general.[8] He is considered one of the best and most famous coaches in the history of American football.

KNUTE ROCKNE ALL AMERICAN captures Rockne's story in classical biopic form typical for studio-era Hollywood.[9] It dramatizes a couple of more or less well-

---

[7] The term "All-American" refers to the tradition of selecting an "All-American team" in college and high school sports at the end of a season. Such a team usually consists of the best players voted for by media experts, the audience and/or sports professionals such as coaches and other players. The equivalent with regard to professional/non-amateur sports would be the "All-Star" or "All-Pro" team. While the latter often competes in an actual game (the "All-Star game"), the "All-American team" usually remains a hypothetical, quasi-fictional construct, as such itself pointing to the productive interdependence of an ever reshaping national collectivity (as an imagined community, see chapter 3.2) and the (outstanding) individuals it recognizes and honors. Central to such concept of a 'heroically' forming society is not only the idea of exceptionalism, but also of endless inclusiveness, as the term "All-America(n)" also indicates. Lately, the term has made a comeback in sports film titles, see for example MY ALL-AMERICAN (A. Pizzo, 2015) or the TV drama series ALL AMERICAN (A. Blair, 2018).

[8] Although Rockne cannot be credited with the *invention* of the forward pass as the film seems to indicate, he certainly played a very significant role in its adequate, regular and successful implementation in the game. One of the most important games regarding this development was the 1913 defeat of the much-favored Army team, during which Rockne and his friend, Notre Dame's quarterback Gus Dorais, outscored their physically superior opponent by a series of forward pass plays. The game is not only dramatized in Bacon's film, but also in the 1955 production THE LONG GRAY LINE by John Ford. For more historical background on Rockne's career and his influence on the game of football, see for example Sperber 2002 or Robinson 1999.

[9] For a rich discussion of how the film is deeply embedded within Hollywood's classical genre period and this period's history of the biopic form, see the fourth chapter of Sperber 1998. Murray Sperber's extensive study, in which he grasps the crisis-filled and scandal-ridden history of intercollegiate athletics of the 1930s through the 1950s as explicitly one of media sports, is also a

known events at different stages of its hero's lifetime: the emigration of Rockne's family from Norway to Chicago, the young boy's discovery of "the most wonderful game in the world" (TC 00:07:10), Rockne working at a post office to earn enough money to finally attend college, him excelling in both chemistry and as a football player, and becoming a research assistant, a married man and father all before then committing to a long-term tenure as a successful and celebrated football head coach. With regard to the film's form, at least three things are remarkable from a macro perspective: first, the relative high number of legendary games that are depicted and subdivide the movie, often by means of integrating original footage; second, how throughout the whole film, the Rockne character clearly is the mediated center of the mise en scène (Figure 36); and third, how the movie as a whole presents a strikingly unshaken filmic world and dramaturgical progression and thereby establishes a more or less uncontested success story. It needs literally two plays in a children's pickup football game on the street for little Knute to not only become a football player, but also an American: "Papa, don't talk Norwegian. Talk American. We're all Americans now. Especially me, I'm left end" (TC 00:04:59). The "six years of hard work that brought me here," which Rockne mentions when starting college,[10] are shown in a one-minute sequence of consistent flow (TC 00:07:41), with a superimposed close-up series of postage stamps moving steadily from left to right through the image, while we see Rockne sorting letters in a post office and hear lightheartedly springing marching music.

The movie received subsequent fame through Ronald Reagan's performance of the role of star player George Gipp. About halfway through the film though, Gipp gets sick – what first only seems to be a sore throat kills him quite suddenly and quickly after four days of fever.[11] The whole event, from Rockne taking notice of Gipp's coughing to the mourning teammates and family in the

---

good source for comprehending the great impact and defining role of KNUTE ROCKNE ALL AMERICAN for its American audience and the history of the genre of the (college) sports film. For a more general approach towards the biographical film of the Studio Era, see Custen 1992. Pearson et al. certainly do not strive for proper historical analysis, but rather for a study of statistical overview, mentioning "biographies" as "characteristic [for the sports film] of the 1940s and 1950s," while also saying that "[a]ltruism, self-sacrificing, and character building were themes frequently employed in sport films of the 1930s" (2003, 147). Besides JIM THORPE – ALL-AMERICAN, which I will look more closely at in the next chapter, they name PRIDE OF THE YANKEES (S. Wood, 1942) and THE STRATTON STORY (S. Wood, 1951) as examples for sports films with a biographical form during the 1940s and 1950s. Sperber adds HARMON OF MICHIGAN (C. Barton, 1941), THE SPIRIT OF STANFORD (C. Barton, 1942), and SMITH OF MINNESOTA (L. Landers, 1942).

10 A text plate shortly before says "ten years of hard work and sacrifice."
11 The real George Gipp died of pneumonia in December 1920, probably after a strep throat infection. For a detailed description of his last weeks, see Cavanaugh 2010, 160–183.

Figure 36: Rockne as the center of the mise en scène (KNUTE ROCKNE ALL AMERICAN).

hospital, is staged quite briefly, and as a rather sober incident, making up no more than four minutes of screen time (TC 00:42:46–00:46:40, Figure 37).[12] While Gipp's death is interwoven with the fact that he is a senior player and hence would not be eligible for the following season anyway – Rockne tells him that he "will be missed" – the funeral or memorial service is not depicted at all. This contrasts greatly with the extensive memorial scene on the occasion of Rockne's death at the end of the movie, which I will analyze in detail in a moment.

Nonetheless, there is a melodramatic center to this scene's otherwise quite soberly operating tableau, which lacks any strong expression of suffering. And that is the staging of Gipp's famous last words on his deathbed, after he has heard about his nomination for the All-American team and reassured Rockne that he could not complain and was not afraid of dying: "Rock, sometime when

---

[12] The indicated time codes refer to the US 2006 Warner Bros. DVD, played on VLC media player for macOS X.

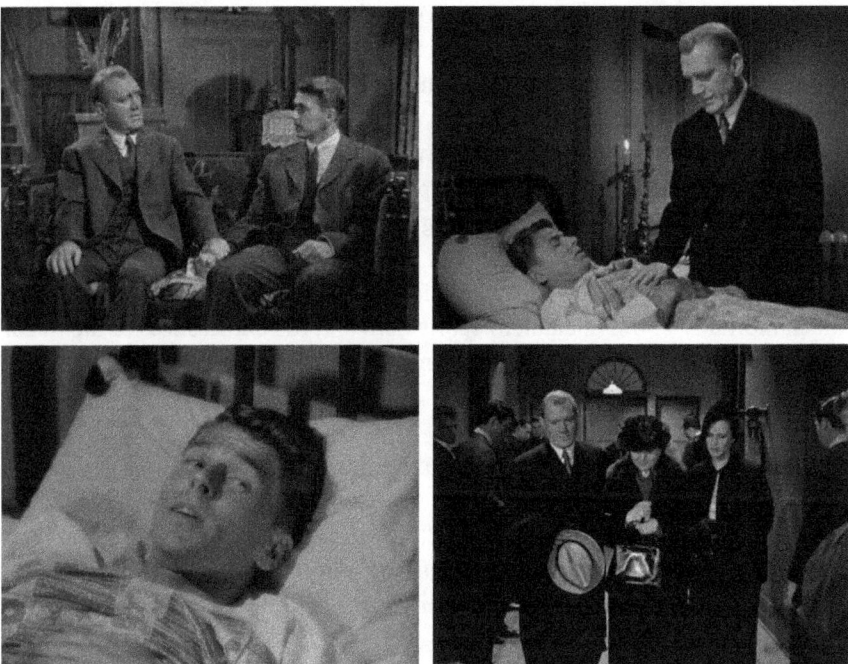

Figure 37: The brief staging of George Gipp's death.

the team is up against it and the breaks are beating the boys, tell them to go out there with all they've got ... and win just one for the Gipper" (TC 00:45:30).[13] "[T]he most rallying cry in sports history" (Cavanaugh 2010, 181) and one of the most famous movie quotes in the history of US cinema, the last part of the sentence got picked up by Reagan himself, becoming one of his political slogans and earning him a nickname. At the 1988 Republican National Convention, Reagan used the sentence to send George H.W. Bush on the journey to become his successor as president of the United States: "George, go out there and win one for the Gipper!" The quote is also referenced in several movies and TV shows, not least in rather parodic ways. Perhaps the most famous spoof of it can be found in the

---

13 As Jack Cavanaugh mentions, it remains unclear until today how that sentence actually came into being, as Rockne seemingly was alone with Gipp at his deathbed when the latter supposedly said it. There is also some doubt about the nickname "Gipper" (see Cavanaugh 2010, 181, and also 226–227). What is supposed to finally have fueled the legend is Rockne's use of the situation for a pep talk before or during the halftime of a 1928 game between Notre Dame and Army at Yankee Stadium, almost eight years after Gipp had died (Cavanaugh 2010, 224–227). This incident also made its way into the movie (TC 01:18:30).

comedy film AIRPLANE! (J. Abrahams / D. Zucker / J. Zucker, 1980), when Leslie Nielsen's character Dr. Rumack slips into a Rockne parody telling an old war story about a heavily wounded pilot named George Zipp, using the sentence "Win one for the Zipper!"[14]

While it would definitely be worthwhile to further detect such traces with regard to the web of creative (re-)appropriations, the focus will be shifted a little bit now and turned towards the ending of KNUTE ROCKNE ALL AMERICAN and how the film here not only depicts the death and mourning of its main character, but participates in the production of an audiovisual discourse of supratemporality, of the immortality of the (mediated) sports hero and the endlessness of the (mediated) media community creating him and being created by him.

Rockne's Death as Media Discourse and Absent Presence

Knute Rockne himself died in an airplane crash in 1931, at only 43 years old. Rockne's death was a nationwide tragedy, garnering massive attention as the country lost "a towering national hero" (Niemi 2006, 210). As Robert Niemi writes and archival pictures testify (Figure 38),[15] Rockne's demise was a huge media event:

> Most of the nation's 1,700 newspapers carried Rockne editorials the week of his death. His funeral was broadcast live on the radio throughout the United States and in parts of South America, Europe, and Asia. A crowd of over 100,000 mourners lined his funeral procession in South Bend, Indiana [...]. (Niemi 2006, 210)

The film incorporates this newspaper coverage throughout its running time and especially during its last ten minutes, which I will now analyze in more detail. The depiction of newspapers – often by means of short dramatic zooms and musical interludes and with headlines functioning as a form of connecting or puncturing intertitle – is thereby only one component of the audio-vision's reflexive addressing of a historical and at the same time seemingly infinitely extendable media community of future remembrance. By means of the integration of historical imagery and a specific poetics of worship and reproduction, the film reproduces this 'eternal community' anew in the (and as an) act of film-viewing, thus realizing an audiovisual discourse of the rigorous media heroization of Rockne, of which KNUTE ROCKNE ALL AMERICAN is

---

14 For another example, see episode 20 of season 1 of M.A.S.H. ("The Army-Navy Game," 1973).
15 Photo fragments of *The Detroit News*, Michigan, and *The Cleveland Sunday News*, Ohio, from 5 April 1931, https://www.worthpoint.com/worthopedia/knute-rockne-death-funeral-notre-dame-107197371 (accessed 21 February 2020).

Figure 38: Fragments of historical newspaper articles on Rockne's death.

obviously itself part of in the first place. Another significant reference point of this discourse of images of images is a *Universal Newspaper Newsreel* capturing the proceedings of the funeral ceremony,[16] to which the film at its ending clearly refers, even though it seems like the original footage was not directly utilized.

As is quite typical for the film, its last ten minutes figure less as a series of distinct scenes but rather as a long sequence with different subparts and an overarching dramaturgical arc. Up until the actual funeral ceremony, there are four smaller scenic vignettes. The first one shows Rockne and his family enjoying their long-awaited Florida beach vacation together, before Rockne has to leave on short notice and go to California. During the second one, we follow him traveling by plane. This sequence is connected to the first one by means of a telegram conversation between Rockne and his wife and also includes a significant 'goodbye scene' at an airport where Rockne has to change planes. The third vignette comprises of the plane crash, while the fourth shows the spreading of the tragic news of Rockne's death through media coverage and by means of images of technical transmission and an expressive movement of rush and overturning.

Strikingly, the crash itself is staged entirely off-screen and through the depiction of a farmer, who works on a field and witnesses the accident, as well as through two explosive bangs and a dramatic trumpet sequence on the audio track (TC 01:30:55, Figure 39).

---

16 See here: https://www.gettyimages.de/detail/video/mourners-attend-the-funeral-and-burial-of-nachrichtenfilmmaterial/1B012255_036 (accessed 22 April 2022).

Figure 39: A plane crash off-screen (KNUTE ROCKNE ALL AMERICAN).

Similar to WE ARE MARSHALL analyzed in chapter 4.2, the moment of (the devastating, fatal) impact of the plane is left outside of the frame, leaving it only indirectly addressed. While this omission of the moment of catastrophe is achieved in WE ARE MARSHALL on the level of montage with the help of a sudden black screen, it becomes first and foremost a question of framing and off-screen here. Especially because not being resolved by means of a reverse shot (of the plane or wreck),[17] the resulting constellation of spectatorship clearly creates an imaginary (negative) space to be charged or occupied by the film viewer's perception of past and present as images of images, and an audiovisual discourse of a 'remembering into the future,' which the film previously prepared for and further pushes in what follows.

To this effect, KNUTE ROCKNE ALL AMERICAN engages in a melodramatic interplay of a mode of foreshadowing (generating future in the present) and of a mode of remembrance (invoking past in the present), while interweaving its hero in an audiovisual play of present absence and absent presence.[18]

---

[17] In WE ARE MARSHALL, a reverse shot (of the burning wreck) is slightly delayed, but ultimately occurs as the center of an audiovisual rhetoric of shocking realization. Interestingly, both historical incidents – the one KNUTE ROCKNE ALL AMERICAN and the one WE ARE MARSHALL refers to – got a lot of (media) attention, as a demanding public inquiry into the causes and circumstances of the crashes even led to far-reaching changes in aircraft design, maintenance and accident policy. With regard to this and the crash in which Rockne and nine others lost their lives, see for example O'Leary 2010.

[18] Even though I do not want to refer to this present absence and absent presence on a theoretical level here, it has of course been heavily discussed in both philosophy (and here especially by and in reference to Jacques Derrida) and film theory. For recent approaches, see Peretz 2017 and also Lie 2020.

6.1 Immortality as the Multiplication of Immediacy — 211

Too Late and Too Early: A Mediated Possibility to Say Goodbye

About three and a half minutes earlier, KNUTE ROCKNE ALL AMERICAN shows Rockne, his wife Bonnie (Gale Page) and their kids in a lively beach scene (TC 01:27:26). After the end of the season and after years of postponing, the family is finally on vacation in Florida. But even here, football is never far away. We see Rockne watching a group of kids playing football in the sand, then talking to his wife about going to Florida every winter from now on. A young postman turns up and hands over a letter to Rockne. "Well, I've gotta go to California." His wife is not amused about the news, but Rockne says that he promised to be there if his help is needed.[19] To save time and be back with his family as soon as possible, he decides to travel by airplane. His wife, fearful about this (at the time still) very dangerous mode of travel, asks him not to fly. He nonetheless takes the plane.

During a stopover in Kansas City, a friend at the airport tells him about an incoming storm and asks Rockne if he does not want to wait for the next aircraft (TC 01:29:30). But Rockne is unwavering: "I can't waste any time. I've gotta be back in Florida by Monday. It's my vacation."

What follows is a sequence strikingly staged as a farewell scene. While the camera follows Rockne's walk across the runway to the airplane in lateral movement, a small crowd can already be spotted in the background.[20] After a medium shot depicting Rockne and his acquaintance shaking hands, the scene switches to a long shot, which not only shows us the airplane but also a rear view of a group of people lined up behind a barrier. With a slow pan to the right, the camera not only follows the plane as it starts its engines, but also reveals more and more people waving it goodbye. The following shot captures Rockne behind and framed by an airplane window. Significantly, he looks directly into the camera for about

---

19 The reason why he has to go is not revealed. The historical Rockne was about to make his way to California to participate in the shooting of the movie THE SPIRIT OF NOTRE DAME (R. Mack, 1931) as a kind of technical adviser, when the plane with him and nine other passengers crashed. The film was finally released in October 1931, a couple of months after Rockne's death, and is dedicated to his memory (see Hall 1931).
20 When speaking, in what follows, of the activity of the camera, I do not refer to it simply as a technological reproduction of a previously existent (human) gaze looking at a previously existent world, but rather, following Gilles Deleuze, as a self-referential 'perception and thinking machine,' with a 'cinematic consciousness' and its own, non-personal mode of individuation. At the center of this 'cinematic consciousness' lies the movement-image as a kind of image-producing seeing of the image itself (see Pisters 2003 and also Shaw 2008). Understood in this way, a camera does not primarily show represented objects, but rather offers a sensory perspective, a perceptual form which it itself has taken on (see Kappelhoff 1998, 104, in German and cf. Sobchack 1992).

three seconds, waves and smiles before changing the direction of his gaze and looking out of the window over his right shoulder (Figure 40).

Figure 40: Waving goodbye.

Especially in connection with the hardly synchronized movements depicted in the preceding and following shots, this direct address to the camera clearly stands out as what Francesco Casetti described as a "gesture of interpellation" (Casetti 1998, 16). But instead of 'inviting a virtual spectator to participate in the action' (see Casetti 1998, 16), the film's audio-vision seems to rather transcend or open up the diegetic world here, in order to (re-)create a process of parting by appealing to the perception of remembered and remembering imagery: the newspaper articles and images, as well as the newsreel pictures that frame this marked moment of an early *and* late farewell. In this respect, KNUTE ROCKNE ALL AMERICAN seemingly does not so much strive for accurate representation and a gesture of authentication here, but rather transcends the narrative content of its images, as well as the iconic and indexical charges of the images it incorporates, to produce an expressive movement-image, which enables what these images simply cannot show, and what history was denied: namely, the deliberate act of the sports star saying goodbye to his audience. An audience which is an ever-historical one and forms due to the layering of temporalities at work here in the first place, when the images of the news of Rockne's death and of the funeral ceremony merge with images of the melodramatic airport scene, where a farewell crowd on a runway becomes a film audience and vice versa. By means of the audiovisual gesture of this latter scene, the national hero, who suddenly and unexpectedly died, gets the belated chance to wave farewell to this nation (of film spectators). Here, KNUTE ROCKNE ALL AMERICAN does not only provoke a crystallization of a real life past and invoke the future of its plot, in which Rockne will die and his passing will be mourned again, but also generates, first, an audiovisual space of knowledge of the historical past and, second, a mediated space of historical presence in which the former might find or be given its appropriate (conciliatory) closure. It is already at this point where a comparison to JIM THORPE – ALL-AMERICAN becomes apparent, as the apotheosis of the sports hero undertaken here seems to experience a very interesting inversion in Curtiz' film ten years later, when the latter's protagonist 'comes to terms' with his audience through looking at an iconic picture of his younger self, as described in the following chapter.

Staging Invisibility and the Invisible

KNUTE ROCKNE ALL AMERICAN does not end here though, but rather embraces the audiovisual gesture just described to strengthen its melodramatic structure and prepare for its final sequence. During this sequence, the contraction of the heroic individual and the community making him a hero in the first place finally becomes the center of the film's mise en scène, rendering both the hero and the community of heroism mediated products of an audiovisual discourse as (filmic) images of images.

We see the plane moving towards the camera and taking off, then a second gaze and wave of Rockne (TC 01:30:20). This time, it is directed down to the left side of the image, again evoking the diegetic crowd standing at the gate and seeing off the plane. A shot of his worried facial expression follows, before the film cuts to a parallel shot of Bonnie, as she and the kids receive the telegram that he had sent shortly before boarding the soon-to-be deadly plane in Kansas City. Its message comes too soon and too late: "I'm practically there. Will wire again from Los Angeles. Love to all." The subtle excitement and joyful anticipation of Bonnie reading to her children is immediately undermined: Seemingly hit by some kind of negative energy, which is tonally expressed by the sudden insertion of a low and sinister drum and strings sound and finally announces the forthcoming accident point-blank, Bonnie pulls an anxious face, looks up to the sky and reaches for her jacket: "It seems to have gotten cold all of a sudden" (see Figure 41).

Figure 41: A letter and the wife as melodramatic media.

What follows is the (off screen, indirect) staging of the airplane crash already described above, followed by the rapid spread of the news about Rockne's death far and wide (TC 01:30:54). This latter sequence is made palpable by a short but elaborate sequence of repetitive superimpositions of shots, creating an accelerating, whirling movement. The staged invisibility (but audibility) of the crash from just before is transformed into an expressive illustration of something that is basically invisible in a representational sense: the spreading of the news of Rockne's death. Consistent with how it continues right after, the film (re-)constructs the popularity and remembrance of Rockne as reference system of news media and technologies of transmission: From the witness's telephone, the audio-vision takes the viewer along the phone lines to the female switchboard operators and newspaper headlines: "Rockne is dead! Yes, Rockne is dead! Yes, Rockne is dead!" The expressive movement of explosive repetitive multiplication, triggering an aesthetics of overpowering, will take center stage again shortly after, at the very end of KNUTE ROCKNE ALL AMERICAN.

A Poetics of Clarity and Control and a Mediated Media Community

With images of the apparently shocked Father John Callahan, Notre Dame's university director and Rockne's mentor, sitting at his desk next to a newspaper with the devastating headline, the film transitions into its concluding part, which depicts the memorial service (TC 01:31:54) but is, as will hopefully become clear in the course of this chapter, neither about someone being buried nor about suffering grief really.

Through extended long shots, which, with the exception of two slow vertical pans, eschew any camera movement, the university's Basilica of the Sacred Heart is presented to us in symmetrically composed images (Figure 42).

Figure 42: Visual symmetry.

The rhythmic clarity and control of the visuals is accompanied by a ringing of bells and the singing of a (shortly thereafter also shown) choir on the acoustic level, together creating an atmosphere of devout calmness and melancholic order. The display of a clear and harmonious overview fits well into the dominant imagery of the whole movie so far: Although there is more movement and acceleration at times, the film's audio-vision is almost completely freed from any turmoil or upheaval, especially with regard to the protagonists' bodies, and even more so with regard to the body that figures as the center of a very effective and regulated mise en scène throughout the whole film, even when impaired, that is Rockne's (see again Figure 36).

Here and there, views from above or shots with a clearly ordered image composition allow for the separation from the individual body and greater movement and flexibility within the image, while still offering visuals that suggest mastery or synoptic plentitude, especially with regard to the transmission of perception as powerful gaze. In this sense, the overall poetics of affect of KNUTE ROCKNE ALL AMERICAN is one of orderliness and restraint, and never one of forlornness or threat, plagued by doubt or worry. Here, it is important to note how much the movie sets itself apart from other sports films produced afterwards, as the following analysis of JIM THORPE – ALL-AMERICAN in this chapter for example will show. Most certainly, the distinctiveness of KNUTE ROCKNE ALL AMERICAN in that regard feeds from the movie's production time shortly before the United States' official entry into World War II, when an imaginary pathos of unshaken integration and development was more likely to prevail in cultural production. From that point of view, one can argue that, with films like KNUTE ROCKNE ALL AMERICAN, US culture in a way had entered the war already by putting forward and intervening in appropriate propagandistic efforts. Fittingly, there are also no setbacks when it comes to the film's narrative, with maybe one exception of the death of star player George Gipp, which, as I described above, is nevertheless executed very quickly and heavily embedded in a rhetoric of immediate continuation.

Against this backdrop, the very last, epilogue-like minute of the memorial service scene sticks out and can therefore at the same time be interpreted as historically quite symptomatic for one of the sports film's central topoi, that of eternal succession – not only in the sense of narrative dramaturgy and motif, but as an audiovisual discourse of the sports film genre's constitutive conflict of the American Dream as a time-image of community-building historicity (see chapter 3.2).

Inside the church, the scene's dramaturgy arises especially from the fact that its audiovisual dynamic is strongly interconnected with another, qualitatively different but quite dominant movement, that is the rhetoric of Father Callahan's memorial speech. After a quite complex series of long shots, which in combination with the precisely choreographed movements of the priests and altar servers measure the space of the mise en scène and the crowd inhabiting it, Callahan is shown walking up the pulpit to deliver his address (TC 01:33:49), in which Rockne's name appears strikingly late – a fact that just strengthens the invocation of the mythic hero we are about to witness.

Depicted in a lateral medium shot, he starts his speech not only by directly referring to the hundreds of people just seen gathering in the church, but also by immediately unifying them to draw a bigger picture: "We who are here are but a handful of his friends, come to pay our last tribute of devotion to his mortal remains. Of necessity, we are few in number in this hallowed place, though thousands are without the doors. But we represent millions like ourselves who are here in spirit listening in all over America." The We, present in the here and now of the church service, not only experiences an immediate expansion to become the We of a nation and a mediated public sphere – the film here also refers to the actual funeral having been a nationwide, highly mediatized event, as already indicated above. Further, it is only by means of this We that the exceptional individual Knute Rockne can take shape (again) as sports star and film hero. It is itself not simply represented but also mediated, as it forms through a poiesis of film-viewing and thus includes the audience of KNUTE ROCKNE ALL AMERICAN as a constitutional part.

The (Re-)Production of the Exceptional Individual

When Callahan starts with the second part of his first sentence, a reverse shot captures the coffin from a slightly lower and more centralized angle. It is placed in the central aisle, quite literally *among* the attendants in the rows. Surprisingly though, this configuration is not captured in the same highly symmetrical compositional style we have seen before. Since the camera is not positioned full frontal with regard to the audience and with the coffin as its exact center, the impression that Rockne's "mortal remains" are rather among the many of the crowd is further strengthened. Nonetheless, as the coffin and the audience rows do not completely converge on the same line of perspective here, a slight tension (within the image) remains, the process of full absorption into the community of grievers being delayed (Figure 43).

Figure 43: Among the many, but still outstanding.

Directly after the words "... last tribute of devotion ...", the scene cuts to a short medium tracking shot. In a straight horizontal movement to the right, the camera captures Rockne's family sitting in the first row: his daughter, his wife and his two sons, plus some men in the background. The shot does not last very long, but because of the little overall camera movement in this scene, it sticks out as quite distinct. Here, the film introduces us to a kind of movement of 'generational sequencing and multiplication,' which is picked up again a couple of seconds later, when the camera tracks along some of the players Rockne has coached, while Callahan talks about "the ideals he set up in the lives of young men." Underlining my argument here, Rockne's sons are the last in the row seen in the first shot, followed and thus continued by the young male players in the second one (Figure 44).

Figure 44: Generational sequencing.

While this audiovisually fabricated string of players already anticipates the film's epilogue, which follows shortly after and makes this string 'explode,' it also emphasizes the other vector of the sports film's conflict about how the exceptional individual is both constituted by and constitutive of (the We of a) community. Measuring this relation, the film builds an understanding of how the American nation's heroic ethos is formed and effective both as a *pars pro toto* and a *totum pro parte*. It is exactly through this reciprocity that Knute Rockne is presented and becomes palpable: He is who he is through the community, but the community is also only a community because of him. He is 'one of us,' but at the same time decisively detached from that Us, an exceptional outsider. "Yes. Knute Rockne has gone. And who was he?" asks Callahan rhetorically, and the camera jumps back to a symmetrical long shot depicting the choir room and the first few rows, creating an overview and detaching from the individual bodies and faces (of the priest, of the wife, of the kids and players) before, with the coffin at the center of the composition, being still hauled out but also absorbed by it (and upon the altar) now (Figure 45).

Figure 45: Absorbed and hauled out in symmetry.

The image then captures Callahan at his pulpit once again and via a medium shot from an almost worm's eye perspective (TC 01:35:23): "Ask the president of the United States, ask the King of Norway, ask the thousands of newspapermen ... every heart in America ... the men and women, the children, the boys of America." Here, Rockne is not only and simply elevated into a line of the (global) 'history of the great white men,' but invoked as a product of national mythology and collective perception, as the myth of an exceptional individual being told and retold, but also as images imagined and perceived by a community of exceptionalism – a community that arises out of such imagination and perception in the first place, and out of the tension of the interdependence between individual and communal subjectification. Rockne is at the same time part of and separated from the community that 'made' and 'remakes' him, as much as this community *is* only because of him. As already hinted at before, this imagination of the exceptional individual being the product of a forming community and vice versa is also addressed explicitly as one of media coverage here, and, in that way and more importantly, as a reflexive audiovisual discourse of a poiesis of film-viewing.

A Ghost in an Empty Stadium

The question returns once again, having transcended Callahan as the character who asks: "Who was this man?" As if answering 'all these people are him,' the image shows another long shot, which depicts the congregation and the choir room. It is the presence of the community, through which Knute Rockne not only became who he was but now again still is and can be in the future. By moving away from any individual (figurative) corporeality, the film refrains from the solemn atmosphere here, as the "bowed heads in grief" mentioned by Callahan disappear in the dark of the long shot. At the same time, it also establishes the ornamental crowd attending the ceremony as some kind of vacuum to be filled, as a template of collectivity on which the hero can appear again – a vacuum through which past, present and future are able to come together. A cross-fade leads us out of the church and on the field of the Notre Dame stadium, where Rockne – with the help of another superimposition – appears as a ghost-like figure walking from left to right in front of a stadium wall (Figure 46).

Figure 46: A ghost in the stadium.

A passionate voice-over, whose speed and aggressiveness is underlined by the reintroduction of the rising *Victory March*,[21] that counters the slow and festive speech of Callahan (TC 01:36:08): "And from that field of Notre Dame, the spirit of Knute Rockne is reborn in those who have kept their pledge to carry on for

---

21 The *Victory March* is the fight song of the University of Notre Dame and one of the most famous collegiate team anthems. It was written by Notre Dame graduates and brothers John F. Shea and Michael J. Shea at the beginning of the twentieth century. The song officially appeared under the copyright of the University of Notre Dame in 1928.

him." The impression of a vacuum-like image space is picked up again by the next shot, which shows the huge but empty Notre Dame stadium from a position high up in the stands. The voice-over superimposes Rockne's legacy onto the depicted stadium, thereby positioning it within a rhetoric of national symbolism: "Today, in every corner of this country, they are teaching his standards of clean sportsmanship and right living ..." Quite surprisingly, KNUTE ROCKNE ALL AMERICAN does not use the attending crowd to represent the (national) community addressed before, nor does it immediately show any athletic action on the field. What it shows instead is the emptiness of the space typically occupied by the athletes and their spectators, the space into which they are inscribed through sports and sports films.

Here, the film shows the flip side of its poetics of present absence with regard to the relationship between individual heroic subjectivity and worshiping community: While it was Rockne being invoked by the mourning mass in the church before, it is now this mass, which forms around him only through the film's (non-representational) audiovisual dramaturgic progression. In this way, the scene not only emphasizes the crowd by marking it as strikingly absent in the picture, but, at the same time, affirms the strength of the spectatorial position, addressed to and animated in the film's actual viewers. Confronted with pictures of an empty stadium, we as spectators are thrown back on ourselves *as* spectators to an even greater extent.

This intensified interweaving of the stadium space and the film viewer by means of the film's image space helps to install the final dynamic of the audiovisual rhetoric of KNUTE ROCKNE ALL AMERICAN: an expressive movement of filling and multiplication, which propagates power and superiority by means of overwhelming reproduction. This is obtained through a brimming and banging last sequence, which in a sense attacks its viewer. It amplifies the string of young players presented before into an expressive movement of explosive multiplication, thereby putting these players in action and creating an aesthetic of frenetic chaos and exuberant enthusiasm.

Succession as Exploding Multiplication

With the help of an iris trick shot, the empty field is suddenly filled with play action. While the voice-over calls out the names and school affiliations of all the players who were once coached by Rockne and then became (successful) coaches themselves, a series of different game scenes is shown. Each of them is a found footage fragment only capturing one or two seconds of a play. While the material itself already contains a great deal of movement – the game scenes are depicted in medium long shots relatively close to the field, always showing at least ten athletes moving around – the overall motion is additionally intensified through wipes coming from both sides of the frame and superimpositions that show emblems, flags, mascots, and cheerleaders. In this way, the busy scurry of the players combines with other, opposing movements and fragmentations. This overflowing expressive movement is only held together by the rhythmic voice-over and the fast-paced orchestral music.

Hence, what is staged here is the idea of succession as a passing on, as legacy, as an accelerated sequence, which is less linear but instead quite literally spreads out in all directions, kind of like an explosion. With the help of its overpowering aesthetics, the film here not only enacts the impression of an American community as some kind of invincible steamroller, thereby connecting its hero, the team he created and the mourning nation left behind after the former's death, but also praises the present moment and the future (to come) that is born from and clearly in favor of the past. This ending sequence of KNUTE ROCKNE ALL AMERICAN is about a moving Now rather than any kind of standstill. It counts on or emphasizes an aesthetically produced effect of presentness, which can also be found with regard to the present tense used in the voice-over: "*Today*, in every corner of this country, they are teaching his standards of clean sportsmanship and right living ..." Within or through this presentness, time contracts or overlaps: The found footage images show the mentioned disciples of Rockne ("Rockne's boys") as players on the field under his coaching reign at Notre Dame between 1918 and 1930,[22] while the voice-over addresses them – about ten to twenty years later, given the production year of the movie – as the coaches they have or had become after their career as players, guiding teams and school programs all over the country.

Here, KNUTE ROCKNE ALL AMERICAN clearly refers to the custom of what is known as the coaching tree, which is very common in American football, especially in today's *National Football League* culture. Similar to a family tree, a coaching tree (visually) combines both a linear and a net-like structure of expansion (lineage and spreading). It is this combination of rhythmic succession, on the one hand ('one hero after another') and a less regulated but powerful force of instant multiplication, on the other ('one hero makes for a lot of further heroes'), which the film audiovisually renders, propagating endless multiplication through the condensation and sudden expansion of time and space.

---

22 There are no clear sources, but apparently, director Llyod Bacon used material from the football program of his alma mater Santa Clara University. As the movie was shot with the official permission of the University of Notre Dame, some footage might also come from this university's archives.

Quite similar to the rhetoric of war films of the time when KNUTE ROCKNE ALL AMERICAN was produced, and here especially of what is often referred to as combat films,[23] the movie circles around an idea of a transcendent, masculine corporeality being able to reproduce and multiply itself. But while in those war movies, the seemingly endless chain of self-replicating male power is staged as a linear and serial assembly of military fatalities and therefore linked to a continuous (although often brutally fabricated) gesture of sacrifice, here, the idea of constant, never-ending male replacement turns into a celebration of instant and powerful multiplication. Of course, there are war films that stage it that way, too. But what I want to carve out here is the specificity of the resolving of death into the transcendent participation in national community – tied to a university legacy and thus to the creation and persistence of an institution that is similar to, but also different from the military apparatus.[24] The dialectic between the nation as a society of war and as a society of civil (including athletic) education is negotiated in KNUTE ROCKNE ALL AMERICAN by means of another, very telling scene reflective of its production date. It reconstructs a historical committee hearing on the occasion of the discussion about the form and purpose of (a back then highly unregulated) college sports in the 1920s and 1930s. The Rockne character attends the hearing and gives a passionate speech, in which he argues for the necessity of college sports to provide a 'safer outlet for man's natural spirit of combat than war and revolutions,' to 'build character' and give life experience, especially in times in which "the most dangerous thing in American life is that we're getting soft" (TC 01:22:27). In this sense, the poetics of Bacon's film, as I have analyzed it here, could also be seen as contrasting the temporal (and contemporary) state of emergency of war and the radical disruption and overhaul of time accompanying it with the commemorative, repetitive temporality of continuous enhancement.

At the end, the hero, whose individualization and uniqueness through the community was the film's main concern so far, transcends not as a transtemporal singularity, but as the origin of a process of splitting, which not only seems stronger than its source and its individual parts but also contains or at least indicates an endlessness and repetition, especially through the fusion of the athletic action on the field and the personalized institution forming it, of player and coach. It is the film's overall presentation of Rockne as a successful example of a

---

23 See for example BATAAN (T. Garnett, 1943), GUNG HO! (R. Enright, 1943) or SAHARA (Z. Korda, 1943).
24 With regard to the medial formation and characteristics of this national body, see also especially chapter 5 of this book, where I analyze the film MIRACLE (G. O'Connor, 2004) with regard to the sports film's poetics of flow.

player becoming coach, which KNUTE ROCKNE ALL AMERICAN sharpens here, and through which it is able to think the idea of eternal succession as a movement of condensation and dissemination, of sequentiality and momentum, of a passing on in multiplication.

Rather than simply adding him to an already existing string of collectivity (of great players and coaches) or merging with the mourning community established shortly before, the heroic figure Knute Rockne is shown as a force which *produces* community in the first place. Even as he himself is identified as a product of (myth-creating media) communality in the church service sequence before, he is now presented as a singular and singularized power giving birth to a multitude of players becoming coaches – the hardly visible, ghost-like figure in the huge empty stadium is put in multiplied motion on and off the field and with it the film's viewer off the screen. Significantly in this respect, there are no diegetic spectators shown during this last sequence, except for a very short period of time at its very end. The cheering of the crowd is taken over by the audiovisual representation itself (especially through the level of sound) and the audience affectively relating to it.

A Nation of Heroes in the Here and Now

In this manner, KNUTE ROCKNE ALL AMERICAN at its end confronts us with a conception of heroism, which is neither solely based on an individual's self-sacrifice nor mass worship of such an individual. Rather than understanding exceptionalism in this sense as explicit difference, the film seems to emphasize the mutual relation of individual subject and community that makes for a hero, or, more precisely: that makes for the ritual- and media-based mythologization, which makes for a hero. Knute Rockne is not simply included in the community, he does not merely become part of it through his death. Rather, through commemoration, he produces and at the same time is produced by that community – through stories and images being told and listened to, shown and seen, remembered and actualized, formed and modified. (KNUTE ROCKNE ALL AMERICAN is always already part of this media interweaving.) As much as the church service sequence makes clear that Knute Rockne is who he is through the community that remembers him, this very last sequence emphasizes, on the other hand, that this communal We also is and will only continue to be a We because of him.

Now, the forthright and emphatic audiovisual realization of an impromptu multiplication, analytically described above, constitutes the particularity of KNUTE ROCKNE ALL AMERICAN in regard to this by all means typical sports film formula or constellation. Moreover, it also solidifies the movie's propagandistic appearance shortly before the United States' entry into World War II though, as the sports film's key operation of binding together past and future (*in memoriam* meeting *in providentiam*) and its central topos of endless succession culminate here in a martially charged expressive movement of explosion, as well as in an audiovisual rhetoric of instant and plural reproduction. The endlessness of the line of (repetitive) succession seems to be framed less within a gesture that praises futurity and linear continuation, but is rather related to an immediate presence and an ever-evolving present. As with the war film, the past appears to be gone but not lost. But rather than functioning as a sacrifice and a kind of promise for a (better) time to come, this past here inscribes a 'game-plan' for (the future in) the present, manifested in an experience of a Now, triggered through the described audiovisual action modality and its affective poetics of aggressive exuberance and overpowering. Less about a multitude of individuals who retrospectively become heroes through their victimhood, but more as the basis for a nation and that nation's continued existence (the often invoked 'greater cause'), the ending of KNUTE ROCKNE ALL AMERICAN is about all the new heroes in a here and now.

Roughly eighteen months before the United States' official entry into World War II, the film stages a ceremony of intimidating greatness: a forward-looking declaration of expansive and expanding power, produced by and producing a historical present of strong propagandistic efforts.[25] In the end, the singled-out hero Knute Rockne makes for a nation of heroes. Hence, instead of embedding the tragic event of his death into a rhetoric of finding new power through the sublimation of suffering, this end rather aims at the production of an all-along strong communal We, which (re-)forms itself in commemoration, and at the same time infects itself with the contagious force of heroism it produces: becoming a hero among heroes by making a hero.

In this sense, the audiovisually orchestrated idea of a kind of automatic, self-reproducing unstoppability here also contests Aaron Baker's claim about Bacon's film employing a rhetoric that "emphasizes the price paid for progress" (Baker 2003, 7). Not only because the film's ending, as this analysis has shown, does not simply emphasize a rhetoric of sacrifice, but also because the film as a whole clearly avoids granting this 'price' much time or space. Quite the opposite: It basically spares its protagonist, as well as its viewer, from any turbulence or shattering that accompanies Rockne's rise and successful career, especially when looking at the movie's audiovisual staging.

---

25 Although the United States did not officially enter World War II before the attack on Pearl Harbor in December 1941, the country's involvement started much earlier, especially with regard to industrial and economic action and intervention.

6.2 Cyclical Infinity and Finally Becoming Spectator Again: JIM THORPE – ALL-AMERICAN

Being Denied and Not Fitting In: Thorpe as Tragic Hero

In what follows, I want to mirror the previously analyzed KNUTE ROCKNE ALL AMERICAN (L. Bacon, 1940) with another sports movie of the biographical form produced around ten years later but still clearly resembling Classical Hollywood cinema: Michael Curtiz' JIM THORPE – ALL-AMERICAN (1951), with Burt Lancaster playing the lead as "the greatest athlete that ever lived" (Wheeler 1979, 118).[26] Again focusing especially on the movie's ending, this comparative analysis will not only provide for another formative variation of the sports film's genre poetics and further elucidate the relative idiosyncrasy of Bacon's film, but also present a very illustrative example of the genre's historical variance with regard to what I have described as its constitutive conflict: the tense, oscillating relation between (the production of) communal subjectification and (the production of) individual subjectification, rooted in a specific notion of historicity as temporal crystallization (see chapter 3.2).

The narrative constellation of Curtiz' film is a little different than that of KNUTE ROCKNE ALL AMERICAN from the outset. While the latter presents a rather uncontested story about a good student and football player becoming a successful star coach, the plot of JIM THORPE – ALL-AMERICAN develops from the rise and fall of an exceptionally talented athlete of Native American heritage, whose exposure to racist social structures is blended with the character's personal struggle, especially concerning his stubbornness and temper. Aaron Baker calls such channeling and concealing of problematic systemic structures into/by a character's individual destiny and emotional drama "melodramatic containment" (Baker 2003, 8). He grasps it as a common dramaturgical operation of Hollywood cinema in general and the sports film in particular.

---

26 According to Robert W. Wheeler, it was Martin Sheridan, a successful athlete at the beginning of the twentieth century and five-time Olympic gold medalist, who made that statement after the real Jim Thorpe broke his Amateur Athletic Union's All-Around Championship record in 1912. An anecdote that also found its way into the movie goes that Gustav V, then King of Sweden, said something similar to Thorpe when handing him his prizes at the closing ceremony of the Summer Olympics in Stockholm earlier that year, where Thorpe stunned the world by winning both the pentathlon and the decathlon. While it surely is a somewhat hackneyed term, this formula of "the greatest athlete" might have nonetheless never been more fitting than with regard to Thorpe and his almost surreal sporting achievements – not only in track and field and football, but also in baseball and basketball. For a biographical account, see Buford 2010.

Rather than serving as the beginning of a successful career like in KNUTE ROCKNE ALL AMERICAN, 'becoming coach' appears as an unfulfilled wish of the protagonist and thus a tragedy-inducing desire driving the narrative until the very end of the movie, as described later in this chapter. At the end of the film's first half, during which we follow the young student athlete's life at the Carlisle Indian Industrial School[27] – having troubles with learning, finding friends, falling in love, but first and foremost excelling in track and field and becoming the star player of the university's football team – Thorpe receives a rejection for a much-wished-for coaching job. As the job goes to his white rival Tom Ashenbrunner (Hubie Kerns) of University of Pennsylvania – the film has shown the two as the battling superstars of their respective teams in a long game scene just before – Thorpe suspects racial prejudices underlying the decision. Disappointed and full of anger, he decides to participate in the 1912 Olympics "to work harder" and "make a record they won't be able to ignore." No sooner said than done: An almost four-minute-long sequence,[28] which consists foremost of (medium) close-up shots of the performing protagonist, interspersed newsreel footage of the actual Olympics in Stockholm and images of newspaper headlines, all accompanied by a driving orchestral score, pictures Thorpe ultimately winning both the pentathlon and the decathlon (TC 00:58:29, Figure 47).

After being enthusiastically celebrated back at home, the tables turn quickly though: Due to a minor misconduct regarding the rule of amateurism – Thorpe had played professional baseball over the summer, receiving meager pay while presumably unaware of his wrongdoing and not using an alias as other college players usually did – he gets retrospectively disqualified and stripped of his Olympic medals and records.[29] His bitterness and anger against 'the institutions' grow further and become

---

[27] The United States Indian Industrial School in Carlisle, Pennsylvania, was the first federally-funded off-reservation Indian boarding school. For an account on the history and legacy of one of the most famous examples of educational campaigns of forced assimilation and eventually cultural genocide in US history, see Fear-Segal / Rose 2018. While Curtiz' film addresses this highly problematic background rather selectively but quite directly at the beginning of the film by means of its voice-over ("School, that frightening institution of the white man's world") and a dialogue, during which freshman Thorpe is bullied by the captain of the football team and told to recite the Gettysburg address in English, because "Indian isn't spoken here," the film as a whole responds to it in a rather mediated but nonetheless quite obvious way, especially with its main protagonist being constantly presented as a hero not fitting in. I will come back to this important aspect later in the chapter.
[28] The indicated time codes refer to the US 2007 Warner Home Video DVD, played on VLC media player for macOS X.
[29] This episode more or less matches the real events. Due to the fact of severe racism at that time, there have always been assumptions that Thorpe lost his medals and records because of

an increasing burden on his private life as well. When his beloved son suddenly dies, the tragic spiral of personal as well as athletic downfall finally gathers pace.

Figure 47: A record impossible to ignore (JIM THORPE – ALL-AMERICAN).

---

his ethnicity (see Watterson 2000, 151). In addition, and even though his achievements also received great acclaim during his lifetime and after his death in 1953, his Olympic awards were not reinstated until 1982. Until today, the International Olympique Committee lists him as a co-champion, together with his competitors that he clearly defeated (see Jenkins 2012).

Becoming Coach as Final Reconciliation

At the very end of JIM THORPE – ALL-AMERICAN, the main protagonist's personal conflict of not 'fitting in' and being unable or denied 'to find his place,' which the movie repeatedly makes palpable as a viewer experience through its expressive movement, resolves after all: Thorpe encounters a group of kids playing in the streets in an epilogue-like final scene, which is then followed by yet another epilogue-like final scene (TC 01:43:59). While the former shows Thorpe finally becoming a coach, the latter depicts a banquet in Thorpe's honor and is actually the second part of a framing narrative that parenthesizes the film as a whole, designating its main plot a *récit encadré*, a flashback story within a story, told by Thorpe's former coach and mentor Glenn Scobey "Pop" Warner as an omniscient and homodiegetic narrator. But for now, let us stick to the first of these two last scenes (TC 01:41:35).

Thorpe accidentally runs over the kids' football with his truck. After he is prompted to drive on by a police officer, a cross-fade presents the kids trying to repair the broken ball. Suddenly, an adult body enters the frame from the left, and a backwards tracking shot reveals that it is Thorpe who exchanges the ball for a brand new one. After Thorpe assures them of their new possession, the kids immediately start playing again. Thorpe watches them and after a shot reverse shot construction intervenes: "If you fellows are gonna use a new football, you ought to learn how to use it right." Another brief, now forward tracking shot creates a cramped visual space in which the kids are closely grouped around the centrally positioned Thorpe – a shot typical for this sports film standard scene, in which a coach talks to his players in a huddle (Figure 48).

Figure 48: Becoming coach.

Thorpe gives the kids some advice and they ask him if he is willing to help them with an upcoming game they want to play. He agrees and, after one of the young boys talks enthusiastically about the medals to be won, Thorpe responds: "Well, let's just play to win the game." A medium shot positions Thorpe in the visual center, framed by the backs of two of the boys. The camera films from a low angle, additionally emphasizing Thorpe's upper body and face against the sky – a variation of the *heroic shot* we have encountered many times before during the first half of the movie, but which has been strikingly absent since the protagonist's life began to show cracks (Figure 49).

Figure 49: A heroic shot once again.

Thorpe, looking down to the right for a moment, immediately turns his head when one of the boys shouts: "Okay, coach!" A ringing on the audio track emphasizes the word "coach" and Thorpe's immediate reaction to it. The kids leave the frame, the image jumps to a close shot of Thorpe staring paralyzed 'into the void.' The absent-minded expression of his face is mobilized by the reverberating ringing sound slowly leading into a strings chord sequence. Its quality of an alarming tension reveals itself as the reprise of an earlier part of the film's score, which introduced us to the young Jim Thorpe running away from school and back to his parents' farm on a reservation at the very beginning of the movie (TC 00:03:06).

Thorpe looks down at the football in his hands, the tension of the music dissolves via a decelerando and a decrescendo into a more melodic and solemn sequence. Thorpe, as if suddenly enlightened, looks up once more and repeats the word "coach." Drums set in, the music accelerates and gets louder again. A jump cut leads to a high angle medium (crane) shot of Thorpe walking backwards. He takes three more steps, shouts "Here she comes!" and kicks the ball. With a loud horn section setting in, the montage 'throws' the camera's gaze into the air, imitating the flight of the football kicked: catching a short glimpse of it against the sky and then quickly panning down again to approach the isolated Thorpe on the ground in a steady tracking shot from above.

This movement of inversion – the camera seems to render the flight of the football as rather one of a boomerang – fits in with the audiovisual orchestration of the last nine minutes of the film. Overall, these last minutes, which include a long sequence previous to the two scenes just mentioned, obey a poetic logic that moves from (images of) isolation to (images of) unification. After the film's hero is once again and very clearly shown as an individual *outside* of (sports) communality, he is then included again as spectator, coach and then spectator again, and by means of an audiovisual gesture that directly relates his supposedly narcissistic introspection to the act of honoring and media commemoration. This conflict between isolation and unification, between an individual subjectification of self-reference and a communal subjectification of mediated remembrance (as finally a poiesis of film-viewing), is laid out by means of three consecutive and, in this regard, clearly corresponding scenes. The first one depicts Thorpe attending the opening ceremony of the 1932 Olympic Games in the Los Angeles Memorial Coliseum (TC 01:36:19); the second one encompasses the encounter of Thorpe and the kids described above, while the third one brings us back to the gala of honor (TC 01:43:59), which, as already mentioned, narratively frames the whole movie.

Thorpe is repeatedly set against and isolated from and within images of communality by means of especially montage, image composition and sound: of the historical mass in the newsreel footage, of the honoring society at the beginning and the end of the movie, of the community of the 'new generation.' As a result, Thorpe and with him the film's viewer are constantly (and often quite literally) confronted with Thorpe as mediated image, as the singled-out, exceptional individual made by but also not being part of an also mediated and mediating community of spectators, including those watching JIM THORPE – ALL-AMERICAN. It is this imagined and at the same time quite real community – forming along the perception of the film's audiovisual images in the first place – that opens up the possibility for him to become the national hero he was seemingly denied to be before or, as the movie at least narratively suggests, he denied himself to be. What comes to a head here through the film's poetics of affect seems to be the fundamental tension characterizing heroism as an operating principle of community-building in sports and film: the back and forth between the narcissistic impulse and effort of the individual to distance itself or to give in, versus the impulse and effort of demanding veneration through the collective, as well as the violence taking place when those impulses proceed and collide.

Being Out of Time and the (Filmic) Negotiation of Sociality

Knute Rockne's exceptionalism in KNUTE ROCKNE ALL AMERICAN is presented through and within an aesthetics of flow and control and, at the very end of the film, by means of an expressive movement of spreading reproduction, emphasized as community-produced, community-producing and community-strengthening (see chapter 6.1). In contrast, JIM THORPE – ALL-AMERICAN deals more with the flip side of that exceptionalism: the problem of 'fitting in' in the first place. While Rockne is presented as being consistently integrated (within the mise en scène, within the expressive movement) and in control of time, Thorpe is a hero *out of* time, an outsider whose non-integration lies at the core of the movie's audiovisual and narrative dramaturgy. This is already staged very early on in the film, for example and most pointedly when Thorpe is shown returning home faster by foot than his dad by carriage, or when he beats the professional runners on the university's track in passing when unintentionally crashing a practice (TC 00:15:02).

Even though these scenes of repeatedly failed or rejected integration here might be very susceptive for a reading in the vein of a certain idea of character psychology (of Classical Hollywood), which often and especially in regard to the sports film has been criticized for concealing socio-structural problems and causalities by emphasizing the personality flaws of its protagonists,[30] I suggest to take another route. That is, to show that when we grasp these scenes along their expressive unfolding and the perceptual retracing of their audiovisual orchestration and thus as the product of a poiesis of film-viewing, we are able to

---

30 See again Baker 2003, but also Price 1973, who takes a closer look at the stereotyping of Native Americans in motion pictures, but also assigns JIM THORPE – ALL-AMERICAN to a wave of pro-Native American movies in the 1950s following the Western BROKEN ARROW (D. Daves, 1950). Especially noteworthy in this regard is the sequence that precedes the mentioned scene of Thorpe unintendedly beating the runners on the track and in that way attracting coach Pop Warner's interest. Here, as well as in its very first scene, the film suggests that sports functions as a compensation for Thorpe having problems with learning and educational institutions in general (TC 00:13:50).

learn much more about at least three things: first, about this film's connection to other sports films and especially KNUTE ROCKNE ALL AMERICAN in the sense of its specific intervening in the sports film's audiovisual discourse of communality and historicity; second, about its part in the coproduction of the genre by means of this poetic relationality in the first place; and third, about its politics beyond the representation of narrative content. It is on this level of "the interaction of an indeterminate plurality of spectators with audiovisual images of an indeterminate diversity of cultural production [...] embedded in the history of rhetoric and poetic formations of a shared reality" (Müller / Kappelhoff 2018, 36 et seq.) on which we have to understand genre cinema as being concerned with the processes of negotiation of sociality in the first place: of in- and exclusion, of belonging and non-belonging, of becoming a subject within and without a community through perception, taste and eccentric self-expression (see Kappelhoff 2018a, 349 et seq.). With regard to the sports film, this conflict about the manifestation and relation of an individual I and a collective We becomes especially acute when it concerns notions of individual performance and camaraderie, of heroism, extraordinariness and collective worship, themselves obviously being inscribed in the cultural practice of sports from the very beginning, but thereby also always already playing their part in the production, circulation and consumption of imagery.

Right from the very beginning of JIM THORPE – ALL-AMERICAN, this line of conflict is presented as precarious, as constantly failing or collapsing – for example during the (split) scene that frames the whole movie and shows a festive banquet in honor of Jim Thorpe. Here, we see and hear the honoring crowd and not only one but two speakers, while the honored individual, the old Thorpe, remains uncannily absent for quite a long time – strictly speaking, until the very end of the movie, which of course also provides for a certain dramaturgical blank space then to be filled by Warner's flashback narrative. Or, as another example, the already mentioned first scene of the flashback narrative where the young Thorpe runs away from school, followed by Thorpe's first experiences (of violent segregation) on college campus, where he is intimidated and challenged by the football team's captain.[31]

---

[31] While those first scenes on campus seem to mirror Thorpe's encounter with young players at the end of the movie, they certainly also evoke Ronald's arrival on campus in Buster Keaton's 1927 film COLLEGE, in which the state of being an outsider is not only exploited for comic purpose, but also generated through the confrontation of athletic and intellectual prowess, a controversially discussed topic within the educational system of the USA even today. Remember Ronald's first words during his high school graduation speech about the 'Curse of Athletics' (which we have to read of course, since COLLEGE is a silent film): "The secret of getting a

Now, almost at the end of the movie, Thorpe's singling out climaxes, his state of 'being out of time' finally culminating as a multifaceted question of belonging and, ultimately, of space and position: that is, with regard to the actual audio-vision as the figure's space within the mise en scène, with regard to the space of the mediated Thorpe as an expressive and perceiving body and thus as another image within an audiovisual discourse of a poiesis of film-viewing, and, last but not least, with regard to what we might call the actual Thorpe's standing in society and that society's history.

The Hero as Isolated Spectator of a Collective Subjectivity

Pop Warner, his former, father-like coach and the film's narrator, seeks out Thorpe in a night club, where the latter just got dropped as a Native American cliché-dressed announcer for a dance contest (TC 01:33:04). Having lost his Olympic medals and athletic strength (in the scene before he collapses during a football game), as well as his family and friends (his son has died, his wife has left him, and his former teammates have turned away from him), Thorpe has most definitely reached rock bottom. After Warner presents him with a ticket for the opening ceremony of the Olympic Games in Los Angeles the next day, Thorpe grumpily tears up the ticket and tells Warner to leave him alone. After a short dispute, Warner quits and the camera turns to Thorpe tremblingly sipping liquor from a glass. A cross-fade leads over to the next scene, for a brief moment creating a haunting double image of Thorpe's sweaty, exhausted face, which is surrounded by (a bird's-eye shot of) the huge *Los Angeles Memorial Coliseum*, the stadium that hosted the 10th Summer Olympics in 1932 (Figure 50).

In what follows, JIM THORPE – ALL-AMERICAN combines newsreel footage of the actual opening ceremony with (studio) footage of Lancaster's Thorpe as one of its spectators. Here, the interweaving of film hero and real-life historic example, which at the end of KNUTE ROCKNE ALL AMERICAN is established through the staging of a ghost-like reincarnation of the (already dead) protagonist within an empty Notre Dame stadium and then filled with archival game scene footage aurally attributed to the players trained by Rockne, is performed even more concretely: assembling the film's protagonist and the historical sports event through montage, with the Hollywood star's face at the center of another

---

medal like mine is books not sports. The student who wastes his time on athletics rather than study only shows ignorance."

6.2 Cyclical Infinity and Finally Becoming Spectator Again — 235

Figure 50: Fallen star and saint.

audiovisual reflection of the connection between communal veneration, stardom subjectivity and visual media.

Festive horns set in on the soundtrack (TC 01:36:18). We see the packed stadium from above and then, in a low angle medium close up shot, people walking through an entrance gate. The camera focuses on two hands pulling a provisionally patched ticket out of a coat pocket and then handing it over to a second pair of hands (of a ticket inspector). Thorpe has changed his mind and indeed has come to the opening ceremony. After another long newsreel shot of the stadium, we encounter him coming out of an entrance tunnel, filmed from a frontal and slightly low angle position. The camera approaches the troubled looking Thorpe, the black background setting his body apart from any diegetic world. Another shot slowly panning to the left along the masses in the stadium finally stitches together the newsreel footage of the 1932 Summer Olympics and point of view of Thorpe, who is, once again and, as so often in the first half of the movie, monumentally presented through another extremely low angle shot following this (Figure 51). The scope or symbolic significance of detached sublimity of this, what I call, *heroic shot* is finally measured in its extremes, starting with Thorpe's face becoming the stadium and ending with his solitary body being lost in that same stadium.

Figure 51: Becoming historical spectator.

After Thorpe sits down next to Pop Warner, the viewer is introduced to the third element of the mise en scène. Besides the newsreel footage and the shots of Thorpe watching the spectacle, a radio broadcaster is shown sitting in a commentator booth and announcing the athletes' entry: "Here they come, the athletes of all nations!" A long shot of the first athletes walking into the stadium is followed by a medium shot of Warner and Thorpe, the latter exposed not only through his dark jacket, but also because he is the only person not clapping. A slight turning of Thorpe's head initiates another cut to the marching athletes on the field, with parts of the packed stands in the background. The montage then breaks free from the shot reverse shot of the point of view construction for a brief moment and presents two additional and very different views of the events on the field back to back: another aerial perspective capturing about one third of the stadium, followed by a shot taken directly on the sidelines.[32]

---

[32] All the found footage Curtiz integrated at the end of the movie seems to stem from newsreel clips of Pathé News and Paramount News. Today, the material is located at the Sherman Grindberg Film Library, and a lot of it is accessible online, on the library's website as well as through Getty Images. See for example https://filmlibrary.shermangrinberg.com/?s=file=32837

This measuring of the (huge) dimensions of the stadium is then projected back onto (a close up of) Thorpe's/Lancaster's face.

This back and forth between the proceedings of the historical opening ceremony, during which the entry of the athletes into the stadium is followed by a depiction of the vice president's opening words and an athlete's recitation of the Olympic Oath, the mass audience and Thorpe as the singled-out spectator is repeated multiple times. This combines with the miscellaneous, vigorous and incisive sounds: the radio commentator's energetic announcement, the loud and sharp applause of the crowd, the marching music setting in again and again,[33] the audiovisual staging of the scene produces an expressive movement of pressure built and, in a way, circling around Thorpe. From the very beginning of this scene, it is at least as much about him being watched as it is about him watching.

The huge dimensions of the visual space of the stadium are repeatedly directed towards Thorpe's face, whose expression thereby develops from stubborn ignorance to one of more reflective and emotional involvement. Pop Warner's taunting final words from the previous scene – "All I can say is that when the real battle started, the great Jim Thorpe turned out to be a powder puff" – audiovisually extend to a struggle of enforced integration: Thorpe's disappointment and defiance, channeled in the facial expression of the close-up shots, are placed against the force of the big and loud crowd being united in (watching) sports. The latter is especially rendered by the (extreme) long shots of the stadium as well as by the loud clapping and the well-known national music pieces on the soundtrack, making sure to include the film viewer recognizing them as a constitutive part of this force.

This audiovisual conflict between (national) communality and the hero as an individual outsider is then even further intensified: After the commentator has announced the American athletes separately ("the final contingent"), the montage creates a direct line of sight between those athletes walking past the stands and Thorpe, who noticeably changes his viewing direction and lifts his head in reaction to the marching athletes, some of which then seem to directly return his gaze in the next shot. Once again, the movement on the field is picked up by the head and facial movements of the protagonist Thorpe, whose visual presence is additionally intensified through the temporal extension of the shots depicting him while he reacts to what happens on the field (Figure 52).

(stadium shots, Charles Curtis waving to the crowd, athletes marching during "The Parade of Nations") or https://filmlibrary.shermangrinberg.com/?s=file=32840 (Curtis delivering the opening words) (accessed 18 July 2018).

33 We hear *Semper Fidelis*, the march of the United States Marine Corps, followed by *Hail to the Chief*, the official salute of the US president.

Figure 52: Watching and being watched.

Spectatorship as Mediated Subjective Collectivity

A short gap between the steadily paced ending of *Semper Fidelis* and the start of the much brisker *Hail to the Chief* marks the next expressive movement unit of the scene.[34] Another short extract of the found footage material is semantically charged through the following shot, which, once again, depicts the commentator (and one of his colleagues) in his booth – this time from behind, causing the men's bodies to be projected against the ornamental mass in the stadium stands. He announces the arrival of Vice President Charles Curtis, thereby instantly referring to the audience's reaction in the stadium: "Listen to the ovation the crowd is giving him!" To the planar noise of shouting and clapping, a long shot shows around 150 people getting up from their seats, followed by another take of Thorpe sitting next to Warner. In strong contrast to the overall audiovisual movement of collective enthusiasm and uniformity, which comes across as contagious even outside of the frame, the hero's body remains as if paralyzed and, in this paralysis, excluded (see Figure 53).

---

34 While *Semper Fidelis* was composed by the famous "American March King" John Philip Sousa in 1888, the genesis of *Hail to the Chief* can be traced back to the 1810 narrative poem *The Lady of the Lake* by Scottish poet Sir Walter Scott. The poem, very influential in the nineteenth century, includes, inter alia, the boat song *Hail to the Chief* in its second canto (*The Island*). It was arguably set to music in 1812 by English composer James Sanderson (see Nowlan 2016, 62/63). Apparently, in JIM THORPE – ALL-AMERICAN, the anthem is performed without the usual four ruffles and flourishes, the preceding fanfare for such honors music (with four being the highest honor). I can only guess if this omission might be connected to the fact that it is not the president but 'just' the vice president appearing – due to the Great Depression, US President Herbert Hoover, like many athletes, was prevented from attending the 1932 Olympic Games in Los Angeles – or if the sound was cut because of editing reasons.

Figure 53: Collective enthusiasm vs. individual paralysis.

After Thorpe is informed about the vice president's Native American descent by Warner ("Charles Curtis, Indian."), the music stops and we see Thorpe in another close up shot, again and in contrast to the people around him sadly looking down. Then, the constant audiovisual linking of Thorpe and the ceremony's events, with the former sports star as seemingly the only 'non-affected' spectator, pauses for almost thirty seconds. Additional found footage material shows Curtis, who actually was the first and until this day has been the only (vice) president with Native American ancestry, delivering his opening remarks.[35] Only after two other shots, one showing a group of five fanfare trumpeters, another slowly panning along the athletes on the field, we return to Thorpe's/Lancaster's face.

After the vice president's opening speech, Thorpe is now confronted with another part of "all that flag waving routine, the ra ra stuff," as he called it when

---

35 Charles Curtis served as the 31st Vice President of the United States from 1929 to 1933. Born on 25 January 1860 in Topeka, Kansas Territory, his mother Ellen (Pappan) Curtis was of Kaw, Osage, Potawatomi and French origin (see McKie 2014).

talking to Warner the night before. This time though, it is not the administration or the 'institutional body' that speaks (and with which Thorpe has been in conflict with for such a long time), but the athletes themselves. Once more presented through interwoven historical audiovisual material of the actual 1932 Olympics, the audience and Thorpe witness the recitation of the Athletes' Olympic Oath.³⁶ A medium long shot shows the speaker behind a podium, and in front of a couple of flag bearers and a group of female athletes raising their right hand for the oath. While the found footage's original audio track delivers the oath in full length, the image again jumps back and forth twice between the newsreel images and the seated Thorpe, thereby getting closer to each protagonist respectively (Figure 54).

Figure 54: Witnessing the Athletes' Olympic Oath.

Here, JIM THORPE – ALL-AMERICAN channels the solemn collaborative words of the Athlete's Oath, themselves subject of a ritualistic expressive act of repetition and communitization, upon the film's tragic hero, thereby transforming them into words touching upon the once successful, now embittered individual athlete. In the close up shot of Thorpe's face, which lasts for a little more than ten seconds, these words merge with the micro facial expressions of Lancaster. The seemingly helpless head movements from before devolve into a very slight, almost shivering opening of the mouth, followed by a small widening and then squinting movement of his eyes. The pledge of the collaborative We of the athletes – "We swear, that we will take part in the Olympic Game in loyal competition, respecting the regulations, which govern them, and desirous of participating in the true spirit of

---

36 Beginning with the 2018 Winter Olympics in Pyeongchang, the Olympic Oath consists of one unified oath. Until then, there were three different oaths, one for the athletes, one for the coaches and one for the officials. The 1932 Athlete's Oath, which we also see and hear in the footage, was delivered by fencer and United States Navy officer George Calnan.

sportsmanship, for the honor of our country, and the glory of sports" – inscribes itself into the individualized spectator and ex-star, for whom the cited regulations not only became a big, existential problem, but also, throughout the film, for whom athletic competition has always functioned as an activity of (audiovisual) distinction, separation and escape, rather than one of collaborative participation. At the same time though, this extended close up shot, understood as a Deleuzian *affection-image*, disperses Thorpe as a character, as the figural manifestation or representation of a human-like body with individual agency. In this way and by now at the latest, the question of belonging starts to detach from Thorpe as a historical person or the protagonist of this film's plot and eventually becomes a matter of the audiovisual discourse of the film itself – as the outcome of a poiesis of film-viewing, by means of which images do not appear as artifacts but as the product of the interaction of projected moving images and their audience, as images that come from and relate to other images, as images that reflect (appropriate and modulate) a priori audiovisual forms of a cultural community's world perception. Here, historical time always already appears as or in complex forms of mediated and remediated time.

Hence, as much as the focus on the character's facial expression masks the mass of the stadium and the film's audience, it also 'communitizes' the single spectator Thorpe. In this way, the audiovisual orchestration opens up the resulting close up/affection image of Thorpe's face to this mass once again, thereby creating an audiovisual space of collectivity, in which the depicted historic crowd in the Olympic stadium, the historic newsreel spectators and the spectators of the film JIM THORPE – ALL-AMERICAN are put in contact with and refer to each other. The film stages this encounter as the dissolution-by-isolation of individuality and the restored connection to, or at least recognition of the collectivity produced by the activities of doing and watching sports – whereby sports films often seem to aim at addressing these two activities as one, hence not only claiming that sports is always already media sports, but also making palpable how film can be understood as an experience of subjective collectivity, as an act of individuals coming together to form ever new communities, in the sense of ever new crystallizations of time.

Integrating the Individual by Integrating Time

Through this scene, JIM THORPE – ALL-AMERICAN sutures images of different times and thus makes palpable a historical past and its becoming-present – not by adopting a realistic approach that distinguishes between actual and fictional events, but by emphasizing the ever-new formation of audiovisual discourses through which society becomes able to refer to itself as imagined communities and through which events become graspable as events in the first place. In this sense, culture is an outcome of movement-images and not the other way around.

Rather than communicating any concrete, character-related and character-specific thought, the staging of Thorpe/Thorpe's face itself becomes an expression of the state of being torn between different temporalities and the procedures of inclusion and exclusion associated with them here. Clearly, there is more than the narrative Now of Thorpe as a broken ex-star and, accordingly, the Back Then of the successful times of his earlier career at stake. Indeed, I would argue that the film, in its way of assembling documentary imagery from the past and specifically shot fictional footage, brings the sports film's central conflict to its pinnacle here. What is emphasized is that this conflict is about assimilation, about the (in part quite forcible) integration of an outsider individual (Thorpe) into an institutionalized system of communality (the sporting nation), seemingly for this individual's own sake and this system's 'clear conscience.' The film can be criticized for that, especially from a standpoint concerned with issues of representation and ideology critique: Instead of welcoming and accepting Thorpe's failing otherness or even exposing it as rooted in the racism of a nationalistic society, the film rather reduces the tragedy of its plot lines to the rebellious character of its main protagonist, who, in this way, is presented not only as not fitting in, but as not *wanting* to fit in, and then, eventually, showing some discernment and submission after all. While such criticism is certainly legitimate, it cannot be the final outcome when analyzing the movie by looking more closely at its audiovisual orchestration, especially in regard to its ending.[37]

Rather than charging the film with identity politics that stem from more or less fixed understandings of certain formations, constellations and conflicts ab initio and thus independent from its images and sounds, I propose to bring more attention to how subjectification is developed and negotiated here in the first place – precisely by means of these images and sounds as expressive and perceptual structures. Therefore, while I do not want to absolve JIM THORPE – ALL-AMERICAN of any detectable racist perspective, my claim is that the underlying conflict of belonging, of inclusion and exclusion, is always at the center of

---

[37] Another way of looking at the film could start from a more auteur theoretical angle and the fact that the film is made by a Hungarian Jew, who emigrated to the US in 1926. In that vein, JIM THORPE – ALL-AMERICAN, with its central conflict of systematic exclusion and outsider subjectification, might be read as a work that – under the impression of the Holocaust, which the Allies terminated just a couple of years before the film's production, and in an obviously quite mediated way – deals with the USA's own genocide committed against Native Americans.

its audiovisual dramaturgy anyway, reflected by its images and sounds becoming part of an audiovisual discourse as the outcome of a poiesis of film-viewing.

As much as KNUTE ROCKNE ALL AMERICAN is about the exposition of an individual within a community through a collective act of orientation towards the past as present future (with that individual giving back to this community to stabilize it and guaranteeing its continuation in a future perfect sense: 'Coach Rockne will have had an impact'), Curtiz' film here is very much about the constant attempt to (re-)integrate that outstanding individual – not only into society but into this society's *tradition*, into its line of *passing on*, as superficial, oppressive and violent it might be. As the two very last scenes (apart from the following second part of the film's framing narrative) make clear, this process of integration has much to do with the process of not only becoming coach, but also of becoming spectator.

By analogy, and with regard to my analytical considerations during the first half of this chapter – remember especially Rockne appearing on the field as a ghost-like figure as well as the action-packed game scenes which conclude the movie – the dynamic of the ending of KNUTE ROCKNE ALL AMERICAN could certainly be described as a dramaturgy of becoming player (again). In this context, it is also noteworthy that the transition from player to coach in the Rockne movie is also treated quite prominently, but in a much less tragic sense: Rather than being tied to questions of existence, it is presented more as some kind of bureaucratic act, as the quite mundanely treated decision between sports as the protagonist's 'real' passion, opposed to the more 'reasonable' alternative of an academic career. While an athletic career for the filmic Rockne is more or less the result and an expansion of his freedom and independence, sports for the protagonist Thorpe figures as the (only) possibility to gain this freedom in the first place. In both those early narrative sports movies though, it is the becoming or being coach, which finally functions as the crux of the matter concerning the question of belonging. And even though former players becoming coaches has been a common practice in real life sports until today, sports films seldomly touch upon such a configuration anymore, even though the figure of the coach often features prominently within their plots.[38]

---

[38] Usually, the figure of the coach in later sports films is something of a mixture between a rather eccentric or introvert specialist (COACH CARTER, 2005, WE ARE MARSHALL, 2006, FRIDAY NIGHT LIGHTS, 2004) and a washed-up oldie (THE BAD NEWS BEARS, 1976, HOOSIERS, 1986). For specific analyses of filmic depictions of sports coaches in narrative and documentary cinema, see Bonzel / Chare 2017.

Becoming Singular Plural as Becoming Spectator

After the audiovisual confrontation of Thorpe with the oath-reciting athlete, which ends on another assembling of the protagonist's indecisive face and a bird's-eye shot of the gigantic and crowded stadium, the movie immediately returns to (the inside of) the now vacated stadium. Due to the fact that the transition is conducted with a dissolve, the image here not only renders the stadium from two different perspectives and in two different motions, but also presents it in two very different 'states of being': fully crowded and (almost) completely empty. This not only reminds us of the empty stadium at the end of KNUTE ROCKNE ALL AMERICAN but also seems to once again reinforce the conflict the movie encircles and tries to make palpable by means of both its plot and its audiovisual orchestration: the conflicting successions and feedback loops of the relation between the individual and its community and vice versa, of what Nancy has famously coined "Being Singular Plural." In rethinking the notions of community and the social by not grounding them in individual subjectivity, Nancy argues that being is always 'being with,' that existence is essentially co-existence. This very much fits to what I grasp and want to address here one more time as pivotal to the idea of communality regarding the American Dream as the sports film's constitutive conflict, as Jean-Luc Nancy, with his notion of 'being-with,' does not address "a comfortable enclosure in a pre-existing group, but a mutual abandonment and exposure to each other, one that would preserve the 'I' and its freedom in a mode of imagining community as neither a 'society of spectacle' nor via some form of authenticity" (Nancy 2000 [1996], back cover).

The contrasting rendering of the audiovisual space of the sports stadium, which includes the simultaneous juxtaposition of found footage material and Lancaster's performance for a Hollywood camera, once again makes clear here: Uniqueness (in JIM THORPE – ALL-AMERICAN) means both being a celebrated star and a lonely outsider. This phenomenon of the star being also a kind of an outsider becomes quite vivid when we think of the surplus of strangeness coming along with our (media) perception of the most famous real-life sports stars of our times, which often also bear a certain dimension of a misfit.

At the same time, this uniqueness as a state of singularity does not emerge out of nothing or from an already constituted or consolidated subjectivity. It rather accrues from a dynamic of communality, from the effort of a community, which at the same time makes and is made by its individuals and which, therefore, can never be thought of as separate from its myths and its media or media practices, the latter (like film-viewing) always producing and referring back to the former.

The story of the extraordinary individual Jim Thorpe – from outsider to celebrated star and outsider again – can only become history when it finally (re) inscribes itself into the communal history the film constantly points to: the history of the Olympic Games, itself based on a humanistic tradition of social participation, which not only includes the performing athletes, but also its spectators, the people witnessing the events live in the stadium, in front of their radio or in the movie theater.[39] Hence, becoming a member of (sports) society (again) for Thorpe also means: becoming a spectator.[40] A spectator not only of the opening ceremony of the Olympic Games, which he is not able to attend as an active athlete, or of a children's pick-up game (as in the later scene described above), but also, strikingly, of his previous (filmic) life: After the opening ceremony, after the camera finds Thorpe still sitting in the stands of the empty stadium[41] at the end of a long and rambling tracking and zooming shot that ends on Lancaster's petrified face, a flashback sets in. Superimposed on a freeze frame of Thorpe looking slightly upwards with wide open eyes, we see what narratively accounts for the protagonist's past: images and sounds we as film viewers have seen before during the past one hundred minutes of the movie. Static shots show Thorpe in conversation, first with his father, then with Pop Warner; they alternate with more dynamic parts, which depict Thorpe in athletic action and, in that way, let the scene gain momentum again and again. The close-up of the face of the old, washed up Thorpe is thereby superimposed with figurations of his two father figures, with the younger version of himself at the peak of his athleticism and success, and with Vice President Curtis speaking at the opening ceremony (Figure 55). The third of these superimpositions/recollection-images not only confronts the two Thorpes of different times and captures the dynamic of the huge vertical shooting angles (the *heroic shots*) the film uses to depict its

---

39 The constitutive role of the audience, which is of course quite prominently but nonetheless more implicitly present in the Olympian idea of amateur sports, is made very clear in the Olympic Charter of 1933 for instance, where both "player" and "Spectator" [sic] are explicitly addressed, when the charter asks its readers on the very first page: "Are you a Sportsman?" (International Olympic Committee 1933, 1).
40 Considering that the profession of a coach certainly includes aspects of (very professionalized) spectatorship, becoming coach and becoming spectator cannot be neatly separated of course. Rather, it is exactly this connection which the films aim at here and which is probably most present to us in the humorous expression of the 'couch coach,' of all those spectators in the stadium and at home thinking of themselves as (better) coaches.
41 This shot of the lone hero in the empty stadium is very common in sports films, as we have already seen with FIELD OF DREAMS (P.A. Robinson, 1989) and KNUTE ROCKNE ALL AMERICAN (L. Bacon / W.K. Howard, 1940) in chapters 2.3 and 6.1. In THE PROGRAM (D.S. Ward, 1993), it figures in a similar way to as it does here, as an image-producing audiovisual space – even though finally not functioning as a flashback on the narrative level, but as a flashforward, when protagonist Darnell Jefferson visits the empty college stadium before becoming a student and imagines the crowd and his name on the scoreboard.

protagonist, but also quite strikingly anticipates the very end of the film, when the old Thorpe looks at a painting of his younger self.[42]

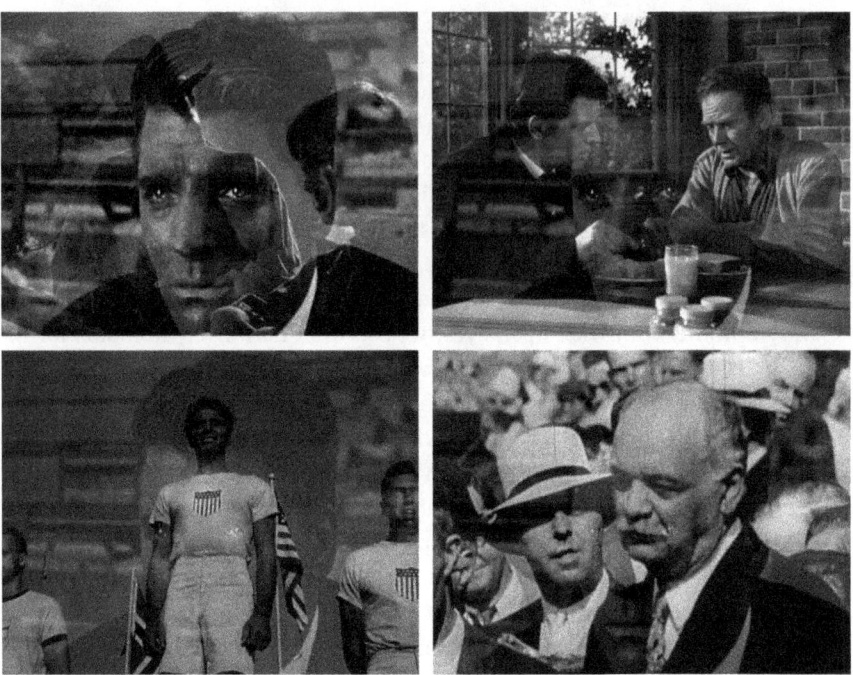

Figure 55: Superimpositions of a mediated past.

To further experience his re-integration into the (film's) society of spectators, as someone who passes on his knowledge and values as a coach and who is worshipped as an extraordinary ordinary person (during the following festive tribute scene), the protagonist Thorpe has to become a spectator himself – a spectator of his own audiovisualization, of a film about him.

It would be hasty, however, to interpret this audiovisually formed gesture of self-reflection merely within a psychological framework of character behavior, as a kind of represented narcissism, or as the result of an ideology loaded star cult primarily located outside of the filmic plot and orchestration. Rather, the argument goes like this: JIM THORPE – ALL-AMERICAN, on the one hand, reflexively

---

[42] Such superimpositions like the last one, of a protagonist and a famous national figure or symbol, occur quite often in sports films. Another striking example can be found at the end of THE JACKIE ROBINSON STORY (A. E. Green, 1950), when Jackie Robinson, played by Jackie Robinson, merges with the Statue of Liberty.

renders film-viewing an experience of doubled corporeality, an intertwined perception of a viewer's and the film's body, an act during which the expression of perceiving and the perception of expressing are constantly related to each other, much in the sense of what Vivian Sobchack describes as the seeing of the seeing of someone else who is "like myself, but not myself" (Sobchack 1992, 136), but also in the sense of Deleuze's conception of the movement-image, which occurs from the encounter of affected and affecting bodies in the first place, beyond any already fixed subjectivity or transcendental consciousness (Deleuze 2013a [1983], 63 et seq.).[43] On the other hand, the film here once again sharpens the driving forces of its dramaturgy and the constitutive conflict of the sports film as genre (see chapter 2.2): the endless process of becoming a subject within or, rather, in constant attunement with others, of being a community-building individual in a community built out of individuals. The cyclical condition of this procedure between belonging and alienation, between dependence/subordination and independence is emphasized here at the end of Curtiz's film, where it is not the hero's death that triggers and signifies the cyclical endlessness of 'passing on,' as in KNUTE ROCKNE ALL AMERICAN, but the re-discovering and re-integration of the hero himself, who is already interwoven in his own (media) remembrance. Where KNUTE ROCKNE ALL AMERICAN puts up an intimidating and rather confrontational performance of exploding multiplication, JIM THORPE – ALL-AMERICAN finally presents an audiovisual gesture of cyclical meeting and unification, by which the hero not only faces himself, but encounters both his intra- and extradiegetic audience in the mutual solidarity of recognition. Thorpe watches his own mythos, as character and historical figure, along with the movie's viewer, and thereby becomes this character and historical figure in the first place – becoming singular plural as becoming spectator.

A Hero's Portrait and the American Dream as Media Imaginary

Especially when finally considering the (meta-)narrative perspectivation and constellation it brings forth, this dynamic of re-integration could of course still provide for a rather ideology critical reading of the film, which aims at problematizing the violence of marginalization and paternalization that always comes along with it and is present in the film. By establishing Thorpe as a spectator of his own mythologization, one might interpret the film as (structurally) suggesting

---

[43] For a critique of Sobchack equating film perception/vision with human perception/vision, see, for example, Frampton 2006, 46.

that the Indigenous identity it nods to multiple times is only legible, only *not* in conflict with a heroic identity 'out of time,' when it can be domesticated and assimilated into a nationalist myth – into a story of reiterated uniqueness, which is not only obviously told by white people, but which also constructs its hero not as the agent but the (recognized) *object* of historical community building. While in such a perspective JIM THORPE – ALL-AMERICAN might be accused of producing the Indigenous identity (of Thorpe as historical person and heroic figure) as a mask, as that what must be dissolved if he is to be a successful athlete and assimilated member of the historical canon of sports,[44] the film nonetheless continues to maintain and reflect the bidirectionality of such a dynamic of (forced) in- and exclusion, as its very last sequence shows once again.

This sequence is itself the continuation (the second part) of the opening scene, which introduced us to the central narrative as a story within a story, as a story told by Pop Warner on the occasion of a festive tribute to the former athlete Thorpe. After having witnessed the isolated Thorpe becoming (one of) his own spectator(s) in the huge but empty Los Angeles Memorial Coliseum and, afterwards, becoming coach of a group of young boys, the film returns at its very end to the ballroom from the beginning (TC 01:43:59). In response to the first part of the scene at the film's beginning, which stages an image of re-beginning and endlessness by means of an expressive movement of repetitive delay, with Warner being literally introduced as a figure of timelessness ("immortal"), the film here also produces a certain sense of repetitiveness and endlessness, also and especially on a macro level, with the juxtaposition of all these potentially final scenes already described.

While the camera horizontally pans along (and in-between) the listening audience, Pop Warner's voice, accentuated by gentle strings, appears on the soundtrack again: "So Jim found himself, and was again on the true path – the bright path, teaching and helping young people everywhere. This was his greatest victory." As the camera arrives near the stage, Warner is depicted standing behind a long table, surrounded by other (seated) officials. Strikingly, and as in the beginning, there is

---

[44] For a good example of such a differently proceeding criticism, for which my methodology here might nonetheless be fruitful, see Briley 2011. Even though giving it some credit for being "somewhat of an innovation in Hollywood's portrayal of Indigenous People as it brings them out of the frontier past and into the twentieth century," Briley criticizes JIM THORPE – ALL-AMERICAN for its problematic stance on race and assimilation, as it does not grant its main protagonist control over his own Native American story, but instead presents "a white narrative of assimilation and social mobility into which Thorpe must be molded" (78), thereby endorsing an idea of assimilation as a process of taming, of bringing a raw force under control and teaching it the 'right way.'

still no sign of Thorpe – only by looking closely, one can recognize him: a still heavily made up Lancaster with now shortened and grayed hair, grumpily looking down on the table in front of him in the background.

Following from what we have seen before and what I have tried to describe analytically in its audiovisual dynamic, this hide-and-seek seems to be a logical consequence, given that the reason for the ceremony – the induction of Jim Thorpe into the state of Oklahoma Hall of Fame – conflates and pinnacles what the film has previously unfolded as its tragic core: the becoming and presentation of an exceptional individual within a community that congregated and formed because of this individual in the first place. The perceived delay signifies the tension that occurs with regard to Thorpe's (first) appearance not as a singular individual but as a singular individual *among* and *worshipped* by *others*. After witnessing his own medialized myth in isolation, after becoming a singular spectator, Thorpe is now part of a festive society coming together to commemorate him. He is or becomes the center of attention – not on the field anymore, but on stage and on film. Quite similar to Knute Rockne at the end of KNUTE ROCKNE ALL AMERICAN, though, the film seems to initially address its hero less through the depiction of a concrete body, but through an (audiovisual) dynamic of mythologization, which emerges between film and spectator as the product of a "poiesis of film-viewing" as "an act of creative production that is to be located in the media consumption itself" (Müller / Kappelhoff 2018, 36). While this dynamic of (filmic) heroism seems to gradually detach or become detached from the film's diegesis and this diegesis' main protagonist in KNUTE ROCKNE ALL AMERICAN (death – funeral – reappearance as ghost – replacement), JIM THORPE – ALL-AMERICAN once more reflexively relates it to the seemingly indestructible body of Thorpe/Lancaster and this body's media representation within and beyond the film.[45]

After a short break, Warner continues his speech: "And tonight, the state of Oklahoma adds another great name, another portrait to its Hall of Fame ..." While the scene jumps to a bird's-eye shot of the assembled crowd, which recalls the shot of the crowded stadium from before and was supposedly taken from found footage material of the actual induction ceremony in 1950,[46] he

---

[45] As Joshua R. Keefe shows, Thorpe himself has been used quite disparately as symbolic object of the highly ambivalent if not schizophrenic self-image of the United States, "as representative of everything from America as colorblind meritocracy to America as racist devourer of its own" (Keefe 2009). Keefe heavily refers to Mark Rubinfeld's study on the history of media representation of Thorpe, where Rubinfeld also analyzes Curtiz's movie, especially with regard to its ideological implications as a text within a historical context (see Rubinfeld 2006).

[46] While I was able to find that the stadium shot was taken from official newsreel footage of the Olympic Games of the time (see footnote 32), the origin of this ceremony footage here (and

once again directly addresses the audience, leading over to another, final introduction and the official induction of Thorpe: "Ladies and gentlemen, the man whose achievements and records will live forever in the annuals of sports. Acclaimed by the American Press as the greatest athlete in the past half century: Jim Thorpe, All American!"

After a cut, the camera exposes the 'old' Thorpe/Lancaster, in a medium close up shot from above, sitting and looking down as if petrified. Applause starts on the audio track and another extremely long shot from above counters this image of (solitary and arrested) consternation: The audience rises to reward the honored Thorpe with a standing ovation. On a drumbeat, the scene proceeds to a symmetric long shot filmed from the back of the crowd. It frontally frames the symmetrical, stage-like arrangement: A long table is horizontally positioned in front of an ensemble of (theater) curtains. Synchronous with the rhythm of the montage and sound, the inner curtain opens up and reveals a painted portrait of (Lancaster as) the young Thorpe, posing with a broad chest and wearing his US Olympic jersey. The painting appears insofar quite familiar as what most certainly served as its template is the heroic shot of Thorpe at the Olympic awards ceremony, which we have just seen again as superimposed on his petrified face during the flashback scene before.

While the camera, positioned slightly above the audience, starts to approach Warner and the unveiled picture, Thorpe, who appears on the right side of the frame, finally gets up and slowly moves towards his former coach, stopping and looking in the direction of the camera almost exactly beneath his own portrait. The camera, still in forward motion, suddenly descends downwards into the crowd and stops, meeting Lancaster's still incredulous gaze (Figure 56).

The question that comes up is why Curtiz and the producers decided not to let Jim Thorpe, who was not only physically on set as an advisor, but also a quite experienced actor, play himself here, especially with regard to the appearance of the real-life governor in the first part of this sequence at the beginning of the film.[47] While the specific reasons for this decision remain unclear, it can certainly

---

at the very beginning of the movie) remains unclear. What can be said for sure is that the real Jim Thorpe was inducted into the Oklahoma Hall of Fame in 1950, about one year before Curtiz' film's US release on 24 August 1951. This happened in the course of the "Oklahoma Hall of Fame Banquet & Induction Ceremony," which has been hosted every year in November since 1928 (see https://oklahomahof.com/history-mission and https://oklahomahof.com/member-archives/t/thorpe-james-jim-francis-1950) (accessed 15 April 2022).

47 According to his IMDb entry, Thorpe appeared in more than seventy films as an almost never credited extra, most of the times representing a Native American character and, sometimes, an athlete. In Curtiz' film, he actually got a very small role as an official.

Figure 56: Exposed and honored as part of the community and as image.

be construed in line with structures and practices of racism and stereotyping not only in everyday life, but specifically within the film production business.[48] At the same time, it quite clearly runs contrary to assumptions about any intentional striving for authenticity, thereby rather strengthening the argument that JIM THORPE – ALL-AMERICAN is less about the real-life historical person Jim Thorpe than about the emergence of a *mediated* mythological figure and its role for and within the self-conception of an (obviously racist) North American society, as well as this society's dynamic of building and re-building a national identity through filmic images of sports. As questions addressing the ways and the extent the film affirms or criticizes this racism and which develop along a reconstruction of the cultural contexts of its production and its represented narrative content should certainly remain the subject of further research, the dimension of the film's audiovisual poetics addressed here certainly have to be taken into account and can hopefully add some value to (such) future discussion.

But let us return one last time to this circle of media mythologization, which still is not yet completed: A jump cut carries the viewer even closer to Thorpe and Warner, who look each other in the eyes and perform a long handshake. Warner pats Thorpe on his shoulder, then leads him to turn around, away from the camera and towards his own portrait. The camera starts moving again, passing Thorpe, who witnesses the heroic epiphany of himself – who becomes a spectator of his visual (re-)appearance as a hero, made and worshipped by a community of which he is now also part, whether he wants to be or not (Figure 57).[49]

---

[48] On that topic and with a specific focus on Native Americans and Hollywood movies, see for example Aleiss 2005.
[49] Even though he is concerned with it in the 'original' context of ancient Greek culture and does not touch upon the moving image, Jorge Bravo has provided a closer look at this interrelation of

252 — 6 Commemorating Futurity, Projecting Pastness: Never-Ending Endings

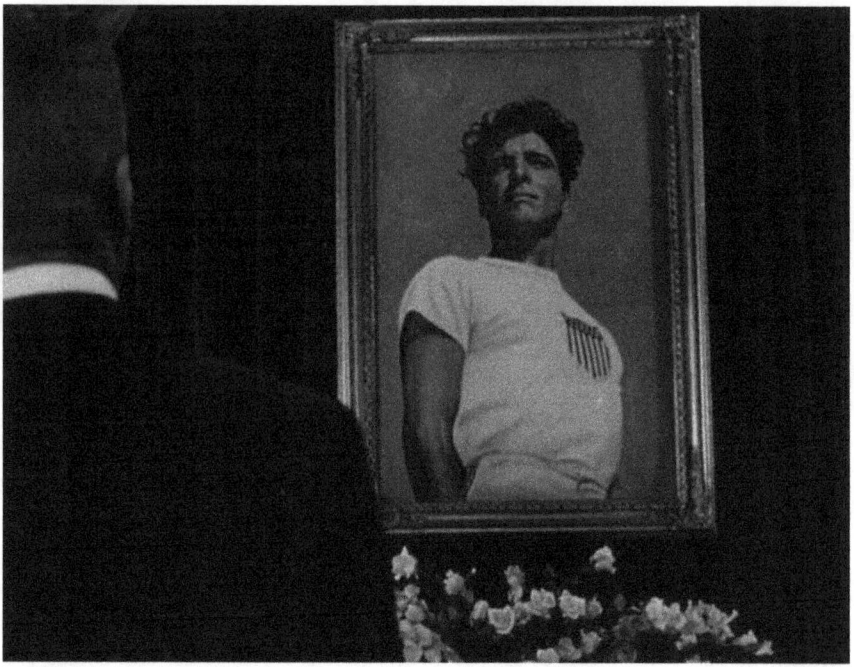

Figure 57: Becoming spectator of one's own visual (re-)appearance as hero.

The process of *becoming spectator* as the audiovisual *rite de passage* of the once exceptional athlete, but also of the viewer of JIM THORPE – ALL-AMERICAN, has reached its next and for the time being final circuit: After Thorpe has been shown first as the singularized spectator of the historically ritualized event of the opening ceremony of the 1932 Olympics and then as the isolated spectator of the film's and his own diegetic past (in form of recurring imagery shared with the film's viewer), and after he has been audiovisually (and quite literally) thrown back on himself when helping to transform a group of kids into possible future players, he now finally merges with his audience by looking at a pictorial representation of himself, at an occasion which is supposed to honor and eternalize his achievements.

While the audiovisual poetics of KNUTE ROCKNE ALL AMERICAN emphasizes the futurity inscribed into the idea of the American Dream as a way of becoming a

---

heroic iconography in votive (narrative as well as visual) representations, under which the portrait here can likely be subsumed, and the cultic contexts of the phenomenon of heroic epiphany, under which the honors banquet here can likely be subsumed (Bravo 2004).

historical community by means of a rather outward-directed movement, which produces an ad hoc and seemingly endless chain of strong individuals set free, JIM THORPE – ALL-AMERICAN rather concentrates on how such strong individuality is captured and contained again by the community it arises from and at the same time produces.

Even though they carry out a different weighting, both films clearly take part in the ever ongoing negotiation of belonging, which constitutes and forms societal and individual identity in the first place, of the processes of inclusion (of the excluded) and exclusion (of the included), hence becoming significant in both ways: As much as it is about the integration of the individual into a community, it is about the integration of the community into the individual (or the question of its place and valence within the individual's self-conception). And as much as KNUTE ROCKNE ALL AMERICAN and JIM THORPE – ALL-AMERICAN show the society of the American Dream as a community of the isolated but vigorous and extraordinary individual among (admired by and producing) other such individuals, they outline it as a community, which tries to catch and domesticate these individuals again and again.

In this way, both films – as two exemplary representatives or rather media of the sports film genre – work on the field of tension between individual distinction and societal usurpation, clarifying that communities do not produce ideology, but arise in the production of ideology, and that this production is inextricably linked to a constant process of in- and exclusion, as well as to image and media circuits of remembrance, worship and admiration, in which the individual hero is always both the excluded and the appropriated other.[50] In KNUTE ROCKNE ALL AMERICAN, the death of the film's central protagonist, who moves through a strikingly unshaken filmic world from the very beginning, causes for a quite intimidating staging of futurity as some kind of a sudden chain reaction, signifying for a multiplication of individual strength in favor of a confident (pre-)war community. The film's overall movement of repetition constitutes as endlessness, while in JIM THORPE – ALL-AMERICAN it rather becomes tangible as a cyclically accelerating, densifying repetition. Here, it is the forceful incorporation (redemption) of the eccentric (fallen) individual, through which the (national) community is able to manifest again, through which American egalitarianism is reinstated and at the same time disclosed – a strong gesture of (inward-oriented) self-affirmation, which seems

---

[50] In this regard, JIM THORPE – ALL-AMERICAN also seems to get to the heart of what Keefe describes as the "malleable social significance" (Keefe 2009) of Jim Thorpe, whose destiny has been symbolically exploited for so many and quite different purposes in the history of the United States' cultural imaginary (see also Oxendine 1995, 203).

to hint at the social unrest of a post-World War II society at the end of the initial US occupation and amid the onset of the Cold War. As well as at a society in the middle of the Second Red Scare, a time at which "a significant shift in the federal government's policy towards Native Americans from the 'Indian New Deal' [...] to 'termination and relocation,' which sought to end all financial support for, and cultural legitimization of, reservation life" (Rubinfeld 2006, 179–180) occurred. In his nuanced representational critique of Curtiz' film, Mark Rubinfeld connects JIM THORPE – ALL-AMERICAN with THE JACKIE ROBINSON STORY (which was released one year earlier) and reads it as Hollywood's ideological answer to the 'scandalous' case of Soviet Union-friendly African American Paul Robeson, a former All-American college football player and then successful and respected singer, actor and political activist, who spoke out against US imperialism and racism at the World Peace Conference in Paris in 1949. At the same time, Rubinfeld's assessment of the movie's huge relevance for American society seems to resonate with what the film anticipates and reflects itself all the time anyway, via what I have called a poiesis of film-viewing and the specific audiovisual discourse it produces. He writes: "Normally, a single movie is not all that culturally significant. [...] But for large numbers of non-Native Americans, much of what they know about Jim Thorpe and, by extension, Native Americans comes from the movie Jim Thorpe – All American" (Rubinfeld 2006, 176).

While in KNUTE ROCKNE ALL AMERICAN, the hero is immortalized through the 'reincarnation of his spirit in those who pledged to carry on for him,' which translates into an explosive multiplication of power and agitation, JIM THORPE – ALL-AMERICAN dissects the central conflict worked through by sports films – the interrelation of individual and collective subjectification, of ordinariness and extra-ordinariness, of in- and exclusion in view of an idea of a communality of permanent reference and renewal of past, present and future – as a self-referential media system of a social imaginary that is, as I claim, the American Dream. While in the former film, the heroic act is audiovisually understood as a dynamic of proliferation (of strength and superiority), which counters the absence/demise of the remembered individual with an aesthetics of immediacy and thereby presents this individual as the primordial source of a strong community and communal effort to come, the latter unfolds this relation of exceptional subject and exceptional community as a loop-like movement of reflexive spectatorship and medialization.

7 Concluding Remarks: The Hill We Climb

On 20 January 2021, as part of the ceremony surrounding the inauguration of Joe Biden as the 46th president and Kamala Harris as the 49th vice president of the United States, the poet Amanda Gorman recited her poem *The Hill We Climb* on the West Front of the United States Capitol in Washington, D.C. She was the third African American woman to take on the role of what is referred to an inaugural poet, a relatively new tradition, which so far has solely been upheld by presidents of the Democratic Party.[1] Gorman was invited by the new first lady, Dr. Jill Biden, and wrote the piece specifically for the occasion of the inauguration and in view of its overall theme "America United." The violent storming of the Capitol by Donald Trump supporters on 6 January took place while Gorman was still drafting the poem – according to Gorman herself, she wrote essential parts of her poem and finished it that very night. At the end of this book, I will provide a brief examination of Gorman's poem and selectively contrast it with President Biden's inaugural address in order to put my findings on the US team sports film into a wider context. What I want to show is how the American Dream as an idea and finally cultural imaginary of crystalline historicity, which is produced and nurtured by the time-image(s) of the genre of the sports film, impregnates (contemporary) American pathos and politics and also how this pathos and politics are to be understood as mutually dependent, intertwined by means of poetic making.

President Biden's inaugural address, which followed shortly after Gorman's performance, conjures the unity or (re-)integration of the American people, though, in its rhetorical simplicity, at times sounds like a desperately placatory echo of Trump's trumpeted "Make America Great Again." Gorman's virtuously spoken-word poetry, on the other hand, proceeds in a far more astute way. Combining an allusive playfulness and strong pathos, *The Hill We Climb*, both text and performance, seem especially telling with regard to navigating that fine line of American exceptionalism, whose right-wing flank Trumpism has certainly brought to new heights in painful fashion, but which is, I claim, ultimately rooted in and must be seen from the foot of that hill, to stay with this

---

[1] The first inaugural poet was Robert Frost at John F. Kennedy's inauguration in 1961, reciting his poem *The Gift Outright*. Maya Angelou read her poem *On the Pulse of Morning* at the first inauguration of Bill Clinton in 1993. At Clinton's second inauguration in 1997, it was Stanley Miller Williams who read his poem *Of History and Hope*. At Barack Obama's first inauguration in 2009, Elizabeth Alexander recited her poem *Praise Sing for the Day*, and at Obama's second inauguration in 2013, it was Richard Blanco with *One Today*.

https://doi.org/10.1515/9783110760354-007

multi-compatible metaphor. Likely the most pivotal reference here is, of course, the "City Upon A Hill." Rooted in the Sermon on the Mount, the metaphor served puritan John Winthrop as a trope for the community of settlers in the 'new world' in one of his sermons in 1630. It further underwent decisive integration into the modern cultural memory of American exceptionalism by means of John F. Kennedy's famous speech of the same name delivered during the Cold War more than 300 years later. This trope or image is less about the arduous climb, though, but rather about the exposed position, the exposure or the process of exposing oneself once on that hill. It is about *being seen* – something that Gorman addresses in her poem and that I have described along the US sports films as one part of its constitutive conflict (see chapter 3.2).

The American Dream as an Imaginary of Audiovisual Culture

With this book on the poetics of historicity of the US team sports film, I have tried to make sense of this elementary dimension of the American self-imagination through the notion of the American Dream. Existing research on the sports film agrees on the importance of the American Dream for the genre, though most scholars work (and thus also approach and apply the American Dream) within theories of representational realism and methods of narrative analysis. In doing so, questions of medialization and aesthetic form are often put aside. While this leads to an understanding of the American Dream as subject matter, signifying along action patterns and/or a narratively structured and conveyed ideologeme, my analysis reconceptualized it as a media cultural imaginary.[2] This imaginary is significantly formed by and takes effect through sports films and sports film-viewing – not only in the sense that it is narrativized as an element of the cultural work of (national) imagination or represented by means of conventionalized mythological, ideological or sociological models, but also in that it is produced, modulated and reflected as filmic thinking. It is this filmic thinking of the sports film which renders the American Dream part of a genuinely audiovisual culture.

This is important to note, as it provides for a change in perspective and hopefully underscores the intervention of my work with regard to a political aesthetics and the relation between a) the work of *poiesis* as creative production, b) the aesthetic experience of film-viewing, and c) the relationality of

---

[2] For a very productive notion of the cultural imaginary, which fits to my work here on many levels, even though it is developed along the history of the American novel of the eighteenth and nineteenth century, see Fluck 1997 (in German).

expressive and perceptual structures as audiovisual discursivity, as thinking in images. While I do not want to question or condemn approaches of mythology and ideology critique in general,[3] the aim of this intervention was to point out the reductive methodology most of these approaches succumb to and to provide new ways of approaching the sports film and genre cinema beyond the concern for narrative content and structures on the basis of an idea of representational realism.

When I talk about a certain idea of temporality and communitization as the central feature or problem of the American Dream as cultural imaginary and then end up recognizing this feature also being worked on in Gorman's poem, this recognition becomes possible from and materializes as an effect of this filmic thinking, in which I am involved as viewer and analyst of the *poiesis of sports film-viewing*. Not primarily because sports films are poetic works, too, or because Gorman's poem uses what can be called a sports metaphor, but because they both work on a specific idea and experience of time and communality central to the American Dream being shaped and taking effect as cultural imaginary. We can only really perceive and understand this imaginary by means of the relationalities between its medializations and poetic redescriptions. To put it bluntly: *The Hill We Climb*, and my reading of it as a poetic and performative contemplation of the American Dream as cultural imaginary, is inextricably linked to the FIELD OF DREAMS, and all the other (sports) films I have watched and analyzed. The same applies to this book's theoretical and historical efforts, to its philosophical projection of and towards the American Dream, which cannot be reduced to a reconceptualization originally external to sports films and then detected in them as represented content. Rather, and in a more Cavellian sense of the notion of projection, the kind of film philosophy that I have striven for here is nourished by a constantly changing stimulation located between the interdependent and tantamount media of image and viewer, word and reader.

American Dream Time

FIELD OF DREAMS has served as a hinge in many ways here. For one thing, it helped to expose the problem of understanding the sports film as genre as a problem of

---

[3] A productive mythological approach could for example build on Hans Blumenberg's notion of myth as a means of interpreting the world through imaginary thinking (see Blumenberg 2010 [1979]).

a genre theory that is oriented towards a rule- and convention-based taxonomy and predominant within the research field. Following Stanley Cavell, Christine Gledhill, Matthias Grotkopp and Hermann Kappelhoff, I carried out a genre theoretical revision, which enables us to understand genre cinema as an always dynamic, open and contingent system of referentiality between expressive and perceptual modalities. Along its formation and reformation, aesthetic experience, media imagination and cultural discourse continuously realign and become retraceable as the genre's cultural work of imagination. On the other hand, and in the vein of this theoretical intervention, FIELD OF DREAMS made it possible to qualify this cultural work of imagination of the sports film as filmic thinking and specify it by means of analytical description as its constitutive conflict, the latter making it a genre in the first place. Thus, besides serving as a genre theoretical intervention, FIELD OF DREAMS also helped to bring forward a genre *historical* reflection. The former was about situating the ritualistic functioning of Hollywood genre cinema on the level of sensory structures and the formation of a feeling of a We, followed by marking the historicity of the American people as a *deep temporality* of that cinema, with sports and film as media of national commemoration and the viewer being part of the correlating processes of integration, appropriation and exclusion. The latter was about the specific forms and formations of that temporality and the specific We that comes along with it. It is ultimately this temporality and this We that become the central elements of the audiovisual discourse of the American Dream as a cultural imaginary, produced and modulated by means of the sports film genre's filmic thinking.

This temporality, which I call *American Dream Time*, is characterized by its crystal-like disposition: interweaving a retrospective 'no longer' and a prospective 'not yet.' It is to be understood as a constantly realigning, multifaceted simultaneity of a present of the past and a present of the future – a contraction or, to use a term that often comes up in the context of Deleuze's discussion of temporal heterogeneity with regard to the filmic (crystal) image and underlines that it is about an amalgamation of elements, which nonetheless remain recognizable as distinct, a coalescence.[4]

Initially, I approached this crystalline temporality from at least two angles: first, from one of time-philosophical film theory, with Deleuze's concept of the crystal image as an image which makes time visible in its dividedness and wholeness, as duration in the sense of an indeterminable processing and reorganization of movement, as "peaks of present and sheets of past" (Deleuze 2013b [1985], 103) in between the dissymmetrical orders of the actual and the

---

4 See for example Hernández-Lemus 2000 or Angelucci / Marchetti 2014.

virtual; and, second, from an angle of the history of ideas of the American Dream, which goes beyond the advent of the notion itself at the beginning of the twentieth century. The idea of connecting these two angles was inspired and at the same time challenged by a) the existing sports film scholarship, b) the few approaches towards an aesthetics of sports, with which one can think of the historical affinity of sports and film not only by means of a discourse of media technology, but also via a (eventually political) theory of spectatorship, and c) the observation of the US team sports film being 'obsessed' with the sensory realization of historical time and the pathos of pastness and possible futurity coming along with this realization.

By consulting a number of philosophical approaches concerning theories of (American) communality, which have not yet been taken into account when it comes to the contouring of the American Dream as ideology or mythos in sports film scholarship (and in most of cultural studies more generally), as well as by analyzing the structure of temporality of the Declaration of Independence as both act and document, I mapped out how the crystalline *American Dream Time* intertwines with a model of exceptional community as a fragmentary, potential and unique collectivity of unique singularities, with these singularities being themselves fragmentary and in a state of becoming. Following Walt Whitman and Herman Melville, Gilles Deleuze takes hold of this fragmentariness with a metaphor that nowadays, in view of the Trump presidency, experiences an ironic twist: Deleuze describes the American Dream as "a wall of loose, uncemented stones" (Deleuze 1998, 86).[5]

In that vein, it became possible to argue for an apprehension of the American Dream not as a self-evident mythologeme or a narrative pattern of ideological misrepresentation of everyday world conditions, but as a specific temporality and communality, through which sports, film and sports film-viewing interrelate, and which only emerge because of these interrelations in the first place. Further, this tempo-communality is to be understood as the imaginary of an audiovisual culture, which crucially forms as and is shaped by the cinematic thinking of the genre of the sports film. It projects a specific We, by which American society recognizes itself as a political and historical community (of exceptionalism).

The Hill's Narrow Ridge and Unreachable Peak

In and with her poem *The Hill We Climb*, Amanda Gorman addresses the American Dream in a similar way: not only as a story or an empty promise of upward

---

5 See chapter 3.2 ("Deleuze on Melville") of this book.

social mobility, but as a poetic and poetically malleable project of conflictual subjectification. This subjectification takes place between exceptional individuality and exceptional (national) collectivity, draws its power from an imaginative reference to and fictional processing of what counts as 'the real world,' and accounts for and takes effect by a contraction of past, present and future, exactly because it does not represent reality: "We, the successors of a country and a time / Where a skinny Black girl, / Descended from slaves and raised by a single mother, / Can dream of becoming president, / Only to find herself reciting for one" (Gorman 2021, 18).

This We is a We of self-reference, even self-testimony, and the main feature through which it describes, reconstitutes and certifies itself is its incompleteness: "Somehow, we've weathered and witnessed / a nation that isn't broken, but simply unfinished" (Gorman 2021, 18). It is an imperfect We of "unattained but attainable self[s]" (Cavell 1991, 57) of a "new, yet unapproachable America" (Cavell 2013 [1989], 104), as Stanley Cavell addresses it by reading Emerson (or rather: by defending him as a philosopher especially concerning his essay *Experience*) to develop his own notion of moral perfectionism.[6] To stay with the metaphor: The hill to climb – as a site of work on the American Dream – not only tapers and becomes a narrow (and therefore exploitable and dangerous) ridge, but also has an unreachable peak shrouded by the clouds. While in Gorman's poem, which clearly appears to be a work of critical affirmation, this idea of unattainability remains rather implicit, it is nonetheless and especially formally communicated, for example with regard to her use of the simple present or her poetry slam-like speaking style gestural movements. All of this points to the poem's topic as truly more about the process of climbing and less about reaching the peak. This We of the American Dream is one of becoming and it reflexively envisions itself as such, within a momentary Now that forms as the interrelatedness of past and future, of anteriority and posteriority. But at the same time, it remains purely superficial in reference to this interrelatedness and these sheets of temporality. The historicity of this We of the American Dream, by means of which the US society reflects itself as a political community, lies in the present moment as an ever-new reference to both past and future, as a moment of remembering into the future and projecting into the past. Ultimately, this moment is a simultaneously homogenous and heterogenous mixture of past and future. It is in this sense that the historicity of the American We and its unfolding "story that tells ages yet to come that we answered the

---

[6] For a critique of Cavell's take, see Urbas 2010.

call of history" (Biden 2021), as President Biden stated it in his inaugural speech, must be understood and can be addressed anew again and again.

The Pain of a Momentous Present as Past and Future

The most defining moment of a present past during the inauguration of the 46th president of the United States certainly was the attack on the Capitol by Trump's supporters only two weeks prior. In his speech, Biden addresses the event early on to then praise the fragile but prevailing system of democracy and to underline his call for unity. He comes back to it at the very end:

> We met the moment. / That democracy and hope, truth and justice, did not die on our watch but thrived. / That our America secured liberty at home and stood once again as a beacon to the world. / That is what we owe our forebearers, one another, and generations to follow. / So, with purpose and resolve we turn to the tasks of our time. (Biden 2021)

Aside from the fact that these lines in a slightly altered version could easily be heard in a locker room when a coach addresses his players in a sports film, they evoke the idea of the moment as simultaneity of a past and a future – of a past to which one refers despite all the violence, guilt, mourning and pain it inflicted, and of a future, by means of which one overcomes this violent and painful past and finally accepts it as tradition (in the sense of a heritage to be carried on and a responsibility for a future that generates pride) exactly because it marks the present as past. The moment of this violence and pain is replaced by the next moment, past and future can deliberately be positioned and qualified – this is where the claim to and feeling of freedom, but also the dangers of the narrow ridge, lies, depending on the length of the steps one takes to determine and combine a before and an after, on how far one is determined or able to look into the past and future. What becomes apparent here is how this historicity can also turn into and be understood and exploited as an idea of timelessness in the sense of oblivion, of historical forgetfulness. This could be a starting point for further research combining stances of ideology critique and sports film aesthetics in productive ways, since sports movies – with their orchestration of de-temporalized time, their poetics of 'pure present/presence' and effects of immediacy – can quite obviously be interpreted towards such an understanding.

The film analytical chapters of this book have especially demonstrated how this violence, pain and grief of American momentousness appear as aesthetic forms of filmic mediality: on the one hand, in WE ARE MARSHALL, as part of a crystallized and crystallizing media remembrance, which is produced and pervaded by a melodramatic suspense structure and addresses the event (of the plane crash) not so much as the ultimate, causal origin of pain and grief, but as an occurrence of empty, non-graspable but all-pervading time; on the other hand, in JIM THORPE – ALL-AMERICAN, as the 'inclusion through exclusion' of the American We, the exposure as isolation and violent rise within an exposed community, which is laid out by the life of the main character in a striking way.

Delayed Democracy and a Poetic Project of Reimagining

Gorman several times also comments on this violence, pain and grief, as well as the endurance necessary to withstand and overcome it. Therein, she uses strong, religiously charged metaphors, especially at the beginning and in the end of her poem, with the maybe most telling one of them regarding the essential ambiguity of the American Dream found in her third sentence: "We've braved the belly of the beast" (Gorman 2021, 14). It is obvious, that it is the beast of racism, fascism and ethnonationalism addressed here, with Trump as its latest and most tangible incarnation. But there is more to it, as the metaphor of the belly as not only a digestive organ but also a birth-giving womb underlines that the We of American society is a constitutive part of this beast, as eventually an always lingering danger from within. It is this dangerous "force" that in its endeavor to "shatter our nation" and "destroy our country [...] very nearly succeeded" (Gorman 2021, 30). The method of this destruction is a question of temporality and communality: of "delaying democracy" (Gorman 2021, 30), with the American Dream as an ongoing fight against this delay and as the ever new realization of acknowledgement and attachment necessary in the light of violence and power: "If we merge mercy with might, and might with right, / Then love becomes our legacy, / And change, our children's birthright. / So let us leave behind a country better than the one we were left" (Gorman 2021, 40 et seq.).

Gorman addresses this striving for a more perfect union and its unfinishedness,[7] which eventually shows itself as inequality very early in her poem. She does so with a good portion of irony, when pointing out that, as a young girl, she could dream of becoming president, only to now recite a poem for one (as cited above). Acknowledging and subtly criticizing the present impossibility of

---

[7] In this regard, see also the opening remarks of Senator Roy Blunt at the inauguration, stating that the endeavor to create a "more perfect Union" is a continuing project and "we are more than we have been and we are less than we hope to be."

an African American woman to become president,[8] Gorman at the same time strengthens her position as a poet and emphasizes the importance of the creative act of imagination with regard to the American Dream as something that must be "form[ed]" and "compos[ed]" (Gorman 2021, 20/22), as a poetic project of remaking, redescribing, reimagining. By reciting and performing her poem, Gorman becomes a critical spectator of the nation, but at the same time a constitutive part of it and its becoming different – comparable to Jim Thorpe, who, at the end of JIM THORPE – ALL-AMERICAN, eventually takes part in the opening ceremony of the Olympic Games as a viewer and comes in contact with the vice president through found footage material, only to be then staged in complete solitude again (see chapter 6.2).

At the same time, Gorman reflects the American Dream here not only as an endless chase for a destination that is never reached, but also as a seductive invitation to share one's personal fortune with that of the nation, and thus as maybe the most obvious manifestation of what Laurent Berlant calls "cruel optimism" (Berlant 2011), taking effect through and within affective and aesthetic structures and a pop culturally formed sentimentality of communality (see Berlant 2008).

A Perfect Union with a Past to Step Into

With this in mind, to hear Biden's inaugural speech – after four years of the Trump administration – feels less calming than one might have expected or hoped for. From the perspective of this book and the American Dream as an audiovisual discourse of crystalline temporality, one reason for this might be that Biden, unlike Gorman, refrains from making clear that "being American is more than a pride we inherit" but "the past we step into, and how we repair it" (Gorman 2021, 28). Instead, he focuses on the proclamation of the idea of absolute inclusion and the new moment, from which to come forth as a global power again, as the "perfect union as beacon of the world" (Biden 2021). What this shows is neither that Biden and Gorman proceed on completely different tracks, nor that Biden is somehow the new Trump, but just how narrow this narrow ridge of the hill of the American Dream actually is and how quickly and differently the idea of American historicity and communitization can be exploited.

---

8 Kamala Harris, the first female, African American and Asian American vice president of the United States, initially sought the 2020 Democratic presidential nomination, but withdrew from the race before the primaries started.

This same idea is also evident in my analysis of KNUTE ROCKNE ALL AMERICAN and its poetics of unwavering hero worship, which finally culminates in an audiovisual rhetoric of limitless imperialistic strength by means of the orchestration of an explosive multiplication (see chapter 6.1). It can also be detected when Cavell talks (with or through Emerson) about the idea of the contemporary human being as material and sign for the human being to come (see Cavell 2013 [1989], 9) – an idea which also has its fascist version, as we know. Last but not least, this narrowness is also to be found in Gorman's text, when she indeed describes the crystalline temporality along the constructions of feeling through which sports films work their way through time and again, but then cannot help but finally add a fierce "victorious" claim (even though she then instantly relativizes): "That even as we grieved, we grew, / That even as we hurt, we hoped, / That even as we tired, we tried. / That we'll forever be tied together, victorious, / Not because we will never again know defeat, / But we will never again sow division" (Gorman 2021, 26). One is again – even though this time rather formally – reminded of the Emersonian (and Thoreauian and Freudian) Cavell and his aphorisms of "finding as founding" (Cavell 2013 [1989], 77) and "morning of mourning" (Cavell 1984, 56)[9] as not only capturing the crystalline configuration of time and experience, but as both ways of life *and* philosophizing.

Audiovisual History and Cultural Complexity

This leads us right to and beyond the film analyses of this book, by means of which I have tried to make palpable the formation of a filmic thinking of the American Dream as a cultural work of imagination at the intersection of aesthetic perception and historical experience and, in that sense, as different time-images, as different versions of a poetics of affect of the (always mediated and always athletic) American Dream. Against the background of the genre theory developed in the second chapter, all of these film analyses work in both an exemplary and a specific manner. As much as each of these poetic modulations of the American Dream as cultural imaginary could be pointed out in any other sports film (as should have become clear by means of the multitude of cross-references throughout the entire work), it is equally important to describe each of them anew in its specific aesthetic shaping. This does not make the work easier, however, but opens it up and frees it with regard to a film based historical engagement beyond taxonomic, epoch-historical or auteur-theoretical approaches. Such

---

9 See also Cavell 2013 [1989], 84.

an engagement could take the direction of a theory of a genuine audiovisual history, with Bernhard Groß' idea of the audiovisual as a mode of thinking historicity (see Groß 2017) and Michael Wedel's notion of visual history as fruitful starting points and directive angles. Following Kracauer and strongly resonating with what I have at least tried to do here in this book, they both demand and practice a visual history that "think[s] history through films, not beyond and above films" (Wedel 2018, 112, my translation). At the center of this visual history and this audiovisual thinking, which historicizes and is to be historicized, lies "the time of experiencing a [filmic] space image [...], which is itself antinomically and cataractically formed and in which neither 'the timeless [can] be stripped of the vestiges of temporality, nor the temporal [does] wholly engulf the timeless'" (Wedel 2018, 111, citing Kracauer 1995 [1969], 200). And which, in turn, produces time-images that take effect socially as mythopoetic structures within (their) different mediatization. Starting from this claim, such a notion of audiovisual history can add to the understanding of culture as the product of a poiesis of film-viewing and thus of the discursivity of audiovisual movement-images achieved through the appropriation of moving images. This way, one could quite easily imagine an interdisciplinary debate to stimulate the field of cultural as well as North American studies more specifically, for example in the sense of Simon Schleusener, who analyzes American literature, film and photography from a media aesthetic perspective and considers a realignment of North American cultural theory through the development of a notion of "cultural complexity" (Schleusener 2015, in German). It is hardly surprising that ideas of an "image of thinking" and "heterochronic or polychronic time" (Schleusener 2015, 364/367) seem to become crucial in this context.

Bibliography

Aab, Vanessa: *Kinematographische Zeitmontagen. Zur Entwicklungsgeschichte des Kinos*. Marburg 2014.
Adams, James Truslow: *The Epic of America*. Westport 2001 [1931].
Adams, James Truslow: *The Epic of America*. Piscataway 2017 [1931].
Agamben, Giorgio: *Potentialities. Collected Essays in Philosophy*. Stanford 1999, 243–302.
Agamben, Giorgio: *The Coming Community*. Minneapolis 2007 [1993].
Aleiss, Angela: *Making the White Man's Indian. Native Americans and Hollywood Movies*. Westport 2005.
Allison, Lincoln: Sport and Politics. In: id. (ed.): *The Politics of Sport*. Manchester 1986, 1–26.
Althusser, Louis: *On the Reproduction of Capitalism*. London / New York 2014 [1971], 232–272.
Altmann, Rick: A Semantic / Syntactic Approach to Film Genre. *Cinema Journal* 3 (1984), 6–17.
Altman, Rick: *The American Film Musical*. Bloomington / Indianapolis 1987.
Altman, Rick: *Film / Genre*. London 1999.
Anderson, Benedict: *Imagined Communities. Reflections on the Origin and Spread of Nationalism*. London / New York 2006 [1983].
Anderson, Sam: 'Moment' Is Having a Moment. *The New York Times* (30 August 2015), https://www.nytimes.com/2015/08/30/magazine/moment-is-having-a-moment.html (accessed 14 February 2020).
Andrews, David L. / Jackson, Steven J.: *Sport Stars. The Cultural Politics of Sporting Celebrity*. London / New York 2001.
Angelucci, Daniela / Marchetti, Sarin: *Deleuze and the Concepts of Cinema*. Edinburgh 2014.
Arendt, Hannah: *On Revolution*. New York 1990 [1963].
Arendt, Hannah: *Lectures on Kant's Political Philosophy*. Chicago 1992.
Asinof, Eliot: *Eight Men Out. The Black Sox and the 1919 World Series*. New York 1963.
Babington, Bruce: *The Sports Film. Games People Play*. London / New York 2014.
Bakels, Jan / Kappelhoff, Hermann: Das Zuschauergefühl. Möglichkeiten qualitativer Medienanalyse. *Zeitschrift für Medienwissenschaft* 5 (2011), 78–96.
Bakels, Jan / Greifenstein, Sarah / Kappelhoff, Hermann: *Die Poiesis des Filme-Sehens. Methoden der Analyse audiovisueller Bilder*. Berlin 2023 (in preparation).
Baker, Aaron / Boyd, Todd: *Out of Bounds. Sports, Media, and the Politics of Identity*. Bloomington 1997.
Baker, Aaron: *Contesting Identities. Sports in American Film*. Urbana 2003.
Bakhtin, Mikhail: Forms of Time and of the Chronotope in the Novel [1975]. In: Michael Holquist (ed.): *The Dialogic Imagination. Four Essays by Mikhail Bakhtin*. Austin 1981, 84–258.
Barthes, Roland / Bellour, Raymond: *Die Körnung der Stimme. Interviews 1962–1980*. Frankfurt a M. 2002 [1970], 78–98.
Barzun, Jacques: *God's Country and Mine. A Declaration of Love Spice with a Few Harsh Words*. London 1955.
Beaulieu, Alain: Gilles Deleuze's Politics. From Marxism to the Missing People. In: Constantin Boundas (ed.): *Gilles Deleuze. The Intensive Reduction*. London 2009, 204–217.
Beck, Daniel / Bosshart, Louis: Sports and Media. *Communication Research Trends* 22/4 (2003), 3–26.

Bellour, Raymond: Das Entfalten der Emotionen. In: Matthias Brütsch / Vinzenz Hediger / Ursula von Keitz / Alexandra Schneider / Margrit Tröhler (eds.): *Kinogefühle. Emotionalität und Film.* Marburg 2005, 51–101.

Bensmaia, Reda: Der 'beliebige Raum' als 'Begriffsperson' / L'espace quelconque comme 'personnage conceptuelle Zeichen'. In: Oliver Fahle / Lorenz Engell (eds.): *Der Film bei Deleuze / Le Cinéma selon Deleuze.* Weimar / Paris 1999, 153–164.

Berger, Hanno: *Thinking Revolution Through Film. On Audiovisual Stagings of Political Change.* Berlin 2022.

Bergson, Henri: *Matter and Memory.* New York 1991 [1896].

Bergson, Henri: *Creative Evolution.* Mineola 1998 [1911].

Berlant, Lauren: *The Female Complaint. On the Unfinished Business of Sentimentality in American Culture.* Durham 2008.

Berlant, Lauren: *Cruel Optimism.* Durham / London 2011.

Biden, Joseph R.: Inaugural Address. *The White House* (20 January 2021), https://www.whitehouse.gov/briefing-room/speeches-remarks/2021/01/20/inaugural-address-by-president-joseph-r-biden-jr/ (accessed 14 February 2020).

Bidermann, David: 11 Minutes of Action. *The Wall Street Journal* (15 January 2010), https://www.wsj.com/articles/SB10001424052748704281204575002852055561406 (accessed 14 February 2020).

Bishop, Greg: Major Florida State Wins Live On in Sod Cemetery. *The New York Times* (1 January 2014), https://www.nytimes.com/2014/01/02/sports/ncaafootball/at-florida-state-major-victories-dont-fade-away.html (accessed 14 February 2020).

Blumenberg, Hans: *Work on Myth.* Cambridge 2010 [1979].

Bogue, Ronald. *Deleuze on Literature.* New York / London 2003.

Bonnet, Valérie: Sport in Films. Symbolism versus Verismo. A France-United States Comparative Analysis. *InMedia* 6 (2017), http://journals.openedition.org/inmedia/883 (accessed 2 March 2020).

Bonzel, Katharina: Reviving the American Dream. The World of Sport. In: Bowdoin Van Riper (ed.): *Learning from Mickey, Donald and Walt. Essays on Disney's Edutainment Films.* Jefferson / London 2011, 201–208.

Bonzel, Katharina: *National Pastimes. Cinema, Sports, and Nation.* Lincoln 2020.

Bonzel, Katharina / Chare, Nicholas (eds.): *Representation of Sports Coaches in Film. Looking to Win.* London 2017.

Boyd, Julian P.: *The Declaration of Independence. The Evolution of the Text as Shown in Facsimiles of Various Drafts by Its Author, Thomas Jefferson.* Princeton 1945.

Boyd, Julian P.: On the Need for 'Frequent Recurrence to Fundamental Principles'. *Virginia Law Review* 62 (1976), 859–871.

Boym, Svetlana. *The Future of Nostalgia.* New York 2001.

Bravo, Jorge: Heroic Epiphanies. Narrative, Visual, and Cultic Contexts. *Illinois Classical Studies* 29 (2004), 63–84.

Briley, Ron: Basketball's Great White Hope and Ronald Reagan's America. Hoosiers (1986). *Film & History. An Interdisciplinary Journal of Film and Television Studies* 35/1 (2005), 12–19.

Briley, Ron: *The Baseball Film in Postwar America. A Critical Study, 1948–1962.* Jefferson 2011, 75–86.

Brohm, Jean-Marie: *Sport, A Prison Measured in Time.* Paris 1978.

Brown, Peter Jensen: From Stuhldreher to Castner and Crowley to Staubach – a Last-Second History of the 'Hail Mary Pass.' *Early Sports and Pop Culture History Blog* (2018), https://esnpc.blogspot.com/2018/02/from-stuhldreher-to-castner-and-crowley.html (accessed 14 February 2020).
Bryant, Levi R.: What are Singularities? *Larval Subjects Blog* (2012), https://larvalsubjects.wordpress.com/2012/06/14/what-are-singularities/ (accessed 2 March 2020).
Buford, Kate: *Native American Son. The Life and Sporting Legend of Jim Thorpe.* Lincoln 2010.
Burch, Noël: Primitivism and the Avant-Gardes. A Dialectical Approach. In: Phil Rosen (ed.): *Narrative – Apparatus – Ideology. A Film Theory Reader.* New York 1986, 483–506.
Butterworth, Michael L.: *Baseball and Rhetorics of Purity. The National Pastime and American Identity During the War on Terror.* Tuscaloosa 2010.
Caillois, Roger: *Man, Play and Games.* London 1962 [1958].
Campbell, Joseph: *The Hero with a Thousand Faces.* Novato 2008 [1949].
Casetti, Francesco: *Inside the Gaze. The Fiction Film and Its Spectator.* Bloomington 1998.
Cashmore, Ellis: *Sports Culture. An A–Z Guide.* New York / London 2000.
Cashmore, Ellis: *Making Sense of Sports.* New York / London 2010.
Cavanaugh, Jack: *The Gipper. George Gipp, Knute Rockne, and the Dramatic Rise of Notre Dame Football.* New York 2010.
Cavell, Stanley: *The World Viewed. Reflections on the Ontology of Film, Enlarged Edition.* Cambridge 1979.
Cavell, Stanley: *Pursuits of Happiness. The Hollywood Comedy of Remarriage.* Cambridge / London 1981.
Cavell, Stanley: The Fact of Television. *Daedalus,* 111/4 (1982), 75–96.
Cavell, Stanley: *Themes Out of School. Effects and Causes.* Chicago 1984.
Cavell, Stanley: *Conditions Handsome and Unhandsome.* Chicago 1991.
Cavell, Stanley: *This New Yet Unapproachable America. Lectures After Emerson After Wittgenstein.* Chicago / Illinois 2013 [1989].
Chat Transcript with Roger Staubach. Pro Football Hall of Fame Official Site (2000), https://www.profootballhof.com/news/chat-transcript-with-roger-staubach/ (accessed 14 February 2020).
Chion, Michel: *Audio-Vision. Sound on Screen.* London 1994 [1990].
Chion, Michel: *The Voice in Cinema.* New York 1999 [1987].
Clarke, Melissa: The Space-Time Image. The Case of Bergson, Deleuze, and Memento. *The Journal of Speculative Philosophy* 16/3 (2002), 167–181.
Colebrook, Claire / Weinstein, Jami: *Deleuze and Gender. Deleuze Studies.* Vol. 2. Edinburgh 2008.
Collins, Jim: Genericity in the Nineties. Eclectic Irony and the New Sincerity. In: Jim Collins / Ava Preacher Collins / Hilary Radner (eds.): *Film Theory Goes to the Movies. Cultural Analysis of Contemporary Film.* London 1993, 242–263.
Colman, Felicity: *Deleuze and Cinema. The Film Concepts.* Oxford / New York 2011.
Cooper, Caroline M.: FIELD OF DREAMS. A Favorite of President Clinton – But a Typical Reaganite Film? *Literature / Film Quarterly* 23/3 (1995), 163–168.
Crosson, Seán. *Sport and Film.* New York 2013.
Crosson, Seán: From Babe Ruth to Michael Jordan. Affirming the American Dream via the Sports / Film Star. *Kinema* 42 (2014), 79–104.

Crosson, Seán: Review: *The Sports Film. Games People Play* (Bruce Babington). *Kinema. A Journal for Film and Audiovisual Media* (2015), https://openjournals.uwaterloo.ca/index.php/kinema/article/view/1320/1730 (accessed 2 March 2020).
Csíkszentmihályi, Mihaly: Flow. The Secret to Happiness. *TED* (2004), https://www.ted.com/talks/mihaly_csikszentmihalyi_flow_the_secret_to_happiness?language=de#t-9095 (accessed 12 November 2020).
Csíkszentmihályi, Mihaly: *Flow. The Psychology of Optimal Experience*. New York 2008.
Csíkszentmihályi, Mihaly / Getzels, Jacob W.: *The Creative Vision. A Longitudinal Study of Problem Finding in Art*. New York 1976.
Csíkszentmihályi, Mihaly / Getzels, Jacob W. / Kahn, Stephen P.: *Talent and Achievement. A Longitudinal Study of Artists* [A Report to the Spencer Foundation]. Chicago 1984.
Csíkszentmihályi, Mihaly / Robinson, Rick E.: *The Art of Seeing. An Interpretation of the Aesthetic Encounter*. Los Angeles 1990.
Cull, Laura: The Politics of Becoming(-Woman). Deleuze, Sex and Gender. *Performance Now and Then* (2009), https://www.academia.edu/199365/The_politics_of_becoming_-woman_Deleuze_sex_and_gender (accessed 29 February 2020).
Cullen, Jim: *The American Dream. A Short History of an Idea that Shaped a Nation*. Oxford 2003.
Custen, George F.: *Bio/pics. How Hollywood Constructed Public History*. New Brunswick 1992.
Dalton, Harlon L.: *Racial Healing. Confronting the Fear between Blacks and Whites*. New York 1995.
DeLanda, Manuel: Deleuzian Social Ontology and Assemblage Theory. In: Martin Fuglsang / Bent Meier Sorensen (eds.): *Deleuze and the Social*. Edinburgh 2006, 250–266.
Deleuze, Gilles: Sur / On Spinoza. *Cours Vincennes* (24 January 1978), https://www.webdeleuze.com/textes/14 (accessed 4 March 2020).
Deleuze, Gilles: *The Logic of Sense*. New York 1990 [1969].
Deleuze, Gilles: Coldness and Cruelty. In: id. / Leopold von Sacher-Masoch: *Masochism*. New York 1991 [1967], 15–142.
Deleuze, Gilles: *Negotiations 1972–1990*. New York 1995 [1990].
Deleuze, Gilles: Whitman. In: id.: *Essays. Critical and Clinical*. London 1998a, 56–60.
Deleuze, Gilles: Bartleby; or, The Formula. In: id.: *Essays. Critical and Clinical*. London 1998b, 68–90.
Deleuze, Gilles: *Francis Bacon. The Logic of Sensation*. Minneapolis 2003 [1981].
Deleuze, Gilles: *Cinema I. The Movement-Image*. London 2013a [1983].
Deleuze, Gilles: *Cinema II. The Time-Image*. London 2013b [1985].
Deleuze, Gilles: *Difference and Repetition*. London 2014 [1968].
Deleuze, Gilles / Guattari, Félix: *A Thousand Plateaus. Capitalism and Schizophrenia*. Minneapolis 1987 [1980].
DeLillo, Don: *Underworld*. New York 1998.
Derrida, Jacques: Otobiographies – The Teaching of Nietzsche and the Politics of the Proper Name [1984]. In: Christie V. McDonald (ed.): *The Ear of the Other. Otobiographie, Transference, Translation*. New York 1985, 1–38.
Derrida, Jacques: Declarations of Independence. *New Political Science* 15 (1986), 7–15.
Derrida, Jacques: OTOBIOGRAPHIEN – Die Lehre Nietzsches und die Politik des Eigennamens [1984]. In: id. / Friedrich Kittler: *Nietzsche – Politik des Eigennamens. Wie man abschafft, wovon man spricht*. Berlin 2000, 7–63.

Derrida, Jacques: *Otobiographies. L'enseignement de Nietzsche et la politique du nom propre.* Paris 2005 [1984].
Doran, Robert: Mimesis and Aesthetic Redemption. In: Saija Isomaa / Sari Kivisto / Pirjo Lyytikainen (eds.): *Rethinking Mimesis. Concepts and Practices of Literary Representation.* Newcastle upon Tyne / Cambridge 2012, 201–225.
Dyer, Richard: Entertainment and Utopia. *Movie* 24 (1977), 2–13.
Dyer, Richard: *Only Entertainment.* New York 2002 [1992].
Elsaesser, Thomas: Specularity and Engulfment. Francis Ford Coppola and Bram Stoker's Dracula. In: Steve Neale / Murray Smith (eds.): *Contemporary Hollywood Cinema.* New York / London 1998, 191–208.
Engels, Friedrich: Engels to Franz Mehring (London, 14 July 1893). In: id.: *Karl Marx and Friedrich Engels. Correspondence 1846–1895.* New York 1968, https://www.marxists.org/archive/marx/works/1893/letters/93_07_14.htm (accessed 31 January 2020).
Englert, Barbara: *Mainstream and Beyond. Wie der US-amerikanische Sportfilm der Siebzigerjahre die Gesellschaft reflektiert.* Frankfurt a. M. 2011.
Eyerman, Ron: False Consciousness and Ideology in Marxist Theory. *Acta Sociologica* 24/1–2 (1981), 43–56.
Fahle, Oliver: Zeitspaltungen. Gedächtnis und Erinnerung bei Gilles Deleuze. *montage a/v* 11/1 (2002), 97–112.
Farred, Grant: The Double Temporality of Lagaan. Cultural Struggle and Postcolonialism. *Journal of Sport and Social Issues* 28/2 (2004), 93–114.
Farred, Grant: When Kings Were (Anti-?)Colonials. Black Athletes in Film. *Sport in Society*, 11/2–3 (2008), 240–252.
Fear-Segal, Jacqueline / Rose, Susan D. (eds.): *Carlisle Indian Industrial School. Indigenous Histories, Memories, and Reclamations.* Lincoln 2018.
Fisher, Mark: *The Weird and the Eerie.* New York 2017.
Fitting, Peter: What Is Utopian Film? An Introductory Taxonomy. *Utopian Studies* 4/2 (1993), 1–17.
Florschütz, Gottlieb: *Sport in Film und Fernsehen. Zwischen Infotainment und Spektakel.* Wiesbaden 2005.
Fluck, Winfried: *Das kulturelle Imaginäre. Eine Funktionsgeschichte des amerikanischen Romans 1970–1900.* Frankfurt a. M. 1997.
Frampton, Daniel: *Filmosophy.* London 2006.
Friedlander, Brett / Reising, Robert: *Chasing Moonlight. The True Story of FIELD OF DREAMS' Doc Graham.* Winston-Salem 2009.
Friedman, Lester D.: *Sports Movies.* New Brunswick 2020.
Frye, Northrop: *Anatomy of Criticism. Four Essays.* Princeton 1957.
Gaertner, David: *Tickets to War. Demokratie, Propaganda und Kino in den USA bis 1945.* Berlin 2022.
Gaines, Jane M.: Even More Tears. In: Christine Gledhill / Linda Williams (eds.): *Melodrama Unbound. Across History, Media, and National Cultures.* New York 2018, 325–340.
Gamper, Michael / Hühn, Helmut (eds.): *Zeit der Darstellung. Ästhetische Eigenzeit in Kunst, Literatur und Wissenschaft.* Hanover 2014.
Gamper, Michael / Geulen, Eva / Grave, Johannes / Langenohl, Andreas / Simon, Ralf / Zubarik, Sabine (eds.): *Zeiten der Form – Formen der Zeit.* Hanover 2016.
Giamatti, A. Bartlett: *Take Time for Paradise. Americans and their Games.* New York 1989.

Gill, Ryan: *Our Country, Our Game, Our Film. A Rhetorical Analysis of American Cultural Values in the Institution of Baseball as Expressed in the Film Field of Dreams* [Graduate Student Theses, Dissertations, & Professional Papers, 3154] (1999).

Gledhill, Christine: Rethinking Genre. In: id. / Linda Williams (eds.): *Reinventing Film Studies*. London 2000, 221–243.

Gledhill, Christine: Überlegungen zum Verhältnis von Gender und Genre im postmodernen Zeitalter. In: Monika Bernold (ed.): *Screenwise. Film, Fernsehen, Feminismus*. Marburg 2004, 200–209.

Gledhill, Christine (ed.): *Gender Meets Genre in Postwar Cinemas*. Urbana 2012.

Gledhill, Christine: Prologue. The Reach of Melodrama. In: id. / Linda Williams (eds.): *Melodrama Unbound. Across History, Media, and National Cultures*. New York 2018, ix–xxvi.

Gorman, Amanda: *The Hill We Climb. Den Hügel hinauf*. Hamburg 2021.

Greifenstein, Sarah: *Tempi der Bewegung – Modi des Gefühls. Expressivität, heitere Affekte und die Screwball Comedy*. Berlin 2020.

Greifenstein, Sarah / Kappelhoff, Hermann: Feeling Gloomy or Riding High. Timings of Melodrama and Comedy. In: Marie-Luise Angerer / Bernd Bösel / Michaela Ott (eds.): *Timing of Affect. Epistemologies of Affection*. Chicago 2014, 263–282.

Greifenstein, Sarah / Kappelhoff, Hermann / Scherer, Thomas: Expressive movements in audio-visual media. Modulating affective experience. In: Cornelia Müller / Alan Cienki / Ellen Fricke / Silva H. Ladewig / David McNeill / Jana Bressem (eds.): *Body – Language – Communication. An International Handbook on Multimodality in Human Interaction*. Berlin / New York 2014, 2081–2092.

Grella, George: Baseball and the American Dream. *The Massachusetts Review* 16, 1975.

Grindon, Leger: Body and Soul. The Structure of Meaning in the Boxing Film Genre. *Cinema Journal* 35/4 (1996), 54–69.

Grindon, Leger: *Knockout. The Boxer and Boxing in American Cinema*. Jackson 2011.

Groß, Bernhard: The Audiovisual as a Mode of Thinking Historicity. In: Diego Cavallotti / Simone Dotto / Leonardo Quaresima (eds.): *A History of Cinema Without Names*. Vol II: *Contexts and Practical Applications*. Milan 2017, 243–252.

Grosz, Elisabeth: Deleuze, Bergson and the Concept of Life. *Revue international de philosophie* 3 (2007), 288–289.

Grotkopp, Matthias. *Cinematic Poetics of Guilt. Audiovisual Accusation as a Mode of Commonality*. Berlin 2021.

Grotkopp, Matthias / Kappelhoff, Hermann: Film Genre and Modality. The Incestuous Nature of Genre Exemplified by the War Film. In: Sebastien Lefait / Philippe Ortoli (eds.): *In Praise of Cinematic Bastardy*. Newcastle upon Tyne 2012, 29–39.

Grotkopp, Matthias / Kappelhoff, Hermann: *Genre, Poetik und Affekt*. Berlin 2023 (in preparation).

Grundy, Pamela / Rader, Benjamin: *American Sports. From the Age of Folk Games to the Age of the Internet*. New York 2018 [1983].

Gruneau, Richard S.: *Sport and Modernity*. Cambridge / Malden 2017.

Gugutzer, Robert: Trendsport im Schnittfeld von Körper, Selbst und Gesellschaft. Leib- und körpersoziologische Überlegungen. *Sport und Gesellschaft* 1/3 (2004), 219–243.

Gugutzer, Robert / Englert, Barbara: *Sport im Film. Zur wissenschaftlichen Entdeckung eines verkannten Genres*. Konstanz 2014.

Gumbrecht, Hans Ulrich: *In Praise of Athletic Beauty*. Cambridge 2006.

Gunning, Tom: The Cinema of Attraction. Early Cinema, Its Spectator, and the Avant-Garde. *Wide Angle* 8/3–4 (1986), 63–70.
Gunning, Tom: Now You See It, Now You Don't. The Temporality of the Cinema of Attraction. In: Lee Grieveson / Peter Krämer (eds.): *The Silent Cinema Reader*. London / New York 2004 [1993], 41–50.
Hall, Mordaunt: Movie Review: THE SPIRIT OF NOTRE DAME. *New York Times* (16 October 1931).
Harootunian, Harry: Remembering the Historical Present. *Critical Inquiry* 33/3 (2007), 471–494.
Heidegger, Martin: *Sein Und Zeit*. Tübingen 1976 [1927].
Heller, Franziska: *Filmästhetik des Fluiden. Strömungen des Erzählens von Vigo bis Tarkowskij, von Huston bis Cameron*. Munich 2010.
Hernández-Lemus, Alberto M.: *The Coalescence of Sign Regimes. Deleuze and Italian Neorealism* [Dissertation, New School for Social Research] (2000).
Herzogenrath, Bernd: *An American Body/Politic. A Deleuzian Approach*. Hanover 2010.
Hildebrandt-Stratmann, Reiner / Probst, Andrea: Ästhetische Erziehung im Sportunterricht der Grundschule. In: Joachim Kahlert / Gabriele Lieber / Sigrid Binder (eds.): *Ästhetisch bilden. Bewegungsintensives Lernen in der Grundschule*. Braunschweig 2006, 183–199.
Hill, Sarah: The Ambitious Young Woman and the Contemporary British Sports Film. *Assuming Gender* 5/1 (2015), 37–58.
Hills, Matt: Listening from behind the Sofa? The (Un)Earthly Roles of Sound in BBC Wales' Doctor Who. *New Review of Film and Television Studies* 9/1 (2011), 28–41.
Horkheimer, Max / Adorno, Theodor W.: *Dialektik der Aufklärung. Philosophische Fragmente*. Frankfurt a. M. 2006 [1944].
Huizinga, Johan: *Homo Ludens. A Study of Play-Element in Culture*. Ranchos de Taos 2016 [1938].
Hundley, Heather L. / Billings, Andrew C.: *Examining Identity in Sports Media*. Los Angeles 2010.
Hutchins, Brett / Rowe, David: Globalization and Online Audiences. In: Andrew C. Billings (ed.): *Routledge Handbook of Sport and New Media*. London / New York 2014, 7–18.
Hutchins, Brett / Rowe, David: *Sport Beyond Television. The Internet, Digital Media and the Rise of Networked Media Sport*. London / New York 2012.
Huyssen, Andreas: Introduction to Adorno. *New German Critique* 6 (1975), 3–11.
International Olympic Committee: *Olympic Charter* (1933), https://library.olympics.com/Default/doc/SYRACUSE/62045/the-international-olympic-committee-and-the-modern-olympic-games-international-olympic-committee (accessed 22 July 2022).
Iser, Wolfgang: *Prospecting. From Reader Response to Literary Anthropology*. Baltimore / London 1989.
Jackson, Susan A. / Csíkszentmihályi, Mihaly: *Flow in Sports. The Keys to Optimal Experiences and Performances*. Champaign 1999.
Jameson, Fredric: Magical Narratives. On the Dialectical Use of Genre Criticism. In: id.:*The Political Unconscious. Narrative as a Socially Symbolic Act*. Ithaca 1981, 103–150.
Jameson, Fredric: *Postmodernism. Or, the Cultural Logic of Late Capitalism*. Durham 1992.
Jefferson, Thomas: *Writings. Autobiography – Notes on the State of Virginia – Public and Private Papers – Addresses – Letters*, ed. Merrill D. Peterson. New York 1984.
Jenkins, Sally: Why Are Jim Thorpe's Olympic Records Still Not Recognized? *Smithsonian Magazine* 7 (2012), https://www.smithsonianmag.com/history/why-are-jim-thorpes-olympic-records-still-not-recognized-130986336/ (accessed 15 August 2016).
Jenkins, Steve: Eight Men Out. *Monthly Film Bulletin* 56/666 (1989), 204–205.

Johnson, Richard: There's tons of other stuff in your football team's playbook. *Banner Society Blog* (15 August 2019), https://www.bannersociety.com/2019/8/15/20726587/what-is-in-a-playbook-football (accessed 21 February 2020).

Jones, Glen: In Praise of an 'Invisible Genre'? An Ambivalent Look at the Fictional Sports Feature Film. *Sport in Society* 11/2–3 (2008), 117–129.

Kamp, David: Rethinking the American Dream. *Vanity Fair* 4 (2009), https://www.vanityfair.com/culture/2009/04/american-dream200904 (accessed 29 February 2020).

Kappelhoff, Hermann: Empfindungsbilder. Subjektivierte Zeit im melodramatischen Kino. In: Theresia Birkenhauer / Annette Storr (eds.): *Zeitlichkeiten. Zur Realität der Künste*. Berlin 1998, 93–119.

Kappelhoff, Hermann. *Matrix der Gefühle. Das Kino, das Melodrama und das Theater der Empfindsamkeit*. Berlin 2004.

Kappelhoff, Hermann: *The Politics and Poetics of Cinematic Realism*. New York 2015.

Kappelhoff, Hermann: Genre and 'Sense of Community.' *Mediaesthetics* 1 (2016), https://www.mediaesthetics.org/index.php/mae/article/view/42/145 (accessed 22 July 2022).

Kappelhoff, Hermann: Visualizing Community. A Look at World War II Propaganda Films. In: Anders Engberg-Pedersen / Kathrin Maurer (eds.): *Visualizing War. Emotions, Technologies, Communities*. New York / London 2017, 133–145.

Kappelhoff, Hermann: *Front Lines of Community. Hollywood Between War and Democracy*. Berlin 2018a.

Kappelhoff, Hermann: *Kognition und Reflexion. Zur Theorie filmischen Denkens*. Berlin 2018b.

Kappelhoff, Hermann. *On the Poiesis of Film Viewing. Filmmaking between Germany and Turkey*. A Talk Given at the IKKM Weimar (21 November 2018c).

Kappelhoff, Hermann / Greifenstein, Sarah: Audiovisual Metaphors. Embodied Meaning and Processes of Fictionalization. In: Kathrin Fahlenbrach (ed.): *Embodied Metaphors in Film, Television, and Video Games. Cognitive Approaches*. New York 2016, 183–201.

Kappelhoff, Hermann / Lehmann, Hauke: Poetics of Affect. In: Jan Slaby / Christian Von Scheve (eds.): *Affective Societies. Key Concepts*. London / New York 2019, 210–219.

Kappelhoff, Hermann / Lehmann, Hauke: Zeit. Zeitkonstruktion, Zeiterfahrung und Erinnerung im Film – Theorien filmischer Zeit. In: Bernhard Groß / Thomas Morsch (eds.): *Handbuch Filmtheorie*. Wiesbaden 2021, 535–553.

Kappelhoff, Hermann / Müller, Cornelia: Embodied Meaning Construction. Multimodal Metaphor and Expressive Movement in Speech, Gesture, and Feature Film. *Metaphor and the Social World* 1/2 (2011), 121–153.

Keefe, Joshua R.: Redskin and All-American. Jim Thorpe's Malleable Symbolic Significance. *Inquiries Journal / Student Pulse* 1/10 (2009), http://www.inquiriesjournal.com/articles/15/redskin-and-all-american-jim-thorpes-malleable-symbolic-significance (accessed 22 July 2022).

Kehrberg, Amanda: And the Crowd Goes Wild. Musical Syntax and the Spectacle of Masculinity in Contemporary Sports Films. *Aethlon. The Journal of Sport Literature* 29/1 (2011), 49–65.

Kilerci, Nazlı / Lehmann, Hauke: Beyond Turkish German Cinema. Affective Experience and Generic Relationality. In: Birgitt Röttger-Rössler / Jan Slaby (eds.): *Affect in Relation. Families, Places, Technologies*. London / New York 2018, 259–280.

King, C. Richard / Leonard, David J. (eds.): *Visual Economies of/in Motion. Sport and Film*. New York 2006.

Køppe, Simo / Harder, Susanne / Vaeveret, Mette: Vitality Affects. *International Forum of Psychoanalysis* 17/3 (2008), 169–79.

Kracauer, Siegfried: *History. The Last Things before the Last*. Princeton 1995 [1969].

Kusz, Kyle W.: Remasculinizing American White Guys in/through New Millennium American Sport Films. *Sport in Society* 11/2–3 (2008), 209–226.

LaRocca, David: The European Authorization of American Literature and Philosophy: After Cavell, Reading Bartleby with Deleuze, then Rancière. In: Corey McCall / Tom Nurmi (eds.): *Melville among the Philosophers*. Lanham 2017, 189–211.

Lauri-Lucente, Gloria: Nostalgia and Nostophobia. Filming Englishness and Italianess in A Room with a View and Where Angels Fear to Tread. *Merope* 61–62 (2015), 35–58.

Lefort, Claude: *Democracy and Political Theory*. Minneapolis 1988.

Lehmann, Hauke: Die Produktion des 'deutsch-türkischen Kinos'. Die Verflechtung von Filme-Machen und Filme-Sehen in Lola und Bilidikid (1998) und Tiger – Die Kralle von Kreuzberg (2006). In: Ömer Alkın (ed.): *Deutsch-Türkische Filmkultur im Migrationskontext*. Wiesbaden 2017, 275–297.

Lehmann, Hauke: *Affect Poetics of the New Hollywood. Suspense, Paranoia, and Melancholy*. Berlin / Boston 2019.

Lehmann, Hauke: *Filmesehen – Filmemachen: Gespräche und Analysen zur Poiesis des „deutsch-türkischen Kinos"*. Berlin 2023 (in preparation).

Lie, Sulgie: *Towards a Political Aesthetics of Cinema. The Outside of Film*. Amsterdam 2020.

Liegl, Michael: *Zum Verhältnis von Philosophie und Demokratie bei Richard Rorty* [unpublished master thesis in German, Philipps-Universität Marburg] (2000).

López Frías, Javier: The Reconstructive and Normative Aspects of Bernard Suits's Utopia. *Reason Papers* 38/1 (2016), 51–64.

Maguire, Joseph A.: Sport, Identity Politics, Gender and Globalization. *Sport in Society* 14/7–8 (2011), 994–1009.

Malachowski, Alan: *A Companion to Rorty*. Hoboken 2020.

Mann, Jack: The Great Wall of Boston. *Sports Illustrated* 22/26 (1965), 42–55.

Marrati, Paola: Time and Affects. Deleuze on Gender and Sexual Difference. *Australian Feminist Studies* 21/51 (2006), https://www.tandfonline.com/doi/abs/10.1080/08164640600947202?journalCode=cafs20 (accessed 29 February 2020).

Massumi, Brian: *A User's Guide to Capitalism and Schizophrenia. Deviations From Deleuze and Guattari*. Cambridge 1992.

Massumi, Brian: *Parables for the Virtual. Movement, Affect, Sensation*. Durham 2002.

Matthews, Daniel: Declarations of Independence. Notes on the Thought of Jacques Derrida. *Law and the Political* (2013), http://criticallegalthinking.com/2013/08/07/declarations-of-independence-notes-on-the-thought-of-jacques-derrida/ (accessed 29 February 2020).

Matthews, Eric: *The Philosophy of Merleau-Ponty*. Chesham 2002.

May, Stefan: *Faust trifft Auge. Mythologie und Ästhetik des amerikanischen Boxfilms*. Bielefeld 2004.

McCall, Dan. *The Silence of Bartleby*. Ithaca 1989.

McDorman, Todd F. / Casper, Kurt / Logan, Aaron / McGinley, Sean: Where Have All the Heroes Gone? An Exploration of Cultural Therapy in Jerry Maguire, For Love of the Game, and Any Given Sunday. *Journal of Sport & Social Issues* 30/2 (2006), 197–218.

McKernan, Luke: Sport and the First Films. In: Christopher Williams (ed.): *Cinema. The Beginnings and the Future*. London 1996, 107–116.

McKie, Scott: Charles Curtis. America's Indian Vice President. *Cherokee One Feather* (4 February 2014), https://www.theonefeather.com/2014/02/charles-curtis-americas-indian-vice-president/ (accessed 29 February 2020).

McLaughlin, Douglas W.: Reinventing the Wheel. On Games and the Good Life (Dissertation, 2008), https://etda.libraries.psu.edu/catalog/8879 (accessed 14 February 2020).

Middlekauff, Robert: *The Glorious Cause. The American Revolution. 1763–1789*. New York 2007.

Miller, Andrew: *Laying Down the Rules. The American Sports Film Genre From 1872 to 1960* (Dissertation, Pittsburgh 2003).

Miller, Andrew: Winning It All. The Cinematic Construction of the Athletic American Dream. In: Ricardo Miguez (ed.): *American Dreams. Dialogues in U.S. Studies*. Newcastle 2007, 103–123.

Miller, John C.: *Origins of the American Revolution*. Stanford 1959.

Miller, Toby: Dawn of an Imagined Community. Australian Sport on Film. *Sporting Traditions* 7/1 (1990), 48–59.

Miller, Toby: Film. In: Wray Vamplew (ed.): *The Oxford Companion to Australian Sport*. Melbourne / New York 1994, 163–165.

Mittell, Jason: *Genre and Television. From Cop Shows to Cartoons in American Culture*. New York 2004.

Montville, Leigh: *The Big Bam. The Life and Time of Babe Ruth*. New York 2006.

Mosher, Stephan D.: The White Dreams of God. The Mythology of Sport Films. *Arena Review* 7/2 (1983), 15–19.

Müller, Cornelia / Kappelhoff, Hermann: *Cinematic Metaphor. Experience – Affectivity – Temporality*. Berlin / Boston 2018.

Nancy, Jean-Luc: *The Inoperative Community*. Minneapolis 1991 [1983].

Nancy, Jean-Luc: *Being Singular Plural*. Stanford 2000 [1996].

National Transportation Safety Board: *Aircraft Accident Report Number NTSB-AAR-72-11* (1972), https://www.ntsb.gov/investigations/AccidentReports/Reports/AAR7211.pdf (accessed 21 February 2020).

Neale, Steve: Questions of Genre. *Screen*, 31/1 (1990), 45–66.

Neale, Steve: *Genre and Hollywood*. London 2000.

Nelson, Murry: Sports History as a Vehicle for Social and Cultural Understanding in American History. *The Social Studies* 96/3 (2005), 118–125.

Niemi, Robert: *History in the Media. Film and Television*. Santa Barbara 2006.

Nigianni, Chrysanthi / Storr, Merl: *Deleuze and Queer Theory (Deleuze Connections)*. Edinburgh 2009.

Nixon, Howard L.: *Sport and the American Dream*. New York 1984.

Nowlan, Robert A.: *The American Presidents. From Polk to Hayes. What They Did, What They Said & What Was Said About Them*. Denver 2016.

O'Leary, Michael: The Plane that Changed the World. *Air Classics* 46/10 (2010), 28–48.

Olivier, Bert. Deleuze's "Crystals of Time", Human Subjectivity and Social History. *Phronimon, Journal of the South African Society for Greek Philosophy and the Humanities* 17/1 (2016), 1–32.

Ott, Michaela: Gilles Deleuze. In: Kathrin Busch / Iris Därmann (eds.): *Bildtheorien aus Frankreich. Ein Handbuch*. Munich 2011, 113–124.

Oxendine, Joseph B.: *American Indian Sports Heritage*. Lincoln 1995.

Pearson, Demetrius / Curtis, Russell / Haney, Allen / Zhang, James: Sport Films. Social Dimensions Over Time. 1930–1995. *Journal of Sport and Social Issues* 27/2 (2003), 145–161.
Péguy, Charles: *Clio. Dialogue de l'histoire et de l'âme Païenne*. Paris 1932.
Peretz, Eyal: *The Off-Screen. An Investigation of the Cinematic Frame*. Stanford 2017.
Philpott, Roger: Sport in the Cinema. In: Lincoln Allison (ed.): *Taking Sport Seriously*. Oxford 1998, 173–192.
Pisters, Patricia: *The Matrix of Visual Culture. Working with Deleuze in Film Theory*. Stanford 2003.
Pogodda, Cilli / Gronmaier, Danny: THE WAR TAPES and the Poetics of Affect of the Hollywood War Film Genre. *Frames Cinema Journal* 7 (2015), http://framescinemajournal.com/article/the-war-tapes-and-the-poetics-of-affect-of-the-hollywood-war-film-genre/ (accessed 31 January 2020).
Pollmann, Inga: *Cinematic Vitalism. Film Theory and the Question of Life*. Amsterdam 2018.
Pomerance, Murray: The Dramaturgy of Action and Involvement in Sports Film. *Quarterly Review of Film and Video* 23/4 (2006), 311–329.
Powell, Anna: *Deleuze and Horror Film*. Edinburgh 2006.
Price, John A.: The Stereotyping of North American Indians in Motion Pictures. *Ethnohistory* 20/2 (1973), 153–171.
Rader, Benjamin G.: *American Sports. From the Age of Folk Games to the Age of Televised Sports*. Englewood Cliffs 1990.
Rader, Benjamin G.: *Baseball. A History of America's Game*. Urbana 2008.
Rancière, Jacques: *Disagreement. Politics and Philosophy*. Minneapolis / London 1999.
Rancière, Jacques: *The Flesh of Words. The Politics of Writing*. Stanford 2004 [1998].
Rancière, Jacques: *The Emancipated Spectator*. London 2009 [2008].
Rancière, Jacques: *Dissensus. On Politics and Aesthetics*. London / New York 2010.
Ransom, Amy J.: Bollywood Goes to the Stadium. Gender, National Identity, and Sport Film in Hindi. *Journal of Film and Video* 66/4 (2014), 34–49.
Rastovic, Milos: Deleuze's and Kant's Apprehension of the Imagination in Difference and Repetition. *Dis/Kurs* 7/1 (2011), 36–56.
Ray, Robert B.: *A Certain Tendency of the Hollywood Cinema. 1930–1980*. Princeton 1985.
Reid, John Phillip: The Irrelevance of the Declaration. In: Hendrik Hartog (ed.): *The Law in the American Revolution and the Revolution in the Law. A Collection of Review Essays on American Legal History*. New York 1981, 46–89.
Richter-Hansen, Tullio: HE GOT GAME. Der Sportfilm als Genre. In: Robert Gugutzer / Barbara Englert (eds.): *Sport im Film. Zur wissenschaftlichen Entdeckung eines verkannten Genres*. Konstanz / Munich 2014, 27–36.
Ricœur, Paul: *Time and Narrative*. Vol. 1. Chicago 1984 [1983].
Robinson, Ray: *Rockne of Notre Dame. The Making of a Football Legend*. Oxford 1999.
Rorty, Richard: Beyond Realism and Anti-Realism. In: Ludwig Nagl / Richard Heinrich (eds.): *Wo steht die analytische Philosophie heute?* Vienna 1986.
Rorty, Richard. *Contingency, Irony and Solidarity*. Cambridge 1989.
Rorty, Richard: *Achieving Our Country. Leftist Thought in Twentieth-Century America*. Cambridge 1998.
Rorty, Richard: Back to Class Politics. In: id.: *Philosophy and Social Hope*. London 1999a, 255–261.
Rorty, Richard: Truth Without Correspondence to Reality. In: id.: *Philosophy and Social Hope*. London 1999b, 23–46.

Rosenstone, Robert A.: *Visions of the Past. The Challenge of Film to Our Idea of History.* Cambridge 1995.
Rowe, David: If You Film It, Will They Come? Sports on Film. *Journal of Sport and Social Issues* 22/4 (1998), 350–359.
Rowe, David: *Sport, Culture and the Media. The Unruly Trinity.* Maidenhead 2004.
Rowe, David: Time and Timelessness in Sport Film. *Sport in Society* 11/2–3 (2008), 146–158.
Rowe, David: *Global Media Sport. Flows, Forms and Futures.* London 2011.
Rowland, Robert C. / Jones, John M.: Recasting the American Dream and American Politics. Barack Obama's Keynote Address to the 2004 Democratic National Convention. *Quarterly Journal of Speech* 93 (2007), 425–448.
Rubinfeld, Mark: The Mythical Jim Thorpe. Re/presenting the Twentieth Century American Indian. *The International Journal of the History of Sport* 23/2 (2006), 167–189.
Samuel, Lawrence R.: *The American Dream. A Cultural History.* Syracuse 2012.
Sauer, Bruno: Kairos. In: Wilhelm H. Roscher (ed.): *Ausführliches Lexikon der griechischen und römischen Mythologie.* Leipzig 1894, 897–901, https://archive.org/details/roscher1/Ro scher21IK/ (accessed 22 July 2022).
Schatz, Thomas: *Hollywood Genres. Formulas, Filmmaking and the Studio System.* Boston 1981.
Schierl, Thomas (ed.): *Handbuch Medien, Kommunikation und Sport.* Schorndorf 2007.
Schleusener, Simon. *Kulturelle Komplexität. Gilles Deleuze und die Kulturtheorie der American Studies.* Bielefeld 2015.
Schmidgen, Henning: *Bruno Latour in Pieces. An Intellectual Biography.* New York 2014.
Schultz, Jaime: The Truth about Historical Sport Films. *Journal of Sport History* 41/1 (2014), 29–45.
Schwier, Jürgen (ed.): *Mediensport. Ein einführendes Handbuch.* Baltmannsweiler 2002.
Schwier, Jürgen / Schauerte, Thorsten: *Soziologie des Mediensports.* Cologne 2008.
Seel, Martin: Die Zelebration des Unvermögens. Zur Ästhetik des Sports. *Merkur. Deutsche Zeitschrift für europäisches Denken* 47/527 (1993), 91–100.
Seel, Martin: Das Glück der Form. Über eine Dimension ästhetischer Bildung. In: Eckart Liebau / Jörg Zierfas (eds.): *Schönheit. Traum – Kunst – Bildung.* Bielefeld 2007, 17–32.
Shannon, Timothy J.: What About That Pursuit of Happiness? In: *History Faculty Publications.* Vol 75. Gettysburg 2016, http://cupola.gettysburg.edu/histfac/75 (accessed 29 February 2020).
Shaughnessy, Dan: The Wall. *The Boston Globe Magazine* (11 April 1999).
Shaw, Spencer: *Film Consciousness. From Phenomenology to Deleuze.* Jefferson 2008.
Sicks, Kai M. / Stauff, Markus: *Filmgenres. Sportfilm.* Stuttgart 2010.
Silverman, Kaja: *The Acoustic Mirror. The Female Voice in Psychoanalysis and Cinema.* Urbana 1988.
Simondon, Gilbert: The Genesis of the Individual. In: Jonathan Crary / Sanford Kwinter (eds.): *Incorporations.* New York 1992, 297–319.
Sipiora, Phillip / Baumlin, James S.: *Rhetoric and Kairos. Essays in History, Theory, and Praxis.* New York 2002.
Sobchack, Vivian: The Scene of the Screen. Envisioning Cinematic and Electronic 'Presence'. In: Hans Ulrich Gumbrecht / Ludwig Pfeiffer (eds.): *Materialities of Communication.* Stanford 1988, 83–106.
Sobchack, Vivian: 'Sorge and Splendor.' A Phenomenology of the Hollywood Historical Epic. *Representations* 29 (1990), 24–49.

Sobchack, Vivian: *The Address of the Eye. A Phenomenology of Film Experience*. Princeton 1992.
Sobchack, Vivian: Baseball in the Post-American Cinema, or Life in the Minor Leagues. In: Aaron Baker / Todd Boyd (eds.): *Out of Bounds. Sports, Media and the Politics of Identity*. Urbana 1997, 175–198.
Sperber, Murray: *Onward to Victory. The Creation of Modern College Sports*. New York 1998.
Sperber, Murray: *Shake Down the Thunder. The Creation of Notre Dame Football*. Urbana 2002.
Staiger, Janet: Rethinking 'Primitive' Cinema. Intertextuality, the Middle-Class Audience, and Reception Studies. In: id. (ed.): *Interpreting Films: Studies in the Historical Reception of American Cinema*. Princeton 1992, 101–123.
Stam, Robert: Bakhtin, Polyphony and Ethnic/Racial Representation. In: Lester Friedman (ed.): *Unspeakable Images. Ethnicity and the American Cinema*. Urbana 1991, 251–277.
Stauff, Markus: [Review] C. Richard King / David J. Leonard (eds.): Visual Economies of/in Motion. Sport and Film. *MEDIENwissenschaft. Rezensionen – Reviews* 25/2 (2008), 193–194.
Streible, Dan: *Fight Pictures. A History of Boxing and Early Cinema*. Berkeley 2008.
Stern, Daniel: *The Interpersonal World of the Infant*. New York 1985.
Suits, Bernard / Hurka, Thomas: *The Grasshopper. Games, Life and Utopia*. Peterborough 2005 [1978].
Tampio, Nicholas: *Deleuze's Political Vision*. Lanham 2015.
Theunissen, Michael: *Pindar. Menschenlos und Wende der Zeit*. Munich 2000.
Thoreau, Henry David: *Walden. Or Life in the Woods*. Oxford 1997 [1854].
Todorov, Tzvetan: *The Fantastic. A Structural Approach to a Literary Genre*. Ithaca 1975 [1970].
Todorov, Tzvetan: The Origin of Genres. *New Literary History* 8/1 (1976), 159–170.
Totaro, Donato: Gilles Deleuze's Bergsonian Film Project. Part 2. *Off Screen* 3/3 (1999), https://offscreen.com/view/bergson2 (accessed 14 February 2020).
Trifonova, Temenuga: Matter-Image or Image-Consciousness. Bergson contra Sartre. *Janus Head* 6/1 (2003), 80–114.
Trifonova, Temenuga: A Nonhuman Eye. Deleuze on Cinema. *SubStance* 33/2 (2004), 134–152.
Tröhler, Margrit: Die sinnliche Präsenz der Dinge oder: die skeptische Versöhnung mit der Moderne durch den Film. In: Christian Kiening (ed.): *Mediale Gegenwärtigkeit*. Zurich 2007, 283–306.
Tudor, Deborah V.: *Hollywood's Vision of Team Sports. Heroes, Race, and Gender*. New York 1997.
Urbas, Joseph: Cavell's "Moral Perfectionism" or Emerson's "Moral Sentiment"? *European Journal of Pragmatism and American Philosophy* (2010), https://journals.openedition.org/ejpap/897 (accessed 14 February 2020).
Vermeulen, Pieter: Community and Literary Experience in (Between) Benedict Anderson and Jean-Luc Nancy. *Mosaic. An Interdisciplinary Critical Journal* 42/4 (2009), 95–111.
Vihalem, Margus: Everyday Aesthetics and Jacques Rancière. Reconfiguring the Common Field of Aesthetics and Politics. *Journal of Aesthetics & Culture* 10/1 (2018), https://www.tandfonline.com/doi/full/10.1080/20004214.2018.1506209?scroll=top&needAccess=true (accessed 14 February 2020).
Vogl, Joseph (ed.): *Gemeinschaften. Positionen zu einer Philosophie des Politischen*. Frankfurt a. M. 1994.

Waitz, Thomas: Die filmische Produktivität des Sports. In: Robert Gugutzer / Barbara Englert (eds.): *Sport im Film. Zur wissenschaftlichen Entdeckung eines verkannten Genres*. Konstanz 2014, 37–54.
Wasserman, Loretta: The Music of Time. Henri Bergson and Willa Cather. *American Literature. A Journal of Literary History* 57/2 (1985), 226–239.
Watterson, John S.: *College Football. History, Spectacle, Controversy*. Baltimore 2000.
Wedel, Michael: Grausame Geschichte. Kracauer, Visual History und Film. In: Bernhard Groß / Vrääth Öhner / Drehli Robnik (eds.): *Film und Gesellschaft denken mit Siegfried Kracauer*. Vienna / Berlin 2018, 107–119.
Wedel, Michael: *Pictorial Affects, Senses of Rupture. On the Poetics and Culture of Popular German Cinema. 1910–1930*. Berlin / Boston 2019.
Wells, Paul: *Animation, Sport and Culture*. New York 2014.
Wenner, Lawrence A.: *Media, Sports, and Society*. Newbury Park / London / New Delhi 1989.
Wenner, Lawrence A.: *MediaSport*. New York / London 1998.
Whannel, Garry: Fields in Vision. Sport and Representation. *Screen* 25/3 (1984), 99–107.
Whannel, Garry. *Fields in Vision. Television Sport and Cultural Transformation*. New York 2005 [1992].
Whannel, Garry. *Media Sport Stars*. New York 2002.
Whannel, Garry: Winning and Losing Respect. Narratives of Identity in Sport Films. *Sport in Society* 11/2-3 (2008), 195–208.
Whannel, Garry: Television and the Transformation of Sport. *The ANNALS of the American Academy of Political and Social Science* 625/1 (2009), 205–218.
Wheeler, Robert W.: *Jim Thorpe, World's Greatest Athlete*. Chicago 1979.
Williams, Linda: Melodrama Revised. In: Nick Browne (ed.): *Refiguring American Film Genres. Theory and History*. Berkeley 1998, 42–88.
Williams, Linda: Film Bodies. Gender, Genre, and Excess. In: Barry K. Grant (ed.): *Film Genre Reader II*. Austin 1999, 140–158.
Williams, Tennessee: *The Glass Menagerie*. New York 2009 [1945].
Wills, Garry: *Inventing America. Jefferson's Declaration of Independence*. New York 2002.
Wilson, Amy: The Night Huntington Died. *Lexington Herald-Leader* (18 December 2006).
Wolfe, Katharine: From Aesthetics to Politics. Rancière, Kant and Deleuze. *Contemporary Aesthetics* 4 (2006), https://digitalcommons.risd.edu/liberalarts_contempaesthetics/vol4/iss1/12/ (accessed 25 August 2022).
Wyllie, Martin: Lived Time and Psychopathology. *Philosophy, Psychiatry, & Psychology* 12/3 (2005), 173–185.
Žižek, Slavoj: *Welcome to the Desert of the Real*. New York 2002.
Žižek, Slavoj: *For They Know Not What They Do. Enjoyment as a Political Factor*. New York 2008 [1991].
Žižek, Slavoj: *Event. Philosophy in Transit*. London 2014.

Filmography

1. Dir. Peter Crowder. Spitfire Pictures / Diamond Docs, USA 2013.
42. Dir. Brian Helgeland. Warner Bros, USA 2013.

AIRPLANE!. Dir. Jim Abrahams / David Zucker / Jerry Zucker. Paramount Pictures, USA 1980.
A LEAGUE OF THEIR OWN. Dir. Penny Marshall. Columbia Pictures, USA 1992.
ALL AMERICAN. Dir. April Blair. CBS Television, USA 2018.
ALL THE RIGHT MOVES. Dir. Michael Chapman. Twentieth Century Fox, USA 1983.
ANGELS IN THE OUTFIELD. Dir. Clarence Brown. MGM, USA 1951.
ANGELS IN THE OUTFIELD. Dir. William Dear. Walt Disney Pictures, USA 1994.
ANY GIVEN SUNDAY. Dir. Oliver Stone. Warner Bros, USA 1999.

BABE COMES HOME. Dir. Ted Wilde. First National Pictures, USA 1927.
BANG THE DRUM SLOWLY. Dir. John D. Hancock. Paramount Pictures, USA 1973.
BATAAN. Dir. Tay Garnett. MGM, USA 1943.
BLUE CHIPS. Dir. William Friedkin. Paramount Pictures, USA 1994.
BLUE IN THE FACE. Dir. Paul Auster / Wayne Wang / Harvey Wang. Miramax, USA 1995.
BODY AND SOUL. Dir. Robert Rossen. Enterprise Productions, USA 1947.
BRIAN'S SONG. Dir. Buzz Kulik. Screen Gems Television, USA 1971.
BROKEN ARROW. Dir. Delmer Daves. Twentieth Century Fox, USA 1950.
BULL DURHAM. Dir. Ron Shelton. The Mount Company, USA 1988.

CHILDREN OF THE CORN. Dir. Fritz Kiersch. Hal Roach Studios / New World Pictures, USA 1984.
COACH CARTER. Dir. Thomas Carter. MTV Films, USA 2005.
COLLEGE. Dir. James W. Horne / Buster Keaton. Joseph M. Schenck Productions, USA 1927.
CRIS CROSS. Dir. Robert Siodmak. Universal International Pictures, USA 1949.

DAYS OF THUNDER. Dir. Tony Scott. Paramount Pictures, USA 1990.

EIGHT MEN OUT. Dir. John Sayles. Orion Pictures, USA 1988.

FIELD OF DREAMS. Dir. Phil Alden Robinson. Gordon Company, USA 1989.
FIGHTING YOUTH. Dir. Hamilton MacFadden. Universal Pictures, USA 1935.
FIREFOX. Dir. Clint Eastwood. The Malpaso Company, USA 1982.
FOR LOVE OF THE GAME. Dir. Sam Raimi. Universal Pictures, USA 1999.
FORD V FERRARI. Dir. James Mangold. TSG Entertainment, USA 2019.
FORREST GUMP. Dir. Robert Zemeckis. Paramount Pictures, USA 1994.
FRIDAY NIGHT LIGHTS. Dir. Peter Berg. NBC Universal Television, USA 2004.

GRAND PRIX. Dir. John Frankenheimer. MGM, USA 1966.
GREASED LIGHTNING. Dir. Michael Schultz. Warner Bros, USA 1977.
GUNG HO! Dir. Ray Enright. Walter Wanger Productions, USA 1943.

HARMON OF MICHIGAN. Dir. Charles Barton. Columbia Pictures, USA 1941.
HARVEY. Dir. Henry Koster. Universal International Pictures, USA 1950.
HE GOT GAME. Dir. Spike Lee. Touchstone Pictures, USA 1998.
HEADIN' HOME. Dir. Lawrence C. Windom. Kessel & Baumann. USA, 1920.
HEAVEN CAN WAIT. Dir. Warren Beatty / Buck Henry. Paramount Pictures, USA 1978.
HERE COMES MR. JORDAN. Dir. Alexander Hall. Columbia Pictures, USA 1941.
HITLER: A CAREER [HITLER: EINE KARRIERE]. Dir. Joachim Fest / C. Herrendoerfer. Interart / Werner Rieb Produktion, GER 1977.
HOOSIERS. Dir. David Anspaugh. Cinema '84, USA/UK 1986.
HORSE FEATHERS. Dir. Norman Z. McLeod. Paramount Pictures, USA 1932.
HURRICANE SEASON. Dir. Tim Story. Dimension Films / IAM Entertainment, USA 2009.

IN THE REALM OF PERFECTION [L'EMPIRE DE LA PERFECTION]. Dir. Julien Faraut. UFO Production, F 2018.

JIM THORPE – ALL-AMERICAN. Dir. Michael Curtiz. Warner Bros, USA 1951.

KELLY'S HEROES. Dir. Brian G. Hutton. MGM / Avala Film, USA 1970.
KNUTE ROCKNE ALL AMERICAN. Dir. Lloyd Bacon / William K. Howard. Warner Bros, USA 1940.

LA GRAN FINAL. Dir. Gerardo Olivares. Greenlight Media AG / Wanda Films, ESP/GER 2006.
LAGAAN: ONCE UPON A TIME IN INDIA. Dir. Ashutosh Gowariker. Aamir Khan Productions / Jhamu Sughand Productions, IND / USA / UK 2001.
LE MANS. Dir. Lee H. Katzin. Cinema Center Films, USA 1971.

M.A.S.H. S01 E20: THE ARMY-NAVY GAME. Dir. Gene Reynolds. 20th Century Fox Television, USA 1973.
MAJOR LEAGUE. Dir. David S. Ward. Paramount Pictures, USA 1989.
MATCH POINT. Dir. Woody Allen. BBC Films, UK / USA 2005.
MIRACLE. Gavin O'Connor. Pop Pop Productions, CAN / USA 2004.
MY ALL-AMERICAN. Dir. Angelo Pizzo. Anthem Productions, USA 2015.

NORTH BY NORTHWEST. Dir. Alfred Hitchcock. MGM, USA 1959.
NORTH DALLAS FORTY. Dir. Ted Kotcheff. Paramount Pictures, USA 1979.

PRIDE OF THE YANKEES. Dir. Sam Wood. The Samuel Goldwyn Company, USA 1942.

REMEMBER THE TITANS. Dir. Boaz Yakin. Jerry Bruckheimer Films / Walt Disney Pictures, USA 2000.
RUSH. Dir. Ron Howard. Exclusive Media Group / Cross Creek Pictures, UK / GER / USA 2013.

SAHARA. Dir. Zoltan Korda. Columbia Pictures, USA 1943.
SCARFACE. Dir. Brian De Palma. Universal Pictures, USA 1983.
SENNA. Dir. Asif Kapadia. Universal Pictures / StudioCanal, UK / F / USA 2010.

SHANE. Dir. George Stevens. Paramount Pictures, USA 1953.
SIGNS. Dir. M. Night Shyamalan. Touchstone Pictures, USA 2002.
SLAP SHOT. Dir. George Roy Hill. Universal Pictures, USA 1977.
SMITH OF MINNESOTA. Dir. Lew Landers. Columbia Pictures, USA 1942.
SOUTH PARK. S6 E22: ASSPEN. Dir. Trey Parker. MTV Entertainment Studios, USA 2002.
SPACE JAM. Dir. Joe Pytka. Warner Bros, USA 1996.
SPEEDY. Dir. Ted Wilde. The Harold Lloyd Corporation, USA 1928.
STRANGERS ON A TRAIN. Dir. Alfred Hitchcock. Warner Bros, USA 1951.

TALENT FOR THE GAME. Dir. Robert M. Young. Paramount Pictures, USA 1991.
TALLADEGA NIGHS: THE BALLAD OF RICKY BOBBY. Dir. Adam McKay. Columbia Pictures, USA 2006.
TEAM AMERICA: WORLD POLICE. Dir. Trey Parker. Paramount Pictures, USA / GER 2004.
THE 24 HOUR WAR. Dir. Nate Adams / A. Carolla. Gearhead Films, USA 2016.
THE ARSENAL STADIUM MYSTERY. Dir. Thorold Dickinson. Greenspan & Seligman Enterprises Ltd., UK 1939.
THE BABE. Dir. Arthur Hiller. Universal Pictures, USA 1992.
THE BAD NEWS BEARS. Dir. Michael Ritchie. Paramount Pictures, USA 1976.
THE BINGO LONG TRAVELING ALL-STARS & MOTOR KINGS. Dir. John Badham. Universal Pictures, USA 1976.
THE CORBETT-FITZSIMMONS FIGHT. Dir. Enoch. J. Rector. Veriscope Company, USA 1897.
THE EXORCIST. Dir. William Friedkin. Warner Bros, USA 1973.
THE EXPRESS. Dir. Gary Fleder. Relativity Media / IDEA Filmproduktions, USA / GER, 2008.
THE GODFATHER. Dir. Francis Ford Coppola. Paramount Pictures, USA 1972.
THE GREAT WHITE HOPE. Dir. Martin Ritt. Lawrence Turman Films, USA 1970.
THE JACKIE ROBINSON STORY. Dir. Alfred E. Green. Jewel Pictures, USA 1950.
THE LAST AMERICAN HERO. Dir. Lamont Johnson. Twentieth Century Fox, USA 1973.
THE LONG GRAY LINE. Dir. John Ford. Columbia Pictures, USA 1955.
THE LONGEST YARD. Dir. Robert Aldrich. Paramount Pictures, USA 1974.
THE MAN. Dir. Joseph Sargent. ABC Circle Films / Lorimar Productions, USA 1972.
THE NAKED GUN: FROM THE FILES OF POLICE SQUAD! Dir. David Zucker. Paramount Pictures, USA 1988.
THE NATURAL. Dir. Berry Levinson. TriStar Pictures, USA 1984.
THE PINCH HITTER. Dir. Victor Schertzinger. New York Motion Picture / Kay-Bee Pictures, USA 1917.
THE PROGRAM. Dir. David S. Ward. Touchstone Pictures / The Samuel Goldwyn Company, USA 1993.
THE SECOND GAME [AL DOILEA JOC]. Dir. Corneliu Porumboiu. 42 Km Film, RO 2014.
THE SET-UP. Dir. Robert Wise. RKO Radio Pictures, USA 1949.
THE SPIRIT OF NOTRE DAME. Dir. Russell Mack. Universal Pictures, USA 1931.
THE SPIRIT OF STANFORD. Dir. Charles Barton. Columbia Pictures, USA 1942.
THE STRATTON STORY. Dir. Sam Wood. MGM, USA 1949.
THE WIZARD OF OZ. Dir. Victor Fleming. MGM, USA 1939.
THREE [DREI]. Dir. Tom Tykwer. X Filme Creative Pool, GER 2010.
TOUCHDOWN! Dir. Norman Z. McLeod. Paramount Pictures, USA 1931.
TROUBLE WITH THE CURVE. Dir. Robert Lorenz. Warner Bros, USA 2012.

WE ARE MARSHALL. Dir. Joseph 'McG' McGinty Nichol. Warner Bros / Legenday Entertainment, USA 2006.
WEEDS ON FIRE [DIAN WU BU]. Dir. Chi Fat Chan. Film Development Fund of Hong Kong / Flash Glory, HK 2016.
WINNING. Dir. James Goldstone. Universal Pictures, USA 1969.

ZIDANE: A 21ST CENTURY PORTRAIT [ZIDANE, UN PORTRAIT DU 21E SIÈCLE]. Dir. Douglas Gordon / Philippe Parreno. Anna Lena Films / Arte France Cinéma, F/ISL 2006.

Table of Figures

All screenshots from films were captured by the author.

Figure 1–13, 15–18	FIELD OF DREAMS (Phil Alden Robinson, USA 1989).
Figure 14	FIELD OF DREAMS, THE EXORCIST (William Friedkin, USA 1973), CRIS CROSS (Robert Siodmak, USA 1949).
Figure 19–32	WE ARE MARSHALL (Joseph 'McG' McGinty Nichol, USA 2006).
Figure 33–35	MIRACLE (Gavin O'Connor, CAN / USA 2004).
Figure 36–37, 39–46	KNUTE ROCKNE ALL AMERICAN (Lloyd Bacon / William K. Howard, USA 1940).
Figure 38	Photo fragments of The Detroit News, Michigan, and The Cleveland Sunday News, Ohio, from 5 April 1931, https://www.worthpoint.com/worthopedia/knute-rockne-death-funeral-notre-dame-107197371.
Figure 47–57	JIM THORPE – ALL-AMERICAN (Michael Curtiz, USA 1951).

Name Index

Aab, Vanessa 188
Abrahams, Jim 208
Adams, James Truslow 87, 120–121, 130, 134
Adams, Nate 5
Adorno, Theodor W. 111
Agamben, Giorgio 119–120
Aldrich, Robert 133
Aleiss, Angela 251
Allen, Woody 3
Allison, Lincoln 89
Althusser, Louis 90
Altman, Rick 20, 22, 30–33, 37, 42, 49, 93
Anderson, Benedict 86, 109
Anderson, Sam 140
Andrews, David L. 99
Angelucci, Daniela 258
Anspaugh, David 9, 51
Antonioni, Michelangelo 119
Arendt, Hannah 48, 122, 131, 141
Aristotle 14, 21, 42–43
Asinof, Eliot 49
Auster, Paul 66

Babington, Bruce 10, 27, 47–48, 50, 69, 81
Bacon, Lloyd 5, 12, 81, 119, 139, 162, 201, 222–223, 225–226, 245
Badham, John 51, 78
Bakels, Jan-Hendrik 183
Baker, Aaron 51, 90, 95, 99, 102–105, 142, 225–226, 232
Bakhtin, Mikhail 104, 156
Balázs, Béla 131
Barthes, Roland 26
Barton, Charles 205
Barzun, Jacques 9
Baumlin, James S. 141
Beatty, Warren 81, 119
Beaulieu, Alain 119
Beck, Daniel 1
Bellour, Raymond 147–148
Benjamin, Walter 141
Bensmaia, Reda 119
Berger, Hanno 141–142

Bergson, Henri 18, 123–125, 127
Berlant, Lauren 263
Biden, Joseph R. 255, 261, 263
Biderman, David 158
Billings, Andrew C. 95
Blair, April 204
Blumenberg, Hans 257
Bogue, Ronald 116
Bonnet, Valérie 4
Bonzel, Katharina 129, 243
Bosshart, Louis 1
Boyd, Julian P. 121
Boyd, Todd 95
Boym, Svetlana 48
Bravo, Jorge 252
Bresson, Robert 119
Briley, Ron 51, 248
Brohm, Jean-Marie 90
Brown, Clarence 81
Brown, Peter J. 151
Brown, Wes 160
Bryant, Levi R. 124
Buford, Kate 226
Burch, Noël 98
Busfield, Timothy 73
Butterworth, Michael L. 83

Caan, James 183
Cahill, Eddie 195
Caillois, Roger 189
Campbell, Joseph 50, 52
Carolla, Adam 5
Casetti, Francesco 212
Cashmore, Ellis 1, 24, 28
Casper, Kurt 33
Cavanaugh, Jack 207
Cavell, Stanley 12–14, 21–23, 29, 39–40, 82, 94, 140, 145, 258, 260, 264
Certeau, Michel de 7
Chan Chi Fat 25
Chapman, Michael 155, 203
Chare, Nicholas 243
Chion, Michel 53, 167
Clarke, Melissa 40

Colebrook, Claire 116
Colman, Felicity 38
Cooper, Caroline M. 51
Coppola, Francis Ford 69
Costner, Kevin 49, 52, 54, 56–57, 77–78
Crosson, Seán 4, 15, 20, 25, 27, 29, 37–38, 41, 49, 84, 89–91, 93–105
Crowder, Peter 5
Csíkszentmihályi, Mihály 183, 186–190, 193, 199
Cull, Laura 116
Cullen, Jim 120–121, 129, 134
Curtis, Russell 30, 39, 205
Curtiz, Michael 12, 70, 102, 115, 162, 201, 213, 226–227, 236, 243, 247, 249–250, 254
Custen, George F. 205

Dalton, Harlon L. 85
Daves, Delmer 232
De Palma, Brian 185
Dear, William 81
DeLanda, Manuel 73
Deleuze, Gilles 7, 15, 18, 35, 38, 42, 53, 71–72, 107, 112, 114–120, 123–125, 127–128, 131, 134, 142–143, 157–159, 182, 193, 199, 211, 247, 258–259
Derrida, Jacques 128, 210
Dickinson, Thorold 2
Doran, Robert 132
Dostoevsky, Fyodor 104
Dreyer, Carl Th. 119
Dyer, Richard 93–94, 100–101, 104, 142

Eastwood, Clint 81
Eisenstein, Sergei 7, 107, 131
Elsaesser, Thomas 79
Engels, Friedrich 89
Englert, Barbara 15, 28, 41
Enright, Ray 223
Eyerman, Ron 90

Fahle, Oliver 15
Faraut, Julien 4
Farred, Grant 15, 40–41, 84
Fear-Segal, Jacqueline 227

Fest, Joachim 65
Fisher, Mark 53
Fitting, Peter 142
Fleder, Gary 139
Fleming, Victor 69
Florschütz, Gottlieb 27, 33
Fluck, Winfried 87, 97, 256
Ford, John 204
Fox, Matthew 160
Frampton, Daniel 247
Frankenheimer, John 5
Freud, Siegmund 131
Friedkin, William 69, 122
Friedlander, Brett 67, 71
Friedman, Lester D. 13, 16
Frye, Northrop 28, 113–114

Gaertner, David 86
Gaines, Jane M. 175
Gamper, Michael 127
Garnett, Tay 223
Geraghty, Brian 167
Getzels, Jacob W. 188
Giamatti, A. Bartlett 179
Gill, Ryan 15, 83–84
Gledhill, Christine 10, 21, 25, 28, 34–36, 39, 94, 258
Godard, Jean-Luc 7, 42
Goldstone, James 5
Gordon, Douglas 4, 38, 102
Gorman, Amanda 259–260, 262–264
Gowariker, Ashutosh 40
Gramsci, Antonio 90
Green, Alfred E. 84, 246
Greifenstein, Sarah 6–7, 61, 131, 183
Grella, George 15, 84
Grindon, Leger 4, 42, 94
Groß, Bernhard 265
Grosz, Elisabeth 123
Grotkopp, Matthias 21, 39, 42, 94, 131–132, 258
Gruneau, Richard S. 91
Guattari, Félix 72
Gugutzer, Robert 28, 191
Gumbrecht, Hans Ulrich 188
Gunning, Tom 33, 93

Name Index

Hall, Alexander 81
Hall, Mordaunt 211
Haney, C. Allen 30, 39, 205
Harder, Susanne 148
Harootunian, Harry 109
Heidegger, Martin 18, 71, 136–137
Helgeland, Brian 139
Heller, Franziska 190
Henry, Buck 81, 119
Hernández-Lemus, Alberto M. 258
Herrendoerfer, Christian 65
Herzogenrath, Bernd 115–116, 135
Hildebrandt-Stratmann, Reiner 12
Hill, George Roy 133
Hill, Sarah 95
Hiller, Arthur 100
Hills, Matt 53
Hitchcock, Alfred 3, 54
Hoffman, Gaby 57
Horaz 42
Horkheimer, Max 111
Horne, James W. 5
Howard, Ron 5
Howard, William K. 81, 201, 245
Hühn, Helmut 127
Huizinga, Johan 191
Hume, David 157
Hundley, Heather L. 95
Husserl, Edmund 18
Hutchins, Brett 1, 91
Hutton, Brian G. 167
Huyssen, Andreas 111

Iser, Wolfgang 97

Jackson, Steven J. 99
Jackson, Susan A. 183, 186–190, 199
Jameson, Frederic 72–73, 113–114
Jefferson, Thomas 126
Jenkins, Sally 228
Jenkins, Steve 49
Johnson, Lamont 5
Johnson, Richard 173
Jones, Glen 13, 28
Jones, James Earl 49, 78

Kamp, David 111
Kant, Immanuel 48, 118, 131, 134, 189
Kapadia, Asif 5
Kappelhoff, Hermann 2, 6–8, 10–14, 17, 21–22, 30, 32, 35–36, 39, 41–45, 48, 61, 94, 102, 106–107, 127, 130–132, 148, 152, 175, 177, 183, 187–190, 192–193, 211, 233, 249, 258
Katzin, Lee H. 5
Keaton, Buster 5, 233
Keefe, Joshua R. 249, 253
Kehrberg, Amanda 147, 153, 185
Kerns, Hubie 227
Kiersch, Fritz 54
Kilerci, Nazli 32, 79
King, C. Richard 3
Køppe, Simo 148
Korda, Zoltan 223
Koster, Henry 69
Kotcheff, Ted 26, 122, 162
Kracauer, Siegfried 265
Kulik, Buzz 203
Kusz, Kyle W. 95

Lancaster, Burt 49, 69–70, 226, 234, 237, 239–240, 244–245, 249–250
Landers, Lew 205
LaRocca, David 119
Lauri-Lucente, Gloria 73
Lee, Spike 31
Lefort, Claude 126
Lehmann, Hauke 2, 32, 35, 44, 73, 79, 127, 171, 190
Leonard, David J. 3
Levinson, Berry 51
Lie, Sulgie 210
Liegl, Michael 130
Liotta, Ray 49, 56–58, 82
Logan, Aaron 33
López Frías, Javier 142
Lorenz, Robert 81

MacFadden, Hamilton 5
Mack, Russell 211
Madigan, Amy 49, 62
Maguire, Joseph A. 1

Malachowski, Alan 131
Mangold, James 5
Mann, Jack 66
Marchetti, Sarin 258
Marker, Chris 119
Marrati, Paola 116
Marshall, Penny 26
Marx, Karl 89
Massumi, Brian 128, 159
Matthews, Daniel 92, 128–129
May, Stephan 4
McCall, Dan 117
McConaughey, Matthew 146, 163
McDorman, Todd F. 33
McGinley, Sean 33
McGinty Nichol, Joseph 'McG' 12, 119, 144–145
McKay, Adam 5
McKernan, Luke 93
McKie, Scott 239
McLaughlin, Douglas W. 142
McLeod, Norman Z. 5
Middlekauff, Robert 121
Miller, Andrew 4–5, 15–16, 20, 24, 30–33, 37–38, 45–46, 51, 85–86, 93, 201
Miller, Toby 3, 24, 134
Mittell, Jason 37
Montville, Leigh 100
Mosher, Stephan D. 28
Müller, Cornelia 2, 7–8, 11, 22, 107, 131, 148, 152, 177, 233, 249

Nancy, Jean-Luc 109, 244
Neale, Steve 20, 34, 37, 39
Nelson, Murry 8–9
Nielsen, Leslie 208
Niemi, Robert 208
Nietzsche, Friedrich 112
Nigianni, Chrysanthi 116
Nixon, Howard L. 89
Nowlan, Robert A. 238

O'Connor, Gavin 12, 139, 191, 223
O'Leary, Michael 210
Olivares, Gerardo 38

Olivier, Bert 134
Ott, Michaela 199
Oxendine, Joseph B. 253

Page, Gale 211
Parker, Trey 184–185
Parreno, Philippe 4, 38, 102
Patrick, Robert 161
Pearson, Demetrius 30, 39, 205
Péguy, Charles 142–143
Peretz, Eyal 210
Philpott, Roger 103
Pisters, Patricia 211
Pizzo, Angelo 139, 204
Pogodda, Cilli 44
Pollmann, Inga 144
Pomerance, Murray 3, 5–6, 8, 11, 17, 33, 137
Porumboiu, Corneliu 4
Powell, Anna 38
Price, John A. 232
Probst, Andrea 12
Pytka, Joe 96

Rader, Benjamin G. 1, 78, 89, 100
Raimi, Sam 144
Rancière, Jacques 44, 118, 127
Ransom, Amy J. 95
Rastovic, Milos 117
Ray, Robert 104
Ray, Robert B. 98, 104
Rector, Enoch J. 5
Reid, John Phillip 121
Reising, Robert 67, 71
Richter-Hansen, Tullio 31
Ricœur, Paul 13, 22, 71, 79
Ritt, Martin 78
Robinson, Phil Alden 13, 22, 46–47, 49, 245
Robinson, Ray 204
Robinson, Rick E. 188
Rorty, Richard 48, 116, 127, 130–134
Rose, Susan D. 227
Rosenstone, Robert A. 103
Rossen, Robert 28
Rowe, David 1, 3, 9, 24, 37–41, 91, 95
Rowland, Robert C. 113

Rubinfeld, Mark 249, 254
Russell, Kurt 191

Samuel, Lawrence R. 87, 96, 112
Sargent, Joseph 78
Sauer, Bruno 141
Sayles, John 49
Schatz, Thomas 14, 20, 31, 93
Schauerte, Thorsten 91
Scherer, Thomas 131
Schertzinger, Victor 5
Schierl, Thomas 91
Schiller, Friedrich 189
Schleusener, Simon 265
Schmidgen, Henning 143
Schultz, Jaime 89
Schultz, Michael 5
Schwier, Jürgen 1, 91
Scott, Tony 5
Seel, Martin 127, 199
Shannon, Timothy J. 134
Shaughnessy, Dan 66
Shaw, Spencer 211
Sheffer, Craig 183
Shelton, Ron 51
Shyamalan, M. Night 54
Sicks, Kai Marcel 23–26, 28
Silverman, Kaja 54
Simondon, Gilbert 124
Siodmak, Robert 70
Sipiora, Phillip 141
Sobchack, Vivian 17, 48, 82, 131, 153, 188, 211, 247
Sperber, Murray 204–205
Spinoza, Baruch de 35
Staiger, Janet 98
Stam, Robert 104
Stauff, Markus 3, 23–26, 28
Stern, Daniel 147
Stevens, George 60
Stone, Oliver 33
Storr, Merl 116
Streible, Dan 4
Suits, Bernard 142

Tampio, Nicholas 114
Theunissen, Michael 141
Thompson, Steve 70
Thoreau, Henry David 117, 120
Todorov, Tzvetan 21
Totaro, Donato 182
Trifonova, Temenuga 124–125
Tröhler, Margrit 188
Tudor, Deborah 50–51, 62, 66, 78–79, 89, 95, 153
Tykwer, Tom 71

Urbas, Joseph 260

Vaeveret, Mette 148
Vermeulen, Pieter 109
Vihalem, Margus 127
Vogl, Joseph 87

Waitz, Thomas 3
Wang, Wayne 66
Ward, David S. 51, 183, 203, 245
Washington, Denzel 180
Wasserman, Loretta 123
Watterson, John Sayle 228
Wedel, Michael 22, 34, 71–72, 79–80, 148, 265
Weinstein, Jami 116
Wells, Paul 28
Wenner, Lawrence A. 1, 91
Whaley, Frank 49
Whannel, Garry 1, 15, 25–27, 84, 87–89, 91, 95, 99
Wheeler, Robert W. 226
Wilde, Ted 100
Williams, Linda 36
Williams, Tennessee 134
Wills, Gary 121
Wilson, Amy 174
Windom, Lawrence C. 100
Winthrop, John 121, 256
Wise, Robert 28
Wolfe, Katharine 118
Wood, Sam 205
Wyllie, Martin 92

Yakin, Boaz 119, 180
Young, Robert M. 51

Zemeckis, Robert 3
Zhang, James 30, 39, 205

Žižek, Slavoj 126, 141–143
Zucker, David 3, 208
Zucker, Jerry 208

Film Index

1 5
42 139

A LEAGUE OF THEIR OWN 26
AIRPLANE! 208
ALL AMERICAN 204
ALL THE RIGHT MOVES 155
ALL THE RIGHT MOVES 203
ANGELS IN THE OUTFIELD (1951) 81
ANGELS IN THE OUTFIELD (1994) 81
ANY GIVEN SUNDAY 33, 95

BABE COMES HOME 100
BANG THE DRUM SLOWLY 139
BATAAN 223
BLUE CHIPS 122
BLUE IN THE FACE 66
BODY AND SOUL 28
BRIAN'S SONG 203
BROKEN ARROW 232
BULL DURHAM 51

CHILDREN OF THE CORN 54
COACH CARTER 243
COLLEGE 5, 233
CRIS CROSS 69

DAYS OF THUNDER 5

EIGHT MEN OUT 49, 51

FIELD OF DREAMS 12–13, 22, 46–52, 57, 59–63, 66, 69–73, 76–80, 82–83, 145, 245, 257–258
FIGHTING YOUTH 5
FIREFOX 81
FOR LOVE OF THE GAME 139, 144, 196
FORD V FERRARI 5
FORREST GUMP 3
FRIDAY NIGHT LIGHTS 243

GRAND PRIX 5
GREASED LIGHTNING 5
GUNG HO! 223

HARMON OF MICHIGAN 205
HARVEY 69, 81
HE GOT GAME 31, 51
HEADIN' HOME 100
HEAVEN CAN WAIT 81, 119
HERE COMES MR. JORDAN 81
HITLER: A CAREER [HITLER: EINE KARRIERE]. 65
HOOSIERS 9, 51, 243
HORSE FEATHERS 5
HURRICANE SEASON 139

IN THE REALM OF PERFECTION [L'EMPIRE DE LA PERFECTION] 4

JIM THORPE – ALL-AMERICAN 12, 70, 102, 115, 122, 139, 145, 155, 162, 196, 201, 203, 205, 213, 216, 226, 229, 231–234, 238, 240–242, 244, 246–249, 251–254, 262–263

KELLY'S HEROES 167
KNUTE ROCKNE ALL AMERICAN 119, 201–205, 208, 210–214, 216–217, 221–227, 232–234, 243–245, 247, 249, 252–254, 264

LA GRAN FINAL 38
LAGAAN: ONCE UPON A TIME IN INDIA 40
LE MANS 5

M.A.S.H. 208
MAJOR LEAGUE 51, 203
MATCH POINT 3
MIRACLE 12, 139, 145, 183, 191–192, 194, 196, 198–200, 223
MY ALL-AMERICAN 139, 204

NORTH BY NORTHWEST 54
NORTH DALLAS FORTY 26, 122, 162

PRIDE OF THE YANKEES 119, 205

REMEMBER THE TITANS 139, 145, 180
RUSH 5

https://doi.org/10.1515/9783110760354-012

SAHARA 223
SCARFACE 185
SENNA 5
SHANE 60
SIGNS 54
SLAP SHOT 133
SMITH OF MINNESOTA 205
SOUTH PARK 185
SPACE JAM 96
SPEEDY 100
STAR WARS 78
STRANGERS ON A TRAIN 3

TALENT FOR THE GAME 51
TALLADEGA NIGHTS: THE BALLAD OF RICKY BOBBY 5
TEAM AMERICA: WORLD POLICE 184, 186, 190, 198
THE 24 HOUR WAR 5
THE ARSENAL STADIUM MYSTERY 2
THE BABE 100
THE BAD NEWS BEARS 243
THE BINGO LONG TRAVELING ALL-STARS & MOTOR KINGS 51, 78
THE CORBETT-FITZSIMMONS FIGHT 5
THE EXORCIST 69
THE EXPRESS 139
THE GODFATHER 69
THE GREAT WHITE HOPE 78

THE JACKIE ROBINSON STORY 84, 246, 254
THE LAST AMERICAN HERO 5
THE LONG GRAY LINE 204
THE LONGEST YARD 133
THE MAN 78
THE NAKED GUN: FROM THE FILES OF POLICE SQUAD! 3
THE NATURAL 51
THE PINCH HITTER 5
THE PROGRAM 51, 183, 186, 245
THE SECOND GAME 4
THE SET-UP 28
THE SPIRIT OF NOTRE DAME 211
THE SPIRIT OF STANFORD 205
THE STRATTON STORY 139, 205
THE WIZARD OF OZ 69
THREE [DREI] 71
TOUCHDOWN! 5
TROUBLE WITH THE CURVE 81

WE ARE MARSHALL 12, 16–17, 119, 139, 144–153, 155, 157–159, 162–164, 168, 171, 173, 175–179, 181–182, 194, 196, 210, 243, 261
WEEDS ON FIRE [DIAN WU BU] 25
WINNING 5

ZIDANE: A 21ST CENTURY PORTRAIT [ZIDANE, UN PORTRAIT DU 21E SIÈCLE] 4, 38, 102

www.ingramcontent.com/pod-product-compliance
Lightning Source LLC
Chambersburg PA
CBHW050516170426
43201CB00013B/1978